Mental Illness in the Workplace

Psychological and Behavioral Aspects of Risk Series

Series Editors: Professor Cary L. Cooper and Professor Ronald J. Burke

Risk management is an ongoing concern for modern organizations in terms of their finance, their people, their assets, their projects and their reputation. The majority of the processes and systems adopted are very financially oriented or fundamentally mechanistic; often better suited to codifying and recording risk, rather than understanding and working with it. Risk is fundamentally a human construct; how we perceive and manage it is dictated by our attitude, behavior and the environment or culture within which we work. Organizations that seek to mitigate, manage, transfer or exploit risk need to understand the psychological factors that dictate the response and behaviors of their employees, their high-flyers, their customers and their stakeholders.

This series, edited by two of the most influential writers and researchers on organizational behavior and human psychology explores the psychological and behavioral aspects of risk; the factors that:

- define our attitudes and response to risk;
- are important in understanding and managing "risk managers"; and
- dictate risky behavior in individuals at all levels.

Titles Currently in the Series Include:

Creating Healthy Workplaces
Stress Reduction, Improved Well-being, and Organizational Effectiveness
Edited by Caroline Biron, Ronald J. Burke and Cary L. Cooper

The Fulfilling Workplace
The Organization's Role in Achieving Individual and Organizational Health
Edited by Ronald J. Burke and Cary L. Cooper

Occupational Health and Safety
Edited by Ronald J. Burke, Sharon Clarke and Cary L. Cooper

Corporate Reputation
Managing Opportunities and Threats
Edited by Ronald J. Burke, Graeme Martin and Cary L. Cooper

Mental Illness in the Workplace

Psychological Disability Management

HENRY G. HARDER, SHANNON L. WAGNER, AND JOSHUA A. RASH

GOWER

Gower Applied Business Research
Our programme provides leaders, practitioners, scholars and researchers with thought provoking, cutting edge books that combine conceptual insights, interdisciplinary rigour and practical relevance in key areas of business and management.

Published by
Gower Publishing Limited
Wey Court East
Union Road
Farnham
Surrey, GU9 7PT
England

Gower Publishing Company
110 Cherry Street
Suite 3-1
Burlington, VT 05401-3818
USA

www.gowerpublishing.com

British Library Cataloguing in Publication Data
A catalogue record for this book is available from the British Library

ISBN: 9781409445494 (hbk)
ISBN: 9781409445500 (ebk – ePDF)
ISBN: 9781472402417 (ebk – ePUB)

Library of Congress Cataloging-in-Publication Data
The Library of Congress Cataloging-in-Publication Data has been applied for.

Printed in the United Kingdom by Henry Ling Limited,
at the Dorset Press, Dorchester, DT1 1HD

Contents

List of Figures

List of Tables

About the Authors

Dr Henry G. Harder is Professor and past Chair of the School of Health Sciences at the University of Northern British Columbia. He currently holds the Dr Donald B. Rix BC Leadership Chair in Aboriginal Environmental Health. He is a registered psychologist. Dr Harder has been in the fields of mental health, rehabilitation, psychology, and disability management for over 25 years. His research interests are in aboriginal health, disability issues, workplace mental health, and suicide prevention. He is a Canadian Institutes of Health Research funded scholar. Dr Harder is a published author and has made presentations and conducted workshops throughout Canada, the United States, Europe and Australia. He is a member of the College of Psychologists of British Columbia, Network Environments for Aboriginal Research in BC, Canadian Psychological Association, American Association of Marriage and Family Therapy, International Society of Physical and Rehabilitation Medicine, and other professional organizations. Dr Harder can be reached at henry.harder@unbc.ca

Dr Shannon L. Wagner is a Professor in the School of Health Sciences at the University of Northern British Columbia, as well as a registered psychologist working in private practice. Her research focus is occupational mental health, especially as it relates to disability management, occupational stress, trauma and family-work interface. She has published widely in the fields of occupational mental health and disability management, and works actively with the stakeholder community to increase knowledge regarding mental health accommodation in the workplace. Dr Wagner's teaching interests are focused on topics of occupational health and safety, disability management, psychological assessment, and methodology (for example, statistics and epidemiology). She also maintains active service commitments in both the academic and practitioner communities, including regular collaborations with disability management stakeholders. In addition to her research, teaching and service, Dr Wagner maintains a small clinical practice. Her practice provides general psychological assessment for both children and adults and provides specific expertise for issues of occupational mental health, especially workplace related traumatic stress.

Mr Joshua A. Rash is a Doctoral student in Clinical Psychology at the University of Calgary. He holds a Master's degree in Health Psychology from the University of Northern British Columbia where he has worked as a Research Assistant and Senior Laboratory Instructor. His research is focused on developing a better understanding of the bio-behavioural mechanisms involved in the development and progression of chronic illnesses. He is also involved in the design and evaluation of behavioural interventions aimed at improving outcomes among patients suffering from chronic illnesses. He has published in pain expression and perception, fetal programming, patient adherence, indigenous youth suicide, cardiovascular psychophysiology, and mental health in the workplace.

Reviews for
Mental Illness in the Workplace

Harder and colleagues have produced a much needed, eminently accessible text focussed on mental illness and the workplace. With predictions of major labour shortages in many industrialised nations, employers urgently need to preserve their valuable human resources, including those workers with mental health issues. This book provides employers and others with practical management strategies to prevent and manage mental illness at work.

Nicholas Buys, Griffith University, Australia

This text provides a useful overview of mental illness, its impact on individuals, society and the workforce, and practical strategies for addressing it in the workplace. The strategies outlined will not only benefit workers with existing mental illness, but all workers and employers via the creation of healthier workplaces that optimize the mental health and productivity of all members.

Christine Randall, Griffith University, Australia

Mental Illness in the Workplace *fills a large void in the existing literature by defining common psychological health conditions and broadening the readers understanding of how mental health conditions impact in the workplace. It explores current evidence, diagnostic challenges and treatment complexities. The authors' articulate and present solid and well thought out solutions for prevention and management. Disability Management Professionals will benefit greatly from this resource.*

Liz R. Scott PhD, Principal / CEO, Organizational Solutions

The book provides richly detailed information on how to deal with challenges of mental health in the workplace. Bringing expertise in both areas, mental health and the workplace, together is crucial in order to improve labor market participation by one of the most disadvantaged social groups, heavily stigmatized and generally ignored in their needs for social, medical and workplace support.

Thomas Geisen, University of Applied Sciences
Northwestern Switzerland, Switzerland

Chapter 1

Introduction

Mental health needs a great deal of attention. It's the final taboo and it needs to be faced and dealt with.

Adam Ant

On an international scale, treatment of individuals with mental health issues has been a source of historical embarrassment. In decades and centuries past, individuals with mental illness have been segregated, stigmatized, and shunned. Sufferers of mental illness have been exposed to experimental treatments, institutionalized, and in the most horrific of situations have endured physical, mental, and/or sexual abuse. Despite more recent efforts to improve treatment, inclusion, and opportunity for those with mental illness, societies still struggle to adequately and respectfully meet the needs of persons with mental illness. Mental illness also continues to be a source of significant fear and stigma. As a consequence, individuals with mental illness are under-represented in important facets of society such as work and recreation. Further, it is clear that societies have a long way to go in changing perceptions so that individuals with mental illness are viewed as valued members who can contribute fully given appropriate treatment and accommodation.

This textbook specifically addresses the topic of workplace issues for individuals with mental illness. Times are changing. Treatments for mental health concerns have improved drastically over recent decades, as has the understanding that individuals with mental illness can be meaningful, contributing members of occupational environments. Access to more effective treatments along with suitable accommodation strategies have increased the number of individuals with mental illness available to engage in the workforce, providing employers with a new, traditionally undervalued contingent of workers. Improvements in treatment have also allowed workers who may have previously been required to leave the workplace as a result of poor mental health to maintain their working situation. This has, in turn, improved employee retention, and reduced employee turnover and the loss of expertise held by employees with mental health concerns.

Legislative requirements surrounding issues of mental illness in the workplace have also changed. Specifically, many countries around the world are making, or have made, steps to increase legal protections for individuals with mental illness. New legislative environments ensure that employers are responsible to avoid harassment and discrimination related to mental health. Further, requirements to accommodate for mental illness are also common. However, such protections are not without complications. More and more, employers are becoming versed in their responsibilities to employees with respect to avoidance of discrimination and the need for accommodation. They have also continued to increase knowledge and competency regarding the requirement for and the know-how surrounding accommodation for physical disabilities. On the other hand, in the experience of the authors, it seems that employers find mental illness less well defined. They report feeling unsure about issues of assessment, intervention, and accommodation in the area of mental health. Consequently, this text is intended to provide a global review of mental health in the workplace, while, at the same time, providing some practical advice to employers about how to approach the more daunting areas of workplace mental health.

Employer familiarity with mental illness and related approaches in the workplace is integral to a healthy workplace for many reasons. First, individuals with mental illnesses have been, and continue to be, under-represented in the workplace. Similar to individuals with other types of disabilities, individuals with mental illness represent a contingent of working capital whose value has been traditionally underestimated. Second, disability costs related to issues of mental health are known to be among the highest of all types of disabilities, and they are continuing to increase at an alarming rate. In order to be competitive locally, nationally, and internationally, employers will have to acquire knowledge and skills related to the management of issues surrounding mental illness. Third, competency for management of mental health in the workplace will assist employers in maintaining compliance with legislative requirements and avoiding potential litigation related to inappropriate management. Fourth, increased knowledge and skills for employers will lead to better accommodation and treatment of individuals with mental illness in the workplace. Such improvements will lead to better inclusion, access, and accommodation for working persons with mental health issues. Finally, individuals with mental illness will experience the benefits that often result from participation in meaningful work. Increases in self-competency, self-esteem, and social/occupational functioning for individuals with mental health should never be overlooked as a justification for ensuring workplaces are adequately prepared to assist and accommodate where necessary.

This text gives employers and others interested in learning about mental health in the workplace a single source intended to provide both knowledge as well as recommendations regarding how to approach assessment, intervention, and accommodation. The authors came together as researchers and practitioners in mental health and disability to write a text that could use available peer-reviewed research to supplement a practical guide to mental health in the workplace. With this in mind, we started our text with an overview of the reasons why issues related to mental illness in the workplace can no longer be ignored, as well as an overview of the prevalence, costs, and potential future growth of mental illness in the workplace. Next, we provide four chapters outlining common mental illnesses reported in workplace environments and present a business case for the effective management of these disorders. Specifically, our chapters discuss research and workplace aspects of depression, anxiety, occupational stress, and post-traumatic stress disorder. Finally, in our last set of chapters we pull the specific reviews back into the general and discuss workplace issues and recommendations for action. Important and timely issues discussed include toxic workplaces, worksite reactions, psychological assessment, healthier workplaces, and accommodation for mental health in the workplace. Taken together, the chapters provide a review of mental health in the workplace, and give the reader "hands-on" recommendations for appropriately addressing workplace mental illness. We hope we have achieved our goal and that you find the text both informative and useful.

Chapter 2
The Scope of Mental Illness

To confess ignorance is often wiser than to beat around the bush with a hypothetical diagnosis.

William Osler

Introduction

DEFINITION OF MENTAL DISORDER

The term mental disorder is often used to refer to a disorder of the mind. This, unfortunately, implies that there is a distinction between "mental" disorders such as depression and "physical" disorders such as cardiovascular disease. In reality, this is an artificial dichotomy as the mind and body are inseparable and there is often as much physical anguish in mental disorders as there is metal anguish in physical disorders. Perhaps more appropriately, the term mental disorder is used to refer to a condition that defies typical biomedical explanations (that is, a condition in which the pathophysiological mechanisms are largely unknown). That is, mental disorders often lack the same etiological understanding as do physical disorders. For example, bacteria or viruses cause typical "flu-like" symptoms and are often treated with antibiotics or a flu-shot whereas the causes of depression are still unclear.

In order to propose a pragmatic definition of mental disorder let us first consider the intended purpose of this definition. At the highest level, a definition of mental disorder should help distinguish normal distress from disorder, aid communication between professionals, and inform clinical practice. Five models have been recommended to accomplish this task. The *statistical model* equates disorder with statistical rarity (Lilienfeld and Landfield, 2008). By this convention, disorders are abnormal because they are infrequent in the general population. Yet, a statistical model provides no guidance as to where to set limits or boundaries on what constitutes disordered behavior. Further, some disorders are relatively rare while others are more prolific throughout society.

The *Subjective Distress Model* maintains that psychological pain is the core feature distinguishing disordered from non-disordered. According to this model, psychological pain underlies mental disorder analogous to the way that physical pain underlies most physical disorders. Yet, there are disorders that are not accompanied by self-distress. For example, anorexia nervosa is not accompanied by feelings of distress and is considered ego-syntonic, meaning that it is consistent with the individual's self concept. The subjective distress model cannot account for disorders that are not accompanied by distress.

The *Biological Model* (Kendell, 1975) stipulates that disorders are characterized by biological or evolutionary disadvantage. This disadvantage may include premature mortality or reduced fitness (for example, a decreased likelihood of reproducing). The biological model fails to account for disorders that do not result in premature mortality or reduced fitness (for example, specific phobias), and is over-inclusive (for example, smoking increases the risk of mortality but is not a disorder).

The *Need for Treatment* model contends that disorders are a heterogeneous class of conditions that all share one common feature—the need for treatment (Taylor, 1971). Many mental disorders such as schizophrenia, bipolar disorder, and depression are viewed by society as needing treatment. The need for treatment model fails to explain life events that require treatment but are not considered mental disorders, such as pregnancy.

The *harmful dysfunction* model (Wakefield, 1992) contends that mental disorders are harmful dysfunctions (that is, socially devalued breakdowns of evolutionary systems). For example, panic disorder would be considered a disorder because it is devalued by society and the inflicted individual, and results in activation of the sympathetic nervous system in the absence of a typical evolutionary cue. Yet, the environment is constantly changing and some disorders may be considered adaptive reactions within their environment.

Each of the reviewed models provides useful indicators for mental disorder, but different situations may call for different definitions for defining disordered (Stein, Phillips, Bolton, et al., 2010). For the purposes of this book we will adopt the definition of mental disorder given by the American Psychiatric Association (APA) and refined by the Diagnostic and Statistical Manual (5th Edition) task force: refer to Table 2.1 (APA, 2004; First and Wakefield, 2010;

Table 2.1   Suggested definition of mental disorder adapted from First and Wakefield, 2010 and Stein et al. 2010

A. A behavioral or psychological syndrome or pattern that occurs in an individual

B. That is a manifestation of a behavioral, psychological or biological dysfunction in the individual

C. The consequences of which are clinically significant distress (e.g. a painful symptom) or disability (i.e. impairment in one or more important areas of functioning), or substantial increased risk of future distress or disability. Increased risk of distress or disability is not in itself a disorder unless due to a dysfunction.

D. The syndrome or pattern must not be merely an expectable response to common stressors and losses (for example, the loss of a loved one), or a culturally sanctioned behavior or belief (for example, trance states in religious rituals)

E. Neither deviant behavior (e.g. political, religious or sexual) nor conflicts that are primarily between the individual and society are mental disorders unless the deviance or conflict is a symptom of a dysfunction in the individual.

Stein, Phillips, Bolton, et al., 2010). According to this definition, a mental disorder is a behavioral or psychological syndrome that manifests in behavioral, psychological, or biological dysfunction, and results in clinically significant distress or disability, or risk thereof. Further, mental disorders extend beyond reactions to normal circumstances and cannot be explained by adjustment to stressors or loss, culturally sanctioned behavior, or conflicts with society.

CLASSIFICATION SYSTEMS

Mental disorders are latent constructs that are diagnosed based upon the clustering of typical signs and symptoms within a person. This diagnosis is generally performed in a dichotomous fashion meaning that an individual is either assigned a disorder or not based upon the abundance and clustering of specified symptoms. For example, a major depressive episode is classified based upon the experience of any five of nine typical symptoms in a two-week period so long as one symptom is depressed mood or loss of interest. This method of classification, while effective, can lead to significant heterogeneity in expression and can result in over 70 different combinations of symptoms that meet the criteria for depression.

Two global classification systems have undertaken the task of providing a common language and standardized diagnostic criteria for classifying mental disorders. These are the International Classification of Diseases and Related Health Problem (10th revision; ICD-10) developed by the World Health Organization (WHO, 2011), and the Diagnostic and Statistic Manual

(4th Edition; DSM-IV; APA, 2000). In 2013 the DSM-V was introduced amidst substantial controversy. As most readers will have familiarity with earlier versions of the DSM we have presented information as per the DSM-IV as well as the DSM-V. The DSM and ICD classification systems converge with each successive iteration, moving towards a global standard in the diagnosis of mental disorders.

The DSM and the ICD incorporate aspects from many of the previously discussed models for identifying mental disorders. For example, the DSM-IV utilizes a multiaxial coding system designed to assess several domains of information that may help clinicians plan treatment and predict outcome. There are five such axes included in the DSM-IV:

Axis I:　　Clinical Syndromes

Axis II:　　Developmental Disorders and Personality Disorders

　　　　　–　Developmental disorders include autism and mental retardation; disorders which are typically first evident in childhood.

Axis III:　　Physical Conditions

　　　　　–　Physical conditions are those such as brain injury or HIV/AIDS which can result in symptoms of mental illness.

Axis IV:　　Severity of Psychosocial Stressors

　　　　　–　Events in a person's life, such as the death of a loved one, starting a new job, college, unemployment/underemployment, and even marriage can impact the disorders above in Axis I and II.

Axis V:　　Highest Level of Functioning

　　　　　–　A clinician rates a person's level of functioning both at the present time and the highest level in the previous year.
　　　　　–　This helps the clinician to understand how the above four Axes are affecting the person and what changes should be expected.

These axes allowed for a clear-cut system of understanding when it comes to mental illness and how they can be categorized by clinical professionals. What is important to note is the difference between each of the axes which highlight the broad range of mental illness and contributing factors across the dimensions.

The DSM V contains important changes to the diagnostic procedures and the reader is referred to the American Psychiatric Association's online resources such as http://www.dsm5.org/Documents/changes%20from%20dsm-iv-tr%20 to%20dsm-5.pdf that clearly identify these changes. In summary, the first three axes have been combined and the fifth has been eliminated in favor of other more specific assessment tools. However, the general diagnostic criteria remain essentially the same.

LIMITATIONS OF CLASSIFICATION SYSTEMS IN OCCUPATIONAL SETTINGS

The use of explicit diagnostic systems in the workplace poses some problems. First, the DSM and ICD contain many nuances that necessitate specialized knowledge and training. Such knowledge and training is costly both in terms of time and financial resources. It takes more than familiarity with a diagnostic system to properly diagnose mental disorders. Similar to medical training, proper diagnosis of mental disorders often takes years of training, and specialty practicum placements. There is no substitute for clinical experience when it comes to proficiency in diagnosis of mental disorders. It would likely be more cost-effective for an employer to "hire-out" the job of assessment to a trained and certified mental health professional.

The second challenge with assessing mental health conditions in the workplace is the typical length of an assessment interview. Structured clinical interviews represent the "gold standard" for diagnosing mental disorders. These are highly structured interviews that contain question algorithms designed to assess nearly every mental disorder in a comprehensive manner. Each classification system has its own structured interview. The Structured Clinical Interview for DSM-IV disorders (SCID) was developed to assess DSM-IV-based disorders while the Composite International Diagnostic Interview (CIDI) was developed to assess ICD-10 disorders. Each interview is modularized and clinicians need not administer the entire interview to every subject. As such, the length of each interview can vary depending on a number of factors, including diagnostic purposes, case conceptualization, and number of suspected comorbidities. The average interview can be expected to span one and one half to two hours.

ALTERNATIVES TO CLASSIFICATION SYSTEM DIAGNOSIS

Several brief screening measures have been developed to screen for common mental disorders in the general population. Two particularly brief and well-studied measures are the Kessler 10 (K-10) and Kessler 6 (K-6) that screen for non-specific psychological distress (Kessler, Andrews, Colpe, et al., 2002). Measures such as the K10/6 were originally used as first-stage screens to identify individuals with emotional problems who may have a disorder or who are at risk for developing a disorder. Once identified, these individuals could be referred for more in-depth clinical assessment. The scales were designed to detect clinically significant nonspecific distress in order to discriminate serious mental illness from non-cases (Kessler, Barker, Colpe, et al., 2003). While originally developed as screens, the K 10/6 have proven effective in discriminating between disordered and non-disordered and have often been used without clinical follow-up.

The K-10/6 have proven effective at discriminating between cases and non-cases of mental disorders in the community. The scales have good precision in identifying individuals with high psychological distress (that is, individuals who score in the 90–99th percentile) (Kessler, Andrews, Colpe, et al., 2002). In a field trial, the K10/6 correctly identified 87–88 percent of individuals with psychopathology in a sample that included low, moderate, and high functioning individuals (that is, global assessment of functioning scores between 0–70). When considering individuals who were functioning poorly (that is, individuals who have global assessment of function between 0 and 50) the K 10/6 correctly identified 95–96 percent of those with disorders (Kessler, Andrews, Colpe, et al., 2002).

The K-6 is the shorter version that has been found to perform equally as well or better at discriminating psychological distress as the K-10 (Kessler, Barker, Colpe, et al., 2003). The K-6 consists of six questions that are responded to using a 1-to-5 point LikeRT scale. Scores on the K-6 range between 6 and 30 with the optimal cutpoint being 6–18. Scores on the K-6 can place individuals at low, moderate, high, or very-high risk of mental disorder. It has been reported that approximately 50 percent of individuals with moderate K-6 scores will meet diagnostic criteria for a mental disorder (ABS, 2007). Those interested in the K-6 can find more information at http://www.hcp.med.harvard.edu/ncs/k6_scales.php.

Prevalence of Mental Disorders

Mental disorders are more common than one might think. The World Health Organization (WHO) has carried out a World Mental Health (WMH) survey initiative designed to assess the prevalence and correlates of mental disorders throughout the world. In order to accomplish this task, the WHO has provided instruments, training, and data analysis to countries that would not otherwise be able to conduct nationally representative epidemiological surveys. All WMH surveys use a structured research diagnostic interview—the Composite International Diagnostic Interview (CIDI; Kessler and Ustun, 2004)—to identify mental disorders. Importantly, the CIDI includes the Sheehan Disability Scale (SDS; Sheehan, Harnett-Sheehan, and Raj, 1996)—a disorder-specific measure of role impairment in three domains: 1) work/school, 2) social life, and 3) family life.

As of 2009, 28 countries had completed the WMH surveys, the majority of which were completed in a nationally representative manner. Results were unanimously clear; mental disorders are prevalent across the globe. Across all countries studied, the lifetime prevalence of mental disorders was approximately one-third of the population (Kessler, Aguilar-Gaxiola, Alonso, et al., 2009). The highest estimates were found in the United States (47.4 percent), Columbia (39.1 percent), and France (37.9 percent). The lowest estimates were found for China (13.2 percent) and Nigeria (12.0 percent) which had considerably lower prevalence estimates that were likely to be underestimated (Gureje, Lasebikan, Kola, et al., 2006). It has been argued that the current diagnostic criteria are restrictive, and evidence suggests that clinically significant sub-threshold manifestations of many mental disorders are more prevalent than the disorders themselves, indicating that the prevalences found in the WMH survey initiative represents conservative estimates of the true global burden of mental disorders.

In order to gain an accurate representation of the burden of mental disorders it is important to consider disorder severity. The WMH surveys had the added benefit of assessing the severity of mental disorders. Disorder severity was classified as mean number of days with role impairment that was attributable to the disorder. Results suggested that the 12-month prevalence of serious mental disorders ranged between 2.3 percent and 6.8 percent of the population (Kessler, Aguilar-Gaxiola, Alonso, et al., 2009). These prevalence estimates vary across country but showed a positive association with prevalence of any disorders. Unsurprisingly, countries with a higher prevalence rate of mental disorders also had a higher prevalence of inhabitants who suffered from a disorder that was judged to be serious ($r = .46$), or moderate ($r = .77$) in severity.

We know that many individuals with mental disorders do not participate in the workforce. The previously described prevalence of mental disorders has been taken from population estimates. While the prevalence of mental disorders is lower in the workforce than in the general population it is reportedly quite common. The one-month prevalence of mental disorders in employees ranges between 10.5 percent and 18.2 percent (Dewa, Lesage, Goering, et al., 2004; Kessler and Frank, 1997; Lim, Sanderson, and Andrews, 2001). These are likely conservative estimates and do not account for sub-threshold cases which are more prevalent than severe mental disorders and merit attention and treatment.

Burden of Mental Disorders

It is becoming increasingly clear that mental disorders are associated with profound social and economic costs. Globally, mental disorders are the leading causes of disability, and, in some high-income countries, account for as much as 40 percent of all disabilities. It has been estimated that depression will emerge as one of the leading causes of disability by the year 2020, second only to heart disease (WHO, 2001).

Government and organizations across the globe are collaborating to quantify the burden of mental disorders and to arrive at suitable strategies to address the issue. One such undertaking was conducted by the European Brain Council, a federation of European-wide organizations with an interest in the brain and its disorders, who attempted to quantify the economic cost and morbidity associated with mental disorders in the Europe Union-27. This undertaking constituted a series of literature reviews assessing the costs of disorders of the brain in Europe conducted by panels of experts in epidemiology and health economics. Population-based studies conducted in European countries were used to derive estimates of the burden of mental disorders. Currencies were converted into Euros (€) and costs were imputed for countries where no data were available. Initial reviews were performed in 2005 (Wittchen and Jacobi, 2005) and updated in 2010 (Olesen, Gustavsson, Svensson, et al., 2012; Wittchen, Jacobi, Rehm, et al., 2011). One of the variables of interest in the most recent iteration was disability adjusted life years (DALY's) which capture years of life lost due to premature mortality as well as years of life lost due to living with a disability. Results indicated that in Europe, mental and other disorders of the brain are responsible for one-third of all DALY's in women and one quarter of all DALY's in men. Mental disorders alone accounted for 12,072,826 DALY's (20.2 percent) which equates to 289.7/1,000 DALY's (Wittchen, Jacobi,

Rehm, et al., 2011). Stated more directly, 2 out of 10 years of healthy life lost in Europe is due to a mental disorder.

THE ECONOMIC BURDEN OF MENTAL DISORDERS

The burden of mental disorders extends beyond that of disability and permeates all facets of the global economy. Many important investigations have been conducted that highlight the total economic costs of mental disorders in various parts of the world.

The Sainsbury Centre for Mental Health (SCMH; 2007) used data obtained from a nationally representative sample of 8,000 adults in the United Kingdom (UK) surveyed by the Office for National Statistics and extrapolated costs to the population of the UK. According to this report, mental disorders among staff cost organizations in the UK an estimated £26 billion each year. This is equivalent to £1,035 for every employee in the UK workforce (SCMH, 2007). Importantly, these costs do not account for disability adjusted life years and represent only indirect costs borne to the employer in terms of absenteeism, presenteeism, and turnover.

The economic costs of mental disorders across the Europe Union-27 were calculated in the previously mentioned series of reviews conducted by the European Brain Council (Wittchen, Jacobi, Rehm, et al., 2011). Conservative estimates into the annual cost of mental disorders in Europe were calculated at €247 billion per year adjusted for 2004 price purchasing parody (Andlin-Sobocki, Jönsson, Wittchen, et al., 2005; Wittchen and Jacobi, 2005). Importantly, 60 percent of this cost could be attributed to a loss in productivity. This estimate was considerably lower than the 2010 estimated cost of mental disorders in Europe. When prices were adjusted for inflation, the total cost of mental disorders (that is, addiction, anxiety disorders, eating disorders, mood disorders, personality disorders, psychotic disorders, sleep, and somatoform disorders) in the European Union-27 in 2010 was €430 billion (Wittchen, Jacobi, Rehm, et al., 2011). This equates to €4,527.5 per patient with a mental disorder. When broken down, the omnibus cost translates into €162 billion in direct healthcare costs, €32 billion in direct non-medical costs (nursing homes, and so on), and €238 billion in indirect costs (absenteeism from work, pensions, and so on) (Olesen, Gustavsson, Svensson, et al., 2012).

Cost accounting for mental disorders has been performed in North America with similar results to Europe. Depression alone was estimated to cost the US economy $83.1 billion USD at prices adjusted for the year 2000 (Greenberg,

Kessler, Birnbaum, et al., 2003). The bulk of this cost, $51.5 billion USD, was attributable to indirect workplace costs. The 2002 US National Comorbidity Survey Replication (NCS-R) was used to assess the prevalence and burden of mental disorders in a nationally representative sample of 4,982 Americans. Data from the NCS-R was used to estimate the economic costs of serious mental disorder. An estimated 6.5 percent of the sample had a serious mental disorder (Kessler, Heeringa, Lakoma, et al., 2008). Individuals with a serious mental disorder earned $16,306 (42 percent) less than the sample's average. Loss of earnings was greater among males ($26,435) than among females ($9,302). When extrapolated to the US population, serious mental illness resulted in a societal reduction of earnings equivalent to $193.2 billion USD (Kessler, Heeringa, Lakoma, et al., 2008). This represents a substantial loss of taxable income for government. Interestingly, only 25 percent of this reduction in earning could be accounted for by societal-level effects such as education status, household size, and marital status.

Data from approximately 77,000 Canadians completing the 1996/1997 National Population Health Survey was used to calculate the economic burden of mental disorders (Stephens and Joubert, 2001). Results suggested that mental disorders cost the Canadian economy $14.4 billion CAD per annum. This analysis was admittedly conservative and more recent estimates indicate that short-term and long-term disability associated with mental disorders cost the Canadian economy $15 to $33 billion (CAD) alone (Sroujian, 2003). The burden of mental disorders is similar in Australia. According to Australia's largest private healthcare provider that covers more than 3 million employers, workplace stress (generally referring to anxiety and depression) results in organizational costs of $14.8 billion AUD (Medibank Private, 2008).

Data from the WMH survey initiative has been used to quantify the economic impact of serious mental illness on the global economy. Data was used from 19 countries (n = 44,561) to determine that serious mental illness results in a 32.5 percent global reduction of earnings (Levinson, Lakoma, Petukhova, et al., 2010). At the societal level, reduction in earnings associated with serious mental disorder account for 0.8 percent of gross domestic product (GDP) in high-income countries. In low-income countries the estimate is slightly lower at 0.3 percent GDP (Levinson, Lakoma, Petukhova, et al., 2010). One must remember that these costs only reflect serious mental disorders and the cost associated with moderately severe mental disorders is likely higher given the higher prevalence.

The economic burden of mental disorders is typically calculated using full-cost accounting. This means that many estimates include direct costs as well as indirect costs borne unto individuals, employers, and society. In the following section we will deconstruct the economic burden of mental disorders and highlight the impact on employers and society.

Economic burden of mental disorders—unemployment

Work is a highly valued activity that has important implications for mental health and well-being. A career is perhaps the single greatest source of self-worth and social identity. Exclusion from the workforce can erode self-efficacy, create social isolation, and result in feelings of marginalization (Stuart, 2006). Most individuals with a mental disorder are willing and able to work yet their unemployment rates remain high (Macias, DeCarlo, Wang, et al., 2001).

Individuals with a mental disorder are less likely to be employed due to their inability to obtain or retain employment (Lerner, Adler, Chang, et al., 2004). Mechanic et al. analyzed data from four nationally representative US population surveys and found that individuals with a mental disorder have an employment rate of approximately two-thirds that of individuals without a mental disorder (Mechanic, Bilder, and McAlpine, 2002). Definition of a mental disorder varied across the four populations studied and, with it, so did estimates of employment. Between 48 percent and 73 percent of individuals with a mental disorder were employed while between 32 percent and 61 percent of individuals with a serious mental disorder were employed. Population surveys that used items identifying DSM-based diagnoses provided higher and likely more accurate estimates of employment than population surveys using self-report diagnosis. Individuals may be reluctant to self-identify with a diagnosis or may not realize that their symptoms reflect a mental disorder.

Similar estimates of unemployment among individuals with mental disorders have been found in England. Data from the 1996/1997 Family Resources Survey (n = 23,940) indicated that employment was nearly 40 percent lower among individuals with mental disorders in England (Berthoud and Britain, 2006). Mental disorders were the one class of disorders that led to markedly lower employability. Disability in general was associated with a 23 percent lower likelihood of finding employment. Comparable trends have been found in Australia. In an Australian survey of 134 disability employment service providers assisting 3,025 jobseekers, individuals with mental disorders represented the largest category of jobseekers at 30 percent (Commonwealth Department of Family and Community Services, 2002). Jobseekers with a mental disability were less likely to find or retain employment than any other disability category. At 16-month follow-up, 44 percent of jobseekers with mental disorders remained unemployed.

It is often difficult to distinguish the direction of cause and effect between unemployment and mental disorders. In some cases mental disorders cause employees to leave the workforce (Murphy, 1998). Some individuals who develop mental disorders fail to perform adequately at their job or are forced to leave the job market due to stigma and bullying. In other cases unemployment can be the trigger that results in the expression of a mental disorder. As some form of reassurance that mental disorders lead to poor labor market outcomes, the strong relationship between mental disorders and unemployment persists when the possibility that employment may cause the worker's poor mental health has been accounted for (Ettner, Frank, and Kessler, 1997; Ettner and Grzywacz, 2001).

Several barriers to competitive employment exist among individuals with mental disorders. Many of these barriers are discussed by Waghorn and Lloyd (Waghorn and Lloyd, 2005). First, mental disorders often produce cognitive, perceptual, affective, and interpersonal deficits which may contribute to unemployment (Anthony and Jansen, 1984). Such cognitive symptoms likely cause employment restrictions that limit occupational choices and restrict the type of work that can be performed (Waghorn and Chant, 2005). Second, the symptoms of mental disorders can serve as barriers to obtaining and retaining employment. Symptoms of mental disorders may necessitate job accommodation such as restricted work hours, and need for ongoing employment assistance. Yet, symptomatology is not a consistent predictor of employment outcome (see Tsang, Lam, Ng, et al., 2000). Third, side-effects of pharmacotherapy may act as a barrier to vocational outcomes. Finally, stigma surrounding mental disorders can act as a barrier to gainful employment. The public often does not understand the impact of mental disorders and carry misperceptions about the abilities and needs of those who experience such disorders. Individuals with mental disorders are often viewed in a more negative manner than other individuals and this negative view can restrict opportunities (Corrigan, 2003, 2004; Corrigan, Markowitz, and Watson, 2004). All else being equal, employers will often not hire or advance individuals with mental disorders (Spillane, 1999; Stuart, 2006).

The government incurs substantial costs due to unemployment. Unemployment results in less taxable income, and increased use of public services, such as unemployment benefits, disability insurance, welfare programs, and healthcare. Indeed, people with mental disorders constitute one of the largest groups of social security recipients (Murphy, Mullen, and Spagnolo, 2005; Sanderson and Andrews, 2006). Employers also stand to incur substantial costs due to unemployment. Employers incur substantial costs through rehiring and training new employees. It has been estimated that mental disorders among staff cost the United Kingdom £2.1 billion each year due to replacing personnel (SCMH, 2007).

Economic burden of mental disorders—absenteeism

Many mental disorders are cyclical in nature meaning that the presence and severity of symptoms associated with some mental disorders typically wax and wane. Sometimes symptoms are severe and debilitating while other times they are mild or, in the case of remittance, non-existent. As such, individuals with mental disorders have both good and bad days, weeks, and months. One thing is certain; symptoms associated with mental disorders often necessitate the individual to miss additional time from work. Time missed from work is generally termed absenteeism. A great deal of time and effort has been placed into determining the additive effects of mental disorders on absenteeism. While there is no agreed upon or "gold standard" (Lofland, Pizzi, and Frick, 2004), absenteeism is usually recorded as hours or days missed from the workplace during a specified period of time and most commonly assessed through occupational records or by way of self-report questionnaires.

Mental disorders are one of the leading causes of absenteeism from work and early retirement across Europe. In the UK, stress (generally referred to as anxiety and depression) is the greatest cause of work absence, accounting for nearly 30 percent of all work-related absences (UKHSE, 2011). Work-related stress caused workers in Great Britain to lose an estimated 10.8 million working days in 2010/2011. On average, each person suffering from work-related stress lost 27 business days. This burden is not exclusive to Great Britain or high-income countries but rather persists across the entire world. Data from the previously described WMH survey indicated that individuals with any mental disorder experienced 31.1 more absenteeism days per year than individuals with no conditions (Alonso, Petukhova, Vilagut, et al., 2010). Mental health conditions accounted for 62.2 percent of all days out of role. Further, this effect persisted after sociodemographic variables and comorbidities were adjusted for.

Workplace absenteeism related to mental disorders account for an estimated 7 percent of the global payroll across all organizations (Watson Wyatt Worldwide, 2000). Previously described data suggests that mental disorders among staff cost UK employers an estimated £8.4 billion each year in terms of absenteeism (SCMH, 2007). Similar estimates have been found for Australia. Absenteeism alone has been found to cost Australian employers an estimated $3.5 billion AUD each year (Medibank Private, 2008). Further, the total absenteeism and long-term disability cost of mental disorders in the Netherlands has been estimated to be 0.5 percent of GDP or €1.44 billion annually (Järvisalo, Andersson, Boedeker, et al., 2005).

Economic burden of mental disorders—presenteeism

Presenteeism is an indirect cost that refers to an illness-related reduction in work productivity. Individuals with mental disorders often report to work but operate at reduced levels resulting in presenteeism. Mental disorders at work can increase error rate, lead to poor decision-making, decreased motivation and commitment, and increased tension and conflict, all of which result in poor work performance (Harnois and Gabriel, 2000). While there is no "gold standard", many measures of presenteeism exist and the majority of these have adequate statistical properties (see Lofland, Pizzi, and Frick, 2004; Prasad, Wahlqvist, Shikiar, et al., 2004 for reviews of common measures). The majority of these measures capture self-reported time (hours) or proportion (percent) of illness-related loss-of-work performance.

Mental disorders can be characterized as disorders of presenteeism, or the working wounded. Without a doubt, the greatest costs incurred as a result of mental disorders are due to presenteeism. The work-related cost of presenteeism on the UK economy has been estimated at £15.1 billion each year (SCMH, 2007). This is nearly double the £8.4 billion attributable to absenteeism. Similarly, in 2003 it was estimated that the loss of work productivity attributable to mental disorder-related long-term disability cost the Canadian economy $8.47 billion CAD (Lim, Jacobs, Ohinmaa, et al., 2008). An assessment of mental disorder-related presenteeism in Australia yielded similar conclusions. Mental disorder-related presenteeism cost the Australian economy an estimated $6.63 billion AUD (Medibank Private, 2008). This estimate was once again nearly twice the $3.5 billion AUD attributable to absenteeism.

One way to assess presenteeism is through partial disability days. Partial disability days are a measure of the days in which an individual has a functional limitation in their daily activities. These are days where individuals were unable to carry out normal work activities because of a disability. Bruffaerts et al. (2012) assessed partial disability days among 26 international samples of individuals completing the WMH survey. Individuals with mental disorders experienced an average of 4.37 disability days per month (Bruffaerts, Vilagut,

Demyttenaere, et al., 2012). This equates to 1.42 partial disability days per month more than those without a physical or mental disorder. In fact, there was some indication that mental disorders are more debilitating than physical disorders. Individuals with mental disorders consistently reported 15–28 percent more partial disability days than those with physical disorders. The authors calculated population attributable risk portions (PARP's) for partial disability days attributable to mental disorders at 14.7 percent, indicating that 14.7 percent of societal partial disability days could be reduced if mental disorders were reduced.

Economic burden of mental disorders—workplace accidents

Workplace accidents can cost employers substantial amounts in terms of loss or damage to equipment or goods, reduced production, medical/insurance expenses, and associated absenteeism (Hilton and Whiteford, 2010). Some have suggested that the costs associated with workplace accidents outweigh the costs of absenteeism and presenteeism (Wang, Beck, Berglund, et al., 2003).

Many recent studies have assessed the relationship between mental disorders and workplace accidents. Some have concluded that the symptom associated impairment of mental disorders can increase the risk of workplace accidents. These studies have limitations and do not assess diagnosed mental disorders directly but often assess depressive symptomatology or psychological distress.

In a study of 1,324 Australian heavy goods vehicle drivers, the presence of severe or very severe depressive symptoms assessed using the Depression, Anxiety, Stress Scale (DASS) was associated with an increased risk of being involved in an accident or a near miss (Hilton, Staddon, Sheridan, et al., 2009). Drivers with severe depressive symptoms were 4.5-fold more likely to experience an accident or near-miss in the preceding 28 days while those with very severe symptoms were 5-fold more likely. The authors concluded that driving with severe depression is akin to impaired driving with a blood alcohol content of 0.08.

The risk of experiencing a workplace accident attributable to psychological distress has been quantified using two nationally representative samples. Both studies quantified psychological distress using the Kessler 6 (K6) psychological stress inventory. Kim (2008) analyzed data from the 2000–03 US National Health Interview Survey (n = 101,855) and found that serious psychological distress was associated with an increase in three-month age-adjusted prevalence of occupational injury. The prevalence of workplace injury among individuals with serious psychological distress was 0.8 which was 37 percent higher than the prevalence in workers without serious psychological distress (Kim, 2008). This increase in risk was only slightly attenuated to 34 percent (OR = 1.34) after controlling for sex, age, race, education, and occupation. The second study used data from the 2004/2005 Australian Work Outcomes Research Cost-Benefit (WORC) survey (n = 60,566) to quantify the association between psychological distress and workplace accidents, arriving at similar conclusions (Hilton and Whiteford, 2010): 4.5 percent and 9 percent of employees had moderate and high psychological distress, respectively. High and moderate psychological distress each increased the likelihood of workplace accidents by 40 percent (OR = 1.40) after education status, employment sector, and job status were adjusted for. Additionally, moderate and high psychological distress increased the likelihood of experiencing a workplace failure in the previous month by 2.3-fold and 2.6-fold, respectively. This increased risk of workplace failure attributable to psychological distress was greater than the risk associated with having six or more physical health conditions (Hilton and Whiteford, 2010).

Comparing Mental Disorders and Physical Disorders

While chronic medical conditions and physical disorders are prevalent and costly, the burden associated with mental disorders is consistently found to be greater than that of physical disorders. For example, depression is associated with greater work-related loss and disability days than most chronic health conditions (Dewa and Lin, 2000; Grzywacz and Ettner, 2000).

In 2002 a total of 7,797 full-time employees working for Dow in the United States completed a survey reporting on the costs and burden associated with physical and mental disorders (Collins, Baase, Sharda, et al., 2005). Mental disorders were found to cost employers more financially than other chronic medical conditions. Fifty-eight percent of employees reported having a primary health condition and 9.2 percent of employees reported a mental disorder (for example, anxiety, depression). Collins et al. calculated the direct (that is, medical/pharmaceutical) and indirect (that is, absenteeism and presenteeism) costs of each disorder. The highest total cost per worker, per year was for mental disorders ($18,864 USD in 2002). The majority of this cost was due to presenteeism. The costs associated with mental disorders were more than $5,000 USD greater than the costs associated with the next most costly medical condition—breathing disorders.

Mental disorders also appear to be more pervasive and debilitating than common physical conditions. Dewa et al. used short-term disability data from a Canadian resource sector company that had been collected between 2003 and 2006 (n = 12,407) to compare incidence and costs of mental and physical disabilities (Dewa, Chau, and Dermer, 2010). The yearly incidence of disability was 14.5 percent, indicating 145 disability cases per 1,000 employees annually. The incidence of mental disorders (2.1 percent) was comparable to respiratory disorders (2.4 percent) and musculoskeletal disorders (2.0 percent). Disability episodes for mental disorders were longer than those for other types of disorders (67.0 days versus 33.8 days). Further, mental disorders resulted in the highest cost per episode at $17,734.41 CAD, which was significantly greater than the average disability cost of $9,026.68 CAD.

Mental disorders not only cost more than the average chronic medical condition but they are also more debilitating. Data from 15 countries completing the WMH survey across (n = 73,441) was used to compare the disability associated with mental and physical disorders (Ormel, Petukhova, Chatterji, et al., 2008). Sheehan Disability Scale scores were generally higher for mental disorders than physical disorders, indicating that mental disorders are associated with greater work, social, and personal disability. Ormel et al. selected the 100 most logical mental/physical disorder comparisons and found that mental disorders were associated with greater disability in 91 out of 100 comparisons, leaving no doubt that mental disorders are more debilitating than physical conditions. These results persisted after controlling for sociodemographic variables and treatment status, indicating that differences in treatment modalities cannot explain this discrepancy: while convincing, comorbidities were not accounted for and the discrepancy between mental and physical disorders was more pronounced for social and personal disability, and less so for work disability (19.4–21.7 percent vs 17.9–18.1 percent). Thus, while mental disorders are more debilitating than physical conditions, these results may not transfer directly to the workplace.

Mental and physical conditions are not mutually exclusive and the two often co-occur. Considerable evidence suggests that psychological distress is comorbid with other health conditions and can worsen health outcomes (Benton, Staab, and Evans, 2007; Demyttenaere, Bonnewyn, Bruffaerts, et al., 2006; Fortin, Bravo, Hudon, et al., 2006; Moussavi, Chatterji, Verdes, et al., 2007). The loss of functional capacity often associated with the occurrence of a physical disorder often leads to psychological distress and may result in a clinically diagnosable mental disorder. Evidence suggests that comorbid mental and physical conditions cost employers and society substantially more than either condition in isolation. Results from the previously described WORC suggest that absenteeism and presenteeism is greater among employees that have psychological distress (Holden, Scuffham, Hilton, et al., 2011). The incidence relative risk for absenteeism adjusted for demographic and work variables was consistently greater if the employee experienced a health condition with comorbid psychological distress. The greatest risk was found for cancers (OR = 1.08 vs 1.83), arthritis (OR = 1.07 vs 1.41), and neck/back pain (OR's = 1.02 vs 1.33). The risk for presenteeism adjusted for demographic and work variables was consistently greater if the employee experienced a health condition with comorbid psychological distress. The most elevated risk was found for arthritis (OR = 0.90 vs. 5.06), cancers (OR = 0.80 vs 4.44), and neck/back pain (OR's = 0.91 vs 4.20).

Individuals with Mental Disorders are not Receiving Minimally Adequate Treatment

Few individuals with mental disorders are receiving treatment. This appears to be a global phenomenon that is not reliant on country income level or socio-political structure. Few individuals with a mental disorder across 15 countries who completed the WMH survey (n = 73,441) self-reported receiving treatment in the previous 12 months (Ormel, Petukhova, Chatterji, et al., 2008). While the proportion of individuals in high-income countries (23.7 percent; n = 2637) who received treatment in the previous 12 months was greater than in middle and low-income countries (7.3 percent; n = 319), overall treatment rates were dismal. Across the entire sample, only a small minority of individuals with a mental disorder (19.3 percent; n = 2,956) self-reported receiving treatment in the previous 12 months. While the proportion of individuals with serious mental disorders who received treatment was higher at 29.7 percent (n = 1,523), it was still incredibly low. The proportion of individuals receiving treatment for a mental disorder was substantially lower than those receiving treatment because of a physical disorder (60.9 percent; n = 9,604).

The proportion of individuals in the workforce who are receiving treatment for a mental disorder is similar to that of the general population. Australian evidence indicates that only 15 to 20 percent of employees with a mental disorder have received treatment in the previous month (Hilton, Scuffham, Sheridan, et al., 2009; D. Lim, Sanderson, and Andrews, 2001). These findings suggest that there are many employees who suffer silently with a mental disorder that would benefit from treatment. It is, however, important to ensure that the treatments being offered are evidence based and supported by research.

Not all treatments are made equal and it is important to determine what portion of individuals with a mental disorder are receiving minimally adequate treatment, usually defined as a treatment that has been supported by research evidence. Wang et al. (2007) used WMH survey data from 17 countries (n = 88,848) to answer this question. Respondents receiving any mental health services in the previous 12 months varied by country (1.6 percent in Nigeria to 17.9 percent in the US). Excluding China, there was a dose-response relationship between mental disorder severity and service use (Wang, Aguilar-Gaxiola, Alonso, et al., 2007). Despite this relationship, only 11 percent (China) to 62.1 percent (Belgium) of individuals with a serious mental disorder received treatment in the previous 12 months. Respondents who received treatment often received follow-up treatment. Between 70.2 percent (Germany) and 94.5 percent (Italy) of treated individuals received follow-up treatment. One discouraging finding was that the vast majority of individuals using services were receiving treatment that was less than minimally adequate. Minimally adequate treatment was defined as receiving either pharmacotherapy ($\geq$ 1 month of medication plus $\geq$ 4 visits to any type of medical doctor), or psychotherapy ($\geq$ 8 with any professional). According to this definition, only 26.6 percent (n = 1175) of individuals accessing services were receiving treatment defined as minimally adequate. Respondents receiving "minimally adequate treatment" varied between 10.4 percent (Nigeria) and 42.3 percent (France) but were generally lower in lower-income countries with one notable exception being the US (18.1 percent) (Wang, Aguilar-Gaxiola, Alonso, et al., 2007).

The low and inadequate treatment among individuals with mental disorders is consistent with the low recognition and rate of treatment in primary care settings. Individuals with mental disorders often have their signs and symptoms overlooked by their primary healthcare provider and this does not appear to change if the provider is further educated about the disorder (Thompson, Kinmonth, Stevens, et al., 2000; Tiemens, Ormel, Jenner, et al., 1999). In one large study across the UK, physicians evidenced approximately 36 percent sensitivity in detecting depression and this did not change following education or treatment seminars (Thompson, Kinmonth, Stevens, et al., 2000).

To make matters worse, substantial delays exist between onset of mental disorders and first treatment contact. Wang et al. analyzed data from the WMH survey to determine the delay between onset of common mental disorders (that is, anxiety disorders, mood disorder, and substance abuse disorders) and the utilization of treatment (Wang, Angermeyer, Borges, et al., 2007). The delay between onset of disorder and service utilization was substantial across all mental disorders. Individuals with anxiety disorder exhibited a median delay of onset of 20 years before seeking treatment. Only 0.8–36.4 percent of individuals with anxiety disorders sought treatment in the year of disorder onset. For mood disorders, the median delay of treatment service contact was 4 years with 6–52.1 percent of individuals seeking treatment contact in the year of disorder onset. The median delay between disorder onset and treatment contact was 6.62 for individuals with substance use disorders with only 0.9–18.6 percent making treatment contact within the year of disorder onset (Wang, Angermeyer, Borges, et al., 2007). Across all disorders, female sex was associated with earlier treatment contact.

Poor service utilization may be due to many factors, including individual, societal, and environmental. Across the European Union-27, poor service provision has been attributed to underutilization of resources that are already available, under-recognition of psychological distress and existing mental disorders, and a lack of resources needed to adequately treat individuals with mental disorders (Wittchen Jacobi, Rehm, et al., 2011).

Treatment of Mental Disorders is Effective

The finding that individuals with mental disorders experience a prominent delay in seeking treatment after disorder onset and often do not receive minimally adequate treatments is perplexing given that empirically supported treatments have proven highly effective. Empirically supported treatments such as CBT, pharmacotherapy, or some combination are effective in reducing symptomatology of common mental disorders (for example, depression, anxiety) in up to 75 percent of individuals (Katon, Von Korff, Lin, et al., 1995; NICE, 2009; Simon, Chisholm, Treglia, et al., 2002). Westen and Morrison conducted a multidimensional meta-analysis on treatments for depression, panic disorder, and generalized anxiety disorder and found impressive initial and sustained treatment effects (Westen and Morrison, 2001). Across studies, approximately 54 percent, 63 percent, and 52 percent of patients with depression, panic disorder, and generalized anxiety disorder showed clinically significant improvement at the end of treatment, respectively. These effects were deemed large by standard convention and were approximately a Cohen's d (that is, a mean standardized difference) of 2. Of those who initially improved, in most cases there were small to moderate decreases in efficacy over 18 months' time.

Many meta-analyses have been performed in the last two decades attesting to the efficacy of psychological treatments for mental health disorders. For example, cognitive behavioral therapy (CBT) is one of the most extensively researched forms of psychotherapy that has proven incredibly effective at treating common mental disorders. An underlying presumption of CBT is that symptoms and dysfunctional behaviors are often cognitively mediated and improvement can be produced, modifying these dysfunctional thoughts and beliefs (Dobson and Dozois, 2001). In a review of meta-analyses, Butler et al. convincingly illustrated that CBT is exceptionally effective at treating symptoms of a wide range of common mental disorders (Butler, Chapman, Forman, et al., 2006). Large effect sizes were found for CBT for depression, generalized anxiety disorder, panic disorder, social phobia, and post-traumatic stress disorder. Medium effects were found for CBT for marital distress, anger, and chronic pain. These effects are often found when compared to placebo or other active control conditions. There are numerous other examples of empirically supported treatments for common mental disorders but the point will not be belabored here. The take home message is that many psychological treatments are highly effective at treating mental health concerns. The problem appears to be linking patients with effective treatments. We will now turn our attention to reviewing evidence that suggests treating mental disorders can result in cost savings to employers.

Treating Mental Disorders is Beneficial for Employers

Employers who treat mental disorders stand to incur substantial benefits. Some of these benefits will be highlighted in the proceeding paragraphs while others will be addressed throughout the chapters of this book. As one would expect, treating mental disorders and psychological distress improves employee mental health and well-being. As you will see in our final chapter, a happy worker is a hard worker. Alleviating the signs and symptoms of mental disorders and psychological distress improves employees personal, social, and occupational functioning. Employees whose mental disorders are being attended to provide better customer service, and experience more favorable co-worker interactions, less absenteeism, higher productivity, and less healthcare-related expenses.

Hilton et al. used cross-sectional data from the previously described WORC project (n = 60,556) to evaluate the association between mental disorder treatment and work productivity, defined as a combination of presenteeism and absenteeism (Hilton, Scuffham, Sheridan, et al., 2009). In general, employees with greater psychological distress rated lower on productivity and this relationship persisted independent of treatment status. Further, employees with psychological distress were less likely to work more hours than required (that is, evidenced less extensionism). Given that this data was cross-sectional, it was impossible to track treatment effects and link treatment gains to productivity.

With this limitation in mind, Hilton et al. calculated the productivity benefits that were accrued as psychological distress moved from severe to moderate to mild among treated employees. Moving from a high distress treated group to a low distress treated group indicates an increase in productivity of 11.1 percent. These benefits were found in terms of absenteeism and presenteeism. For example, moving from high distress treated to moderate distress treated resulted in a 7.4 percent reduction in absenteeism while moving from high distress treated to low distress treated resulted in 9.4 percent improvement in presenteeism. These effects occurred after controlling for significant covariates of gender, age, marital status, number of children, education, and physical conditions. Interestingly, the incremental gains in productivity among the "treated" group were greater than gains among untreated employees (11.1 percent vs 1.7 percent). We can safely conclude that treatment that is effective in alleviating psychological distress will result in substantial improvements in productivity.

A recent review summarized evidence on workplace-based work disability prevention interventions for workers with common mental health conditions (Pomaki, Franche, Murray, et al., 2012). Articles located by the authors were screened, subject to a 29-item quality rating form, and synthesized using best evidence synthesis (Slavin, 1995). Eight articles were included that identified four interventions and four work outcomes. Results suggest that facilitating access to treatment, and workplace-based high-intensity psychological interventions have moderate effects in improving work functioning, quality of life, and economic outcomes among employees with mental disabilities. Facilitating access to treatment has limited additional benefits in reducing work absence. Workplace-based low-intensity psychological interventions were found to have moderate effects in reducing work absences, limited effects in improving quality of life, and moderate effects in improving economic outcomes. In sum, employers stand to gain most from ensuring that their employees with mental disabilities have access to, and utilize treatment services.

One method that has proven successful in reducing stigma and facilitating the identification and treatment of mental disorders in the workplace is an occupational mental health first aid training course. Mental health first aid consists of a 12-hour standardized, manual-based course designed to give employees the skills to work through a mental health crisis in the workplace similar to how one would work their way through a medical emergency. Evaluation of a workplace-based mental health first aid course has yielded encouraging results (Kitchener and Jorm, 2004). Employees (n = 301) from Australian government departments were randomized to a mental health first aid course or a waitlist control. The benefits of the mental health first aid course included: greater confidence about providing help, greater likelihood of advising help-seeking behavior, and decreased stigma.

Concluding Remarks

Mental disorders are conditions that defy biomedical explanations. There have been numerous pragmatic attempts to define mental disorders (for example, statistical rarity, subjective distress, harmful dysfunction), but these attempts do not fully account for mental disorders and leave exceptions that cannot be overlooked. Such discrepancies have led to two internationally recognized classification systems that are based on clustering of signs and symptoms. While classification systems have proven valid, reliable, and important for research and clinical practice, they may be overly cumbersome and intensive for use in the workplace. Brief screening measures for mental disorders have a number of benefits for use in the workplace. Research surveys from around the world indicate that mental disorders are a common occurrence affecting between 20 and 48 percent of the population at any given time. Mental disorders result in substantial personal and economic consequences. Individuals with mental disorders are more likely to experience unemployment and take time away from work. They are also more likely to operate at reduced levels when at work and to be involved in a workplace accident. The economic and personal burden associated with mental disorder has been estimated to exceed the burden associated with physical disorders, such as cardiovascular disease and cancer. Luckily, several effective treatments for mental disorders have been developed, and have been shown to reduce burden and improve outcomes. Yet, individuals who suffer from mental disorders are not receiving empirically supported treatments. Research indicates that a substantial portion of those who suffer from a mental disorder will suffer for many years before seeking treatment and will not receive empirically supported treatments when they do seek them. Using brief screening measures to identify employees who may be suffering from mental illness, and referring those employees for a thorough evaluation and subsequent empirically validated treatments, represents one of the most effective means for improving the economic outlook of a company as well as the quality of life of employees.

More information can be found at the following sources:

World mental health survey initiative at http://www.hcp.med.harvard. edu/wmh/

World Health Organization mental health action plan at http://www.who.
  int/mental_health/en/

ICD-10 classification for mental and behavioral disorders at http://www.
  who.int/classifications/icd/en/index.html

DSM-V classification of mental disorders at http://www.psychiatry.org/
  dsm5

Cost of disorders of the brain in Europe at http://www.europeanbraincouncil.
  org/meetings/launch-study-cost-disorders.asp

References

ABS, Australian Bureau of Statistics. (2007). National Survey of Mental Health
  and Wellbeing: summary of results: Australian Bureau of Statistics Canberra.
Alonso, J., Petukhova, M., Vilagut, G., Chatterji, S., Heeringa, S., Üstün,
  T.B., et al. (2010). Days out of role due to common physical and mental
  conditions: results from the WHO World Mental Health surveys. *Molecular
  Psychiatry*, 16(12), 1234–46.
Andlin-Sobocki, P., Jönsson, B., Wittchen, H.U., and Olesen, J. (2005). Cost of
  disorders of the brain in Europe. *European Journal of Neurology*, 12(s1), 1–27.
Anthony, W.A. and Jansen, M.A. (1984). Predicting the vocational capacity
  of the chronically mentally ill: Research and policy implications. *American
  Psychologist; American Psychologist*, 39(5), 537.
APA, American Psychiatric Association. (2000). Diagnostic and Statistical
  Manual of Mental Disorders DSM-IV-TR (Text Revision). American
  Psychiatric Association. Washington, DC.
Benton, T., Staab, J., and Evans, D.L. (2007). Medical co-morbidity in depressive
  disorders. *Annals of Clinical Psychiatry*, 19(4), 289–303.
Berthoud, R. and Britain, G. (2006). *The Employment Rates of Disabled Oeople*
  (Vol. 298): Corporate Document Services London.
Bruffaerts, R., Vilagut, G., Demyttenaere, K., Alonso, J., AlHamzawi, A., Andrade,
  L.H., et al. (2012). Role of common mental and physical disorders in partial
  disability around the world. *The British Journal of Psychiatry*, 200(6), 454–61.
Butler, A.C., Chapman, J.E., Forman, E.M., and Beck, A.T. (2006). The empirical
  status of cognitive-behavioral therapy: a review of meta-analyses. *Clinical
  psychology review*, 26(1), 17–31.
Collins, J.J., Baase, C.M., Sharda, C.E., Ozminkowski, R.J., Nicholson, S., Billotti,
  G.M., et al. (2005). The assessment of chronic health conditions on work

performance, absence, and total economic impact for employers. *Journal of Occupational and Environmental Medicine*, 47(6), 547.

Commonwealth Department of Family and Community Services. (2002). *Case Based Funding Trial Evaluation. Interim Report.* Canberra: Australian Government.

Corrigan, P. (2003). Beat the stigma: come out of the closet. *Psychiatric Services*, 54(10), 1313–1313.

Corrigan, P. (2004). How stigma interferes with mental health care. *American Psychologist; American Psychologist*, 59(7), 614.

Corrigan, P.W., Markowitz, F.E., and Watson, A.C. (2004). Structural levels of mental illness stigma and discrimination. *Schizophrenia Bulletin*, 30(3), 481–91.

Demyttenaere, K., Bonnewyn, A., Bruffaerts, R., Brugha, T., De Graaf, R., and Alonso, J. (2006). Comorbid painful physical symptoms and depression: prevalence, work loss, and help seeking. *Journal of affective disorders*, 92(2–3), 185.

Dewa, C.S., Lesage, A., Goering, P., and Caveen, M. (2004). Nature and prevalence of mental illness in the workplace. *Healthcare Papers*, 5(2), 12–25.

Dewa, C.S., Chau, N., and Dermer, S. (2010). Examining the comparative incidence and costs of physical and mental health-related disabilities in an employed population. *Journal of Occupational and Environmental Medicine*, 52(7), 758–62.

Dewa, C.S. and Lin, E. (2000). Chronic physical illness, psychiatric disorder and disability in the workplace. *Social Science & Medicine*, 51(1), 41–50.

Dobson, K. and Dozois, D.J. (2001). Historical and philosophical bases of the cognitive-behavioral therapies. In K. Dobson (ed.), *Handbook of Cognitive-behavioral Therapies* (2nd ed., pp. 3–38). New York, NY: Guilford Press.

Ettner, S.L., Frank, R.G., and Kessler, R.C. (1997). The impact of psychiatric disorders on labor market outcomes: National Bureau of Economic Research. *Industrial and Labor Relations Review*, 51(1) 64–81.

Ettner, S.L. and Grzywacz, J.G. (2001). Workers' perceptions of how jobs affect health: A social ecological perspective. *Journal of Occupational Health Psychology*, 6(2), 101–13.

First, M.B. and Wakefield, J.C. (2010). Defining "mental disorder" in DSM-V. A commentary on: "What is a mental/psychiatric disorder? From DSM-IV to DSM-V" by Stein et al. (2010). *Psychol Med*, 40(11), 1779–82. DOI: 10.1017/S0033291709992339.

Fortin, M., Bravo, G., Hudon, C., Lapointe, L., Dubois, M.F., and Almirall, J. (2006). Psychological distress and multimorbidity in primary care. *The Annals of Family Medicine*, 4(5), 417–22.

Greenberg, P.E., Kessler, R.C., Birnbaum, H.G., Leong, S.A., Lowe, S.W., Berglund, P.A., and Corey-Lisle, P.K. (2003). The economic burden of depression in the United States: how did it change between 1990 and 2000? *Journal of Clinical Psychiatry*, 64(12), 1465–75.

Grzywacz, J. and Ettner, S.L. (2000). Lost time on the job: the effect of depression versus physical health conditions. *Econ Neurosci*, 2(6), 41–6.

Gureje, O., Lasebikan, V.O., Kola, L., and Makanjuola, V.A. (2006). Lifetime and 12-month prevalence of mental disorders in the Nigerian Survey of Mental Health and Well-Being. *Br J Psychiatry*, 188, 465–71. DOI: 10.1192/bjp.188.5.465.

Harnois, G. and Gabriel, P. (2000). Mental health and work: impact, issues and good practices. Geneva, SUI: World Health Organization. Available at: http://www.who.int/mental_health/media/en/712.pdf.

Hilton, M.F., Scuffham, P.A., Sheridan, J., Cleary, C.M., Vecchio, N., and Whiteford, H.A. (2009). The association between mental disorders and productivity in treated and untreated employees. *Journal of Occupational and Environmental Medicine*, 51(9), 996–1003.

Hilton, M.F., Staddon, Z., Sheridan, J., and Whiteford, H.A. (2009). The impact of mental health symptoms on heavy goods vehicle drivers' performance. *Accident Analysis & Prevention*, 41(3), 453–61.

Hilton, M.F. and Whiteford, H.A. (2010). Associations between psychological distress, workplace accidents, workplace failures and workplace successes. *International Archives of Occupational and Environmental Health*, 83(8), 923–33.

Holden, L., Scuffham, P.A., Hilton, M.F., Ware, R.S., Vecchio, N., and Whiteford, H.A. (2011). Health-related productivity losses increase when the health condition is co-morbid with psychological distress: findings from a large cross-sectional sample of working Australians. *BMC Public Health*, 11(1), 417. DOI: 10.1186/1471-2458-11-417.

Järvisalo, J., Andersson, B., Boedeker, W., and Houtman, I. (2005). *Mental Disorders as a Major Challenge in Prevention of Work Disability. Experiences in Finland, Germany, the Netherlands and Sweden*: The Social Insurance Institution, Helsinki, Finland.

Katon, W., Von Korff, M., Lin, E., Walker, E., Simon, G.E., Bush, T., et al. (1995). Collaborative management to achieve treatment guidelinesImpact on depression in primary care. *JAMA: the Journal of the American Medical Association*, 273(13), 1026–31.

Kendell, R.E. (1975). The concept of disease and its implications for psychiatry. *Br J Psychiatry*, 127, 305–15.

Kessler, R.C., Aguilar-Gaxiola, S., Alonso, J., Chatterji, S., Lee, S., Ormel, J., et al. (2009). The global burden of mental disorders: an update from the WHO World Mental Health (WMH) surveys. *Epidemiologia e psichiatria sociale*, 18(01), 23–33.

Kessler, R.C. and Frank, R.G. (1997). The impact of psychiatric disorders on work loss days. *Psychological Medicine*, 27(4) 861–873. DOI: 10.1017/S0033291797004807.

Kessler, R.C. and Ustun, T.B. (2004). The World Mental Health (WMH) Survey Initiative Version of the World Health Organization (WHO) Composite International Diagnostic Interview (CIDI). *Int J Methods Psychiatr Res*, 13(2), 93–121.

Kessler, R.C., Andrews, G., Colpe, L.J., Hiripi, E., Mroczek, D.K., Normand, S.L.T., et al. (2002). Short screening scales to monitor population prevalences and trends in non-specific psychological distress. *Psychological Medicine*, 32(6), 959–76.

Kessler, R.C., Barker, P.R., Colpe, L.J., Epstein, J.F., Gfroerer, J.C., Hiripi, E., et al. (2003). Screening for serious mental illness in the general population. *Archives of General Psychiatry*, 60(2), 184–9.

Kessler, R.C., Heeringa, S., Lakoma, M.D., Petukhova, M., Rupp, A.E., Schoenbaum, M., et al. (2008). The individual-level and societal-level effects of mental disorders on earnings in the United States: Results from the National Comorbidity Survey Replication. *The American Journal of Psychiatry*, 165(6), 703–11.

Kim, J. (2008). Psychological distress and occupational injury: findings from the national health interview survey 2000–2003. *Journal of Preventive Medicine and Public Health*, 41(3), 200–207.

Kitchener, B.A. and Jorm, A.F. (2004). Mental health first aid training in a workplace setting: A randomized controlled trial [ISRCTN13249129]. *BMC Psychiatry*, 4(1), 23. DOI: 10.1186/1471-244X-4-23.

Lerner, D., Adler, D.A., Chang, H., Lapitsky, L., Hood, M.Y., Perissinotto, C., et al. (2004). Unemployment, job retention, and productivity loss among employees with depression. *Psychiatric Services*, 55(12), 1371–8.

Levinson, D., Lakoma, M.D., Petukhova, M., Schoenbaum, M., Zaslavsky, A.M., Angermeyer, M., et al. (2010). Associations of serious mental illness with earnings: results from the WHO World Mental Health surveys. *The British Journal of Psychiatry*, 197(2), 114–21.

Lilienfeld, S.O. and Landfield, K. (2008). Issues in diagnosis: Categorical vs. dimensional. In E.W. Craighead, D.J. Miklowitz and L.W. Craighead (eds), *Psychopathology: History, Diagnosis, and Empirical Foundations* (pp. 1–33). New Jersey, NJ: John Wiley & Sons, Inc.

Lim, D., Sanderson, K., and Andrews, G. (2001). Lost productivity among full-time workers with mental disorders. *The Journal of Mental Health Policy and Economics*, 3(3), 139–46.

Lim, K.L., Jacobs, P., Ohinmaa, A., Schopflocher, D., and Dewa, C.S. (2008). A new population-based measure of the economic burden of mental illness in Canada. *Chronic Diseases in Canada*, 28(3), 92–8.

Lofland, J.H., Pizzi, L., and Frick, K.D. (2004). A review of health-related workplace productivity loss instruments. *Pharmacoeconomics*, 22(3), 165–84.

Macias, C., DeCarlo, L.T., Wang, Q., Frey, J., and Barreira, P. (2001). Work interest as a predictor of competitive employment: policy implications for psychiatric rehabilitation. *Administration and Policy in Mental Health and Mental Health Services Research*, 28(4), 279–97.

Mechanic, D., Bilder, S., and McAlpine, D.D. (2002). Employing persons with serious mental illness. *Health Affairs*, 21(5), 242–53.

Medibank Private. (2008). *The Cost of Workplace Stress in Australia*: Medibank Private. Available at: http://www.medibank.com.au/Client/Documents/ Pdfs/The-Cost-of-Workplace-Stress.pdf.

Moussavi, S., Chatterji, S., Verdes, E., Tandon, A., Patel, V., and Ustun, B. (2007). Depression, chronic diseases, and decrements in health: results from the World Health Surveys. *The Lancet*, 370(9590), 851–8.

Murphy, Ann A, Mullen, Michelle G, and Spagnolo, Amy B. (2005). Enhancing individual placement and support: promoting job tenure by integrating natural supports and supported education. *American Journal of Psychiatric Rehabilitation*, 8(1), 37–61.

Murphy, M.A. (1998). Rejection, stigma, and hope. *Psychiatric Rehabilitation Journal*, 22, 185–8.

NICE, National Institute for Health Clinical Excellence. (2009). Managing long-term sickness absence and incapacity for work. London: National Institute for Health Clinical Excellence. Available at: http://www.nice.org.uk/nicemedia/ pdf/ph19guidance.pdf.

Olesen, J., Gustavsson, A., Svensson, M., Wittchen, H.U., Jonsson, B., group, Cdbe study, and European Brain, Council. (2012). The economic cost of brain disorders in Europe. *Eur J Neurol*, 19(1), 155–62. DOI: 10.1111/j.1468-1331.2011.03590.x.

Ormel, J., Petukhova, M., Chatterji, S., Aguilar-Gaxiola, S., Alonso, J., Angermeyer, M.C., et al. (2008). Disability and treatment of specific mental and physical disorders across the world. *The British Journal of Psychiatry*, 192(5), 368–75.

Pomaki, G., Franche, R.L., Murray, E., Khushrushahi, N., and Lampinen, T.M. (2012). Workplace-based work disability prevention interventions for workers with common mental health conditions: a review of the literature. *Journal of Occupational Rehabilitation*, 1–14.

Prasad, M., Wahlqvist, P., Shikiar, R., and Shih, Y.C.T. (2004). A review of self-report instruments measuring health-related work productivity: a patient-reported outcomes perspective. *Pharmacoeconomics*, 22(4), 225–44.

Sanderson, K. and Andrews, G. (2006). Common mental disorders in the workforce: recent findings from descriptive and social epidemiology. *Can J Psychiatry*, 51(2), 63–75.

SCMH, Sainsbury Centre for Mental Health. (2007). *Mental health at work: developing the business case*. London: Sainsbury Centre for Mental Health. Available at: http://www.centreformentalhealth.org.uk/pdfs/mental_health_at_work.pdf.

Sheehan, D.V., Harnett-Sheehan, K., and Raj, B.A. (1996). The measurement of disability. *International Clinical Psychopharmacology*, 11, 89–95.

Simon, G.E., Chisholm, D., Treglia, M., and Bushnell, D. (2002). Course of depression, health services costs, and work productivity in an international primary care study. *General Hospital Psychiatry*, 24(5), 328–35.

Slavin, R.E. (1995). Best evidence synthesis: an intelligent alternative to meta-analysis. *Journal of Clinical Epidemiology*, 48(1), 9–18.

Spillane, R. (1999). Australian managers' attitudes to mental illness. *Journal of Occupational Health and Safety Australia and New Zealand*, 15, 359–64.

Sroujian, C. (2003). Mental health is the number one cause of disability in Canada. *Insurance Journal*, 8.

Stein, D.J., Phillips, K.A., Bolton, D., Fulford, K.W., Sadler, J.Z., and Kendler, K.S. (2010). What is a mental/psychiatric disorder? From DSM-IV to DSM-V. *Psychol Med*, 40(11), 1759–65. DOI: 10.1017/S0033291709992261.

Stephens, T. and Joubert, N. (2001). The economic burden of mental health problems in Canada. *Chronic Diseases in Canada*, 22(1), 18–23.

Stuart, H. (2006). Mental illness and employment discrimination. *Current Opinion in Psychiatry*, 19(5), 522–6.

Taylor, F. Kräupl. (1971). Part 1. A logical analysis of the medico-psychological concept of disease. *Psychological Medicine*, 1(05), 356–64. DOI: DOI:10.1017/S003329170004472X.

Thompson, C., Kinmonth, A.L., Stevens, L., Pevele, R.C., Stevens, A., Ostler, K.J., et al. (2000). Effects of a clinical-practice guideline and practice-based education on detection and outcome of depression in primary care: Hampshire Depression Project randomised controlled trial. *The Lancet*, 355(9199), 185–91.

Tiemens, B.G., Ormel, J., Jenner, J.A., Van der Meer, K., Van Os, T., Van Den Brink, R.H.S., et al. (1999). Training primary-care physicians to recognize, diagnose and manage depression: does it improve patient outcomes? *Psychological Medicine*, 29(04), 833–45.

Tsang, H., Lam, P., Ng, B., and Leung, O. (2000). Predictors of Employment Outcome for People with Psychiatric Disabilities: A Review of Literature Since the Mid'80s. *Journal of Rehabilitation-Washington*, 66(2), 19–31.

UKHSE, United Kingdom Health and Safety Executive. (2011). *Stress and Psychological Disorders*. Retrieved from: http://www.hse.gov.uk/statistics/causdis/stress/stress.pdf.

Waghorn, G. and Chant, D. (2005). Labour force activity by people with depression and anxiety disorders: a population-level second-order analysis. *Acta Psychiatrica Scandinavica*, 112(6), 415–24.

Waghorn, G. and Lloyd, C. (2005). The employment of people with mental illness. *Advances in Mental Health*, 4(2), 129–71.

Wakefield, J.C. (1992). The concept of mental disorder. On the boundary between biological facts and social values. *Am Psychol*, 47(3), 373–88.

Wang, P.S., Aguilar-Gaxiola, S., Alonso, J., Angermeyer, M.C., Borges, G., Bromet, E.J., et al. (2007). Worldwide use of mental health services for anxiety, mood, and substance disorders: results from 17 countries in the WHO World Mental Health (WMH) Surveys. *Lancet*, 370(9590), 841–50.

Wang, P.S., Angermeyer, M., Borges, G., Bruffaerts, R., CHIU, W.A.I.T.A.T., DE GIROLAMO, G., et al. (2007). Delay and failure in treatment seeking after first onset of mental disorders in the World Health Organization's World Mental Health Survey Initiative. *World Psychiatry*, 6(3), 177–85.

Wang, P.S., Beck, A., Berglund, P., Leutzinger, J.A., Pronk, N., Richling, D., et al. (2003). Chronic medical conditions and work performance in the health and work performance questionnaire calibration surveys. *Journal of Occupational and Environmental Medicine*, 45(12), 1303–11.

Watson Wyatt Worldwide. (2000). Staying at Work 2000/2001—the dollars and sense of effective disability management. Vancouver: Watson Wyatt Worldwide.

Westen, D. and Morrison, K. (2001). A multidimensional meta-analysis of treatments for depression, panic, and generalized anxiety disorder: an empirical examination of the status of empirically supported therapies. *Journal of Consulting and Clinical Psychology*, 69(6), 875.

WHO, World Health Organization. (2001). *The World Health Report 2001 Mental Health: New Understanding, New Hope*. Geneva, SUI: WHO Press.

WHO, World Health Organization. (2011). *ICD-10: International Classification of Diseases and Related Health Problems—10th revision*. Geneva, SUI: WHO Press.

Wittchen, H.U. and Jacobi, F. (2005). Size and burden of mental disorders in Europe--a critical review and appraisal of 27 studies. *Eur Neuropsychopharmacol*, 15(4), 357–76. DOI: 10.1016/j.euroneuro.2005.04.012.

Wittchen, H.U., Jacobi, F., Rehm, J., Gustavsson, A., Svensson, M., Jonsson, B., et al. (2011). The size and burden of mental disorders and other disorders of the brain in Europe 2010. *Eur Neuropsychopharmacol*, 21(9), 655–679. DOI: 10.1016/j.euroneuro.2011.07.018.

Chapter 3

Current Thinking about Mental Illness in the Workplace

What remains visible in the public eye are the newspaper accounts of violence, the homeless mentally ill, the untreated illness in friends, family, and colleagues. What is not seen are all the truck drivers, secretaries, teachers, lawyers, physicians, and government officials who have been successfully treated, who work, compete, and succeed. (Jamison, 2006)

Introduction to Mental Health/Mental Illness

The incidence of mental health conditions in the workplace are not easily recognized and are definitely not a rare occurrence according to recent research. From a worldwide perspective, the conditions that are most often reported are depressive and anxiety disorders. The invisibility of mental ill-health is often the reason it goes unnoticed in society. Many mental health conditions are only revealed through disclosure by the individual. Both invisibility of mental health conditions and the likelihood to disclose an illness are sustained by low levels of what is known as mental health literacy, to be discussed at the end of this chapter. Understanding and knowing how to support individuals with mental illness can contribute to the unmet needs of individuals with mental disorders. As a result of these issues specific to the invisibility of many conditions and the lack of mental health literacy in society. Heavy burdens are placed not only on the emotional environment and unmet needs of employees with mental illness; there is also a substantial economic burden that organizations must face (Bartlett, Travers, Cartwright, et al., 2006; Pomaki, Franche, Murray, et al., 2012).

There exists a tremendous lack of understanding in society when it comes to mental health and mental illness. Most information is distributed through media outlets and secondary sources of information. However, the general lack of what is referred to as mental health literacy does not stop people from making their own assumptions about mental health or illness. This lack of accurate knowledge pertaining to the risk factors of mental illness is a contributing barrier to actually understanding mental health and mental illness. Case in point, we know less about the risk factors for mental disorders than we do about those for heart disease, diabetes, and cancer (Jorm, 2012). While these physical conditions are important to understand, it is important to note the imbalance occurring as mental health takes a secondary position in the discussion of overall health. Extensive focus on physical health has traditionally taken precedence over understanding mental components of health that often go unseen in daily life. The harmful effects of undeveloped mental health literacy present as misconceptions of mental illness held by society in general. Simply put, conditions that are more readily visible are often perceived as more "real" than mental disorders which are not always physically expressed. Beyond the reality of the condition, mental illness is often perceived as a lack of "moral fibre". This becomes an issue when external perceivers readily come to the conclusion that those with mental illness should be able to "snap out of it" on their own (Kendell, 2001). This process coupled with lack of any real knowledge is what is largely behind the stigma attached to having a mental illness. One of the results of this stigmatization is that people with mental illness tend to isolate themselves and avoid contact with society. This behavior can become an integral part of an individual's social identity and then be woven into their activities of daily living and their relationships with others. As a result, people with mental illness face the challenge of wanting to belong but not to a group that holds negative perceptions about them (Hall and Cheston, 2002).

Mental health can be influenced by social and economic factors in society including having access to: employment, safe working conditions, education, income, housing, family/social/community supports, and other opportunities that offer autonomy, and freedom from discrimination and violence (Kobau, Seligman, Peterson, et al., 2011). How it is addressed varies between the ability to recognize mental illness early on and having sufficient information pertaining to interventions available (Bartlett, Travers, Cartwright, et al., 2006). Topics in this chapter will address in-depth information on mental health and mental illness, perceptions of mental illness, stigmatization, and how mental illness impacts the individual and the workplace. Before proceeding, the interested reader may wish to refer to Chapter 2 for a detailed description of how mental disorders are classified.

Overview of Mental Health/Mental Illness

MENTAL HEALTH AND MENTAL ILLNESS TODAY

Since 1994, trends in mental health have been tracked through the National Population Health Survey and a series of cross-sectional studies conducted in 2001, 2003, 2005, and 2007 through the Canadian Community Health Survey. As a result, researchers have been able to track this data over time to understand how mental health has or has not changed in Canada. According to Simpson et al. (2012) there has been little change across 15 years of data that were targeted. However, the proportion of people using anti-depressants has increased while self-evaluations of extreme stress have decreased. The authors note that this may in fact be a result of mental health literacy increasing in the population as opposed to being viable changes in mental health status (Simpson, Meadows, Frances, et al., 2012).

Still today there is little attention drawn to the need for mental illness as a global priority, even when lifetime prevalence of mental illness in the general population has been estimated to be between 12.2 and 48.6 percent globally (WHO, 2000). Using a sample inclusive of seven countries, the WHO produced a report of mental illness prevalence using data from 1990–91. Out of 6,261 respondents there is a 37.5 percent prevalence rate of some form of mental disorder at some point in the life-course for Canadians. Of those disorders, one-third were found to be anxiety (21.3 percent)—the most prevalent out of those disorders surveyed (anxiety, mood, and substance-use)—and one third were found to be substance use (19.7 percent) (WHO, 2000). A startling statistic out of the United Kingdom states that in our lifetime, one in every four people will experience some form of mental health problem (Sinclair and Patel, 2012), Even despite these overwhelming numbers, mental health budgets are typically the first to be cut when health budgets face loss of funds (Tomlinson and Lund, 2012).

SOCIETAL PERCEPTIONS OF MENTAL ILLNESS

Mental illness is perceived very differently in society and oftentimes can be over-exaggerated in terms of its severity and rates of recovery to the extent of regaining functionality in daily living. Mental health literacy survey research has shown that many people are unable to correctly recognize mental disorders to begin with (Jorm, 2012). A recent study in Australia found that upon hearing about mental illness, society often goes directly to schizophrenia rather than the more common affective and anxiety disorders (Jorm and Reavley, 2012). The definition of mental illness over time has become singular to severe disorders while disregarding the less severe but more commonly experienced adverse mental health conditions. Using public perceptions of mental illness, Rusch et al. (2012) presented six mental illnesses alongside one another to gauge which were perceived as "Mental Illness". Of the six, participants regularly defined schizophrenia, bipolar disorder, and depression as being a mental illness. The three that were not identified as mental illnesses were drug addiction, stress, and grief.

These findings suggest that there is still a substantial belief in society that only major psychiatric disorders are mental illnesses while the more commonly occurring affective and anxiety conditions are not. This belief has gained support through research calling for people to examine scenarios of depressed individuals. Of those that participated, Canada averaged a 75 percent recognition rate for depression. Unfortunately, while a majority of the population can recognize depression, those that don't are unable to label depression as something that might need treatment or other help-seeking (Jorm, 2012). This deeply ingrained societal belief challenges people with mental illness to successfully establish social networks and various other means of support in their lives. While membership in a group brings positive components to an individual's life, associating oneself with mental illness can potentially compromise a positive social identity (Hall and Cheston, 2002). Ultimately, this struggle for an identity consequently influences an individual's quality of life by exacerbating the burdens of their illness (Ekeland and Bergem, 2006). Recognition of a mental disorder is the first step toward obtaining support and ultimately recovery, not simply as an act of stigmatization (Jorm, 2012).

PERCEIVED OUTCOMES OF MENTAL ILLNESS DIAGNOSIS

Those who experience severe mental illness are often thought to have a poor prognosis and face pessimistic views surrounding their abilities to function on a daily basis. Severe mental illness is defined as causing one or more major areas of functioning to be markedly below expectations for a significant period of time. It has even been found that those who provide services for those with mental illness can carry negative attitudes regarding poor outcomes (Corrigan, Markowitz, and Watson, 2004). Investigations in a nursing environment in Sweden (among 140 staff and 141 patients in a service provider environment) revealed that negative attitudes towards mental illness were prevalent among staff. Examples of the negative viewpoints ranged from: the possibility of the person being hired with their illness, willingness to date someone with a mental illness, and hiring a patient to care for children (Hansson, Jormfeldt,

Svedberg, et al., 2011). On the other hand, negative attitudes from the patient's perspective revealed thoughts about: personal failure because of entering a mental health facility, believing people think less of them, and not being taken seriously (Hansson, Jormfeldt, Svedberg, et al., 2011).

Attitudes toward mental illness vary in their degree but for the most part commonly occurring ones are: 1) authoritarianism—believing that life decisions should be made by others, 2) benevolence—mental illness makes a person childlike and need to be cared for, 3) fear, 4) avoidance, and 5) exclusion (people with mental illness should be segregated). However, important to note is that younger generations, people with higher educational levels, and contact with people experiencing mental illness reduces these attitudes (Arvaniti, Samakouri, Kalamara, et al., 2009).

SEEING THE PERSON, NOT THE ILLNESS

When discussing mental illness it is important to remember to see the person before the illness. It is common for people to become defined by the mental health diagnosis they receive when it becomes common knowledge to others. Unfortunately due to the treatment many receive from society based on their mental illness, they have come to brand themselves by engaging in self-stigmatisation. Some individuals who live with mental illness have very few demands and keep their expectations low (Jamison, 2006). As a result, they begin to accept the expectations society has laid upon them and increasingly expect less of themselves; however it is important to note that this may not always be the case. There are many options to consider when negotiating mental illness and the stigmas associated with it. First and foremost, it is important that everyone involved is kept informed and ensures the respect and privacy of individuals with mental illness is maintained.

A joint effort between the person with mental illness and service providers should focus on the individual's life path and what will work in their unique situation. Recovery is highly dependent upon re-engagement with society and taking control of developing that positive sense of self again (Ekeland and Bergem, 2006). This can be accomplished through attempting return to work programs among other supports for people with mental illness. However, taking on deeply ingrained beliefs in society surrounding mental illness remains a challenge.

The ability to classify people as either 'us' or 'them' derives from deeply ingrained processes by which people engage in group building. It is also a means of quick and dirty classification, better known as "cognitive economy" wherein people take in a large amount of information which has to be processed quickly by simplifying, filtering, and organizing. This ability was formed as a necessary evolutionary survival process wherein people were able to minimize potential dangers with minimal cognitive effort; thus, the stereotype was born.

Stereotypes become the few negative pieces of prototypical information that are used to define a person within a group (Baumann, 2007). While disturbing as some stereotypes have become and how they have been used in negative ways, it is important to understand how this thinking developed over time in order to understand how deeply inset it is within the human mind. This enables us to build an understanding of what it will take for people to look beyond quick classifications of people in order to assess and categorize the risk and then slot them into a box, thereby creating the stereotype leading to the creation of the stigma. When we understand how stigmas are formed we can move beyond the stigma to a true understanding of mental illness that is based on accurate information.

Mental Health/Mental Illness in the Workplace

> *Common Mental Disorders (CMDs) can have negative effects on work as they can impair work functioning and increase sickness absence. (Gartner, Ketelaar, Smeets, et al., 2011, 290)*

Discussing mental health and mental illness in the workplace is gaining momentum as a relevant topic as research begins to show how the workplace is adversely affected. Canadian businesses are affected by mental illness and return to work in regards to loyalty and retention. Mental illness accounts for high turnover, low productivity, and increased disability leave. As a result, mental illness is ranked in the top three reasons for short-term disability and is reported in 72 percent of long-term disability cases (Mental Health Commission of Canada, 2010). These facts show how important and urgent it is for employers to implement workplace disability management programs. Important to note is that employees are not the only ones to benefit from such programs. Workers who are supported and cared for by their employer, as witnessed by effective disability management programs that are dedicated to the overall wellness of employees, will experience improvement in employees returning to work post-injury or illness, staying at work, as well as increased productivity. Such programs also facilitate, through education and awareness campaigns, an increase in accurate knowledge of mental illness issues in the organization. There is ample evidence of this in the literature and many insurers have recognized this trend and have been actively endorsing these programs for the past two decades (Dyck, 2009).

Models of mental health have been developed over time that look at the overall conditions involved in occupations in order to understand how the workplace can cause and/or exacerbate illness. Three of which will be discussed in this section: 1) the demand-control model, 2) the effort-reward imbalance model, and 3) the person-environment fit model. The demand-control model looks at decision latitude and psychological demands involved in the workplace by assessing the degree individuals are able to utilize their skills at their discretion and the demands of work volume and time. While similar to demand-control, the effort-reward model targets an individual's need for control by analyzing a person's flexibility to work situations that require high demand but low reward. This model reveals an employee's ability to manage their work and perception of rewards in work situations based on their coping styles. Finally, the person-environment model assesses the fit between employee skill-set, job demand, the employee's goals/aspirations, and the supplies offered by the work environment. When these dichotomies are not balanced employees run the risk of becoming stressed, disease prone, and strained (Wilhelm et al., 2004).

Mental illness is a complex issue within the workplace and places a burden on the labour force in general. This burden is multiplied when you consider that many employees who become disabled are between 36 and 55 years of age with many years of experience in the industry (Dewa, Lesage, Goering, et al., 2004). These employees have years of training and have remained loyal to their respective industries. The costs of losing them are multiplied when you consider all the factors taken into consideration with disability leave:

- Paid employee sick leave, weekly indemnity, and/or short-term disability insurance costs

- Salary for replacement workers

- Healthcare benefits

- Extended supplementary healthcare benefits

- Rising provincial Workers' Compensation Board rates

- Long-term disability insurance premium rates and costs

- Supervisory time to reschedule work

- Supervisory time to work with the disabled employee

- Disability claim and case management time and costs

- Recruitment and training of replacement workers

- Lowered employee morale

- Lowered productivity

- And lost business opportunities (Dyck, 2009).

CAUSED BY THE WORKPLACE

In the workplace it appears as though stress is a leading illness affecting employees for various reasons. While stress is a normal part of life that is necessary for individual survival, growth, and development, it can easily become distressing when it is experienced in excess (Trudel, Vonarx, Simard, et al., 2009). The factors commonly associated with excessive exposure to stress involve: methods of worker supervision, the type and volume of work, an individual's performance and profitability within the organization, conflicts between workers and supervisors, employment uncertainty, repetitive work, low utilization of skills, workplace harassment, and methods of promotion and remuneration (Trudel, Vonarx, Simard, et al., (2009. An example of a workplace in which employees are vulnerable to injuries and mental health issues is in the healthcare sector. Nurses are in a line of work that exudes characteristics of stress resulting from high job demands, low job control, and low social support. As such, nurses have a higher risk of developing mental health problems than those outside of the healthcare sector. This field is an extreme example in that it demonstrates the person experiencing such stress is not only individually affected. Nurses facing these issues can potentially cause further negative consequences to their patients if the distress is not addressed in a way that supports the maintenance of their health (Gartner, Ketelaar, Smeets, et al., 2011). Mealer et al. (2009) suggest that novel therapies and interventions are required in order to improve the quality of the working environment for nurses because of the stressors they face. When it comes to the high risk of post-traumatic stress disorder (PTSD) and burn out syndrome

(BOS), the health sector faces high levels of nurses exiting their professions, or reducing their involvement, in order to maintain their own health.

Mental illness can also be the cause of physical injuries. When this happens these injuries and having to deal with the consequences of these injuries (that is pain, impairment) often exert a co-morbid mental toll and we are confronted with a closed loop in that, for example, depression = injury = depression. This is not of minor consequence. Accidents in the workplace between 1993 and 1996 resulted in more lost days of work than did situations of labour unrest in Canada (Barling, Kelloway, and Iverson, 2003). Each workplace injury in this total was estimated to cost the workplace $6,000 while workplace fatalities were estimated to be approximately $492,000 (Marshall, 1996, as cited in Barling, Kelloway, and Iverson, 2003). The Association of Workers' Compensation Boards identified 329,357 workplace injuries serious enough to require compensation and 976 fatalities in the workplace (2007). Workplace injuries can happen for various reasons due to safety education and behaviors of employees. Those physical injuries that do take place have a mental component when it comes to employees in their recovery time and fear of future occurrences.

Beliefs surrounding workplace safety are influenced by the acute or chronic perceptions of accidents. An event is acute when it is able to reach its 'low point' almost immediately—meaning that an individual is not likely to believe such an accident will happen again. On the other side of the scale, chronic events are those that do not reach their 'low point' and employees believe that the same accident is likely to happen again or that the negative consequences of the accident remain present (Barling, Kelloway, and Iverson, 2003).

Looking at the full picture of workplace injuries we also need to consider the impact injuries have on other employees who may witness or be the first responders to accident victims. Vicarious exposure to workplace injuries can also cause beliefs of risk to self (Barling, Kelloway, and Iverson, 2003) and possible development of post-traumatic stress disorder, discussed in detail in Chapter 7.

ADVERSE PSYCHOLOGICAL OUTCOMES IN THE WORKPLACE

Much is made of accidents in the workplace due to excessive job demands. However, consideration also needs to be given to workplaces which extol a huge amount of psychological stress in both acute and chronic doses such as for those working in emergency services. Demands from emergency service jobs impact physical and mental health in similar ways as being exposed to critical incidents. Furthermore, jobs that demand continuous exposure to situations that are demanding, stressful, and potentially traumatizing can result in traumatic stress symptoms, burn out, fatigue, post-traumatic stress disorder (PTSD), and other elements of ill-health. Employees exposed to critical incidents deal with a wide range of chronic stressors that impact the health and well-being of themselves and their overall workforce (Tuckey and Hayward, 2011) and require due care and attention based on the best available scientific information.

PERCEPTIONS, STIGMA AND DISCLOSURE

Disclosure or self-disclosure can be defined as the process of communicating information about oneself verbally to another person. Mental health services users face difficulties in deciding whether to disclose a mental health problem in the employment context. (Brohan, Henderson, Wheat, et al., 2012)

Not all disabilities are disclosed by persons with mental illness. Recent studies have shown that people's understandings of mental illness vary, and depending on the individual's view, they may or may not disclose their disability at work (Irvine, 2011).

A major reason for lack of disclosure arises from the fear of stigmatization by co-workers, supervisors, managers, and other personnel in the workplace. However, an issue related to this and not commonly discussed surrounding mental illness and individuals who have mental illness is the question of personal identity. Since mental illness often defines an individual for society (stereotype, stigma), it can become an integral piece of personal identity: often people with mental illness struggle with the positive need associated with belonging to a group that could support them but are afraid to reach out to such groups because of the negativity associated with that group being other people with a mental illness like them. This same behavior and thinking process may impact on their willingness to disclose a mental illness or any mental health-related information in the workplace.

Mental illness is very much at the mercy of visibility in the workplace and plays a key role in an individual's social identity. While some mental illness can move through an organization without detection, there are characteristics and behaviors that may be apparent in others or caused by the medication used to control their symptoms (Brohan, Henderson, Wheat, et al., 2012). Since an employer can only accommodate a disability that is disclosed, the lack of willingness to disclose a mental illness, regardless of the motivation behind such lack of disclosure, limits in an extreme way the employer's ability to accommodate such a worker.

As a result of the fact that some mental illness can remain concealable, some employees enjoy the opportunity to control when or if disclosure needs to happen in the workplace. However, there are four dimensions to consider when the act of disclosure comes up in the workplace. These four dimensions are: 1) Voluntary or Involuntary, 2) Full or Partial, 3) Selectiveness (to which people do you disclose), and 4) Timing of Disclosure (prior to employment or after employed). To be mindful of mental illness it is important to note that many individuals who have various illnesses are very much aware of public perceptions. To that end, many truly believe that they won't be considered for employment in the first place or that they would be let go after disclosing their mental illness. "I don't think you'd get a foot in through the door that way. You wouldn't get taken on in the first place if you told them you had a big mental history" (Brohan, Henderson, Wheat, et al., 2012, p. 6).

International data still suggest that stigma and discrimination of mental illness have devastating effects and must be addressed at various levels (Kirby, 2008). Certainly, stigmatizing beliefs surrounding mental illness cause society to see any kind of disorder as an intractable health problem (Tomlinson and Lund, 2012). This derails any movement towards innovative solutions to addressing stigma of mental disorders. In virtually all societies there is evidence of some form of stigma of mental illness that permeates tolerance, beliefs, and treatment of those who suffer from them (Jamison, 2006). Jamison also believes that being able to identify those who are different even in subtle ways is deeply wired into the human brain. At the same time she does note that there are instances where violence is possible with untreated mental illness; as well that some moods are contagious (depression for example). However, society needs to be able to look beyond these fears and remember the person with the mental illness first.

Unfortunately research has shown that the most common means of avoiding stigma are to remove oneself from society and/or move to a larger city to become more anonymous (for example, Ekeland and Bergem, 2006). The workplace can contribute to reducing stigma through education and awareness campaigns whose effectiveness has recently received support from research. According to Kobau et al. (2010), people who had contact with someone who had a mental illness, or had a mental illness at one point in time themselves, were less likely to have stigmatizing attitudes. Until stigmatizing attitudes are addressed and remedied in the workplace, many mental illnesses will go undiagnosed, untreated, and underestimated (Baumann, 2007), and will continue to have an ongoing negative impact on all concerned.

ACCOMMODATION AND RETURN TO WORK

Mental illness was previously thought to prevent individuals from participating as functional members of society. However, many advances in treatment and programs which return autonomy to individuals have proved to be very successful in regards to persons with mental illness being able return to society and to work as well (Pernice-Duca, Case, and Conrad-Garisi, 2012). Increasingly, those with severe mental illness are returning to productive lives with the help of improved treatment and support systems within the community (Wahl, Wood, and Richards, 2002). Small communities of support and return-to-work programs for those with mental illness serve to facilitate the transition back into society and avoidance of stigma and/or isolation.

For those with mental illness, the loss of work and place in their organization influences the ability to make meaningful use of time outside of work. That is, without the structure provided by work, people with mental illness often struggle with the capability to structure the rest of their lives including personal time when not working (Becker and Kilian, 2008). Return-to-work programs aid people with disabilities to rejoin the workforce within their respected fields. Not only is it important to implement such support programs within the workplace but to also educate the workplace on disability issues and to focus on adjusting work according to abilities instead of disabilities.

Future directions should include policy change initiatives that aim to integrate evidence-based health promotion programs in the community and workplaces in order to improve overall population health. Creating a balance between mental health awareness and the possibility of incorporating positive mental health within that model may help to incite innovative programs targeting population health (Kobau, Seligman, Peterson, et al., 2011).

MENTAL ILLNESS: IMPACTS AND COSTS FOR THE WORKPLACE

In the Canadian Community Health Survey of 2002 mental health and well-being were examined in regards to their prevalence. Major depressive episodes were found to have a 4.2 percent prevalence rate and social phobias 3.1 percent in the working population (Wang, Smailes, Sareen, et al., 2010). Ultimately it is of most benefit to support current employees with programs that enable and support them in returning to the workplace. It is of benefit for workplaces to create and support a disability management program within their organization for the benefit of all employees, including those with mental illness. This should be seen as a critical initiative as it has been predicted that depression will be one of the leading causes of disability globally by 2020 (WHO, 2000). With depressive disorders already being a leading cause of disability in high-income countries (Dewa, Lesage, Goering, et al., 2004), proactive measures need to be taken.

A key player in this field is the insurance sector and more work is needed between the workplace and insurance agencies in order to cooperate and develop strategic plans surrounding diagnosis and treatment plans for employees who may require mental health supports (Pomaki, Franche, Murray, et al., 2011). The costs to the workplace, and society at large, are far too high to ignore mental health.

Promoting and Supporting Mental Health: Solutions for the Workplace

Researchers such as Tuckey and Hayward (2011) have shown that elements of workplace culture and camaraderie are essential for creating healthier workplaces. This is especially noticeable in workplaces where employees are continuously exposed to critical incidents on the job (emergency services). However, lessons from these workplaces serve to inform other organizations on key components of creating healthy changes and maintaining them over time. When switching gears to a mentally healthy workplace, a cultural change might be required in order to instill the values and actions of safe work environments:

> *Elements of trust, common identity, and understanding, along with general positive social bonds, are embedded within the concept of camaraderie. As such, culture change, team building, and leadership development initiatives could all play a role ... (Tuckey and Hayward, 2011)*

The positive psychology movement focusing on what is right about people targets competencies and resources already available in society that can help promote mental health. Fostering positive mental health through programs can prevent mental illness and improve health altogether. This approach to mental health takes attention away from the idea that health is simply the absence of disease which is the cause of the majority of issues we face today dealing with stigma. The disease model of mental health describing treatment and support services has confused the terminology away from its actual root meaning, health (Kobau, Seligman, Peterson, et al., 2011).

Cognitive behavioral therapy and psycho-pharmacotherapy have been shown to alleviate clinical symptoms of mental illness in some cases. However, with that said, individual treatments rarely consider targeting the workplace in order to assess these impacts in regards to functional outcomes such as return to work. As individuals enjoy the improved quality of life that comes with these treatments, it would stand to reason that the workplace could also benefit from lost time and costs as well. A workplace dedicated to supporting its employees could enjoy sustained employment and productivity as opposed to the $51 billion in losses due to disability incurred in 2003 alone.

MENTAL HEALTH LITERACY

To promote and support the attainment of good mental health, organizations can take on a campaign of mental health literacy to broaden the understanding of various disorders. Mental health literacy is the knowledge and beliefs surrounding mental disorders that can aid in recognition, management, and/or prevention (Jorm, 2012). A depth of understanding mental health issues can help those in management positions in the workplace to: a) learn prevention skills, b) help recognize a developing disorder, c) be aware of treatments and other support strategies, and d) be able to provide mental health first aid for others who are in a mental health crisis (Jorm, 2012). All these components of mental health literacy support a working knowledge of mental illness in the workplace and can help create systems within the organization that are mobilized to support workers in various ways when an issue arises. A recent report from Australia on mental health literacy compared results of people asked to diagnose a vignette referring to depression. Findings were positive in that recognition of depression was higher (81 percent) in the 2004 sample than it was in a previous sample from 1995 using the same depression vignette. These results reflect the growing levels of mental health literacy in an Australian sample and indicate the potential for success of programs designed to educate the community about mental health (Bartlett, Travers, Cartwright, et al., 2006).

Concluding Thoughts

When addressing mental health and mental illness it is of utmost importance that a clear distinction be made between physical and mental illness in order to understand the implications of mental illness. Mental illness is not a condition experienced by only a very few people nor is it something to be ignored because of its invisibility. Mental health concerns need to be addressed up front and help should be sought out sooner rather than later. Society plays a role in the perception of mental illness and mental health literacy is a potential solution for increasing the accuracy of information available to those in need or those interested in providing supports. As Sinclair and Patel state, some form of mental illness will affect one out of every four people at some point in their lives. What is more shocking is that these individuals will also live 5–10 years less than the general population due to their quality of life with mental illness (Sinclair and Patel, 2012).

When discussing mental health and impacts on the workplace it is important to remember that preparation for these issues is imperative before an issue arises. Employers and insurers would be best served by establishing protocols and policies within the organization to ensure services are available and accessible when needed.

Key Terms to Remember:

Mental Health

Mental Illness

Mental Health Literacy

Stigmatisation

More information can be found at the following sources:

Workplace strategies for mental health at http://www. workplacestrategiesformentalhealth.com/

Mental health works: why workplace mental health matters at http://www. mentalhealthworks.ca/why-it-matters

Canadian Mental Health Association: Fast facts about mental illness at http://www.cmha.ca/media/fast-facts-about-mental-illness/#. UgLVv9LCai1

Centre for Addiction and Mental Health: Mental health and addiction statistics at http://www.camh.ca/en/hospital/about_camh/ newsroom/for_reporters/Pages/addictionmentalhealthstatistics. aspx

Mental Health Commission of Canada: The facts at http://strategy. mentalhealthcommission.ca/the-facts/

Public Health Agency of Canada: Mental illness at http://www.phac-aspc. gc.ca/cd-mc/mi-mm/

References

Association of Workers' Compensation Boards of Canada (2007). National Work Injury Statistics Program. Retrieved from: http://www. Awbc.org/en/ nationalworkinjurydiseasesandfatalitystatistic.asp on July 30th, 2012.

Arvaniti, A., Samakouri, M., Kalamara, E., Bochtsou, V., Bikos, C., and Livaditis, M. (2009). Health service staff's attitudes towards patients with mental illness. *Social Psychiatry & Psychiatric Epidemiology*, 44, 658–65. DOI: 10.1007/ s00127-008-0481-3.

Barling, J., Kelloway, E.K., and Iverson, R.D. (2003). Accidental outcomes: attitudinal consequences of workplace injuries. *Journal of Occupational Health Psychology*, 8(1), 74–85. DOI: 10.1037/1076-8998.8.1.74.

Bartlett, H., Travers, C., Cartwright, C., and Smith, N. (2006). Mental health literacy in rural Queensland: results of a community survey. *Australian and New Zealand Journal of Psychiatry*, 40(9), 783–9. DOI: 10.1111/j.1440-1614.2006.01884.x.

Baumann, A.E. (2007). Stigmatization, social distance and exclusion because of mental illness: The individual with mental illness as a 'stranger'. *International Review of Psychiatry*, 19(2), 131–5. DOI: 10.1080/09540260701278739.

Becker, T. and Kilian, R. (2008). Daily living: does this matter for people with mental illness? *International Review of Psychiatry*, 20(6), 492–7. DOI: 10.1080/09540260802564417.

Brohan, E., Henderson, C., Wheat, K., Malcolm, E., Clement, S., Barley, E.A., Slade, M. and Thornicroft, G. (2012). Systematic review of beliefs, behaviours, and influencing factors associated with disclosure of a mental health problem in the workplace. *Biomed Central Psychiatry*, 12(11). Retrieved from: http://www.biomedcentral.com/1471-244X/12/11.

Corrigan P.W., Markowitz, F.E., and Watson, A.C. (2004). Structural levels of mental illness stigma and discrimination. *Schizophrenia Bulletin*, 30(3), 481–91.

Dewa, C.S., Lesage, A., Goering, P. and Caveen, M. (2004). Nature and prevalence of mental illness in the workplace. *Healthcare Papers*, 5(2), 12–25.

Dyck, D.E.G. (2009). *Disability Management: Theory, Strategy & Industry Practice* (Third Edition). LexisNexis: Canada.

Ekeland, T. and Bergem, R. (2006). The negotiation of identity among people with mental illness in rural communities. *Community Mental Health Journal*, 42(3), 225–32. DOI: 10.1007/s10597-006-9034-y.

Hall, S. and Cheston, R. (2002). Mental health and identity: the evaluation of a drop-in centre. *Journal of Community & Applied Social Psychology*, 12, 30–43. DOI: 10.1002/casp.639.

Hansson, L., Jormfeldt, H., Svedberg, P., and Svensson, B. (2011). Mental health professionals' attitudes towards people with mental illness: Do they differ from attitudes held by people with mental illness? *International Journal of Social Psychology*, 59(1), 48–54. Accessed online at: http://isp.sagepub.com/content/early/2011/09/27/0020764011423176.short.

Gartner, F.R., Ketelaar, S.M., Smeets, O., Bolier, L., Fischer, E., van Dijk, F.J.H., Nieuwenhuijsen, K. and Sluiter, J.K. (2011). The Mental Vitality @ Work study: design of a randomized controlled trial on the effect of a workers' health surveillance mental module for nurses and allied health professionals. *Bio Med Central Public Health*, 11(290).

Irvine, A. (2011). Something to declare? The disclosure of common mental health problems at work. *Disability & Society*, 26(2), 179–92. DOI: 10.1080/09687599.2011.544058.

Jamison, K.R. (2006). The many stigmas of mental illness. *The Lancet*, 367, 533–4.

Jorm, A.F. (2012). Mental health literacy: empowering the community to take action for better mental health. *American Psychologist*, 67(3), 231–43. DOI: 10.1037/a0025957.

Jorm, A.F. and Reavley, N.J. (2012). Public confusion caused by differing understandings of the term "mental illness". *Australian & New Zealand Journal of Psychiatry*, 46, 397–9.

Kendell, R.E. (2001). The distinction between mental and physical illness (editorial). *British Journal of Psychiatry*, 178, 490–493.

Kirby, M. (2008). Mental health in Canada: out of the shadows forever. *Canadian Medical Association Journal*, 178(10), 1320–1322. DOI: 10.1503/cmaj.071897.

Kobau, R., Seligman, M.E.P., Peterson, C., Diener, E., Zack, M.M., Chapman, D. and Thompson, E. (2011). Mental health promotion in public health: perspectives and strategies from positive psychology. *American Journal of Public Health*, 101(8), 1–9.

Marshall, K. (1996). A job to die for. Available at: http://www.statcan.gc.ca/studies-etudes/75-001/archive/e-pdf/2889-eng.pdf on September 24th, 2013.

Mealer, M. Burnham, E. L., Goode, Colleen, J., Rothbaum, B., and Moss, M. (2009). The prevalence and impact of post traumatic stress disorder and burnout syndrom in nurses. *Depression and Anxiety*, 26, 1118–26. DOI: 10.1002/da/20631.

Mental Health Commission of Canada (2010). Why Investing in Mental Health Will Contribute to Canada's Economic Prosperity and to the Sustainability of our Health Care System. Retrieved from: http://www.mentalhealthcommission.ca/English/site-search/72%25%20long%20term%20disability?retain-filters=1&type_filters= on September 24th, 2013.

Pernice-Duca, F., Case, W., and Conrad-Garisi, D. (2012). The Role of Intentional Communities to Support Recovery from Mental Illness, Mental Illnesses – Evaluation, Treatments and Implications, Luciano L'Abate (ed.), ISBN: 978-953-307-645-4, InTech. Available at: http://www.intechopen.com/books/mental-illnesses-evaluation-treatments-and-implications/the-role-of-intentional-communities-to-support-recovery-from-mental-illness.

Pomaki, G., Franche, R.L., Murray, E., Khushrushahi, N., and Lampinen, T. (2012). Workplace-based work disability prevention interventions for workers with common mental health conditions: a review of the literature. *Journal of Occupational Rehabilitation*, 22, 182–95. DOI: 10.1007/s10926-10926-011-9339-9.

Rusch, N., Evans-Lacko, S., and Thornicroft, G. (2012). What is mental illness? Public views and their effects on attitudes and disclosure. *Australian & New Zealand Journal of Psychiatry*. DOI: 10.1177/0004867412438873.

Schiebe, S., Bagby, R.M., Miller, L.S. and Dorian, B.J. (2001). Assessing posttraumatic stress disorder with the mmpi-2 in a sample of workplace accident victims. *Psychological Assessment*, 13(3), 369–74. DOI: 10.1037//1040-3590.13.3.369.

Simpson, K.R., Meadows, G.N., Frances, A.J., and Patten, S.B. (2012). Is mental health in the Canadian population changing over time? *Canadian Journal of Psychiatry*, 57(5), 324–31.

Sinclair, J.M. and Patel, M.X. (2012). No health without mental health: core competencies for all doctors (Editorial). *Medicine*, 40(11), 567.

Tomlinson, M. and Lund, C. (2012). Why does mental health not get the attention it deserves? an application of the Shiffman and Smith Framework. *PLoS Med* 9(2). DOI: 0.1371/journal.pmed.1001178.

Trudel, L., Vonarx, N., Simard, C., Freeman, A., Vezina, M., Brisson, C., Vinet, A., Bourbonnais, R., and Dugas, N. (2009). The adverse effects of psychosocial constraints at work: A participatory study to orient prevention to mitigate psychological distress. *Work*, 34, 345–57. DOI: 10.3233/WOR-2009-0933.

Tuckey, M.R. and Hayward, R. (2011). Global and occupation-specific emotional resources as buffers against the emotional demands of fire-fighting. *Applied Psychology: An International Review*, 60(1), 1–23. DOI: 10.111/j.1464-0597.2010.00424.x.

Wahl, O.E., Wood, A., and Richards, R. (2002). Newspaper coverage of mental illness: is it changing? *Psychiatric Rehabilitation Skills*, 6(1), 9–31.

Wang, J.L., Smailes, E., Sareen, J., Fick, G.H., Schmitz, N. and Patten, S. (2010). The prevalence of mental disorders in the working population over the period of global economic crisis. *The Canadian Journal of Psychiatry*, 55(9), 598–605.

WHO International Consortium in Psychiatric Epidemiology (2000). Cross-national comparisons of the prevalences and correlates of mental disorders. *Bulletin of the World Health Organization*, 78(4), 413–26.

Wilhelm, K., Kovess, V., Rose-Seidel, C. and Finch, A. (2004). Work and mental health. *Social Psychiatry Epidemiology*, 39, 865–73. DOI: 10.1007/s00127-004-0869-7.

Chapter 4
Depression in the Workplace

If depression is creeping up and must be faced, learn something about the
nature of the beast: You may escape without a mauling.

Dr R.W. Shepherd

Introduction

The most prevalent mental illness inside and outside of the workforce is depression. Occurring across the lifespan, depression is a chronic, recurrent condition that typically spans several decades. An international investigation examining the worldwide burden of depression found that the average major depressive episode lasts for 26 weeks in duration (Ustun, Ayuso-Mateos, Chatterji, et al., 2004). Indeed, helping workers acquire and maintain remission from depression is quickly proving a valuable cost-saving strategy for businesses worldwide.

Depression is referred to as the common cold of mental disorders. Most of the time people describe depressed affect as a mild mood consisting of feeling down, sad or blue. Clinical depression, on the other hand, differs qualitatively from mere depressed affect. Diagnosable clinical depression is defined by the experience of significant sadness that lasts most of the day, and occurs nearly every day. In addition to sad mood, depressed individuals often report experiencing disturbances in sleep and eating, chronic fatigue, difficulties making decisions or concentrating, feelings of worthlessness, thoughts of suicide and anhedonia or a loss of pleasure derived from previously pleasurable experiences.

Depressed employees seem sad, withdrawn, angry, unmotivated or tired with diminished, erratic or error-prone performances (Kahn, 2008). Furthermore, their interpersonal relationships appear to be isolated, turbulent or diminished. These are all warning signs indicating the need for thoughtful consideration and possible referral in order to stave off a depressive episode.

Depressive disorder exists on a severity gradient from mild forms termed dysthymia to severe crippling forms termed melancholic depressive disorder (Kahn, 2008). See Table 4.1 for a list of the most typical presenting symptoms indicative of dysthymia, atypical depression, major depressive disorder, and melancholic depression.

This chapter discusses the impact, cost, and burden of depression in the workplace along with treatment options. First, etiological theories of depression are given followed by workplace influences that perpetuate the illness. Next, diagnosis of depression is discussed along with its nuances. Following this, the costs of workplace depression in terms of unemployment, absenteeism, presenteeism, retention, and disability are given. Finally, this chapter concludes with a discussion about treatment and prevention of depression in the workplace.

Theories of Depression

Researchers have proposed a variety of different theories in an attempt to explain the development of depression, some having received more support than others.

One of the oldest and most influential theories is the diathesis stress model. The *diathesis-stress model* recognizes that a combination of vulnerability (that is, diathesis) may interact with stress and bring about depression. In essence, every person is born with varying degrees of susceptibility to mental illness that is initiated by various life stressors. The diathesis-stress model recognizes that severe, chronic stress can reach toxic levels and result in the development of depression. This is true even for individuals with low vulnerability to depression. Henceforth, the difference between individuals with no, low, and high predispositions to developing depression is not the process itself but rather how much stress is needed to reach toxic levels.

As the diathesis-stress model would suggest, twin studies have found a strong genetic component to depression. If one identical twin experiences unipolar or bipolar depression there is a 40 to 80 percent chance that the other will also experience depression. This is higher than the 10 to 25 percent likelihood of non-identical fraternal twins each experiencing depression

Table 4.1   Mental health in the workplace

Dysthymic Disorder	Atypical Depression	Major Depressive Disorder	Melancholic Depression
1. During most days for at least 2 years, depressed mood is reported or apparent most of the time.	1. Individual experiences mood reactivity and can be cheered up, at least temporarily, in response to positive events.	1. 5 or more of the following symptoms are present for at least 2-weeks.	1. At least one of:
2. Two of the following are present when depressed:	2. Two of the following are presented:	• Depressed mood most of the day, nearly every day.	• Loss of pleasure in all or most activities
• Decrease or increase in appetite	• Significant weight gain, increase in appetite or cravings	• Anhedonia or significantly decreased interest or pleasure in nearly all activities of the day, nearly everyday	• Lack of mood reactivity (cannot be cheered up)
• Insomnia or hypersomnia	• Oversleeping	• Significant weight loss or weight gain	2. At least three of:
• Fatigue or low energy	• Perceived physical lethargy	• Significant increase or decrease in appetite	• Distinct quality of depressed mood (i.e., qualitatively distinct from bereavement, etc)
• Low self-esteem	• Pattern of, and sensitivity to personal rejection that results in distress or occupational impairment	• Insomnia or oversleeping nearly everyday	• Depression is regularly worse in the morning
• Difficulty concentrating or making decisions	3. Symptoms are not better captured by melancholic depression during the episodes.	• Psychomotor agitation or retardation	• Early morning awaking (at least 2 hours prior normal)
3. Symptoms do not remit for longer than 2 months during the 2-year period.		• Fatigue or loss of energy	• Severe psychomotor retardation
4. Symptoms are not better captured by a Major Depressive Disorder.		• Feelings of worthlessness or excessive guilt	• Significant appetite loss or weight gain
5. No manic, hypomanic or mixed episodes occurred		• Troubles concentrating or being indecisive	• Excessive or inappropriate guilt.
6. Symptoms are not the result of a general medical condition or other substance use (including prescription medications).		• Recurrent thoughts of death or suicidal ideation	
7. Symptoms cause significant distress or impair work, social, or personal functioning.		2. Symptoms do not meet criteria for mixed episode	
		3. Symptoms cause significant distress or impairment in social, occupational or personal roles	
		4. Symptoms are not the result of a medical condition or substance use	
		5. Symptoms are not better accounted for by bereavement or significant interpersonal loss.	

(Sullivan, Neale and Kendler, 2000). This means that genetically identical twins are more than twice as likely to co-experience depression, as twins who only share 50 percent of their genetic information.

One of the most common diathesis-stress models of depression is *Beck's Cognitive Theory of Depression*. Beck believed that our thoughts and interpretations of events are responsible for the feelings we experience following those events. Thus, Beck believed that depressed individuals have a tendency to view and interpret events in a more pessimistic and negative manner than are warranted by such events. This negativity can be seen in three negative cognitive distortions termed the *Cognitive Triad* (Beck, 1970). The three cognitive distortions are negative views of oneself, negative views of the world, and hopelessness for the future. These three cognitive distortions are thought to be the cause of low self-esteem, enhanced cynicism and pessimism, and the sense of hopelessness commonly found in depressed individuals.

Interestingly, interpreting an event in a negative manner makes the event more stressful and increases the likelihood of developing a depressive episode (Langlieb and DePaulo, 2008). If this was not bad enough, experiencing a depressive episode increases the likelihood of interpreting an event as negative. This line of reasoning nicely illustrates how the negative cycle of depression becomes a recursive vortex of despair. Depression acts to alter thinking patterns, leading to negative schemas regarding one's social, work, and personal environments, further perpetuating the cycle of depression.

Perpetuating Workplace Factors

Several workplace factors have been identified which exacerbate and contribute to the genesis of depression. Among these workplace factors, some stand out as more pronounced than others, with the most prominent factors being:

a)   High job strain

   – High psychological demands
   – Low decision latitude

b)   Exposure to high-stress, high-threat work environments

c)   Low co-worker and supervisor support.

A. JOB STRAIN

The most indicative workplace factor of mental illnesses including depression is working at a job that is high in job strain (Karasek, 1979). Robert Karasek advocated a revolutionary theory of work stress and illness in proposing the *job-demand-control* (JD-C) model. The JD-C stipulates that job strain is comprised of two interdependent facets, being job demands and decision latitude (See Figure 4.1). Job demands represent the mental load placed on employees by their working conditions. Time constraints, unrealistic deadlines, excessive amounts of work, conflicting demands, and having to work at an unrealistically hard and fast pace in order to meet these demands are all examples of job demands common to employees. Employees are at a great risk of developing job strain and a concurrent mental illness when the job demands under- or over-exceed the individual's resources to cope with such demands.

The second facet of the JD-C model, decision latitude, represents job control or the amount of freedom and decision-making authority at work.

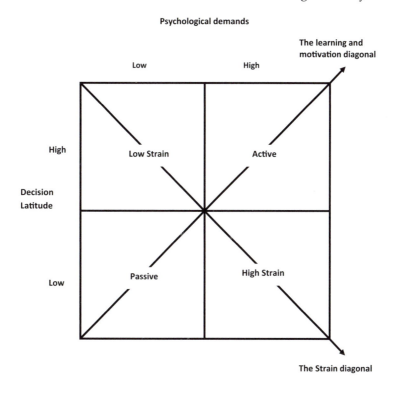

Figure 4.1   Karasek's Job Demand Control Model of Workplace Strain (JD-C)

Having the personal freedom to plan tasks, decide the order in which tasks will be completed, and having flexibility in scheduling are examples of high decision-making latitude. Decision latitude and job demands interact to create a work environment that facilitates either personal growth and well-being or job strain and mental illness. The highest level of job strain is found in jobs in which employees have high demands but low decision latitude to cope with such demands.

Having a job high in decision latitude and job demands are what Karasek considered active jobs leading to well-being, learning, and personal growth (Karasek and Theorell, 1990). In essence, job strain results when an employee's autonomy and skill-set is not recognized and matched to the job demands presented at work. This is often recognized as a job in which the employee does not take ownership of and control over. In fact, women and men in high-strain jobs are four and five times more likely to be dissatisfied with their jobs, respectively (Shields, 2006).

A landmark study examined the relationship between occupational variables and three forms of depression (major depressive disorder, depressive syndrome and dysphoria), firmly linking the JD-C model to depression (Mausner-Dorsch and Eaton, 2000). The authors examined 905 full-time employees and concluded that working in occupations high in job strain (high psychological demands and low decision latitude) is associated with a greater prevalence of all three forms of depression, especially major depressive disorder. Interestingly, these effects were stronger for women, suggesting that women may suffer from a greater degree of job strain.

Data from a 2002 Canadian Health Survey provides support for the theory that women may experience a higher degree of job strain at work than do men. A survey of almost 37,000 Canadian citizens revealed that, on average, women experience higher work-related psychological demands and less decision latitude, resulting in significantly higher job strain (Shields, 2006). This effect persisted after controlling for occupation, work schedule, working hours, and personal income, suggesting that all things being equal, women experience more job strain than men do. Interestingly, men appear to be more susceptible to depression as a result of job strain than are women. Men in high-strain jobs have been found to be 2.5 times as likely to experience depression as are men who work in low strain jobs; women in high-strain jobs on the other hand were only at an elevated risk of 1.6 times the likelihood (Shields, 2006).

In summary, the JD-C model does a good job at predicting job strain. Furthermore, job strain is strongly implicated in the genesis of depression; a robust finding in the literature. However, job strain is a complex phenomenon that may be better linked to depression through the development of stress and low social support.

BOX 4.1: IMPLICATIONS OF THE JD-C MODEL

Modern jobs place a great deal of demand and stress on their employees. These job demands are often harmful to employee mental health but they do not have to be. Having autonomy over their work and a skill-set that is recognized and matched for the job gives employees a positive perception of their work. Employers should try to match an employee's skill-set and aptitude with the demands of their position. This includes offering additional training and clear guidelines for how employees can make the most of their position and further their career. Employer's who maximize employee skill-sets and increase the number of situations requiring some degree of decision latitude are sure to reduce the occurrence of mental illness and promote healthy living among employees.

B. STRESS AND THREAT

Stress is a complex process familiar to everyone in the workforce. Anyone who works experiences stress from time to time. Undoubtedly, some positions carry more stress than do others. Being a manager or a CEO is likely more stressful than being a front-end service employee. Interestingly, stress is largely a subjective construct with objective outcomes that not everyone can detect and accurately verbalize. Therefore, it is with great difficulty that one defines the level at which stress becomes particularly problematic.

There exist no clear-cut rules to define when stress at work has reached toxic levels. However, from an employee's perspective, stress at work becomes problematic at the point in which it exceeds the individual's innate capacity to effectively cope with the stressors. This could mean that the stressor is chronic in nature or that no resources are being allocated to the employee to deal with the stressor. Workplace stressors can be exacerbated by job strain, low emotional and social support, a toxic work climate, or a number of other factors discussed in later chapters.

Both males and females working in occupations prone to threats and violence face an elevated risk of developing an affective- or stress-related disorder (Wieclaw, Agerbo, Mortensen, et al., 2006). Occupational threats and violence are most prevalent in the health services, education, and social work professions. Men and women working in these jobs are at a 45–48 percent greater likelihood of developing an affective disorder and 14–32 percent greater likelihood of developing a stress-related disorder than are employees working in jobs classified as low in occupational threat and violence (that is, technicians, construction workers, and plant and machine operators) (Wieclaw, Agerbo, Mortensen, et al., 2006).

There exists a clear link between threat, violence, stress, and the development of depression, however the mechanism underlying this process appears quite complex. One idea is that high-risk jobs may be associated with greater amounts of psychological distress, job dissatisfaction, and job strain which in turn leads to stress, depression, and mental illness (Collins and Long, 2003; Gerberich, Church, McGovern, et al., 2004). Workers in high-strain jobs are more than twice as likely to find most days stressful (Shields, 2006). However, it cannot be ruled out that individuals with a natural diathesis to the development of depression are drawn to high-risk occupations.

C. SUPERVISOR AND CO-WORKER SUPPORT

A vast literature is amassing which places a high-quality social support system as a buffering agent against the negative impacts of stress and mental illness, depression in particular. Conversely, low social support from supervisors and in particular co-workers has been linked to depressive symptomatology and severity (Plaisier, de Bruijn, de Graff, et al., 2007). Findings suggest that one in every three employees do not receive adequate support from their co-workers and one in every six experience inadequate support from their supervisors (Shields, 2006). More disturbingly, almost twice as many employees who experience low social support at work also develop a severe depressive disorder, suggesting that employers should facilitate a team atmosphere at work where supervisors and employees can bond and develop close, supportive relationships.

Social support, pair bonding, and the formation of deep connections have been linked to a regulatory hormone called oxytocin. Oxytocin is released during social contact and acts to buffer stress, reduce threat appraisals, lower defensive mechanisms, and facilitate social contact (Heinrichs, Baumgartner, Kirschbaum and Ehlert, 2003). Furthermore, oxytocin has been shown to be a hormone important in mediating the effects of antidepressants for the reduction of depression and depressive symptoms (Uvnas-Moberg, Bjokstrand, Hillegaart et al., 1999). In sum, groundbreaking research is beginning to reveal biological mechanisms by which social support contributes to the genesis of depression and can act to buffer against it. One of the most cost-effective mechanisms for preventing depression may well be through companies' ingenious ideas to foster a positive work environment that create a team atmosphere.

Diagnosis of Depression

The most useful and accurate diagnoses of depression are made by trained clinicians during interviews of substantial length. Following the DSM-IV-TR (Refer to Chapter 2), a major depressive episode is diagnosed if the individual experiences five or more criteria such as: recurrent thoughts of death, depressed mood most of the day, insomnia or hypersomnia, psychomotor agitation or retardation, fatigue or loss of energy nearly every day, or feelings of worthlessness. These features must be present during a two-week period, and cause significant distress or impairment.

Unfortunately, using clinical diagnosis as a screening tool is not cost-effective in the workplace. Instead, easy to administer, short, self-report measures of depression exist that employers may use to pre-screen employees. These measures can be administered during yearly evaluations with no recourse. Test results offer a good initial starting point to identify employees that may require referral to a trained clinician for proper diagnosis. Self-report measures *do not* offer employers grounds to diagnose, suspend, discipline, or terminate employees that appear depressed. Rather, such measures open the lines of communication between the employee and the employer, offering a vantage point for both parties to discuss such alternatives as referral.

One of the most widely utilized, reliable, and valid measures of depression is the *Beck Depression Inventory* (second edition) (BDI-II). Developed by Aaron Beck 1961, revised in 1978 and with a second edition in 1996, the BDI-II is a 21-item self-report form asking participants to rate personal statements on a scale from 0–3. The BDI-II was originally developed to provide a quantitative assessment of the intensity of depression. Because it is designed to reflect the depth of depression, it can monitor changes over time and provide an objective measure for judging improvement and the effectiveness of treatment methods. However, like all self-report questionnaires, it is easy for participants to exaggerate their scores and the test may be impacted by administration (that is, given to a person in isolation versus administered to a group). The BDI-II can be accessed online from http://www.ibogaine.desk.nl/graphics/3639b1c_23.pdf. A score of 0–13 represents minimal depression, 14–19 represents mild, 20–28 moderate, and 29–63 severe.

A second widely utilized, reliable, and valid measure of depression is the *Hamilton Rating Scale for Depression* (HRSD) (Hamilton, 1960). Developed by Max Hamilton, the HRSD is a 21-item self-report questionnaire measuring a patient's level of major depressive symptoms. The first 17 statements contribute to the HRSD-17 global score, assessing the severity of depression, while questions 18–21 offer further information for professionals. A structured interview guide for the questionnaire is available. The HRSD is available online from http://healthnet.umassmed.edu/mhealth/HAMD.pdf or http://apps.cignabehavioral.com/web/basicsite/provider/treatingBehavioralConditions/HamiltonRatingScaleForDepression.pdf, with scoring instructions provided in the latter.

One final measure that may prove useful for diagnosis and identification of depression in the workplace is the *Depression Anxiety Stress Scale* (DASS; Lovibond and Lovibond, 1996). Developed by the Psychological Foundation of Australia, the DASS is a 42-item self-report questionnaire assessing the degree of severity for depression, anxiety, and stress (14 items per condition). Participants are asked to rate personal statements on a zero (did not apply to me) to three (applied to me very much, most of the time) scale. The DASS is also available in a 21-item short form. The manual for the DASS is available for $55 from the website http://www2.psy.unsw.edu.au/groups/dass/.

The BDI-II, HRSD, and the DASS are all adequate scales when used for screening depression. Selection of one scale over another may be simple preference of the employer. However, the BDI-II is likely the most extensive questionnaire detailing depression and its severity. The HRSD is more difficult to administer and score while the DASS offers a limited range of questions in assessing each condition. Having that said, the DASS captures three prominent workplace conditions and for ease of convenience may well prove the most utilized measure in the workforce.

Workplace depression is currently under-diagnosed. The workplace prevalence of depression is estimated at 9–11 percent, yet only approximately 2 percent of employees receive diagnosis and treatment (Kessler, Barber, Birnbaum, et al., 1999). One reason for depression being under-diagnosed in the workforce is the stigma attached to mental illnesses.

Many people still view depression as a personal weakness rather than a medical condition that can be successfully treated (Burton and Conti, 2008). Society has placed a negative connotation on being depressed, making depressed workers fearful to come forward and seek help. Co-workers often view depression as some sort of contagious degree and end up treating them unfairly. Employers have concerns about depressed individuals having poor work performance and low productivity (Diksa and Rogers, 1996). This stigmatization marginalizes depressed individuals, removing many supports and social contacts, reducing self-esteem, self-efficacy, and social competence (Cassano and Fava, 2002). Henceforth, organizations and their employees must set aside their preconceived notions of depression and disseminate knowledge, understanding, and acceptance of mental illnesses in the workplace.

Nuances that Influence the Prevalence and Diagnosis of Depression

There are a few key nuances that affect the identification, diagnosis, and treatment of depression in the workplace. First, depression exists in various levels of severity, accompanied by a myriad of presenting symptoms making detection and diagnoses difficult. Second, reliable gender differences have been reported with women being more likely than men to experience (or at least display) depression. Finally, there are key cultural differences in the manifestation of depression.

Depression is a mood disorder that appears to exist on a continuum of severity. At one end of the spectrum, dysthymia and atypical depression are subtle forms of the illness. The detection of sub-threshold depressive symptoms vastly improves the prediction of future depression (Andrews, 2008), suggesting that depression may be a chronic illness, taking years to develop with symptoms becoming progressively worse.

Fogel, Eaton and Ford (2006) found that prior episodes of depression are indicative of future episodes that are more severe in nature. Additional data from the 15-year Baltimore Epidemiological Catchment Area sample showed that 18.8 percent of individuals suffering from a minor depressive disorder in 1981 developed a major depressive disorder by 1996. Individuals with symptoms of minor depression were five times more likely to suffer from a future major depressive disorder. The evidence has surfaced and it seems that depression perpetuates its own negative cycle, making prevention and early identification essential.

Depression is far more common in women than it is in men. The annual prevalence rate in women is 12.9 percent, almost double the 7.7 percent prevalence rate found in men (Birnbaum, Leong, and Greenberg, 2003). Furthermore, a burgeoning literature places women as twice as likely to develop a depressive disorder (Kessler, Sharp and Lewis, 2005). These findings do not necessarily mean that women are more vulnerable to depression than are men. On the contrary, men and women have been found to suffer from similar levels of depression following significant and stressful work and marriage events (Wieclaw, Agerbo, Mortensen, et al., 2006; Langlieb and DePaulo, 2008). The higher rate in prevalence of depression among women is likely due to the marginalization that women still experience and the preference in coping mechanisms.

Women may report greater rates of depression due to the tendency to internalize and ruminate as coping mechanisms. Research finds that men externalize depressive symptoms and search for outside influences as a means of coping while women tend to internalize their problems, resulting in rumination and typical depressive symptoms (Billings and Moos, 1984). Therefore, it should not be surprising that men are more likely to present with depression with an increase in physical symptoms, complaints, and comorbid substance abuse while women are more likely to present with cognitive and affective impairments.

Brinbaum and colleagues (2003) examined the economics of women and depression using administrative claims from over 100,000 beneficiaries of a Fortune 100 company. A total of 13,907 employees suffered from a major depressive disorder, of which 8,155 were female. Interestingly, depressed men used inpatient care 45 percent more frequently than depressed women who used 27 percent more outpatient services and 37 percent more office services. Women were engaging in more self-reporting of symptoms and seeking psychiatric care while men were denying symptoms were present until inpatient care was required. This suggests that the early identification of depressive symptoms among women and in particular men is an imperative step in reducing the economic burden of depression.

Finally, signs of depression manifest differently among individuals from different cultures. Nakao and Yano (2006) analyzed healthcare data gathered from 1,027 adult Japanese workers and found that depressed workers reported a disproportionate amount of somatic complaints such as headaches, lower back pain, constipation, joint pain, and dizziness (Nakao and Yano, 2006). In addition, somatic complaints were typically expressed a year prior to diagnosis of depression. A similar study of Japanese men found that somatic complaints of sleep disturbances, fatigue, tachycardia, and constipation made in 1985 could be used to predict the occurrence of a major depressive episode by 2005 (Takeuchi, Nakao and Yano, 2008). Thus, Asian cultures experience a heightened sensitivity to somatic disturbances prior to the development of depression. Somatic complaints in this population may well compromise sub-syndromal depressive symptoms that offer a great target for early preventative measures.

Economic Burden of Depression in the Workplace: Development of an ROI Equation

The following section gives an accurate assessment of true costs associated with workplace depression. Later sections in this chapter will show how the costs of identifying and treating depression is offset by the benefits gained in terms of improved productivity and a reduction in disability claims. The ROI equation developed in the proceeding sections are outlined in Appendix A along with instructions on their use.

Depression is one of the most costly conditions in the world. The immense international costs of depression are not due to its severe crippling effects but to its high prevalence and sustained adverse effects. As a condition once believed only to affect the unemployed, current findings are implicating depression as the single leading cause of disability in the workplace (Langlieb and Kahn, 2005). Kessler et al. (2008) administered the World Health Organization's Health and Work Productivity questionnaire (HPQ) to a sample of 20,000 employees, finding that 8.3 percent of them suffered from mild to severe forms of depression. Similarly, a health risk appraisal performed on over 16,500 employees found that over 9.0 percent of full-time employees were being treated for depression (Burton, Pransky, Conti, et al., 2004).

In the past few years, several researchers have worked painstakingly to place monetary values on the burden of depression. This research has illuminated four fronts where depression costs employers and the public economy: unemployment, absenteeism, presenteeism, and healthcare utilization. These four facets of burden are the most accurate method reflecting full-cost accounting of depression available; however, these methods still likely underestimate the true economic burden.

Impact of Depression—Cost of Unemployment

A large body of research is amassing which suggests that a high labour force non-participation and unemployment exists in the mentally ill. Estimates obtained from the United States, the United Kingdom and Australia place between 60–90 percent of the mentally ill as unemployed (Hughes 1999; Waghorn and Chant, 2006). The estimates of unemployment due to mood disorders like depression are better than such mental illnesses as schizophrenia, but are still painstakingly high. Three independent research teams have shown that the depressed population is highly susceptible to unemployment. One study measured unemployment at 13 percent among depressed individuals (El-Guebaly, Currie, Williams, et al., 2007), while another study reported gender-specific rates at 26 percent for women and 13 percent for men (Ettner, Frank and Kessler, 1997). An Australian population survey pegged depression as carrying a lofty 46.4 percent reduction in the male labor force and a 28.6 percent reduction in the female labor force (Waghorn and Chant, 2006). Another similar investigation reported an unemployment rate of individuals with depression at 50 percent (Elinson, Houck, Marcus, et al., 2004).

The wide range of estimates for unemployment attributable to depression is a result of the severity of depression considered. When measuring unemployment due to depression, the inclusion of more common and less debilitating dysthymia and atypical depression results in lower estimates of unemployment ranging around 13–20 percent (Lerner, Adler, Chang, et al., 2004b), whereas restricting the sample to only those suffering from major depressive disorder results in estimates around 50 percent (Elinson, Houck, Marcus, et al., 2004). For this reason, and because mild depressive symptoms predict later onset severe depression, it is imperative that workplace studies of depression identify and report mild to severe depression.

Depressed employees have higher job turnover rates than do non-depressed employees. Longitudinal analysis of depression and unemployment indicates that depressed employees are 20–40 percent more likely to become unemployed due to their condition (Dooley, Prause and Ham-Rowbottom, 2000). Lerner and colleagues (2004b) substantiated this claim, finding that a sample of depressed employees had a 15 percent job loss rate relative to the 3.5 percent job loss rate found in non-depressed controls. Making matters worse, depressed employees are less likely to find another avenue of employment up to 18 months following termination and when they do re-enter the workforce they do so at reduced wages and hours.

Lerner et al. (2004b) examined work-related consequences of depression by assessing 229 depressed employees against a control group and a rheumatoid arthritis group. At the six-month follow-up, the authors found that 7 percent of initially employed participants were unemployed. This number was due almost solely to the inclusion of depressed employees, who suffered greater unemployment than did the rheumatoid arthritis or the control group. The authors found that unemployment rates were 14 percent in the dysthymic group, 12 percent in the major depressive group, and 15 percent in the group with comorbid dysthymia and major depression compared to a 3 percent unemployment rate in the rheumatoid arthritis group, and 2 percent in controls. More surprisingly, job turnover consistently resulted in lower pay grades only for the depressed workers.

The economic burden of depression as a result of unemployment is very difficult to assess and has been largely overlooked in the current research. However, it can be safely argued that the economic burden of unemployment due to depression costs taxpayers and economies billions of dollars every year in terms of employment insurance and financial aid. At this point, it is difficult to say if the costs of providing treatment for depressed employees are fewer than the costs of hiring and training new employees. Certainly, evidence that will be presented later in this chapter suggests that the costs of treatment can be completely offset by gains in workplace performance.

Some 50–85 percent of employees considered as suffering from mild to severe forms of depression still participate in the workforce. Data from the National Health Interview Survey-Disability Supplement (NHIS-D) indicates that depressed employees maintain a better self-view, seeing themselves as healthier physically, cognitively, and socially than do unemployed depressed individuals (Elinson, Houck, Marcus, et al., 2004). Just the mere act of working may stave off more severe depressive episodes, acting as a proxy treatment by its own means. Employers should not only consider the bottom line figures but should factor in the loss in social capital as a result of releasing a depressed employee before first investigating such alternatives as treatment options that are largely paid for by employee benefits in the long run.

Impact of Depression—Cost of Absenteeism

Absenteeism is work loss represented as either hours or days missed from work due to extenuating circumstances. Figures representing absenteeism are usually gathered by way of self-report and substantiated using employment records. This method for obtaining absenteeism data is not immune to error but has proven to be both accurate and reliable. Studies have shown that self-reporting of work absenteeism shows a high degree of convergence with employer and medical records on the issue.

Employees suffering from severe forms of depression at work are unable to handle a full-time work schedule and it should not be surprising that depression has been linked to a significant increase in absenteeism. The first study monetizing the burden of depression due to workplace absenteeism was performed in 1999. This study investigated the direct and indirect costs related to lost work performance and bringing employees in to work overtime (Greenberg, Kessler, Nells, et al., 1996). Workplace absenteeism as a result of depression was found to cost the US economy an estimated $US24.5 billion in 1996 alone (see Figure 4.2).

Depressed affect drains an individual's energy reserves, leaving them feeling lethargic and unmotivated to work and resulting in a substantial increase in workplace absences. The majority of the literature examining absenteeism due to depression has found that depressed employees miss on average an additional 0.3–3.8 work days each month (Lerner and Henke, 2008). However, once again we see that workplace absenteeism depends on the severity of depression. One study examining workplace absenteeism and mild to severe forms of depression found that employees with a major depressive

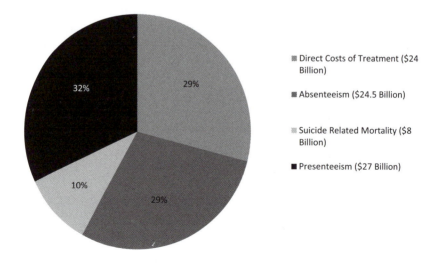

Figure 4.2   The Annual Cost of Depression on the U.S. Economy ($83.5 Billion)

disorder, double depression, and dysthymia missed 3.4, 2.4, and 1.8 more work days a month than did non-depressed controls, respectively (Lerner, Adler, Chang, et al., 2004b). With absenteeism at around 2.5 missed work days a month, the work absence cost has been estimated at $4,600 per annum for employed woman and $3,540 per annum for employed man (Birnbaum, Leong and Greenberg, 2003).

Looking at the average yearly employee absenteeism cost, it is becoming clear that depression should be identified and treated before it develops into more severe forms of major depression. A naturalistic survey of 25,000 primary care patients in 14 different countries found that 48 percent of respondents reported moderate to severe occupational role impairments, missing an average of 7.7 work days per month (Ormel, van den Brink, van der Meer, et al., 1994). This suggests that as severity of depression goes from mild to severe, the cost of workplace absenteeism increases three-fold. Using the aforementioned workplace absenteeism costs, severe forms of major depressive disorder costs employers an estimated $12,000 per-employee per-annum.

Impact of Depression: Cost of Presenteeism

Presenteeism is a reduction in an employee's work-related performance as a result of coming to work in spite of an illness. Presenteeism is likely the greatest cost accrued as a result of workplace depression, costing employers tens of billions of dollars every year (Greenberg, Kessler, Nells, et al., 1996). In fact, a recent employer study suggests that presenteeism is a more costly workplace component than medical care, absenteeism, and disability combined (Goetzel, Long, Ozminkowski, et al., 2004). With such high costs accumulating as a direct result of lost workplace productivity, it should come as no surprise that there is a growing interest on the part of employers and insurers to generate estimates of productivity decrements related to common health and disease conditions.

A commonly used scale capturing presenteeism in the workplace is the Work Limitations Questionnaire (WLQ) (Lerner, Amick, Rogers, et al.,2001). The WLQ is a self-report instrument measuring on-the-job work impairment in four domains: time, physical, mental-interpersonal, and output demands. The recall period varies between 2–4 weeks depending on the application of the instrument (Prasad, Wahlqvist, Shikiar, et al., 2004). The instrument is available in a short and easy-to-administer 25-question written format that has been proven both reliable and valid (Lerner, Reed, Massarotti, et al.,2002).

Lost productivity due to depression comes in many forms. Depressed employees often have a preoccupation with unexplained aches and pains that detracts them from maintaining consistency in and completing their work (Langlieb and DePaulo, 2008). Furthermore, the behavior of depressed employees at work is commonly less cooperative and collegial, creating a negative work atmosphere (Langlieb and DePaulo, 2008). This negative work atmosphere may result in a loss of clientele or employee morale. Finally, depression can impair an employee's judgment, contributing to cognitive impairments and occupational injuries.

Several studies have been able to quantify the adverse impacts of depression on work performance: one such study administered the World Health Organization's Health and Work Performance Questionnaire (HPQ) in the fourth quarter of 2005 to some 20,000 employees with at least 11 months of medical-pharmacy enrollment. The HPQ is an instrument developed in part by the World Health Organization that reliably and validly measures both work productivity and absenteeism. Kessler and colleagues (2008) examined work productivity deficits due to a host of mental and physical diseases ranging from arthritis and back pain to depression and anxiety, with everything in-between. The results revealed depression to be the condition having the greatest negative impact on work performance (β = -3.0) followed by chronic fatigue (β = -2.6) and then anxiety (β = -2.3). In fact, migraine was the only medical condition remaining a significant predictor of lost work productivity after controlling for depression. Furthermore, the effects of depression persisted even after all of the remaining 15 medical conditions were controlled for, suggesting that underlying depressive symptoms are the greatest cause of lost work productivity in nearly every medical condition.

Workplace depression has greater impacts on workplace performance than any other medical condition or mental illness. These depression-related workplace performance deficits are sometimes physical, but are primarily cognitive in nature. Studies using the HPQ to measure deficits in workplace performance have shown that depression limits employees' performance of physical job demands only 20 percent of the time. However, time management, mental and interpersonal demands, as well as output demands are limited in 35 percent or more of cases (Adler, McLaughlin, Rogers, et al., 2006; Lerner, Adler, Chang, et al., 2004a; Lerner, Adler, Chang, et al., 2004b).

One unique method of objectively capturing losses in workplace performance is the experience sampling method. In this method, employees are given a diary and a pager and are asked to record prior events and what they are presently working on every time their pager goes off. The pagers are set to page employees at five random times each day over the course of seven days. Results from one experiential sampling study found depression to be the only condition associable with decrements in workplace task focus as well as productivity (Wang, Beck, Berglund, et al., 2004). This study found that workplace depression accounts for approximately 18 percent reduction in task focus and 7 percent reduction in overall productivity. These findings are in line with research using self-report measures that have found workplace depression results in a 6–10 percent increase in presenteeism (Lerner, Adler, Chang, et al., 2004b).

The presenteeism-related increase due to depression exists on a continuum of severity from dysthymia to major depressive disorder. The most representative study investigating presenteeism as a function of severity of depression found that the average two-week productivity loss reported due to depression was 11.4 percent, 10.1 percent, 6.6 percent, and 2.6 percent for major depressive disorder, double depression, dysthymia, and controls, respectively (Lerner, Adler, Chang, et al. 2004b). It should not be surprising that more severe forms of depression are associated with greater presenteeism because as depression severity increases so too do the number of symptoms and comorbid conditions. Indeed, the impact of depression is worse when it is comorbid with other medical conditions. The reduction in work performance due to pure depression has been found to be 3.5 lost work days a month, which increases to 6.6 lost work days with comorbid sleep disorders, and to 14.9 lost work days with comorbid anxiety disorders (Kessler, White, Birnbaum, et al., 2008).

Interestingly, there have been some reports of depression-related presenteeism increasing as the day goes on, suggesting that depression causes employees to lose their continuity at work and disrupts overall workflow. General trends show that employee work productivity naturally decreases as the work day progresses. However, this trend is even more dramatic in depressed individuals, suggesting that the natural fatigue and monotony of the average work day may bear a disproportionately negative impact on this population of employees. Furthermore, these effects are exacerbated through discrimination, low seniority, low-status positions, job accommodation barriers, difficulty coping with job stress, as well as receiving inadequate treatment (Lerner, Adler, Chang, et al. 2004a). Clearly, there are many avenues for employers to improve the work climate to better accommodate depressed individuals to gain work productivity and reduce presenteeism as a return on their investment. Many of these strategies will be discussed shortly.

Impact of Depression: Cost of Disability

Even the popular press has addressed this issue. A recent Globe and Mail Mental Health Roundtable Report found that 40 percent of short- and long-term disability claims in Canada involve a mental illness (Picard, 2008). Since the mid-1990s many workplaces have seen a steady increase in the number of disability cases attributable to mental illnesses, depression in particular. One examination of the short-term disability cost for a financial service company found that mental health was the third greatest contributor to short-term disability costs at 12 percent; third only to pregnancy (28 percent) and other (22 percent) categories (Burton and Conti, 2008). Furthermore, depression accounts for 60 percent of the total burden of mental illness-related short-term disability. Depression-related short-term disability has been found to affect more employees, lasts longer, and is more apt to recur than are other mental illnesses or nervous system-related short-term disabilities (Dewa, Goering, Lin, et al., 2002).

An analysis of two US national surveys examining depression and short-term disability found that 30-day depression was linked to an increase of 1.5–3.2 short-term disability days (Kessler, Barber, Birnbaum, et al., 1999). Taking these statistics and extrapolating them to encompass the entire US working population, the authors found depression results in an increase of 20 million lost work days a year due to short-term disability.

Perhaps more disturbing, the cost of depression-related long-term disability may be even greater than that of short-term disability. The Globe and Mail Roundtable Report found that mental illnesses cost Canadian employers and insurers $8.5 billion in terms of long-term disability each year. Furthermore, depression was found to comprise 70 percent of long-term disability-related mental health spending in 2004 (Cubic Health Inc, 2007). Thus, depression-related long-term disability costs the Canadian economy an estimated $5.95 billion in mental health expenditures each year.

Treatment for Depression

The information presented in the treatment section provides bits and pieces from the most cost-effective and promising treatments for employees with depression. This section will be presented on five fronts:

a)   The effectiveness of treatment for depression

b)   The cost-effectiveness of treatment for depression

c)   Specific interventions proven effective

d)   Workplace components to treatment

e)   Treatment-resistant depression

A. THE EFFECTIVENESS OF TREATMENT FOR DEPRESSION

At least 80 percent of patients suffering from depression can be treated successfully with medication, psychotherapy or a combination of the two (Horwath, Johnson, Klerman, et al., 1992). Although 80 percent of patients with depression can be successfully treated, many individuals meeting the criteria for diagnosable depression do not receive the treatment they require. It is estimated that only half of the individuals meeting the criteria for diagnosable depression receive treatment (Burton and Conti, 2008). Furthermore, only about one-third of the approximately 50 percent of depressed individuals receiving treatment are receiving minimally adequate treatment. Three nationally representative samples from the United States and one from Australia place the percentage of depressed individuals receiving adequate treatment between 17–30 percent, and 32 percent, respectively (Andrews, Sanderson, Corry, et al., 2000; Miranda, Schoenbaum, Sherbourne, et al., 2004; Wang, Berglund and Kessler, 2000; Young, Klap, Sherbourne, et al., 2001).

Employers stand to accrue large financial gains if employees are screened for depression and referred to clinicians for treatment. Adler and colleagues (2006) examined the effectiveness of primary care treatment for employees with a major depressive disorder and/or dysthymia. Primary care treatment offered by the Tufts Health Plan decreased the severity of employee depression at six months. Severity of depressive symptoms was further reduced from month six to month 18. In all cases, clinical improvement of depression in the first six months significantly improved job performance on all four domains of the Work Limitations Questionnaire (that is, physical demands, time-management, output demands, and mental-interpersonal demands). However, only 21 percent of depressed patients experienced remission during the 18 months, calling the adequacy of care into question. In this case treatment for depression was proven somewhat effective in an employee benefit setting.

Another study examined the efficacy of naturalistic care in 46 clinics with the participation of 181 trained clinicians (Schoenbaum, Unutzer, McCaffrey, et al., 2002). Nearly 44 percent of the 938 patients were assigned to an author-designed intervention that achieved appropriate care through the training of care providers and the provision of additional practice resources, whereas the other 56 percent of patients received only the usual care. Results were hopeful. More than 70 percent of patients receiving appropriate care experienced remission of symptoms compared to 40 percent of patients receiving usual care. Furthermore, after controlling patient factors and covariates, patients receiving appropriate care were more likely to be employed, had better health outcomes, and received lower depression scores. The findings from this study are encouraging and suggest that appropriate care makes vast differences in alleviating depression and aiding the effective return to work for employees. Furthermore, employers should thoroughly evaluate the depression treatment options available through their company to ensure that appropriate care will be given in order to gain maximum financial returns on benefits paid.

Depression has a wide range of antecedents and consequences and often co-occurs with medical conditions. Employees suffering from medical conditions who are believed to be depressed should be pre-screened for depression to conclude whether referral is required. This is important because the treatment of depression comorbid with medical conditions has proven effective in alleviating both depressive symptoms and medical conditions. In a sample of 439 patients at clinics for Group Health Cooperative (a pre-paid health plan serving approximately 450,000 members in Washington), treatment for depression reduced depression scores by over 50 percent for individuals suffering from depression comorbid with ischemic heart disease, diabetes, or obstructive lung disease (Simon, Von Korff and Lin, 2005). Furthermore, the authors found improvement in depression to be associated with reductions in disability days and restricted work activities. One study has noted that comorbid chronic medical conditions are associated with poorer depression outcomes, however the benefits of systematic treatment are at least equivalent in the medically ill (Koike, Unutzer and Wells, 2002).

In summary, when administered appropriately, the treatment of depression is effective at reducing disability and promoting a better quality of life, a quicker return to work, and better work functioning. Furthermore, appropriate treatment for depression appears just as beneficial for pure depression as it is for depression comorbid with chronic or acute medical conditions.

B. THE COST-EFFECTIVENESS OF TREATMENT FOR DEPRESSION

There has been some disagreement as to whether treatment for depression is cost-effective for employers. The emerging literature strongly suggests that the treatment of depression is cost-effective. In one of the most recent, well-defined, and informative studies, Rost, Smith and Dickinson (2004) quantified the employer financial gains accompanied by treatment for depression. The authors examined 12 community primary care practices either offering enhanced care or typical care for depression. Findings revealed that enhanced treatment of depression in consistently employed patients reduced both presenteeism and absenteeism. At 24 months following treatment, the intervention improved productivity by 8.2 percent at an estimated annual savings of $1,982 per full time equivalent. Additionally, absenteeism was reduced by 28.4 percent or 12.3 days over the 24-month period, putting an estimated $619 back into employers' pockets. Findings from this study suggest that treatment for depression is cost effective in the workforce.

Zang et al. (1999) used data from residents in Arkansas with recent symptoms of depression to compare the costs of lost earnings (measured by absentee days multiplied by subjects' wages) to the costs of treatment for depression (using provider and insurance records). Results from this study revealed that the cost of depression treatment was fully offset by the savings due to a reduction in absenteeism alone. Another study extending these findings concluded that it is feasible for savings to fully offset the cost of an intervention program in a long-term disabled population (Leon, Walkup and Portera, 2002). Based on conservative estimates, it was found that if 2,500 claimants were screened for depression, and if as few as ten claimants ultimately returned to work, the program would have net financial benefit. Rost and colleagues (2004) examined 230 employees seeking psychotherapy as a means of treatment for their depression and found that psychotherapy was associated with a 26.1 percent improvement in absenteeism over one year. Employees undergoing psychotherapy as treatment for their depression reduced their absenteeism from 24.3 lost work hours per month at baseline down to 2.5 lost work hours per month reported 12 months later. These findings are informative in suggesting that reductions in absenteeism can fully offset the cost of treatment for depression at work. In fact, estimates suggest that depression-free-days save employers $10–$35 per depression free day (Wang, Simon and Kessler, 2003).

Studies employing full-cost accounting for depression are finding the benefits of reduced absenteeism and presenteeism as a result of treatment far outweigh the costs. More importantly, these estimates are conservative estimates that underestimate the true cost savings of treatment for depression for two reasons. First, depression screening and disease management programs increase the number of workers receiving treatment that is of a high quality. Treating nearly 100 percent of depressed employees with high-quality treatments gives employers a greater return on investment. Second, in terms of absenteeism, employers who pay replacement workers overtime or hire temporary workers may accrue additional financial benefits by treating depressed employees.

C. SPECIFIC TREATMENTS PROVEN EFFECTIVE

The two most well-reviewed and utilized treatment methods for depression are pharmacotherapy and psychotherapies, each having their own strengths and limitations.

Pharmacotherapy (that is, medication) is generally considered effective for about 50 percent of depressed individuals. Selective Serotonin reuptake inhibitors (SSRI's) are currently the prescribed drug of choice for adults with a major depressive disorder. Nevertheless, there is debate as to whether the selective publication of clinical trials has inflated the effectiveness ratings of pharmacotherapy. The Canadian Depression Study found that antidepressant therapy has fallen short of a desired level of efficacy considering their adverse side-effects (Kennedy and Paykel 2004a, b). Antidepressants only substantially alleviated symptoms of depression in one-third of individuals and completely alleviated symptoms of depression in one-quarter of individuals.

Pharmacotherapy has the advantage of being quick and easy to prescribe and administer. However, antidepressant medications have been shown to impair performance on a wide range of laboratory measures, impacting attention, vigilance, memory, problem solving, and motor coordination (Edwards 1995; Lawrenson, Tyrer, Newson, et al., 2000; Tilson, 1990). Additionally, antidepressants are quite costly and carry with them many adverse side-effects including blurred vision, dry throat, constipation, drowsiness, weight gain, and sexual dysfunction. These adverse effects make the use of pharmacotherapy hazardous in the workplace where the risk of accidents are heightened. As a general consensus, employees should receive pharmacotherapy only if psychotherapies prove ineffective.

Psychotherapies are identified as the best method for managing and treating depression. There are two psychotherapies which have proven highly effective in treating depression: *cognitive behavioral therapy* (CBT) and *inter-personal therapy* (IPT). Developed by Aaron Beck, CBT is considered the gold standard of psychotherapies for the treatment of depression. Depressed individuals think discouraging, negative, and painful thoughts such as "I am no good" or "I will always fail". During CBT, the clinician targets the client's fundamental thinking errors that cause them to interpret themselves, people around them, and the world in a negative manner. The first goal is to teach depressed individuals to identify and monitor their dysfunctional thoughts. Next, the client is taught to recognize the link between dysfunctional thoughts, moods, and behaviors. Finally, these automatic dysfunctional thoughts are in turn evaluated. It is through the repeated evaluation of many thoughts and activities that depressed clients become aware of and begin to alter dysfunctional cognitions lying at the core of their depression.

Using CBT, patients learn not to take negative thinking for granted but rather weigh and evaluate the actual evidence for and against such thinking. Patients are taught a "skill-set" such as keeping a "dysfunctional thought record" that they can use to ward off such thoughts during recurrent future episodes (Hollon, DeRubeis, Shelton, et al., 2005). Numerous random control trials attest to the efficacy of CBT as a cost-effective and timely treatment for depression that generally spans 20 or fewer sessions with a trained clinician (Markowitz, 2008). When compared, CBT has been shown to have effects equal to or greater than pharmacotherapy (Hollon, Thase and Markowitz, 2002; DeRubeis, Hollon, Amsterdam, et al., 2005). Furthermore, no adverse side-effects or performance deficits occur.

Inter-personal therapy (IPT) is another form of psychotherapy that has proven effective in the treatment of depression. Depression is characterized by social withdrawal, passivity, and poor social functioning (Markowitz, 2008). Developed by Klerman and colleagues (1984), IPT addresses and treats social functioning. An assumption of IPT is that depression will be resolved by treating the depressed individual's social circumstance. Like CBT, IPT is brief spanning 12–16 sessions which focus on interpersonal disputes, role transitions, grief, and interpersonal deficits. Several random control trials show IPT to relieve depression severity and improve interpersonal skills (Weissman, 1979). Results show that IPT is an effective form of treatment both during depressive episodes and as a form of maintenance to prevent recurrent depressive episodes (Elkin, Shea, Watkins, et al., 1989). Like CBT, IPT teaches depressed patients a "skill-set" that they may rely on to treat recurrent depressive episodes and should be favored over pharmacotherapy.

D. WORKPLACE COMPONENTS TO TREATMENT

Social support has been consistently shown to ameliorate the negative effects of depression (Plaisier, de Bruijn, de Graff, et al., 2007). A key component for the successful treatment of depression is supervisor and co-worker support. Deconstructing the stigma of mental illnesses at work and providing "genuine" care and support will greatly improve the recovery time of depressed employees. Furthermore, depressed individuals would benefit greatly from workplace interventions targeting work performance domains and tasks. It is recommended that supervisors and fellow employees offer support, give advice, and aid depressed co-workers when possible. Helpful tips and hints on how to make work easier and the work environment more user-friendly would also be of benefit.

Beyond offering social support, creating a workplace with lower psychological demands would be of benefit to depressed employees. Since workplace psychological demands are perceived by the individual making them somewhat unique, it is imperative to include the depressed employee when discussing his/her workplace demands and viable solutions. Options include, but are by no means limited to: creating a somewhat flexible schedule, having the employee work on less demanding projects, having two employees work together and share their workloads, offering constructive criticism, or creating an easier-to-operate template through which work should be maintained. Studies have shown that the little things matter when dealing with depressed individuals and that benefits may be gained simply by increasing the number of weekly reminders, developing daily schedules and routines, and having an increased number of follow-ups regarding work performed (Gilbody, Whitty, Grimshaw, et al., 2003).

One avenue promising to be a great asset to depressed employees is the use of an Employee Assistance Plan (EAP). With a significant portion of their clientele base suffering from depression, EAPs have the potential to provide screening, workplace assessments, brief counseling and referral for treatment (Myette, 2008a, b). Furthermore, EAPs can provide workplace services such as stress management, education to reduce stigma and discrimination, as well as supervisor education and consultation. While being costly at the forefront, offering comprehensive benefit packages providing adequate services at the cost of reasonable deductions is the most cost-effective way of retaining a depressed employee in the long run.

The Workplace Accommodation Network provides a list of typical accommodations that can be used to assist depressed employees. This list is provided in Table 4.2. The recommended workplace accommodations are centered around the symptoms of depression, allowing employers flexibility in the accommodation strategy that they tailor to the individual employee.

Table 4.2   Workplace accommodations for depression provided by the Job Accommodation Network

Presenting Concern—Stamina During the Work Day:
• Provide flexible scheduling
• Allow longer or more frequent work breaks
• Allow employee to work from home during part of the day or week
• Provide part-time work schedules
• Move closer to frequently accessed office equipment
Presenting Concern—Concentration:
• Reduce distractions in the work area
• Provide space enclosures or a private office
• Allow for use of white noise or environmental sound machines
• Allow the employee to play music and use a headset
• Increase natural lighting or provide full spectrum lighting
• Plan for uninterrupted work time and allow for frequent breaks
• Divide large assignments into smaller tasks and goals
• Restructure job to include only essential functions
Presenting Concern—Memory Deficits:
• Allow the employee to tape record meetings and provide written checklists
• Provide type written minutes of each meeting
• Provide written instructions and allow additional training time
• Implement color-coding scheme for priority projects
Presenting Concern—Difficulty Staying Organized and Meeting Deadlines:
• Make daily TO-DO lists and check items off as they are completed
• Use calendar to mark meetings and deadlines
• Remind employee of important deadlines
• Use electronic organizers
• Divide large assignments into smaller tasks and goals
Presenting Concern—Difficulty Handling Stress and Emotions:
• Provide praise and positive reinforcement
• Refer to counseling and employee assistance programs
• Allow telephone calls during work hours to doctors and others for needed support
• Allow the presence of a support animal
• Allow the employee to take breaks as needed
Presenting Concern—Attendance Issues:
• Provide flexible leave
• Provide a self-paced work load and flexible hours
• Allow employee to telework

Source: available at http://askjan.org/media/depr.htm.

Preventing Workplace Depression

The successful prevention of workplace mental illnesses requires coordinating efforts at the micro (individual), meso (organizational), and macro (system/policy) levels (Myette, 2008a). At the individual level, having all employees complete a Chronic Disease Self Management Program (CDSMP) yearly may reduce the genesis of depression, dampen the severity and debilitation associated with recurrent episodes, and double back as a safe avenue for depression pre-screening. The CDSMP is a community-based patient self-management course, educating and empowering individuals in effective ways to recognize and overcome the symptoms associated with a range of chronic conditions (Browne, Steiner, Roberts, et al., 2002). Program content should include: the importance of exercise and diet; fatigue and sleep management; use of cognitive symptom management techniques; information about available community resources; use of medication; how to deal with negative emotions such as fear, anger, and dysthymia; problem-solving; decision-making; and ways to effectively communicate with others including health professionals (Myette, 2008b). Thus, CDSMPs will act to reduce the stigma associated with mental illnesses, pre-screen employees, foster a team environment which supports one another, and empower employees by giving them the tools they need to effectively deal with mental health issues.

At the meso level, employers need to build mental health prevention initiatives into the core business goals of the organization. This includes designing, implementing, supporting, and promoting human resource policies regarding items such as conflict resolution, work-life balance, mental health promotion, and recognizing contributions made by employees (Caruso, 2008).

Finally, employers need to use their political influence to affect change at the macro level. Employers must unite with EAPs and medical insurance providers to lobby for incentives, tax relief, cutbacks, and other forms of government funding to build more effective mental health prevention and treatment programs. There exists a research-practice gap, preventing efficient mental health programs from operating in organizational, clinical, and insurance populations. This gap exists because of inadequate communication and conflicting priorities between diverse stakeholders including: researchers, policymakers, service providers, and employers (Myette, 2008). Employers, unions, EAPs, and other service providers have the power to affect changes to policies that are required to effectively prevent and treat workplace depression. The Canadian Institutes for Health Research (CIHR, 2004) has recognized this issue and introduced a stakeholder engagement process to gain a more holistic perspective for the development of their long-term research agenda on mental health in the workplace.

More information can be found at the following sources:

Global Business and Economic Roundtable on Addiction and Mental Health at http://www.mentalhealthroundtable.ca/documents.html

Canadian Mental Health Association at http://www.cmha.ca/mental_health/depression-in-the-workplace/#.Ukeo3D8qNat

Mental Health Works at http://www.mentalhealthworks.ca/

World Health Organization programs in the workplace at http://www.who.int/mental_health/policy/services/13_policies%20programs%20in%20workplace_WEB_07.pdf

National Institute for Health and Clinical Excellence at http://www.nice.org.uk/cg023

References

Adler, D.A., McLaughlin, T.J., Rogers, W.H., Hong, C., Lapitsky, L., and Lerner, D. (2006). Job performance deficits due to depression. *American Journal of Psychiatry*, 163(9), 1569–76.

Andrews, G. (2008). Reducing the burden of depression. *Canadian Journal of Psychiatry-Revue Canadienne De Psychiatrie*, 53(7), 420–427.

Andrews, G., Sanderson, K., Corry, J., and Lapsley, H.M. (2000). Using epidemiological data to model efficiency in reducing the burden of depression. *Journal of Mental Health Policy and Economics*, 3(4), 175–86.

Beck, A.T. (1970). The core problem in depression: The cognitive triad. In J.H. Masserman (ed.), *Depression: Theories and therapies* (pp. 47–55). New York, NY: Grune & Stratton.

Beck A.T., Steer R.A., and Brown, G.K. (1996). *Manual for the Beck Depression Inventory-II*. San Antonio, TX: Psychological Corporation.

Billings, A.G. and Moos, R.H. (1984). Coping, stress, and social resources among adults with unipolar depression. *Journal of Personality and Social Psychology*, 46(4), 877–91.

Birnbaum, H.G., Leong, S.A., and Greenberg, P.E. (2003). The economics of women and depression: an employer's perspective. *Journal of Affective Disorders*, 74(1), 15–22.

Browne, G., Steiner, M., Roberts, J., Gafni, A., Byrne, C., Dunn, E., et al. (2002). Sertraline and/or interpersonal psychotherapy for patients with dysthymic disorder in primary care: 6-month comparison with longitudinal 2-year follow-up of effectiveness and costs. *Journal of Affect Disords*, 68(2–3), 317–30.

Burton, W.N. and Conti, D.J. (2008). Depression in the workplace: The role of the Corporate Medical Director. *Journal of Occupational and Environmental Medicine*, 50(4), 476–81.

Burton, W.N., Pransky, G., Conti, D.J., Chen, C.Y., and Edington, D.W. (2004). The association of medical conditions and presenteeism. *Journal of Occupational and Environmental Medicine*, 46(6), S38–S45.

Canadian Institute for Health Research (2004). Establishing a long-term agenda for workplace mental health research. Report of the Working Group mandated by the Institute of Population and Public Health and the Institute of Neurosciences, Mental Health and Addiction. Ottawa: Canada.

Caruso, G.M. (2008). A clinical perspective on workplace depression: Current and future directions. *Journal of Occupational and Environmental Medicine*, 50(4), 501–13.

Cassano, P. and Fava, M. (2002). Depression and public health—An overview. *Journal of Psychosomatic Research*, 53(4), 849–57.

Collins, S. and Long, A. (2003). Working with the psychological effects of trauma: consequences for mental health-care workers – a literature review. *Journal of Psychiatric Mental Health Nursing*, 10(4), 417–24.

Cubic Health Inc (2007). *Phase I: General context & co-morbidities with depression*: Global Business and Economic Rountable on Addicition and Mental-Health.

DeRubeis, R.J., Hollon, S.D., Amsterdam, J.D., Shelton, R.C., Young, P.R., Salomon, R.M., et al. (2005). Cognitive therapy vs medications in the treatment of moderate to severe depression. *Archives of General Psychiatry*, 62(4), 409–16.

Dewa, C.S., Goering, P., Lin, E., and Paterson, M. (2002). Depression-related short-term disability in an employed population. *Journal of Occupational and Environmental Medicine*, 44(7), 628–33.

Diksa, E. and Rogers, E.S. (1996). Employer concerns about hiring persons with psychiatric disability: Results of the employer attitude questionnaire. *Rehabilitation Counseling Bulletin*, 40(1), 31–44.

Dooley, D., Prause, J., and Ham-Rowbottom, K.A. (2000). Underemployment and depression: longitudinal relationships. *Journal of Health and Social Behavior*, 41(4), 421–36.

Edwards, J.G. (1995). Depression, antidepressants, and accidents. *BMJ*, 311(7010), 887–8.

El-Guebaly, N., Currie, S., Williams, J., Wang, J.L., Beck, C.A., Maxwell, C., et al. (2007). Association of mood, anxiety, and substance use disorders with occupational status and disability in a community sample. *Psychiatric Services*, 58(5), 659–67.

Elinson, L., Houck, P., Marcus, S.C., and Pincus, H.A. (2004). Depression and the ability to work. *Psychiatric Services*, 55(1), 29–34.

Elkin, I., Shea, M.T., Watkins, J.T., Imber, S.D., Sotsky, S.M., Collins, J.F., et al. (1989). National-Institute-of-Mental-Health Treatment of Depression Collaborative Research-Program – General Effectiveness of Treatments. *Archives of General Psychiatry*, 46(11), 971–82.

Ettner, S.L., Frank, R.G., and Kessler, R.C. (1997). The impact of psychiatric disorders on labor market outcomes. *Industrial & Labor Relations Review*, 51(1), 64–81.

Fogel, J., Eaton, W.W., and Ford, D.E. (2006). Minor depression as a predictor of the first onset of major depressive disorder over a 15-year follow-up. *Acta Psychiatrica Scandinavica*, 113(1), 36–43.

Gerberich, S.G., Church, T.R., McGovern, P.M., Hansen, H.E., Nachreiner, N.M., Geisser, M.S., et al. (2004). An epidemiological study of the magnitude and consequences of work related violence: the Minnesota nurses' study. *Occupational and Environmental Medicine*, 61(6), 495–503.

Gilbody, S., Whitty, P., Grimshaw, J., and Thomas, R. (2003). Educational and organizational interventions to improve the management of depression in primary care: a systematic review. *Journal of the American Medical Association*, 289(23), 3145–51.

Goetzel, R.Z., Long, S.R., Ozminkowski, R.J., Hawkins, K., Wang, S.H., and Lynch, W. (2004). Health, absence, disability, and presenteeism cost estimates of certain physical and mental health conditions affecting US employers. *Journal of Occupational and Environmental Medicine*, 46(4), 398–412.

Greenberg, P.E., Kessler, R.C., Nells, T.L., Finkelstein, S.N., and Berndt, E.R. (1996). Depression in the workplace: An economic perspective. In J.P. Feighner and W.F. Boyer (eds), *Selective seratonin re-uptake inhibitors: Advances in basic research and clinical perspective* (2nd ed., pp. 327–63). New York: Wiley.

Hamilton, M. (1960). A Rating Scale for Depression. *Journal of Neurology Neurosurgery and Psychiatry*, 23(1), 56–62.

Heinrichs, M., Baumgartner, T., Kirschbaum, C., and Ehlert, U. (2003). Social support and oxytocin interact to suppress cortisol and subjective responses to psychosocial stress. *Biological Psychiatry*, 54(12), 1389–98.

Hollon, S.D., DeRubeis, R.J., Shelton, R.C., Amsterdam, J.D., Salomon, R.M., O'Reardon, J.P., et al. (2005). Prevention of relapse following cognitive therapy vs medications in moderate to severe depression. *Archives of General Psychiatry*, 62(4), 417–22.

Hollon, S.D., Thase, M.E., and Markowitz, J.C. (2002). Treatment and prevention of depression. *Psychological Science*, 39–77.

Horwath, E., Johnson, J., Klerman, G.L., and Weissman, M.M. (1992). Depressive symptoms as relative and attributable risk-factors for 1st-onset major depression. *Archives of General Psychiatry*, 49(10), 817–23.

Hughes, R. (1999). Psychosocial rehabilitation—New protocols, ethics, and outcomes. *International Journal of Mental Health*, 28(1), 3–33.

Kahn, J.P. (2008). Diagnosis and referral of workplace depression. *Journal of Occupational and Environmental Medicine*, 50(4), 396–400.

Karasek, R.A. (1979). Job demands, job decision latitude, and mental strain—implications for job redesign. *Administrative Science Quarterly*, 24(2), 285–308.

Karasek, R. and Theorell, T. (1990). Health work. *Stress, Productivity and the Reconstruction of Working Life*. New York: Basic Book Inc.

Kennedy, S.H. (2004). *The Canadian Depression Study*. Science & Medicine Canada Incorporated.

Kennedy, N. and Paykel, E.S. (2004a). Residual symptoms at remission from depression: impact on long-term outcome. *Journal of Affective Disorders*, 80(2–3), 135–44.

Kennedy, N. and Paykel, E.S. (2004b). Treatment and response in refractory depression: results from a specialist affective disorders service. *Journal of Affective Disorders*, 81(1), 49–53.

Kessler, D., Sharp, D., and Lewis, G. (2005). Screening for depression in primary care. *British Journal of General Practice*, 55(518), 659–60.

Kessler, R.C., Barber, C., Birnbaum, H.G., Frank, R.G., Greenberg, P.E., Rose, R.M., et al. (1999). Depression in the workplace: Effects on short-term disability. *Health Affairs*, 18(5), 163–71.

Kessler, R., White, L.A., Birnbaum, H., Qiu, Y., Kidolezi, Y., Mallett, D., et al. (2008). Comparative and interactive effects of depression relative to other health problems on work performance in the workforce of a large employer. *Journal of Occupational and Environmental Medicine*, 50(7), 809–16.

Klerman, G.L., Weissman, M.W. and Rounsaville, B.J. (1984). *Interpersonal Therapy for Depression*. New York: Basic Books.

Koike, A.K., Unutzer, J., and Wells, K.B. (2002). Improving the care for depression in patients with comorbid medical illness. *American Journal of Psychiatry*, 159(10), 1738–45.

Langlieb, A.M. and DePaulo, J.R. (2008). Etiology of depression and implications on work environment. *Journal of Occupational and Environmental Medicine*, 50(4), 391–5.

Langlieb, A.M. and Kahn, J.P. (2005). How much does quality mental health care profit employers? *Journal of Occupational and Environmental Medicine*, 47(11), 1099–109.

Lawrenson, R.A., Tyrer, F., Newson, R.B., and Farmer, R.D.T. (2000). The treatment of depression in UK general practice: selective serotonin reuptake inhibitors and tricyclic antidepressants compared. *Journal of Affective Disorders*, 59(2), 149–57.

Leon, A.C., Walkup, J.T., and Portera, L. (2002). Assessment and treatment of depression in disability claimants: a cost-benefit simulation study. The *Journal of Nervous and Mental Disease*, 190(1), 3–9.

Lerner, D., Adler, D.A., Chang, H., Berndt, E.R., Irish, J.T., Lapitsky, L., et al. (2004a). The clinical and occupational correlates of work productivity loss among employed patients with depression. *Journal of Occupational and Environmental Medicine*, 46(6), S46–S55.

Lerner, D., Adler, D.A., Chang, H., Lapitsky, L., Hood, M.Y., Perissinotto, C., et al. (2004b). Unemployment, job retention, and productivity loss among employees with depression. *Psychiatric Services*, 55(12), 1371–8.

Lerner, D., Amick, B.C., Rogers, W.H., Malspeis, S., Bungay, K., and Cynn, D. (2001). The work limitations questionnaire. *Medical Care*, 39(1), 72–85.

Lerner, D. and Henke, R.M. (2008). What does research tell us about depression, job performance, and work productivity? *Journal of Occupational and Environmental Medicine*, 50(4), 401–10.

Lerner, D., Reed, J.I., Massarotti, E., Wester, L.M., and Burke, T.A. (2002). The Work Limitations Questionnaire's validity and reliability among patients with osteoarthritis. *Journal of Clinical Epidemiology*, 55(2), 197–208.

Lovibond, S.H. and Lovibond, P.F. (1996). *Manual for the Depression Anxiety Stress Scales*. Psychology Foundation of Australia.

Markowitz, J.C. (2008). Evidence-based psychotherapies for depression. *Journal of Occupational and Environmental Medicine*, 50(4), 437–40.

Mausner-Dorsch, H. and Eaton, W.W. (2000). Psychosocial work environment and depression: epidemiologic assessment of the demand-control model. *American Journal of Public Health*, 90(11), 1765–70.

Miranda, J., Schoenbaum, M., Sherbourne, C., Duan, N., and Wells, K. (2004). Effects of primary care depression treatment on minority patients' clinical status and employment. *Arch Gen Psychiatry*, 61(8), 827–34.

Myette, T.L. (2008a). Integrated management of depression: improving system quality and creating effective interfaces. *Journal of Occupational and Environmental Medicine*, 50(4), 482–91.

Myette, T.L. (2008b). Research on depression in the workplace: Where do we go from here? *Journal of Occupational and Environmental Medicine*, 50(4), 492–500.

Nakao, M. and Yano, E. (2006). Prediction of major depression in Japanese adults: somatic manifestation of depression in annual health examinations. *Journal of Affective Disorders*, 90(1), 29–35.

Ormel, J., van den Brink, W., van der Meer, K., Jenner, J., and Giel, R. (1994). Prevalence, indication and course of depression in family practice. *Ned Tijdschr Geneeskd*, 138(3), 123–6.

Picard, A. (2008, June 23, 2008). The working wounded. *The Globe and Mail*, pp. 1–5. Retrieved July 22, 2009, from http://www.mentalhealthroundtable. ca/jun_2008/globeandmail.com_%20The%20working%20wounded.pdf.

Plaisier, I., de Bruijn, J.G., de Graaf, R., ten Have, M., Beekman, A.T., and Penninx, B.W. (2007). The contribution of working conditions and social support to the onset of depressive and anxiety disorders among male and female employees. *Social Sciences & Medicine*, 64(2), 401–10.

Prasad, M., Wahlqvist, P., Shikiar, R., and Shih, Y.C.T. (2004). A review of self-report instruments measuring health-related work productivity — A patient-reported outcomes perspective. *Pharmacoeconomics*, 22(4), 225–44.

Rost, K., Fortney, J., and Coyne, J. (2004). The relationship of depression treatment quality indicators to employee absenteeism. *Mental Health Services Research*, 7(3), 161–9.

Sasha-Corporation (January 2007). Compilation of turnover cost studies Retrieved July 15, 2009, from http://www.sashacorp.com/turnframe.html.

Schoenbaum, M., Unutzer, J., McCaffrey, D., Duan, N.H., Sherbourne, C., and Wells, K.B. (2002). The effects of primary care depression treatment on patients' clinical status and employment. *Health Services Research*, 37(5), 1145–58.

Shields, M. (2006). Stress and depression in the employed population. *Health Reports*, 17(4), 11–29.

Simon, G. E., Von Korff, M., and Lin, E. (2005). Clinical and functional outcomes of depression treatment in patients with and without chronic medical illness. *Psychological Medicine*, 35(2), 271–9.

Sullivan, P.F., Neale, M.C., and Kendler, K.S. (2000). Genetic epidemiology of major depression: review and meta-analysis. *American Journal of Psychiatry*, 157(10), 1552–62.

Takeuchi, T., Nakao, M., and Yano, E. (2008). Symptomatology of depressive state in the workplace. *Social Psychiatry and Psychiatric Epidemiology*, 43(5), 343–8.

Tilson, H.H. (1990). Medication monitoring in the workplace — toward improving our system of epidemiologic intelligence. *Journal of Occupational and Environmental Medicine*, 32(4), 313–9.

Ustun, T.B., Ayuso-Mateos, J.L., Chatterji, S., Mathers, C., and Murray, C.J.L. (2004). Global burden of depressive disorders in the year 2000. *British Journal of Psychiatry*, 184, 386–92.

Uvnas-Moberg, K., Bjokstrand, E., Hillegaart, V., and Ahlenius, S. (1999). Oxytocin as a possible mediator of SSRI-induced antidepressant effects. *Psychopharmacology (Berl)*, 142(1), 95–101.

Waghorn, G. and Chant, D. (2006). Work performance among Australians with depression and anxiety disorders—A population level second order analysis. *Journal of Nervous and Mental Disease*, 194(12), 898–904.

Wang, P.S., Beck, A.L., Berglund, P., McKenas, D.K., Pronk, N.P., Simon, G.E., et al. (2004). Effects of major depression on moment-in-time work performance. *American Journal of Psychiatry*, 161(10), 1885–91.

Wang, P.S., Berglund, P., and Kessler, R.C. (2000). Recent care of common mental disorders in the United States: prevalence and conformance with evidence-based recommendations. *Journal of General Internal Medicine*, 15(5), 284–92.

Wang, P.S., Simon, G., and Kessler, R.C. (2003). The economic burden of depression and the cost-effectiveness of treatment. *International Journal of Methods in Psychiatric Research*, 12(1), 22–33.

Weissman, M.M. (1979). Psychological treatment of depression—evidence for the efficacy of psychotherapy alone, in comparison with, and in combination with pharmacotherapy. *Archives of General Psychiatry*, 36(11), 1261–9.

Wieclaw, J., Agerbo, E., Mortensen, P.B., Burr, H., Tuchsen, F., and Bonde, J.P. (2006). Work related violence and threats and the risk of depression and stress disorders. *Journal of Epidemiology and Community Health*, 60(9), 771–5.

Young, A.S., Klap, R., Sherbourne, C.D. and Wells, K.B. (2001). The quality of care for depression and anxiety disorders in the United States. *Archives of General Psychiatry*, 58, 55–61.

Zhang, M., Rhost, K.M., Fortney, J.C. and Smith, G.R. (1999). A community study of depression treatment and employment earnings. *Psychiatric Services*, 50, 1209–13.

Chapter 5
Anxiety in the Workplace

Our anxiety does not empty tomorrow of its sorrow, but only empties today of its strength.

Charles Spurgeon

Introduction

Anxiety falls along a spectrum ranging from mild forms of worry, tension, and apprehension to constant and debilitating fear and nervousness. Everyone has experienced anxiety at some point throughout his or her life. Concerns over the quality of one's work, one's appearance, the ability to meet deadlines, or aptitude for a new vocation are common experiences. Mild anxiety can convey an adaptive advantage by motivating people to prepare for an anticipated event. For example, nervousness over a company presentation may prompt an employee to spend additional time preparing and rehearsing. However, unchecked anxiety can quickly turn maladaptive. Anxiety is maladaptive when nervous worry becomes so overwhelming, constant, and difficult to control that it interferes with one's life in a negative manner. For example, anxiety over an upcoming presentation may cause muscle aches and heart palpitations, and result in the avoidance of work. Pathologically high anxiety is characterized by excessive fear and avoidance behavior that is typically elicited in response to a specific object or situation in the absence of true threat.

All workplaces have aspects that can provoke feelings of anxiety. The workplace is a hierarchically organized structure in the shape of a pyramid. Atop this pyramid sits owners, CEO's, and executives that have power over lower level subordinates. The subsequent levels represent consecutive degrees of subordination, each having less power and decision latitude. Individuals at the top of this hierarchy can exert pressure by instituting new policies, placing demands on workers, or applying sanctions for misbehaviors. Within each level there are also occupational features that can result in anxiety. For example, occupational demands can result in failure, and competition can create rivalry between co-workers. In addition, influences external to the hierarchy also bear an influence. For example, the risk of workplace accidents or customer abuse/ violence can cause employees to become hyper vigilant.

When aggregated, the anxiety disorders are the most prevalent mental illness with 12-month and lifetime prevalence rates of 18.1 percent and 28.8 percent, respectively (Kessler, Berglund, Demler, et al., 2005; Kessler, Chiu, Demler et al., 2005). Cognitive biases, behavioral avoidance, and somatic sensations are characteristic features of anxiety disorders. Individuals suffering from anxiety disorders show automatic and effortful attentional biases towards threat-relevant stimuli (Bar-Haim, Lamy, Pergamin, et al., 2007) The cognitive experience of anxiety is often accompanied by prominent somatic sensations resulting in disproportionately high medical utilization among this population (Barsky, Delamater, and Orav, 1999; Deacon, Lickel, and Abramowitz, 2008; Marciniak, Lage, Landbloom, et al., 2004). Common somatic symptoms associated with anxiety include: elevated heart rate, skipped heartbeats, rapid breathing, sweating, trembling, dizziness, dry mouth, problems swallowing, or an overactive bladder or bowel. The behavioral symptoms of anxiety can mimic many medical conditions and are often so concrete and physical that individuals will visit the hospital emergency room complaining of severe pain (Olfson and Gameroff, 2007). For example, the physical symptoms of panic disorder may mimic a heart attack, and are often misdiagnosed as such.

Anxiety disorder is a diagnostic classification referring to a series of mental disorders that involve abnormal and pathological fear, anxiety, and somatic manifestations of psychological angst. According to the *Diagnostic and Statistical Manual of Mental Disorders* (DSM-IV-TR, refer to Chapter 2; (American Psychiatric Association, 2000)), the anxiety disorder category includes: generalized anxiety disorder (GAD), panic disorder, agoraphobia, specific phobia, social phobia, obsessive compulsive disorder, post-traumatic stress disorder (PTSD), and acute stress disorder. The central feature common among these disorders is the presence of anxiety—an affective state characterized by feelings of threat about the occurrence of a future event (Barlow, 2002). The anxiety experienced by individuals who meet criteria for an anxiety disorder differs from the everyday experience of anxiety, worry, or apprehension in both duration and intensity. Pathological anxiety is more intense, occurs more frequently, spans longer durations, and is more difficult to control than is everyday worry (Dupuy, Beaudoin, Rheaume, et al., 2001).

Etiology of Anxiety Disorders

Recent research has greatly improved and elucidated our understanding of anxiety disorders. It is general consensus that anxiety disorders are complex disorders that are best understood with an integrative understanding of biological, psychological, and social processes.

BIOLOGY

Epidemiological studies of families and twins have shown that virtually every anxiety disorder evidences a moderate level of concordance within the family. A comprehensive meta-analysis and systematic review of the genetic epidemiology of anxiety disorders concluded that individuals with a first degree relative with an anxiety disorder are four- to six-fold more likely to develop an anxiety disorder themselves (Hettema, Neale, and Kendler, 2001). The estimated heritability fluctuates slightly by the specific anxiety disorder but ranges from a low of 32 percent for GAD to a high of 43 percent for panic disorder. Further, non-shared-environmental factors that are specific to the individual are reportedly stronger determinants of the development of anxiety disorders than are non-shared-environmental factors (Hettemma, Neale and Kendler, 2001; Tambs, Czajkowsky, Roysamb, et al., 2009). These findings suggest that anxiety is a neurodevelopmental disorder with genetic vulnerabilities. The same genetic underpinnings appear to be consistent across all anxiety disorders (Gregory and Eley, 2007), meaning that the mechanism of transmission may not be specific to anxiety disorders but rather may be a more general risk factor towards psychopathology and distress. Indeed, the genetic risk towards anxiety disorders appear to be non-specific and may be passed on through personality or temperamental style (Hettema, Prescott, and Kendler, 2004; Scherrer, True, Xian, et al., 2000).

Studies on the neurobiology of anxiety disorders are limited. At present, there is no integrated neurobiological theory of the development of anxiety disorders. Theory and research does, however, implicate brain regions and neurotransmitters. Symptoms of mood disorders are thought to result from disruption in the emotional centers of the brain. Anxiety disorders share hyper-reactivity in the limbic region of the brain, particularly the amygdala, and an inability of higher cortical executive areas to normalize this limbic response (Martin, Ressler, Binder, et al., 2010; Schienle, Hettema, Cáceda et al., 2011). Dysfunction of several neurotransmitter systems also appear to be involved in the neurobiology of anxiety. For example, gamma-aminobutyric acid (GABA) is one of the primary inhibitory neurotransmitters of the brain and central nervous system that aids the inhibition of subcortical areas that are stimulated by threat (Thayer and Lane, 2000). Individuals with anxiety disorders are believed to have decreased GABA activity and an inability to inhibit thought (Friedman, 2007). Other neurotransmitters that may play a role in the development of anxiety disorders include norepinephrine, serotonin, and cortisol. Norepinephrine is the primary neurotransmitter of the sympathetic nervous system that is responsible for arousal during times of stress and may be chronically elevated in anxious individuals. Serotonin and cortisol are also involved in sympathetic arousal and bodily responses to stress. While evidence is at times inconclusive, there is support for the role of GABA, norepinephrine, serotonin, and cortisol in the etiology of anxiety disorders. Norepinephrine does appear to be elevated in anxiety disorders (Ballenger, 2001), and venlafaxine, a serotonin-norepinephrine reuptake inhibitor, is an effective pharmacological treatment for anxiety disorders (Katz, Reynolds, Alexopoulos et al. 2002). Further, though research is not consistent, some evidence suggests an overproduction of cortisol in anxiety disorders (Tiller, Biddle, Maguire et al., 1988; Vreeburg, Zitman, van Pelt, et al., 2010), implicating increased autonomic arousal and function of hypothalamic-pituitary-adrenal corticoid axis (HPA-axis).

COGNITIVE AND BEHAVIORAL

Biases in information processing may represent a vulnerability factor predisposing an individual to the development of an anxiety disorder (Rapee and Spence, 2004). It is generally believed that anxious individuals are hypervigilant towards threatening stimuli, interpret ambiguous information in a threatening manner, preferentially encode threatening information, and exhibit faster access to the retrieval of such information. In fact, the pinnacle feature of cognitive behavior therapy for anxiety disorders involves modulating these biases in cognition.

Numerous studies have demonstrated that anxious individuals exhibit biased cognitive processing and focus on information that is relevant to their fears. A meta-analytic review of 172 studies reported that anxious individuals preferentially attend to threat-related information, and this effect is comparable across the anxiety disorders with a medium Cohen's d effect of 0.45 (Bar-Haim, Lamy, Pergamin, et al., 2007). This threat-related attention bias has been reliably demonstrated with different experimental paradigms and under a range of experimental conditions. For example, research using the stroop task has determined that anxious individuals have slower reaction times while naming the colors of threat-related words, suggesting that they attend to, and have difficulty ignoring the meaning of threatening words

(Becker, Rinck, Margraf et al., 2001; Bradley, Mogg, Millar et al., 1995; Mogg and Bradley, 2005). Similarly, anxious participants have a better recollection for sentences that have been associated with a threatening context rather than a neutral context (Eysenck, Mogg, May et al., 1991).

The cognitive avoidance theory of worry (Borkovec, Alcaine, and Behar, 2004) posits that anxiety represents a cognitive avoidant-coping strategy whereby anxious individuals try to distract themselves from the full experience of the threat. According to this model, worry functions as a cognitive avoidance strategy that distances oneself from that threat and gives the illusion of control. A short-term reduction of emotional reactivity negatively reinforces worry. Nonetheless, substantial evidence indicates that worry evokes and sustains threat in the long term (Mennin, Heimberg, Turk, et al., 2005). Self-reports of college students with generalized anxiety disorder (GAD) suggest that they use worry to distract themselves from emotional topics that are difficult to deal with (Borkovec and Roemer, 1995). Further, people with GAD report higher levels of experiential avoidance (Roemer, Salters, Raffa, et al., 2005). Wells (1999) proposed a metacognitive model of GAD, suggesting that anxious individuals hold positive beliefs about worry (for example, worrying will help me cope with my problem) causing them to actively select worry to cope. When the individual is unable to terminate his or her worry they activate what Wells calls type 2 worry—worry about the cognitive processes involved in worry (also known as worry about worry). Worrying about worry perpetuates a negative cycle that results in an increased sense of apprehension and anxiety (Wells, 1999). The contract avoidance model (Newman and Llera, 2011) adds to the cognitive avoidance theory and the metacognitive model by postulating that anxious individuals engage in chronic worry in order to experience a sustained state of distress as a way of being prepared for the worst possible outcome.

SOCIAL

Learning and modeling may represent one potential pathway to the development of anxiety disorders. Fears may be learned through direct experience with aversive events (Murthy, 2007), or through verbal transmission (Field and Lawson, 2003). Similarly, overprotective, overcontrolling, and negative or over-critical parenting styles have been associated with the development of anxiety in childhood (Rapee, 1997). Yet, anxious children have been found to elicit different parental responses than do non-anxious children, raising the question as to the direction of effect between parenting style and anxiety disorders. Hudson and colleagues (2009) had mothers of children with anxiety disorders and mothers of normal controls interact with children who did and did not have an anxiety disorder (neither of which was their own child). Mothers were found to give more help to anxious children irrespective of the clinical status of their own child, indicating that anxious children elicit behavioral practices from parents that support their fears (Hudson, Doyle, and Gar, 2009). Thus, parenting may play a role in the development of anxiety disorders though this role may be bi-directional in nature.

Prevalence and Course of Anxiety Disorders

As a group, anxiety disorders are one of the most common classes of mental disorders. Andlin-Soboki and Wittchen (2005) amalgamated data from the German National Health Interview and Examination study—Mental Health Supplement (GHS-MHS), along with prevalence estimates from studies conducted in European countries, Iceland, Norway, and Switzerland and reported that the 12-month prevalence of any anxiety disorder was 12 percent (16.3 percent among women and 7.8 percent among men) (Andlin-Sobocki and Wittchen, 2005; Wittchen and Jacobi, 2005). This estimate is similar to the prevalence rates observed in Canada but slightly lower than US and Australian estimates. According to data from the 2002 Canadian Community Health Survey on Mental Health and Well-Being, the 12-month prevalence estimate for anxiety disorders was 12.2 percent. Estimates from the US National Comorbidity Survey Replication placed the 12-month and lifetime estimate of any anxiety disorder among the US population at 18.1 percent and 28.8 percent, respectively (Kessler, Berglund, Demler, et al., 2005; Kessler, Chiu, Demler, et al., 2005). Similarly, 12-month and lifetime prevalence estimates of anxiety disorders in Australia obtained using the 2007 National Survey of Mental Health and Well-being were found to be 11.8 percent and 20.0 percent, respectively (McEvoy, Grove, and Slade, 2011). While international prevalence estimates vary somewhat, it is reasonably clear that women outnumber men in any class of anxiety disorder by a ratio of approximately 2:1.

Anxiety disorders typically emerge earlier than do other mental disorders, with a modal age of onset in late adolescence or early adulthood. After a thorough review of the literature Kessler and colleagues (Kessler, Amminger, Aguilar-Gaxiola, et al., 2007) reported that the median age of onset for phobias and separation anxiety disorder were 7–14 years. The other anxiety disorders have greater variability in their age of onset but tend to emerge between age 4 and 20. While emerging relatively early in life, clinical reports suggest that patients endure symptoms for 5 to 10 years before being effectively diagnosed and treated, and that fewer than 20 percent of sufferers experience complete remission of their symptoms (Ballenger, Davidson, Lecrubier, et al., 2001; Kessler, Keller, and Wittchen, 2001; Rogers, Warshaw, Goisman, et al., 1999). Without treatment, anxiety disorders are chronic, recurrent, and decline only modestly with age (Kessler, Ruscio, Shear, et al., 2010).

Burden of Anxiety Disorders

Until the mid-1980s anxiety disorders were thought to be relatively benign with little impact on the sufferer. It is now recognized that anxiety disorders are chronic and debilitating disorders that are associated with human-related quality of life impairment that is comparable to that of depression (Kessler, DuPont, Berglund et al., 1999; Kessler, Greenberg, Mickelson, et al., 2001; Kessler and Wittchen, 2002), and major medical illnesses (Roy-Byrne, Davidson, Kessler, et al., 2008; Rubin, Rapaport, Levine, et al., 2000). Aside from personal suffering, anxiety disorders are characterized by significant economic burden.

Secondary analyses indicate that anxiety disorders result in substantial economic burden (DuPont, Rice, Miller, et al., 1996; Greenberg, Sisitsky, Kessler, et al., 1999; Rice and Miller, 1998). Greenberg and colleagues (1999) supplemented data from adults between 15 and 54 years of age who completed the US National Comorbidity Survey with data from a health maintenance organization, national statistics, professional meetings, and written communication from industry to calculate the annual economic burden of anxiety disorders. The annual cost of anxiety disorders on the US economy was estimated at $46.6 billion USD (31.5 percent of the total economic costs of mental disorders). The largest component of this cost was non-psychiatric medical treatment at $23 billion USD (53 percent of the total cost). Psychiatric treatment was the second largest component costing $13.3 billion USD (31 percent of the total cost). Indirect workplace costs were the third largest cost at $4.1 billion USD (10 percent of the total cost). Interestingly, 88 percent of the workplace-associated costs of anxiety disorders were attributable to presenteeism at work, suggesting that anxiety disorders are characterized by the working wounded and bear hidden costs to employers. Finally, mortality costs and pharmaceutical costs were the smallest components at $1.2 and $0.8 billion USD, respectively. Importantly, these costs were adjusted for the presence of other psychiatric disorders and sociodemographic characteristics. This study clearly demonstrated that anxiety disorders are associated with substantial economic burden.

Another method for determining the costs associated with anxiety disorders has been to calculate the per-patient cost and to express this figure in terms of purchase power parity (PPP). For example, Smit and colleagues (2006) calculated the individual (per patient) and population (per million) cost of anxiety disorders using data from 5,504 adults between the ages of 18 and 65 who participated in the Netherlands Mental Health Survey and Incidence Survey (NEMISIS). The costs of healthcare service utilization, out-of-pocket expenses, and production losses were calculated using 2003 currency. The annual per-patient cost of anxiety was €3,587 PPP. This cost translated into a population level estimate of $67.3 million USD PPP per one million inhabitants (Smit, Cuijpers, Oostenbrink, et al., 2006). Andlin-Soboki et al. (2005) calculated the costs of disorders of the brain in European countries using the Organization for Economic Co-operation and Development, and Eurostats databases. The authors determined that the cost of anxiety disorders in Europe in 2004 was €41 billion (Andlin-Sobocki, Jonsson, Wittchen, et al., 2005). This figure works out to be €800 per case, per annum. Importantly, this figure is limited because it does not include direct non-medical costs. Further, the indirect costs only comprised lost work days due to sick leave and do not include the more burdensome loss of productivity that arises due to presenteeism.

A thorough coverage of each anxiety disorder is beyond the scope of this chapter. Instead, this chapter will focus on one of the most common anxiety disorders with the greatest empirical research—generalized anxiety disorder.

Generalized Anxiety Disorder (GAD)

GAD is a chronic and impairing disorder characterized by an excessive degree of worry (apprehensive expectation) pertaining to a wide variety of topics in the absence of genuine danger. According to the DSM-IV-TR (APA, 2000), GAD is characterized by excessive worry that occurs on more days than not, about a number of events and activities. The worries must persist for a minimum of 6 months and can involve a wide variety of topics, such as health, safety, job security, and financial matters (Criteria A). Further, this worry is difficult to control (Criteria B). The worries that are typically observed in patients with GAD do not differ in content from those reported by nonclinical samples (Abel and Borkovec, 1995). However, the frequency and intensity of the worry, along with the perceived inability to control the worry, are the two features that appear to discriminate the worries found in GAD from normal worries (Craske, Rapee, Jackel, et al., 1989). In support of this distinction, Dupuy and colleagues (2001) used a daily-diary study to examine worry behavior among nonclinical controls and GAD patients over a two-week period and found that GAD patients had an increased tendency to worry and reported more time spent worrying on a daily basis.

In addition to the cognitive component of GAD (excessive and uncontrollable worry), the diagnosis of GAD requires that the individual experience three (or more) symptoms indicative of physiological or psychological arousal that accompany anxiety. These symptoms can include: 1) restlessness or feeling keyed up or on edge, 2) being easily fatigued, 3) difficulty concentrating or mind going blank, 4) irritability, 5) muscle tension, or 6) sleep disturbance. Feeling restless, keyed up, or on edge is unique to GAD while the remaining symptoms are not. Nonetheless, individuals with anxiety disorders often present with somatic complaints that can reliably discriminate between clinical and nonclinical samples (Brown, Marten, and Barlow, 1995; Kubarych, Aggen, Hettema, et al., 2005; Turvey, Stevens, and Merikangas, 1999).

The second major diagnostic system for mental disorders is the *International Classification of Diseases-10* (WHO, 1992; refer to Chapter 2). The diagnostic features of GAD listed in the ICD-10 also contain cognitive elements of worry and associated somatic complaints. According to the ICD-10, GAD is accompanied by prominent tension, worry, and feelings of apprehension about everyday events that spans six months and is accompanied by four somatic symptoms. The somatic symptoms include a list of 22 symptoms broken down into categories that include: autonomic arousal, chest and abdomen symptoms, symptoms concerning brain and mind, symptoms of tension, general symptoms, and nonspecific symptoms. This long list of potential symptoms broadens the inclusion criteria, influences empirical research, and changes estimates of prevalence and costs. Of further concern, the ICD-10 does not require that the worry be "excessive", further broadening the diagnostic category.

The diagnostic criteria of GAD have changed markedly over the past three decades. GAD began as a residual diagnostic category for individuals who had excessive worry but did not meet the criteria for another anxiety disorder. It was not until the publication of DSM-III-R (APA, 1987) that GAD became a reliable and discrete entity. This was accomplished by placing anxious worry as the core symptom, requiring a longer duration of symptom presence (six months as opposed to one month), and changing the associated psychic and somatic GAD symptoms. Importantly, DSM-III-R retained a long list of associated psychic and somatic symptoms that was confined to a few "hypervigilance" items in DSM-IV (Kessler, Ruscio, Shear, et al., 2010). Epidemiological studies have investigated the impact that making the definition of GAD more or less conservative had on prevalence estimates. Kessler and colleagues (Kessler, Chiu, Demler, et al., 2005) examined data from the US National Comorbidity Survey Replication and determined that lifetime, 12-month, and one-month prevalence estimates are lower when the duration criteria used is six months as opposed to one month, 6.1 percent vs 12.7 percent, 2.9 percent vs 5.5 percent, and 1.8 percent vs 2.6 percent, respectively. The available evidence appears to favor broadening the diagnostic categories for GAD. Shorter episodes of GAD (one to five months) have been found to be nearly as impairing as longer episodes and similar in other characteristics such as course of illness (Ruscio, Chiu, Roy-Byrne, et al., 2007). Indeed proposed revisions to the DSM-V called for shortening the duration of symptoms to three months, removing the difficulty to control worry specification, and reducing the associated symptoms to two or more symptoms from a reduced list. Of note, these proposed revisions were not incorporated into the DSM-V which remains largely unchanged from DSM-IV.

PREVALENCE OF GAD

Prevalence rates of GAD vary somewhat based upon population examined and diagnostic criteria used, however estimates generally fall within the range of 1–3 percent for 12-month estimates and 5–6 percent for lifetime estimates. The largest community epidemiological studies on GAD are the US National Comorbidity Survey (Kessler, McGonagle, Zhao, et al., 1994) and the German National Health Interview and examination study (Jacobi, Wittchen, Holting, et al., 2002) which have a combined sample of more than 64,000 patients. The 12-month and lifetime prevalence of DSM-III based GAD in the NCS was 3.1 percent and 5.1 percent respectively. These were similar to the 3.1 percent 12-month and 5.7 percent lifetime prevalence estimates of GAD reported in the NCS-replication study (Kessler and Wang, 2008). The 12-month DSM-IV based prevalence rate of GAD found using data from the GHS-MHS along with data available from studies conducted in EU countries, Iceland, Norway, and Switzerland was slightly lower at 1.5 percent (Andlin-Sobocki and Wittchen, 2005). Similar studies performed in Europe place the lifetime prevalence rate of GAD at 5 percent (Lieb, Becker, and Altamura, 2005).

ECONOMIC BURDEN OF GAD IN THE WORKPLACE: DEVELOPMENT OF AN ROI EQUATION

The following section is meant to give an accurate reflection of true costs associated with workplace anxiety. As has been discussed previously, anxiety is a prevalent and debilitating condition worldwide. As a condition once believed to be benign in nature, current findings are indicating that the economic burden of anxiety is real and severe, paralleling that of depression.

Many researchers from around the globe have taken great care and consideration into determining the monetary burden of anxiety disorders. This research has focused on direct and indirect costs. In terms of direct costs, individuals with anxiety disorders have been found to utilize the healthcare system more frequently than any other group of individuals. In terms of indirect costs, anxiety disorders have been found to cost employers and the public economy through unemployment, absenteeism, and presenteeism. Appendix B outlines an ROI equation for GAD along with instructions on how to calculate the ROI that one could anticipate for treating workplace GAD.

Impact of Pure-GAD—Costs of Unemployment

Estimates of the costs of unemployment associated with GAD are perhaps better than any other anxiety disorder but are still less well examined than those of depression. In a US nationally representative survey of primary care physicians (n = 558) and their patients (n = 17,739), pure GAD was associated with a 10.7 percent unemployment rate (Wittchen, Kessler, Beesdo, et al., 2002). Stated alternatively, individuals with pure-GAD were 1.6-fold (95 percent *CI* = 1.6–2.1) less likely to be employed than there non-psychiatric counterparts. A second study surveyed 1,007 consecutive patients with scheduled appointments at a US urban general medical practice (Olfson, Shea, Feder, et al., 2000). The practice was affiliated with a public hospital that served predominantly low-income and uninsured patients. Controlling for sociodemographic factors and psychiatric comorbidity, DSM-IV criterion based pure-GAD was associated with a 2.2-fold increased risk of work loss in the previous month. In a similar study conducted in Belgium and Luxemburg, 380 general practitioners participated in the General Anxiety Disorder Impact Survey-II (GADIS-II) and interviewed 13,699 patients (Ansseau, Fischler, Dierick, et al., 2008). According to this survey, 9.2 percent of patients with pure-GAD were unemployed.

Impact of GAD—Cost of Absenteeism

Absenteeism is work loss represented as either hours or days missed from work due to extenuating circumstances. Figures representing absenteeism are usually gathered by way of self-report and substantiated using employment records. This method for obtaining absenteeism data is not immune to error but has proven to be both accurate and reliable. Studies have shown that self-report of work absenteeism show a high degree of convergence with employer and medical records on the issue.

Employees who suffer from GAD often work reduced hours or miss days as a result of anxious worry. Research indicates that GAD is associated with significant absenteeism. The WHO conducted an international multi-center study on Psychological Problems in General Health Care (PPGHC). Data analysis using a subset of approximately 2,000 individuals from this study attending five centers in Europe revealed that individuals with pure-GAD lost a mean number of 4.6 work days to disability in the past month (Weiller, Bisserbe, Maier, et al., 1998). This estimate was slightly higher than an estimate obtained using a nationally representative sample of 4,181 working-age individuals living in Germany. German individuals with a DSM-IV based diagnosis of pure-GAD experienced 2.9 days in which they were absent due to their disorder in the previous month which was significantly higher than the 0.3 days reported by non-psychiatric controls (Wittchen, Carter, Pfister, et al., 2000). These estimates were somewhat lower than those obtained from the US.

Midlife Development in the United States (MIDUS) was a population-based longitudinal study of health and well-being in the United States. Wave 1 was conducted in 1995/1996 on more than 3,000 participants who were followed up during Wave 2 which occurred between 2002 and 2006. The MIDUS database contains excellent information on psychopathology and work. According to data from Wave 1, US adults who suffer from an anxiety disorder reported experiencing an average of 5.5 work days each month where they were unable to work or had to cut back their work due to their illness (Kessler, Greenberg, Mickelson, et al., 2001). In another study of 965 randomly sampled patients attending US primary care clinics, patients with GAD reported an average of 18.1 days in which they could not work due to disability in the past three months compared to 5.7 disability days reported by non-psychiatric control patients (Kroenke, Spitzer, Williams, et al., 2007).

Estimates of disability days were somewhat lower in a population-based study conducted in the Netherlands. The 1996 Netherlands Mental Health Survey and Incidence Study (NEMISIS) was a population-based study that surveyed 7,147 adults between the ages of 18 and 64. Results from this survey indicated that individuals with pure-GAD reported a higher average number of days with limitations due to their condition. According to these criteria, individuals with pure-GAD reported experiencing an average of 11.8 disability days in the past 12 months which was higher than the 1.1 days reported by individuals without a psychiatric diagnosis (Bijl and Ravelli, 2000). This effect was significant after potential confounds were adjusted.

Finally, Australians with GAD have been found to experience similar rates of disability days as North Americans and Europeans. Hunt et al. (2004) used data from the 1997 National Survey of Mental Health and Well-Being conducted by the Australian Bureau of Statistics to compare the impact of GAD on the workforce. The survey sampled a nationally representative population of 10,641 individuals, 100 of whom met DSM-IV based criteria for pure-GAD. Results indicated that pure-GAD was a significantly impairing disorder independent of depression (Hunt, Slade, and Andrews, 2004). Individuals with pure-GAD experienced more disability-related absenteeism days in the previous month than individuals without mental illnesses (6.2 vs 2.5).

Impact of GAD—Presenteeism

Not everyone who suffers from an illness takes time away from work to recover. Some individuals work throughout the duration of their illness. Presenteeism is a measure used to assess the hidden costs associated with working while suffering from an illness. Employees who work while ill have a reduced production capacity and a limited ability to produce work that is of the highest quality. As such, presenteeism costs employers in terms of reduced productivity as well as below-normal work quality. The presenteeism-related costs attributable to anxiety disorders have been estimated as the greatest workplace related costs of anxiety disorders. An estimated 88 percent of the workplace costs attributable to anxiety disorders are a result of presenteeism (Greenberg, Sisitsky, Kessler, et al., 1999).

There are several methods for measuring presenteeism. At the most basic level, one could ask employees to self-report on how much work that they feel they accomplish from week to week. As it turns out, individuals with anxiety disorders report accomplishing less work than do non-psychiatric controls. Data obtained from the Australian nationally representative 1998 Survey of Disability, Ageing, and Careers indicated that a greater portion of working-age adults with an anxiety disorder (30 percent) reported that they accomplished less work than usual in the preceding four weeks than did their non-psychiatric counterparts (0.45 percent) (Waghorn, Chant, White, et al., 2005). Further, more employed adults with anxiety disorders reported taking less care on their work over the past four weeks (18.9 percent) than controls (0.4 percent). While this study indicates that anxiety disorders are associated with substantial presenteeism it does not provide a monetary estimate of this cost.

One of the few studies to administer validated measures of work productivity (for example, Endicott work productivity scale, work productivity and activity impairment questionnaire, work limitations questionnaire) found that work performance is impaired among individuals with anxiety disorders and that the degree of work impairment corresponds to the severity of anxiety (Erickson, Guthrie, Vanetten-Lee, et al., 2009). Erickson et al. (2009) assessed 81 patients who sought treatment in a university-based anxiety clinic at baseline and following 12 weeks of treatment. At baseline, individuals with mild anxiety reported 24 percent impairment while at work while individuals with severe anxiety reported 45 percent work impairment due to health. Conclusions based upon this study are limited due to the use of a treatment-seeking sample, the absence of a control condition, and the inclusion of a wide variety of anxiety disorders characterized by a small sample of patients who are motivated to seek help. Another study using data from the previously described GHS-MHS concluded that 34 percent of patients with pure-GAD reported a reduction in work productivity of 10 percent or greater (Wittchen, Carter, Pfister, et al., 2000). Similarly, Kennedy et al. examined impairments in work productivity in a sample of 65 individuals with pure-GAD using the Sheehan Disability Scale (Kennedy, Lin, and Schwab, 2002). Scores on the Sheehan Disability Scale range between 0 and 10 with higher scores reflecting greater impairment. Patients with pure-GAD rated their degree of work impairment higher ($M = 3.97$) than did non-psychiatric controls ($M = 0.86$). While there is clear evidence for the adverse influence of anxiety disorders on work productivity, additional research is needed to determine better estimates of the contribution of each anxiety disorder to presenteeism.

Given that few studies have quantified presenteeism attributable to GAD, it is worth mentioning one exceptional study that quantified the cost of presenteeism attributable to any anxiety disorder. Loepkke et al. (2007; 2009) examined the financial impact of 25 chronic physical and mental health problems by polling 49,576 employees at 10 companies (Loeppke, Taitel, Haufle, et al., 2009; Loeppke, Taitel, Richling, et al., 2007). Anxiety disorders were found to be the fifth most costly condition when medical, pharmaceutical, absenteeism, and presenteeism costs were aggregated. Importantly, anxiety disorders had a significant effect on presenteeism and resulted in an additional 10.5 presenteeism days per year when compared to employees without a mental or physical illness. This estimate of presenteeism was adjusted for gender, age, and occupation. It seems reasonable to presume that GAD would account for similar presenteeism given that it is the anxiety disorder believed to result in the highest estimated of presenteeism.

Impact of GAD—Medical Care Costs

Anxiety disorders cost the healthcare system in terms of direct treatment costs, as well as costs related to increased medical service use. The symptoms of anxiety are often somatic in nature, resulting in healthcare seeking behavior among individuals with anxiety disorders. In fact, individuals with anxiety disorders represent the group of individuals with the greatest healthcare visits per year. Those with anxiety disorders use more outpatient and inpatient services, have greater length of hospital stays, and visit the emergency room more frequently than age, sex, and metropolitan matched controls (Jones, Ames, Jeffries, et al., 2001; Kennedy and Schwab, 1997; M. Marciniak, Lage, Landbloom, et al., 2004).

Individuals with anxiety disorders have high medical care utilization. Deacon et al. examined medical care utilization among 171 patients with anxiety disorders visiting an outpatient anxiety clinic (Deacon, Lickel and Abramowitz, 2008). Patients with anxiety disorders, and GAD in particular, accrued 6.2 outpatient visits in the preceding 12 months. Importantly, this estimate failed to include inpatient or surgical treatments, mental health visits, or medical prescriptions and does not accurately reflect the true usage. This data is further limited by the absence of a comparison or control sample. Yet, previous studies that have used a comparison sample have arrived at similar conclusions. Marciniak et al. (2004) found that the outpatient medical utilization rates among patients with anxiety disorder were approximately 50 percent higher than a sample of age, sex, and geographic region matched outpatients. A German nationally representative sample of 558 doctors and more than 20,000 patients indicated that patients with pure-GAD utilized twice as many primary care services as controls (Wittchen, Krause, Hoyer, et al., 2001). Porensky et al. found that elderly patients with pure-GAD utilized healthcare services approximately twice as often ($M = 6.7$) as non-psychiatric controls ($M = 3.3$) in a six month period (Porensky, Dew, Karp, et al., 2009). Similarly, Barsky et al. found that a sample of patients with panic disorder reported more physician visits in the previous 12 months ($M = 10.4$) than did comparison patients attending the same clinic who did not have an anxiety disorder ($M = 4.4$) (Barsky, Delamater, and Orav, 1999). Thus, individuals with anxiety disorder exhibit higher healthcare utilization than do the general population and other patients with various health concerns. Further, these healthcare utilization behaviors appear to persist across the lifespan.

A large portion of patients diagnosed with anxiety disorders are treated pharmacologically. For example, a nationally representative nested case-control design in UK primary care reported that 63 percent of nearly 50,000 patients newly diagnosed with anxiety disorders were treated pharmacologically (Martín-Merino, Ruigómez, Wallander, et al., 2010). Similarly, a retrospective examination of nearly 600,000 US citizens with anxiety disorders or major depression enlisted in a PharMetrics claims database reported that approximately 30 percent and 50 percent of patients with anxiety disorders were prescribed anxiolytics or antidepressants by one-year follow-up, respectively (François, Despiégel, Maman, et al., 2010). Francois et al. reported that the annual pharmacy cost for pure anxiety disorders was $837 USD. This estimate was similar to the $1,100 USD anxiety-related outpatient drug cost previously reported (M. Marciniak, Lage, Landbloom, et al., 2004). A slightly smaller annual pharmacy cost of $420 USD for GAD was reported in a study employing similar methods, assessing a large US health insurance database (Berger, Edelsberg, Bollu, et al., 2011). While anxiety disorders appear to be associated with significant pharmaceutical associated expenditures, it is difficult to take these estimates and extrapolate to other countries and employers given the differences in healthcare coverage and reimbursement systems. It is, however, unlikely that the employer would incur 100 percent of the cost of prescription medications for any medical or psychiatric condition, including that incurred for anxiety disorders. For example, 44.5 percent of the total $32 billion in prescription drug spending in Canada in 2012 was funded by the public sector (for example, the government) with 55.5 percent being funded by the private sector (CIHI, 2013).

Marciniak et al. developed a model to capture the medical care costs associated with treating the various anxiety disorders (M.D. Marciniak, Lage, Dunayevich, et al., 2005). To accomplish this task the authors subject data from 6,497 patients with anxiety disorders recorded in the HPM MedStat's MarketScan Database (1996 to 1999) to multivariate regressions controlling for demographic characteristics and comorbidities. Results indicated that the average individual diagnosed with GAD accrued $2,138.14 in direct medical care costs. These costs include inpatient services, outpatient services, drug costs, and direct medical care costs (for example, testing, diagnosis, and so on). Further, individuals with anxiety disorders incurred an additional cost of $503.16 for each previous medical diagnosis in the previous six months, and $1,514.71 for each previous mental health diagnosis in the preceding six months, indicating that healthcare costs increase with medical and mental health comorbidities.

Tools Used to Diagnose Anxiety Disorders

There are a number of comprehensive tools that can be used to diagnose anxiety disorders. Some of these inventories are short paper-and-pencil-based self-report questionnaires that offer a crude diagnosis while others are lengthier, in-depth interviews that have good specificity. Some of these tools require additional training, and experience. While many tools exist that can aid in the screening of anxiety disorders, there is no substitute for clinical training. Cases that are flagged with the use of a scale provided below should always be referred to a qualified professional for further evaluation.

SELF-REPORT MEASURES OF GENERAL ANXIETY

Several well-developed measures exist through which employers can obtain ratings of more general anxiety. Listed below are just a selection of the more common self-report measures used to assess anxiety. Possibly the most popular self-report anxiety inventory is the *State-Trait Anxiety Inventory-Trait Version* (STAI-T; Spielberger and Gorsuch, 1983). Apprehensiveness, tension, nervousness, and worry are the essential qualities evaluated by the STAI. The STAI-T is a brief 20-item questionnaire that measures the general tendency to experience anxiety. Scores range from 20 to 80 with higher scores reflecting greater anxious tendencies. Some questions relate to the absence of anxiety and are reversed scored. The STAI-T is an inexpensive for-purchase inventory that can be purchased for under $1 per administration. Ordering information can be located through Mind Garden at http://www.mindgarden.com/products/staisad.htm.

Another self-report measure of anxiety is the Beck Anxiety Inventory (BAI; Beck and Steer, 1993). The BAI is a 21-item questionnaire measuring anxious symptoms over the past month. Items assess somatic (for example, shortness of breath and rapid heartbeat), and cognitive (for example, fear of losing control or nervousness) features of anxiety. Adults are asked to rate how much each symptom has bothered them using a 0 to 3 scale. The items are summed to obtain a total score between 0 and 63 with higher scores reflecting greater anxiety. Scores below 21 reflect low levels of anxiety. Scores between 31 and 35 reflect moderate levels, and scores over 36 reflect severe anxiety. The BAI is a for-purchase questionnaire that is comparable in price to the STAI. Purchasing information can be obtained through Pearson Assessment at http://www.pearsonassessments.com/HAIWEB/Cultures/en-us/Productdetail.htm?Pid=015-8018-400.

The Hamilton Anxiety Rating Scale (HAM-A; Hamilton, 1959) is a publicly available self-report inventory used to measure the severity of anxiety symptoms over the past week. It is a 14-item interview-based assessment tool. The interviewer asks the interviewee about 14 anxious symptoms and then rates the responses on a 0 ("none") to 4 ("very-severe") scale. The HAM-A assesses somatic (for example, insomnia, respiratory symptoms, muscular complaints) and cognitive (for example, anxious mood, depressed mood, fears) symptoms. Scores are summed and range between 0 and 52 with higher scores reflecting greater anxiety. Scores below 13 fall within the normal range, between 14 and 17 in the mild range, between 18 and 24 in the moderate range, and over 24 in the severe range. The interested reader can access an electronic version of the HAM-A at http://www.serene.me.uk/tests/ham-a.pdf.

The Generalized Anxiety Disorder 7 (GAD 7) is a brief, 7-item self-report rating scale designed to assess GAD specifically (Spitzer, Kroenke, Williams, et al., 2006). It is a valid and reliable measure with good test-retest reliability. Scores range from 0 to 21 with scores from 0 to 4 reflecting minimal severity, 5 to 9 reflecting mild severity, 10 to 14 reflecting moderate severity, and 15 to 21 reflecting severe cases. At a cut-score of 10, sensitivity and specificity exceed 0.80 and sensitivity is nearly maximized. Finally, scores on the GAD7 are strongly associated with multiple domains of functional impairment and disability days. The GAD7 can be located at http://psychres.washington.edu/clinicaltools/gad7_ref.pdf.

THE COMPOSITE INTERNATIONAL DIAGNOSTIC INTERVIEW (CIDI)

The CIDI is a comprehensive, fully structured interview designed to assess mental disorders according to the definitions and criteria of the ICD-10 and DSM-IV. The World Health Organization first developed the CIDI in 1990, which was revised and released as version 2.1 in 1997, and again as version 3 in 2004. One of the advantages of the CIDI is its comprehension. The CIDI is a reliable and well-validated tool used to assess the presence of every major classification of mental illness. The comprehensiveness of the CIDI makes it rather lengthy and cumbersome to administer. Specialized training is required to administer the CIDI. This training must be obtained at a WHO-authorized CIDI training and reference center. The length, complexity, and training requirements of the CIDI make it a poor choice for use in the workplace.

Issues with Comorbidity

Comorbidity refers to the presence of any additional coexisting ailment within a patient. Comorbidities can alter the progression or trajectory of a condition and require different methods for effective treatment. As such, it is important to understand comorbidity among psychiatric conditions. In general, a high degree of psychiatric comorbidity exists between psychiatric conditions. Anxiety disorders are no exception to this rule. There are often high rates of co-occurrence within the anxiety disorders and between anxiety disorders and other psychiatric/medical illnesses.

One out of every two people with a lifetime diagnosis of an anxiety disorder will meet the criteria for two or more such disorders (Kessler, 1995). Perhaps worse, a substantial portion of individuals with a diagnosis of an anxiety disorder will experience a concomitant psychiatric or medical illness. Using data from the NCS-R, individuals with GAD were found to be 6.28-fold more likely to experience a comorbid mood disorder and 2.78-fold more likely to experience a substance-related disorder after controlling for age, sex, race, education, marital status, and geographic region (Kessler, Chiu, Demler, et al., 2005). Similarly, data from the European Study of the Epidemiology of Mental Disorders (ESEMeD; N = 21,425) indicated that individuals with GAD were 33.6-fold more likely to experience co-occurring major depression (Alonso, Angermeyer, Bernert, et al., 2004). To place this odds ratio into perspective, 4.6 percent of the population sampled in the ESEMeD were found to have a pure anxiety disorder while an additional 1.6 percent were found to experience concomitant mood and anxiety disorders. Further, strong empirical evidence suggests that anxiety disorders are associated with a variety of comorbid medical conditions ranging from asthma and irritable bowel syndrome to cardiovascular disease, chronic pain, and cancer (for a review see Roy-Byrne Davidson, W., Kessler, et al., 2008).

While the workplace-related costs presented previously in this chapter pertain exclusively to pure-GAD it is important to note that the workplace-associated costs of GAD increase sharply when comorbid with another disorder. Unemployment is higher when an individual suffers from GAD with comorbid major depression (17.4 percent) than among individuals who suffer from pure-GAD (10.7 percent) (Wittchen, Kessler, Beesdo, et al., 2002). Similarly, individuals with GAD and comorbid depression experience significantly more disability days in which they are away from work. Hunt et al. found that employees with GAD and comorbid major depression experienced an average of 10.9 disability days in the previous month while individuals with pure-GAD experienced 6.2 days (Hunt, Slade and Andrews, 2004).

Medical care costs are also higher among individuals with GAD and comorbid illnesses. For example, using a US PharMetrics Integrated claims database, Zhu et al. identified 36,435 patients between the ages of 18 and 64 and compared healthcare costs reimbursed between January 2003 and June 2004 among individuals with pure-GAD and those with and without comorbid depression and pain (Zhu, Zhao, Ye, et al., 2009). Results indicated that comorbid depression and pain increased healthcare costs. Compared to GAD-only patients, patients with depression, pain, and depression and pain incurred an additional $762, $2982, and $6,073 in medical costs, respectively.

Treatment

Over the past few decades several effective treatments for anxiety disorders have been developed. Some of these methods are more generic while others are targeted to specific anxiety disorders. Many institutions have provided evidence-based guidelines for managing and treating anxiety disorders. One such guideline is the National Institute for Health and Clinical Excellence (NICE) guideline (http://www.nice.org.uk/nicemedia/live/13314/52599/52599.pdf). The NICE guideline begins with person-centered care. Treatment should take into account the needs and preferences of the individual being treated. Individuals with anxiety disorders should be involved in every step of the decision-making process, along with their healthcare professionals. This means that individuals with anxiety disorders should be fully educated about the particular anxiety disorder, the treatment options, potential side effects, and continued monitoring. The NICE guideline is a stepped-care approach beginning with the least intrusive, most effective intervention first and gradually moving to more involved interventions. The number and nature of steps vary somewhat depending on the specific anxiety disorder being treated but some general guidelines can be conferred. The first step should always involve the identification and assessment for anxiety disorders. It is imperative that a proper diagnosis be made and that any comorbidities be determined. The intervention corresponding to this phase is education and active monitoring. The afflicted individual should be provided with an education and guidance booklet explaining the specific anxiety disorder, symptoms, and treatment options. This step also involves active and continued monitoring to determine whether symptoms improve.

Individuals who do not respond to Step 1 care should be considered for Step 2 care. This involves the use of low intensity psychological interventions such as individual non-facilitated self-help, individual guided self-help, or psychoeducation groups. Individual non-facilitated self-help involves systematically working through written or electronic material that is based on the principles of cognitive behavioral therapy (CBT) for six weeks. Individual, guided self-help adds the support of a trained practitioner who is responsible for facilitating the self-help program and monitoring progress. This support can be conferred in five to seven weekly face-to-face or telephone sessions lasting 20 to 30 minutes. The psychoeducational group is a more intensive, interactive design consisting of six weekly two-hour sessions that are conducted by a trained practitioner. Sessions should encourage observational learning and include the presentation of self-help manuals.

Individuals who do not improve through the use of low-intensity psychological interventions should be informed of high-intensity psychological interventions and pharmacotherapy. The individual should be offered their choice of either psychological interventions or pharmacotherapy with the knowledge that the two have been found to exhibit comparable effects across the anxiety disorders (Mitte, 2005; Mitte, Noack, Steil et al., 2005). These should only be used in combination during a final step for severe cases that are resistant to all other forms of treatment. In addition, these cases may need to be referred to specialty clinics.

PHARMACOTHERAPY

In 2005 the British Association for Psychopharmacology published evidence-based guidelines for the pharmacological treatment of anxiety disorders (Baldwin, Anderson, Nutt, et al., 2005). These are empirically based guidelines developed by a consensus meeting involving experts in the field. According to these guidelines, the first step involves a discussion of the possible benefits and risks of drug treatments with the patient before commencing treatment. This discussion needs to cover some important aspects of pharmacological care such as: responses are not immediate, transient worsening of symptoms can occur, prolonged courses are often required to maintain initial effects, and that proper adherence is essential (Nutt, 2003).

Selective Serotonin Reuptake Inhibitors (SSRIs)

Antidepressant drugs are currently the most commonly-prescribed and effective medication for anxiety disorders. The first line of pharmacological treatment for anxiety disorders is the SSRIs. SSRIs are a class of compounds with a particular affinity for serotonin receptors. These compounds increase the extracellular levels of the neurotransmitter serotonin by binding selectively to serotonin receptors. The SSRIs are effective across a range of anxiety disorders and are generally well tolerated with mild to moderate side-effects. Initial increases in nervousness, insomnia, nausea (Baldwin and Birtwistle, 1998), and sexual dysfunction (Baldwin, 2004) are the potentially problematic side-effects most typical of the SSRIs. Further, abrupt withdrawal can result in dizziness, insomnia, and flu-like symptoms (Schatzberg, Haddad, Kaplan, et al., 1997).

Adverse side-effects and overdose associated with the SSRIs are particularly prevalent when starting or increasing the dose because the body must adjust to a sharp increase in serotonin. For this reason, the United Kingdom Committee of Safety and Medicines (CSM) recommends that patients are monitored frequently and carefully when starting or increasing dosages of antidepressant medications (CSM, 2004). Recent NICE guidelines also recommend that patients with anxiety disorders be reviewed at regular intervals during the first six weeks of treatment (NICE, 2011).

Benzodiazapines

A benzodiazepine is a psychoactive drug that enhances the effectiveness of the neurotransmitter gamma-aminobutyric acid (GABA). The benzodiazepine binds to the $GABA_A$ receptor and results in an increased affinity for the GABA neurotransmitter. GABA is the primary inhibitory neurotransmitter of the central nervous system and this benzodiazepine-mediated GABA-enhanced effectiveness results in sedative, or anxyolitic feelings that calm the mind. While the benzodiazepines are effective in treating anxiety disorders, they have several drawbacks including adverse side-effects and dependence. Benzodiazepines should only be offered during short-term crises for patients with persistent, severe anxiety symptoms (Baldwin, Anderson, Nutt, et al., 2005; NICE, 2011). This class of pharmacological agent can cause troublesome sedation during short-term treatment, and dependence and memory impairments can occur with long-term use (RCP, 2005).

Psychological Interventions

COGNITIVE BEHAVIORAL THERAPY (CBT)

CBT for anxiety is based on the idea that the anxiety disorders are due to faulty, maladaptive, and unhelpful thinking patterns (Dobson and Dozois, 2001). It is a psychological intervention that focuses on identifying and changing the automatic thinking styles that are related to anxiety through a process of self-evaluation and hypothesis testing. Thought patterns of anxious individuals are future-oriented and involve ominous themes or a foreboding for the future. Anxious individuals often overestimate the probability and severity of negative consequences, and underestimate their ability for coping. One of the goals of CBT is to help the patient restructure these unrealistic negative thoughts into healthier and more evidence-based thoughts (Beck, 1985). In order to accomplish this goal the client and therapist must work together to identify problems, test hypotheses, and re-evaluate beliefs.

CBT is used to help the patient gain self-efficacy and insight into the nature of their own maladaptive problems. Treatments are specifically tailored to the needs of the individual clients and responses to treatment are continuously monitored in order to evaluate the effectiveness. A typical CBT program for anxiety disorders involves cognitive restructuring. The client typically begins by developing a thought record with the therapist. Thought records are devices used by patients to make hypotheses and evaluate objective evidence for their patterns of thought. A typical thought record will identify several important pieces of information. First, the situation where the emotion occurred is identified (for example, giving a work presentation to the board). Second, the negative feeling or emotion (for example, nervousness, anxiety, fear) is recorded along with the negative automatic thought (for example, 'My job will be terminated if I stumble on my words and everyone will laugh at me'). The client must then record the evidence that supports the negative thought, and the evidence that does not support the negative thought (for example, 'There is no objective evidence, no one has ever lost their job because of such actions'). The client then indicates an alternative thought that fits with the evidence, and the new feeling or emotion. The therapist often works with the patient to evaluate the evidence for and against the thought and encourages the patient to conduct behavioral experiments to test certain beliefs or assumptions.

Exposure Techniques

Exposure techniques involve exposing the client to the feared stimulus or situation and are often used in conjunction with CBT. Exposure is one of the main effective ingredients across all psychological interventions for anxiety disorders. Facing the anxiety-provoking stimuli with little to no adverse effects extinguishes the fear, allows for the development of new coping skills, and alters the original maladaptive cognition. Exposure therapy usually begins with systematic desensitization. The patient and the therapist generate a fear hierarchy from 0 (representing no anxiety at all) to 100 (representing the worst anxiety the patient has ever experienced). The patient begins by imagining the lowest feared stimuli paired with a relaxation response (for example, muscle relaxation or breathing exercises). Patients gradually work their way up the fear hierarchy as they master lower level feared stimuli. A more fast-tracked in-vivo approach may be preferred in which the patient begins by approaching real-life feared stimuli without paired relaxation. Research has shown that in-vivo exposure is more effective than imagined exposure and that the relaxation does not improve effectiveness (Antony and Barlow, 2002).

Exposure techniques often need to be performed with response prevention. Response prevention involves having the patient abstain from engaging in ritualistic behavior used to reduce anxiety but reinforce the maladaptive thinking pattern. Several response prevention techniques have been developed such as worry exposure for GAD (Brown, O'Leary, and Barlow, 2001). Individuals with anxiety disorders often develop ritualistic behaviors that prevent anxious thoughts. For example, an employee who is anxious about being judged negatively by management may excuse themselves and use the restroom in such situations. These actions maintain the anxious feelings by preventing successful resolution of the anxiety. Therefore, exposure and response prevention involves identifying these ritualistic behaviors and then having patients imagine these anxious situations along with the worst possible outcome and preventing their ritualistic behavior. Conversely, patients may be asked to encounter their anxious-provoking situation in-vivo without engaging in their usual response behavior.

EFFECTIVENESS OF PSYCHOLOGICAL INTERVENTIONS

In a recent systematic review, Norton and Price assessed the efficacy of CBT alone or in combination with either exposure and response prevention or relaxation therapy across the anxiety spectrum (Norton and Price, 2007). Results from 108 CBT trials indicated that CBT alone or in combination with exposure and response prevention or relaxation therapy were efficacious across the spectrum of anxiety disorders with no differential efficacy for any treatment component. Thus, the psychological interventions for anxiety disorders appear to be effective means for treating the gamete of anxiety disorders, providing that they are appropriately tailored to the anxious stimulus. A similar conclusion was reached in a meta-analysis by Richardson and Rothstein who reviewed 55 studies and determined that occupational stress management programs are effective in reducing anxiety (mean *Cohen d* = 2.39). The most efficacious intervention was CBT (Richardson and Rothstein, 2008). Many of the investigations included in these meta-analyses were performed using procedures to maximize control in randomized controlled efficacy trials. Skeptics question whether these findings will generalize to clinical practice settings, arguing that clients in practice settings have more severe anxiety and a higher number of comorbid conditions. Fortunately, this question has been subject to empirical scrutiny. A meta-analysis of 56 effectiveness trials of CBT for adult anxiety disorders in clinical practice yielded large effects similar to those obtained in selected efficacy trials (Stewart and Chambless, 2009).

While psychotherapies such as CBT have proven immensely effective in the treatment of anxiety, delivery of treatment is often delayed and rarely administered in an effective manner (Shafran, Clark, Fairburn, et al., 2009). Empirical evidence from the World Mental Health Survey Initiative indicated that individuals with anxiety disorder suffer with anxiety between 9 and 23 years before seeking treatment (Wang, Berglund, Olfson, et al., 2005). Further, when individuals with anxiety disorders do seek treatment the majority are not referred for the treatments that have proved most effective (Collins, Westra, Dozois, et al., 2004). A study using a large sample from Toronto found that less than one-third of respondents with a mood or anxiety disorder were being treated by a physician (Ohayon, Shapiro, and Kennedy, 2000). This trend persisted despite individuals from this category being among the highest consumers of medical care. A lack of adequate care for individuals with anxiety disorders is not unique to Canada. Fernandez et al. analyzed ESEMeD data and determined that less than half of patients with anxiety disorders in Belgium, France, Germany, Italy, the Netherlands, or Spain received minimally adequate treatment (Fernandez, Haro, Martinez-Alonso, et al., 2007). Only 57.4 percent of patients who attended specialized care, and 23 percent of patients who attended general medical care received minimally adequate treatment. These numbers were similar to those found in the US. Rates of minimally adequate treatment among individuals with anxiety disorders in the US were found to be 52 percent among those attending specialized care and 14.9 percent among those attending general medical care (Wang, Lane, Olfson, et al., 2005).

There are several reasons for poor dissemination, some of which include: the high cost of psychotherapy which may not be offset by government or private insurance; the stigma associated with mental illness; and a lack of adequately trained mental health professionals to deliver psychotherapy. One method for improving the dissemination of psychotherapies is to use computer- or internet-based psychotherapies. Computer-based CBT has been used for treating anxiety disorders for more than a decade with promising results. A meta-analysis comparing the effects of internet-based CBT for anxiety disorders relative to control conditions among six studies reported large effects ($d = .96$) for reducing symptoms and disability (Spek, Cuijpers, Nyklícek, et al., 2007). The effects were slightly larger when internet-delivered CBT was combined with therapist support. A more recent meta-analysis of 16 trials found large effects for CBT across the anxiety disorders that were similar to those obtained when CBT was delivered face to face (Andrews, Cuijpers, Craske, et al., 2010). Computer-delivered CBT represents a cost-effective method for disseminating empirically supported treatments to individuals with anxiety disorders who would not otherwise seek treatment and may also circumvent the barriers such as high stigma, high costs, and the poor supply of registered mental health professionals. It is important to raise awareness that there are a number of effective evidence-based treatments for anxiety disorders. Indeed, there is evidence indicating that employers would benefit from the development of company policy that guides employees to effective treatments for anxiety disorders.

The Centre for Economic Performance published a discussion paper on the cost-effectiveness of psychotherapies in Britain (Layard, Clark, Knapp, et al., 2007). The authors reported that the cost of psychotherapy to the government would be fully offset by the savings in incapacity benefits and extra taxes that would result from increasing the amount of employees in the workforce. According to data presented, 82 percent of those beginning psychotherapy would persevere with it and of those, 61 percent would recover within four months. It was concluded that the low cost of therapy (£750 in total) combined with the high rate of recovery (~50 percent) would fully offset the high cost of incapacity benefits (£750 per month).

WORK-RELATED BENEFITS OF PSYCHOLOGICAL INTERVENTIONS FOR ANXIETY DISORDERS

There is a paucity of research explicitly assessing improvement in work-related outcomes following empirically supported treatments for anxiety disorders. The few studies that have been performed present an encouraging picture.

A longitudinal study using objective measures of productivity to assess the impact of anxiety on the productivity of medical insurance claims processors determined that claims processors with an ICD-9 classification of anxiety (n = 71) recovered a substantial proportion of their pre-treatment productivity (Berndt, Finkelstein, Greenberg, et al., 1997). Similarly, Allgulander et al. compared 186 individuals with GAD who were assigned to a 12-week treatment with an antidepressant Sertraline (n = 147) or a placebo (n = 139) (Allgulander, Dahl, Austin, et al., 2004). Individuals given Sertraline experienced a 10.1 point increase on the Endicott work productivity scale which was significantly greater than the 3.9 point increase observed among individuals given the placebo. Beneficial results were also reported in a three-year longitudinal study of work ability and functional capacity following short-term and long-term psychotherapy for depression and anxiety disorders. During the three-year follow-up of the Helsinki Psychotherapy Study, psychodynamic psychotherapy and solution-focused therapy were found to improve work ability by 16 percent and psychological functioning by 21 percent (Knekt, Lindfors, Harkanen, et al., 2008). In summary, there is limited but encouraging evidence indicating that the treatment of employee anxiety disorders will benefit employers by improving a variety of work outcomes.

These results are particularly promising given that research in this area is in its infancy and has not yet evolved to consider therapeutic dose optimization, timing optimization, or potential mediators/moderators of treatment. In general, education about anxiety disorders should be provided to all employees and supervisors. Company screening for anxiety should also be performed on a regular basis. It is also expert consensus that early interventions for anxiety disorders are preferential. Early intervention is particularly important following short-term disability leave where time away from work can reinforce avoidance behaviors. Instead, the goal should be to discuss workplace accommodation and to facilitate return-to-work.

Job Accommodations

Few studies have been conducted that calculate the direct and indirect costs of workplace accommodations among individuals with psychiatric disabilities. The studies that have been carried out suggest that direct costs are low and benefits are substantial. A study of more than 500 accommodations provided by Sears, Roebuck, and Co. from 1978 to 1997 reported that the majority (72 percent) of workplace accommodations had no direct costs to the employer (Blanck, 1996). Only 1 percent of workplace accommodations cost more than

$500. Workplace accommodations among the few employees in this study that had psychiatric illnesses were found to cost the employer $0 in direct costs. Yet, individuals with psychiatric illnesses may garner higher indirect costs associated with workplace accommodations. MacDonald-Wilson et al. reported that individuals with psychiatric disabilities were more likely to require human assistance such as job coaches rather than changes to their physical environment (MacDonald-Wilson, Rogers, Massaro, et al., 2002). Many of these indirect costs come in the form of additional supervisor and co-worker time. Supervisors of employees with psychiatric disabilities were found to spend an additional 5 hours of supervisory time each month with co-workers spending an additional 11 hours.

The Job Accommodation Network (JAN) publishes an Effective Accommodations Practices (EAP) series that recommends helpful job accommodations for individuals with a variety of mental and physical disabilities. The JAN lists several helpful job accommodations that may be useful for individuals with anxiety disorders (see Table 5.1).

Concluding Remarks

Anxiety disorders are a cluster of disorders characterized by excessive worry or apprehension about future events that causes distress. When combined, the anxiety disorders are the most prevalent class of mental disorders affecting nearly 20 percent of individuals at any given time. The once believed notion that anxiety disorders are not associated with substantial suffering is being overturned with the recognition that anxiety disorders are associated with significant impairment in private, occupational, and social functioning. An economic analysis into the burden of generalized anxiety disorder, the most prevalent and researched anxiety disorder, was presented, highlighting the typical burden of an anxiety disorder that is prevalent among the workforce. The outlook is positive and individuals who suffer from anxiety disorders can be effectively treated using empirically validated treatments. Numerous pharmacological and psychological treatments have been developed for the treatment of anxiety disorders that can be widely disseminated and that have demonstrated cost-effectiveness. In addition, a number of workplace accommodation strategies have been developed to ease employee suffering and facilitate treatment and recovery.

Table 5.1 **Potential accommodations for individuals with anxiety disorders recommended by the Job Accommodation Network**

Presenting Concern: Difficulty Handling Stress and Emotions
- Provide praise and positive reinforcement
- Refer to counseling and employee assistance programs
- Allow telephone calls during work hours to doctors and others for needed support
- Provide sensitivity training to co-workers
- Allow the employee to take a break to use stress management techniques to cope with frustration

Presenting Concern: Attendance Issues
- Provide flexible leave for health problems
- Provide a self-paced work load and flexible hours
- Allow employee to work from home
- Provide part-time work schedule

Presenting Concern: Dealing with Change
- Recognize that a change in the office environment or of supervisors may be difficult for a person with an anxiety disorder
- Maintain open channels of communication between the employee and the new and old supervisor to ensure an effective transition
- Provide weekly or monthly meetings with the employee to discuss workplace issues, and production levels

Presenting Concern: Working Effectively with Supervisors
- Provide positive praise and reinforcement
- Provide written job instructions
- Develop written work agreements that include the agreed upon accommodations, clear expectations of responsibilities, and the consequences of not meeting performance standards
- Allow for open communication to managers and supervisors
- Establish written long-term and short-term goals
- Develop strategies to deal with problems before they arise
- Develop a procedure to evaluate the effectiveness of the accommodation

Presenting Concern: Interacting with Co-workers
- Educate all employees on their right to accommodations
- Provide sensitivity training to co-workers and supervisors
- Do not mandate employees to attend work-related social functions
- Encourage employees to move non-work-related conversations out of work areas

Source: Available from http://askjan.org/media/anxi.htm.

More information can be found at the following sources:

Information on anxiety disorders in the workplace at http://www.adaa. org/managing-stress-anxiety-in-workplace/anxiety-disorders-in-workplace

Information on anxiety disorders at http://www.nimh.nih.gov/health/ topics/anxiety-disorders/index.shtml

National Institute for Health and Clinical Excellence guidelines for the treatment of anxiety disorders at http://guidance.nice.org.uk/CG113

Treatment of anxiety disorders at http://www.anxietyaustralia.com.au/

Workplace accommodations for anxiety disorders at http://askjan.org/media/anxi.htm or http://www.mentalhealthworks.ca/employees/faqs/accommodations/types

References

Abel, J.L. and Borkovec, T.D. (1995). Generalizability of DSM-III-R generalized anxiety disorders to proposed DSM-IV criteria and cross-validation of proposed changes. *Journal of Anxiety Disorders*, 9(4), 303–15.

Allgulander, C., Dahl, A.A., Austin, C., Morris, P.L., Sogaard, J.A., Fayyad, R., and Clary, C.M. (2004). Efficacy of sertraline in a 12-week trial for generalized anxiety disorder. *Am J Psychiatry*, 161(9), 1642–9. DOI: 10.1176/appi.ajp.161.9.1642161/9/1642 [pii].

Alonso, J., Angermeyer, M.C., Bernert, S., Bruffaerts, R., Brugha, T.S., Bryson, H., and Vollebergh, W.A. (2004). 12-Month comorbidity patterns and associated factors in Europe: results from the European Study of the Epidemiology of Mental Disorders (ESEMeD) project. *Acta Psychiatr Scand Suppl* (420), 28–37. DOI: 10.1111/j.1600-0047.2004.00328.xACP328 [pii].

American Psychiatric Association, APA. (2000). *Diagnostic and Statistical Manual of Mental Disorders—Text Revision* (4th ed.). Washington, DC: American Psychiatric Association.

Andlin-Sobocki, P., Jonsson, B., Wittchen, H.U., and Olesen, J. (2005). Cost of disorders of the brain in Europe. *Eur J Neurol*, 12 Suppl 1, 1–27. DOI: ENE1202 [pii]10.1111/j.1468-1331.2005.01202.x.

Andlin-Sobocki, P. and Wittchen, H.U. (2005). Cost of anxiety disorders in Europe. *Eur J Neurol*, 12 Suppl 1, 39–44. DOI: ENE1196 [pii] 10.1111/j.1468-1331.2005.01196.x.

Andrews, G., Cuijpers, P., Craske, M.G, McEvoy, P., and Titov, N. (2010). Computer therapy for the anxiety and depressive disorders is effective, acceptable and practical health care: a meta-analysis. *PloS one*, 5(10), e13196.

Ansseau, M., Fischler, B., Dierick, M., Albert, A., Leyman, S., and Mignon, Annick. (2008). Socioeconomic correlates of generalized anxiety disorder and major depression in primary care: The GADIS II study (Generalized Anxiety and Depression Impact Survey II). *Depression and Anxiety*, 25(6), 506–13. DOI: 10.1002/da.20306.

Antony, M.M. and Barlow, D.H. (2002). Specific phobias. In D.H. Barlow (ed.), *Anxiety and its Disorder* (2nd ed., pp. 380–417). New York, NY: Guilford Press.

Baldwin, D.S. (2004). Sexual dysfunction associated with antidepressant drugs. *Expert Opin Drug Saf*, 3(5), 457–70. DOI: EDS030507 [pii].

Baldwin, D.S., Anderson, I.M., Nutt, D.J., Bandelow, B., Bond, A., Davidson, J. R., et al. (2005). Evidence-based guidelines for the pharmacological treatment of anxiety disorders: recommendations from the British Association for Psychopharmacology. *J Psychopharmacol*, 19(6), 567–96. DOI: 19/6/567 [pii] 10.1177/0269881105059253.

Baldwin, D.S. and Birtwistle, J. (1998). The side effect burden associated with drug treatment of panic disorder. *J Clin Psychiatry*, 59 Suppl 8, 39–44; discussion 45–36.

Ballenger, J.C. (2001). Treatment of anxiety disorders to remission. *J Clin Psychiatry*, 62 Suppl 12, 5–9.

Ballenger, J.C., Davidson, J.R., Lecrubier, Y., Nutt, D.J., Borkovec, T.D., Rickels, K., et al. (2001). Consensus statement on generalized anxiety disorder from the International Consensus Group on Depression and Anxiety. *J Clin Psychiatry*, 62 Suppl 11, 53–8.

Bar-Haim, Y., Lamy, D., Pergamin, L., Bakermans-Kranenburg, M.J., and van IJzendoorn, M.H. (2007). Threat-related attentional bias in anxious and nonanxious individuals: a meta-analytic study. *Psychological bulletin*, 133(1), 1.

Barlow, D.H. (2002). *Anxiety and its Disorders: The nature and treatment of anxiety and panic* (2nd ed.). New York, NY: Guilford Press.

Barsky, A.J., Delamater, B.A., and Orav, J.E. (1999). Panic disorder patients and their medical care. *Psychosomatics*, 40(1), 50–56. DOI: S0033-3182(99)71271-5 [pii] 10.1016/S0033-3182(99)71271-5.

Beck, A.T. (1985). *Anxiety Disorders and Phobias: A cognitive perspective*. New York, NY: Basic Books.

Beck, A.T. and Steer, R.A. (1990). *Manual for the Beck Anxiety Inventory*. San Antonio: Harcourt Brace and Company.

Becker, E.S., Rinck, M., Margraf, J., and Roth, W.T. (2001). The emotional Stroop effect in anxiety disorders: general emotional or disorder specificity? *J Anxiety Disord*, 15(3), 147–59. DOI: S088761850100055X [pii].

Berger, A., Edelsberg, J., Bollu, V., Alvir, J.Ma J., Dugar, A., Joshi, A.V., and Oster, G. (2011). Healthcare utilization and costs in patients beginning pharmacotherapy for generalized anxiety disorder: a retrospective cohort study. *BMC Psychiatry*, 11(1), 193.

Berndt, E.R., Finkelstein, S.N., Greenberg, P.E., Keith, A., and Bailit, H. (1997). *Illness and Productivity: Objective Workplace Evidence*. Cambridge, MA: Massacheusettes Institute of Technology.

Bijl, R.V. and Ravelli, A. (2000). Current and residual functional disability associated with psychopathology: findings from the Netherlands Mental Health Survey and Incidence Study (NEMESIS). *Psychological Medicine*, 30(03), 657–68. DOI: null.

Blanck, P.D. (1996). Transcending title 1 of the Americans with Disabilities Act: A case report on Sears, Roebuck & Co. *Mental and Physical Disability Law Reporter*, 20(2), 278–86.

Borkovec, T.D., Alcaine, O., and Behar, E. (2004). Avoidance theory of worry and generalized anxiety disorder. In R.G. Heimberg, C.L. Turk, and D.S. Mennin (eds), *Generalized Anxiety Disorder: Advances in research and practice* (pp. 77–108). New York, NY: Guilford Press.

Borkovec, T.D. and Roemer, L. (1995). Perceived functions of worry among generalized anxiety disorder subjects: distraction from more emotionally distressing topics? *J Behav Ther Exp Psychiatry*, 26(1), 25–30. DOI: 000579169400064S [pii].

Bradley, B.P., Mogg, K., Millar, N., and White, J. (1995). Selective processing of negative information: effects of clinical anxiety, concurrent depression, and awareness. *J Abnorm Psychol*, 104(3), 532–6.

Brown, T.A., O'Leary, T.A., and Barlow, D.H. (2001). Generalized anxiety disorder. In D.H. Barlow (ed.), *Clinical Handbook of Psychological Disorders* (3rd ed., pp. 154–208). New York, NY: Guilford Press.

Brown, T.A., Marten, P.A., and Barlow, D.H. (1995). Discriminant validity of the symptoms constituting the DSM-III-R and DSM-IV associated symptom criterion of generalized anxiety disorder. *Journal of Anxiety Disorders*, 9(4), 317–28.

CIHI, Canadian Institute for Health Information. (2013). Drug expenditure in Canada, 1985 to 2012. Ottawa, ON.

Collins, K.A., Westra, H.A., Dozois, D.J., and Burns, D.D. (2004). Gaps in accessing treatment for anxiety and depression: challenges for the delivery of care. *Clin Psychol Rev*, 24(5), 583–616. DOI: 10.1016/j.cpr.2004.06.001 S0272735804000492 [pii].

Craske, M.G., Rapee, R.M., Jackel, L., and Barlow, D.H. (1989). Qualitative dimensions of worry in DSM-III-R generalized anxiety disorder subjects and nonanxious controls. *Behav Res Ther*, 27(4), 397–402. DOI: 0005-7967(89)90010-7 [pii].

CSM, Committee on Safety of Medicines. (2004). Safety of selective serotonin reuptake inhibitors and antidepressants. United Kingdom.

Deacon, B., Lickel, J., and Abramowitz, J.S. (2008). Medical utilization across the anxiety disorders. *J Anxiety Disord*, 22(2), 344–50. DOI: S0887-6185(07)00078-3 [pii] 10.1016/j.janxdis.2007.03.004.

Dobson, K.S. and Dozois, D.J.A. (2001). Historical and philosophical bases of the cognitive-behavioral therapies. In K.S. Dobson (ed.), *Handbook of Cognitive-Behavioral Therapies* (2nd ed., pp. 3–39). New York, NY: Guilford Press.

DuPont, R.L., Rice, D.P., Miller, L.S., Shiraki, S.S., Rowland, C.R., and Harwood, H.J. (1996). Economic costs of anxiety disorders. *Anxiety*, 2(4), 167–72. DOI: 10.1002/(SICI)1522-7154(1996)2:4<167::AID-ANXI2>3.0.CO;2-L.

Dupuy, J.B., Beaudoin, S., Rheaume, J., Ladouceur, R., and Dugas, M.J. (2001). Worry: Daily self-report in clinical and non-clinical populations. *Behaviour Research and Therapy*, 39(10), 1249–55.

Erickson, S.R., Guthrie, S., Vanetten-Lee, M., Himle, J., Hoffman, J., Santos, S.F., et al. (2009). Severity of anxiety and work-related outcomes of patients with anxiety disorders. *Depress Anxiety*, 26(12), 1165–71. DOI: 10.1002/da.20624.

Eysenck, M.W., Mogg, K., May, J., Richards, A., and Mathews, A. (1991). Bias in interpretation of ambiguous sentences related to threat in anxiety. *J Abnorm Psychol*, 100(2), 144–50.

Fernandez, A., Haro, J.M., Martinez-Alonso, M., Demyttenaere, K., Brugha, T.S., Autonell, J., et al. (2007). Treatment adequacy for anxiety and depressive disorders in six European countries. *Br J Psychiatry*, 190, 172–3. DOI: 190/2/172 [pii] 10.1192/bjp.bp.106.023507.

Field, A.P. and Lawson, J. (2003). Fear information and the development of fears during childhood: Effects on implicit fear responses and behavioural avoidance. *Behaviour Research and Therapy*, 41(11), 1277–93.

François, C., Despiégel, N., Maman, K., Saragoussi, D., and Auquier, P. (2010). Anxiety disorders, major depressive disorder and the dynamic relationship between these conditions: treatment patterns and cost analysis. *Journal of Medical Economics*, 13(1), 99–109.

Friedman, B.H. (2007). An autonomic flexibility-neurovisceral integration model of anxiety and cardiac vagal tone. *Biol Psychol*, 74(2), 185–99. DOI: S0301-0511(06)00184-0 [pii] 10.1016/j.biopsycho.2005.08.009.

Greenberg, P.E., Sisitsky, T., Kessler, R.C., Finkelstein, S.N., Berndt, E., Davidson, J.R., et al. (1999). The economic burden of anxiety disorders in the 1990s. *J Clin Psychiatry*, 60(7), 427–35.

Gregory, A.M. and Eley, T.C. (2007). Genetic influences on anxiety in children: what we've learned and where we're heading. *Clin Child Fam Psychol Rev*, 10(3), 199–212. DOI: 10.1007/s10567-007-0022-8.

Hamilton, M. (1959). The assessment of anxiety states by rating. *British Journal of Medical Psychology*, 32(1), 50–55.

Hettema, J.M., Neale, M.C., and Kendler, K.S. (2001). A review and meta-analysis of the genetic epidemiology of anxiety disorders. *Am J Psychiatry*, 158(10), 1568–78.

Hettema, J.M., Prescott, C.A., and Kendler, K.S. (2004). Genetic and environmental sources of covariation between generalized anxiety disorder and neuroticism. *Am J Psychiatry*, 161(9), 1581–7. DOI: 10.1176/appi. ajp.161.9.1581 161/9/1581 [pii].

Hudson, J.L., Doyle, A.M., and Gar, N. (2009). Child and maternal influence on parenting behavior in clinically anxious children. *J Clin Child Adolesc Psychol*, 38(2), 256–62. DOI: 909505724 [pii] 10.1080/15374410802698438.

Hunt, C., Slade, T., and Andrews, G. (2004). Generalized Anxiety Disorder and major depressive disorder comorbidity in the National Survey of Mental Health and Well-Being. *Depress Anxiety*, 20(1), 23–31. DOI: 10.1002/da.20019.

Jacobi, F., Wittchen, H.U., Holting, C., Sommer, S., Lieb, R., Hofler, M., and Pfister, H. (2002). Estimating the prevalence of mental and somatic disorders in the community: aims and methods of the German National Health Interview and Examination Survey. *Int J Methods Psychiatr Res*, 11(1), 1–18.

Jones, G.N., Ames, S.C., Jeffries, S.K., Scarinci, I.C., and Brantley, P.J. (2001). Utilization of medical services and quality of life among low-income patients with generalized anxiety disorder attending primary care clinics. *Int J Psychiatry Med*, 31(2), 183–98.

Katz, I.R., Reynolds, C.F., 3rd, Alexopoulos, G.S., and Hackett, D. (2002). Venlafaxine ER as a treatment for generalized anxiety disorder in older adults: pooled analysis of five randomized placebo-controlled clinical trials. *J Am Geriatr Soc*, 50(1), 18–25. DOI: 50003 [pii].

Kennedy, B.L., Lin, Y., and Schwab, J.J. (2002). Work, social, and family disabilities of subjects with anxiety and depression. *South Med J*, 95(12), 1424–7.

Kennedy, B.L. and Schwab, J.J. (1997). Utilization of medical specialists by anxiety disorder patients. *Psychosomatics*, 38(2), 109–12. DOI: S0033-3182(97)71478-6 [pii] 10.1016/S0033-3182(97)71478-6.

Kessler, R.C. (1995). Epidemiology of psychiatric comorbidity. In M.T. Tsuang, M. Tohen, and G.E. P. Zahner (eds), *Textbook in Psychiatric Epidemiology* (pp. 179–97). New York, NY: Wiley.

Kessler, R.C., Amminger, G.P., Aguilar-Gaxiola, S., Alonso, J., Lee, S., and Ustun, T.B. (2007). Age of onset of mental disorders: a review of recent literature. *Curr Opin Psychiatry*, 20(4), 359–64. DOI: 10.1097/ YCO.0b013e32816ebc8c 00001504-200707000-00010 [pii].

Kessler, R.C., Berglund, P., Demler, O., Jin, R., Merikangas, K.R., and Walters, E.E. (2005). Lifetime prevalence and age-of-onset distributions of DSM-IV disorders in the National Comorbidity Survey Replication. *Arch Gen Psychiatry*, 62(6), 593–602. DOI: 62/6/593 [pii] 10.1001/archpsyc.62.6.593.

Kessler, R.C., Chiu, W., Demler, O., Merikangas, K.R., and Walters, E.E. (2005). Prevalence, severity, and comorbidity of 12-month DSM-IV disorders in the National Comorbidity Survey Replication. *Arch Gen Psychiatry*, 62(6), 617–27. DOI: 62/6/617 [pii] 10.1001/archpsyc.62.6.617.

Kessler, R.C., DuPont, R.L., Berglund, P., and Wittchen, H.U. (1999). Impairment in pure and comorbid generalized anxiety disorder and major depression at 12 months in two national surveys. *Am J Psychiatry*, 156(12), 1915–23.

Kessler, R.C., Greenberg, P.E., Mickelson, K.D., Meneades, L.M., and Wang, P.S. (2001). The effects of chronic medical conditions on work loss and work cutback. *J Occup Environ Med*, 43(3), 218–25.

Kessler, R.C., Keller, M.B., and Wittchen, H.U. (2001). The epidemiology of generalized anxiety disorder. *Psychiatr Clin North Am*, 24(1), 19–39.

Kessler, R.C., McGonagle, K.A., Zhao, S., Nelson, C.B., Hughes, M., Eshleman, S., et al. (1994). Lifetime and 12-month prevalence of DSM-III-R psychiatric disorders in the United States. Results from the National Comorbidity Survey. *Arch Gen Psychiatry*, 51(1), 8–19.

Kessler, R.C., Ruscio, A.M., Shear, K., Wittchen, H.U., Stein, M.B., and Steckler, T. (2010). Epidemiology of Anxiety Disorders: Behavioral Neurobiology of Anxiety and Its Treatment (Vol. 2, pp. 21–35): Springer Berlin Heidelberg.

Kessler, R.C. and Wang, P.S. (2008). The descriptive epidemiology of commonly occurring mental disorders in the United States. *Annu Rev Public Health*, 29, 115–129. DOI: 10.1146/annurev.publhealth.29.020907.090847.

Kessler, R.C. and Wittchen, H.U. (2002). Patterns and correlates of generalized anxiety disorder in community samples. *J Clin Psychiatry*, 63(8), 4–10.

Knekt, P.L., Lindfors, O., Harkanen, T., Valikoski, M.L., Virtala, E., Laaksonen, M.A., et al. (2008). Randomized trial on the effectiveness of long- and short-term psychodynamic psychotherapy and solution-focused therapy on psychiatric symptoms during a 3-year follow-up. *Psychological Medicine*, 38(5), 689–704.

Kroenke, K., Spitzer, R.L., Williams, J.B., Monahan, P.O., and Lowe, B. (2007). Anxiety disorders in primary care: prevalence, impairment, comorbidity, and detection. *Ann Intern Med*, 146(5), 317–325. DOI: 146/5/317 [pii].

Kubarych, T.S., Aggen, S.H., Hettema, J.M., Kendler, K.S., and Neale, M.C. (2005). Endorsement frequencies and factor structure of DSM-III-R and DSM-IV Generalized Anxiety Disorder symptoms in women: implications for future research, classification, clinical practice and comorbidity. *Int J Methods Psychiatr Res*, 14(2), 69–81.

Layard, R., Clark, D., Knapp, M., and Mayraz, G. (2007). Cost-benefit analysis of psychological therapy. *National Institute Economic Review*, 202(1), 90–98.

Lieb, R., Becker, E., and Altamura, C. (2005). The epidemiology of generalized anxiety disorder in Europe. *Eur Neuropsychopharmacol*, 15(4), 445–52. DOI: S0924-977X(05)00073-8 [pii] 10.1016/j.euroneuro.2005.04.010.

Loeppke, R., Taitel, M., Haufle, V., Parry, T., Kessler, R.C., and Jinnett, K. (2009). Health and productivity as a business strategy: a multiemployer study. *Journal of Occupational and Environmental Medicine*, 51(4), 411–28.

Loeppke, R., Taitel, M., Richling, D., Parry, T., Kessler, R.C., Hymel, P., and Konicki, D. (2007). Health and productivity as a business strategy. *Journal of Occupational and Environmental Medicine*, 49(7), 712–21.

MacDonald-Wilson, K.L., Rogers, E.S., Massaro, J.M., Lyass, A., and Crean, T. (2002). An investigation of reasonable workplace accommodations for people with psychiatric disabilities: quantitative findings from a multi-site study. *Community Ment Health J*, 38(1), 35–50.

Marciniak, M.D., Lage, M.J., Dunayevich, E., Russell, J.M., Bowman, L., Landbloom, R.P., and Levine, L.R. (2005). The cost of treating anxiety: the medical and demographic correlates that impact total medical costs. *Depress Anxiety*, 21(4), 178–84. DOI: 10.1002/da.20074.

Marciniak, M., Lage, M.J., Landbloom, R.P., Dunayevich, E., and Bowman, L. (2004). Medical and productivity costs of anxiety disorders: case control study. *Depress Anxiety*, 19(2), 112–20. DOI: 10.1002/da.10131.

Martín-Merino, E., Ruigómez, A., Wallander, M., Johansson, S., and García-Rodríguez, L.A. (2010). Prevalence, incidence, morbidity and treatment patterns in a cohort of patients diagnosed with anxiety in UK primary care. *Family Practice*, 27(1), 9–16.

Martin, E.I., Ressler, K.J., Binder, E., and Nemeroff, C.B. (2010). The neurobiology of anxiety disorders: brain imaging, genetics, and psychoneuroendocrinology. *Clin Lab Med*, 30(4), 865–91. DOI: S0272-2712(10)00121-6 [pii] 10.1016/j.cll.2010.07.006.

McEvoy, P.M., Grove, R., and Slade, T. (2011). Epidemiology of anxiety disorders in the Australian general population: findings of the 2007 Australian National Survey of Mental Health and Wellbeing. *Aust N Z J Psychiatry*, 45(11), 957–67. DOI: 10.3109/00048674.2011.624083.

Mennin, D.S., Heimberg, R.G., Turk, C.L., and Fresco, D.M. (2005). Preliminary evidence for an emotion dysregulation model of generalized anxiety disorder. *Behav Res Ther*, 43(10), 1281–310. DOI: S0005-7967(04)00232-3 [pii] 10.1016/j.brat.2004.08.008.

Mitte, K. (2005). Meta-analysis of cognitive-behavioral treatments for generalized anxiety disorder: a comparison with pharmacotherapy. *Psychol Bull*, 131(5), 785–95. DOI: 2005-11504-012 [pii] 10.1037/0033-2909.131.5.785.

Mitte, K., Noack, P., Steil, R., and Hautzinger, M. (2005). A meta-analytic review of the efficacy of drug treatment in generalized anxiety disorder. *J Clin Psychopharmacol*, 25(2), 141–50. DOI: 00004714-200504000-00006 [pii].

Mogg, K. and Bradley, B.P. (2005). Attentional bias in generalized anxiety disorder versus depressive disorder. *Cognitive Therapy and Research*, 29, 29–45.

Murthy, R.S. (2007). Mass violence and mental health—Recent epidemiological findings. *International Review of Psychiatry*, 19(3), 183–92.

Newman, M.G. and Llera, S.J. (2011). A novel theory of experiential avoidance in generalized anxiety disorder: A review and synthesis of research supporting a contrast avoidance model of worry. *Clinical Psychology Review*, 31(3), 371–82.

NICE, National Institute for Health and Care Excellence. (2011). *Generalized Anxiety Disorder in Adults: A NICE guideline on management in primary, secondary and community care*. (GC113-Anxiety). London: NICE.

Norton, P.J. and Price, E.C. (2007). A meta-analytic review of adult cognitive-behavioral treatment outcome across the anxiety disorders. *J Nerv Ment Dis*, 195(6), 521–31. DOI: 10.1097/01.nmd.0000253843.70149.9a 00005053-200706000-00009 [pii].

Nutt, D.J. (2003). Death and dependence: current controversies over the selective serotonin reuptake inhibitors. *J Psychopharmacol*, 17(4), 355–64.

Ohayon, M.M., Shapiro, C.M., and Kennedy, S.H. (2000). Differentiating DSM-IV anxiety and depressive disorders in the general population: comorbidity and treatment consequences. *Can J Psychiatry*, 45(2), 166–72.

Olfson, M. and Gameroff, M.J. (2007). Generalized anxiety disorder, somatic pain and health care costs. *Gen Hosp Psychiatry*, 29(4), 310–316. DOI: S0163-8343(07)00065-5 [pii] 10.1016/j.genhosppsych.2007.04.004.

Olfson, M., Shea, S., Feder, A., Fuentes, M., Nomura, Y., Gameroff, M., and Weissman, M.M. (2000). Prevalence of anxiety, depression, and substance use disorders in an urban general medicine practice. *Arch Fam Med*, 9(9), 876–83. DOI: foc0038 [pii].

Porensky, E.K., Dew, M.A., Karp, J.F., Skidmore, E., Rollman, B.L., Shear, M.K., and Lenze, E.J. (2009). The burden of late-life generalized anxiety disorder: effects on disability, health-related quality of life, and healthcare utilization. *Am J Geriatr Psychiatry*, 17(6), 473–82.

Rapee, R.M. (1997). Potential role of childrearing practices in the development of anxiety and depression. *Clin Psychol Rev*, 17(1), 47–67. DOI: S0272735896000402 [pii].

Rapee, R.M. and Spence, S.H. (2004). The etiology of social phobia: empirical evidence and an initial model. *Clin Psychol Rev*, 24(7), 737–67. DOI: S0272-7358(04)00095-9 [pii] 10.1016/j.cpr.2004.06.004.

RCP, Royal College of Psychiatrists. (2005). Benzodiazepines: risks, benefits or dependence. A re-evaluation. Royal College of Psychiatrists, London.

Rice, D.P.. and Miller, L.S. (1998). Health economics and cost implications of anxiety and other mental disorders in the United States. *Br J Psychiatry Suppl* (34), 4–9.

Richardson, K.M. and Rothstein, H.R. (2008). Effects of occupational stress management intervention programs: a meta-analysis. *J Occup Health Psychol*, 13(1), 69–93. DOI: 2008-00533-007 [pii] 10.1037/1076-8998.13.1.69.

Roemer, L., Salters, K., Raffa, S.D., and Orsillo, S.M. (2005). Fear and avoidance of internal experiences in GAD: Preliminary tests of a conceptual model. *Cognitive Therapy and Research*, 29, 71–88.

Rogers, M.P., Warshaw, M.G., Goisman, R.M., Goldenberg, I., Rodriguez-Villa, F., Mallya, G., et al. (1999). Comparing primary and secondary generalized anxiety disorder in a long-term naturalistic study of anxiety disorders. *Depress Anxiety*, 10(1), 1–7. DOI: 10.1002/(SICI)1520-6394(1999)10:1<1::AID-DA1>3.0.CO;2-9 [pii].

Roy-Byrne, P.P., Davidson, K.W., Kessler, R.C., Asmundson, G.J., Goodwin, R.D., Kubzansky, L., et al. (2008). Anxiety disorders and comorbid medical illness. *Gen Hosp Psychiatry*, 30(3), 208–25. DOI: S0163-8343(07)00259-9 [pii] 10.1016/j.genhosppsych.2007.12.006.

Rubin, H.C., Rapaport, M.H., Levine, B., Gladsjo, J.K., Rabin, A., Auerbach, M., et al. (2000). Quality of well being in panic disorder: the assessment of psychiatric and general disability. *J Affect Disord*, 57(1–3), 217–21. DOI: S0165032799000300 [pii].

Ruscio, A.M., Chiu, W.T., Roy-Byrne, P., Stang, P.E., Stein, D.J., Wittchen, H.U., and Kessler, R.C. (2007). Broadening the definition of generalized anxiety disorder: effects on prevalence and associations with other disorders in the National Comorbidity Survey Replication. *J Anxiety Disord*, 21(5), 662–76. DOI: S0887-6185(06)00168-X [pii] 10.1016/j.janxdis.2006.10.004.

Sasha-Corporation. (January 2007). Compilation of turnover cost studies. Retrieved July 15, 2009, from http://www.sashacorp.com/turnframe.html.

Schatzberg, A.F., Haddad, P., Kaplan, E.M., Lejoyeux, M., Rosenbaum, J.F., Young, A.H., and Zajecka, J. (1997). Serotonin reuptake inhibitor discontinuation syndrome: a hypothetical definition. Discontinuation Consensus panel. *J Clin Psychiatry*, 58(7), 5–10.

Scherrer, J.F., True, W.R., Xian, H., Lyons, M.J., Eisen, S.A., Goldberg, J., et al. (2000). Evidence for genetic influences common and specific to symptoms of generalized anxiety and panic. *J Affect Disord*, 57(1–3), 25–35. DOI: S0165032799000312 [pii].

Schienle, A., Hettema, J.M., Cáceda, R., and Nemeroff, C.B. (2011). Neurobiology and genetics of generalized anxiety disorder. *Psychiatric Annals*, 41(2), 113.

Shafran, R., Clark, D.M., Fairburn, C.G., Arntz, A., Barlow, D.H., Ehlers, A., et al. (2009). Mind the gap: Improving the dissemination of CBT. *Behaviour Research and Therapy*, 47(11), 902–9.

Smit, F., Cuijpers, P., Oostenbrink, J., Batelaan, N., de Graaf, R., and Beekman, A. (2006). Costs of nine common mental disorders: implications for curative and preventive psychiatry. *J Ment Health Policy Econ*, 9(4), 193–200.

Spek, V., Cuijpers, P.I.M., Nyklícek, I., Riper, H., Keyzer, J.,, and Pop, V. (2007). Internet-based cognitive behaviour therapy for symptoms of depression and anxiety: a meta-analysis. *Psychological Medicine*, 37(3), 319–28.

Stewart, R.E. and Chambless, D.L. (2009). Cognitive-behavioral therapy for adult anxiety disorders in clinical practice: A meta-analysis of effectiveness studies. *Journal of Consulting and Clinical Psychology*, 77(4), 595.

Spielberger, C.D. and Gorsuch, R.L. (1983). *State-trait Anxiety Inventory for Adults: Sampler Set: Manual, Test, Scoring Key*. Mind Garden.

Spitzer, R.L., Kroenke, K., Williams, J.B., and Lowe, B. (2006). A brief measure for assessing generalized anxiety disorder: the GAD-7. *Archives of Internal Medicine*, 166(10), 1092.

Tambs, K., Czajkowsky, N., Roysamb, E., Neale, M.C., Reichborn-Kjennerud, T., Aggen, S.H., et al. (2009). Structure of genetic and environmental risk factors for dimensional representations of DSM-IV anxiety disorders. *Br J Psychiatry*, 195(4), 301–7. DOI: 195/4/301 [pii] 10.1192/bjp.bp.108.059485.

Thayer, J.F. and Lane, R.D. (2000). A model of neurovisceral integration in emotion regulation and dysregulation. *J Affect Disord*, 61(3), 201–16. DOI: S0165032700003384 [pii].

Tiller, J.W., Biddle, N., Maguire, K.P., and Davies, B.M. (1988). The dexamethasone suppression test and plasma dexamethasone in generalized anxiety disorder. *Biol Psychiatry*, 23(3), 261–70. DOI: 0006-3223(88)90037-6 [pii].

Turvey, C.L., Stevens, D.E., and Merikangas, K.R. (1999). The validity of the associated symptom criteria for DSM-IV generalized anxiety disorder. *International Journal of Methods in Psychiatric Research*, 8(3), 129–37. DOI: 10.1002/mpr.63.

Vreeburg, S.A., Zitman, F.G., van Pelt, J., Derijk, R.H., Verhagen, J.C., van Dyck, R., et al. (2010). Salivary cortisol levels in persons with and without different anxiety disorders. *Psychosom Med*, 72(4), 340–347. DOI: PSY.0b013e3181d2f0c8 [pii] 10.1097/PSY.0b013e3181d2f0c8.

Waghorn, G., Chant, D., White, P., and Whiteford, H. (2005). Disability, employment and work performance among people with ICD-10 anxiety disorders. *Aust N Z J Psychiatry*, 39(1–2), 55–66. DOI: ANP1510 [pii] 10.1111/j.1440-1614.2005.01510.x.

Wang, P.S., Berglund, P., Olfson, M., Pincus, H.A., Wells, K.B., and Kessler, R.C. (2005). Failure and delay in initial treatment contact after first onset of mental disorders in the National Comorbidity Survey Replication. *Archives of General Psychiatry*, 62(6), 603.

Wang, P.S., Lane, M., Olfson, M., Pincus, H.A., Wells, K.B., and Kessler, R.C. (2005). Twelve-month use of mental health services in the United States: results from the National Comorbidity Survey Replication. *Arch Gen Psychiatry*, 62(6), 629–40. DOI: 62/6/629 [pii] 10.1001/archpsyc.62.6.629.

Weiller, E., Bisserbe, J.C., Maier, W., and Lecrubier, Y. (1998). Prevalence and recognition of anxiety syndromes in five European primary care settings. A report from the WHO study on Psychological Problems in General Health Care. *Br J Psychiatry Suppl* (34), 18–23.

Wells, A. (1999). A cognitive model of generalized anxiety disorder. *Behav Modif*, 23(4), 526–55.

Wittchen, H.U., Carter, R.M., Pfister, H., Montgomery, S.A., and Kessler, R.C. (2000). Disabilities and quality of life in pure and comorbid generalized anxiety disorder and major depression in a national survey. *Int Clin Psychopharmacol*, 15(6), 319–28.

Wittchen, H.U. and Jacobi, F. (2005). Size and burden of mental disorders in Europe—a critical review and appraisal of 27 studies. *Eur Neuropsychopharmacol*, 15(4), 357–76. DOI: S0924-977X(05)00075-1 [pii] 10.1016/j.euroneuro.2005.04.012.

Wittchen, H.U., Kessler, R.C., Beesdo, K., Krause, P., Hofler, M., and Hoyer, J. (2002). Generalized anxiety and depression in primary care: prevalence, recognition, and management. *J Clin Psychiatry*, 63 Suppl 8, 24–34.

Wittchen, H.U., Krause, P., Hoyer, J., Beesdo, K., Jacobi, F., Hofler, M., and Winter, S. (2001). Prevalence and correlates of generalized anxiety disorders in primary care. *Fortschr Med Orig*, 119 Suppl 1, 17–25.

Zhu, B., Zhao, Z., Ye, W., Marciniak, M.D., and Swindle, R. (2009). The cost of comorbid depression and pain for individuals diagnosed with generalized anxiety disorder. *J Nerv Ment Dis*, 197(2), 136–9. DOI: 10.1097/ NMD.0b013e3181963486 00005053-200902000-00010 [pii].

Chapter 6
Occupational Stress

Every stress leaves an indelible scar, and the organism pays for its survival after a stressful situation by becoming a little older.

Dr Hans Selye

Introduction

Occupational Stress is a hot topic among employers, disability providers, disability managers, and other workplace stakeholders. There are many reasons why workplace stress has become such a concern for so many including cost, litigation, prevalence, and lack of clarity about definition and application. Generally, stress can be categorized as belonging to one of two types. The first type, eustress, is stress attached to something that raises our level of physiological and psychological arousal, but that is interpreted as a positive environmental occurrence. For example, getting married or becoming a new parent would be considered eustress. These are both highly anticipated and enjoyable life events, but they are certainly not without some stress. Eustress is typically of little concern to employers, as within the workplace, like in life, eustress would be considered a positive factor. In the workplace, a reasonable level of positively interpreted stress can result in increased productivity and quality of work.

In contrast to the positive outcomes often associated with the experience of eustress, distress is the term used to describe similar types of physiological and psychological arousal; but, in place of the positive interpretation, the arousal is interpreted as distressing to the individual. Distress is the type of stress typically discussed when considering occupational stress, both in science and in practice. Stress (distress) is generally described as a mismatch between individual coping skills or abilities and the physical or psychological demands placed upon them. Specifically, work-related stress is generally considered to be caused by situations where individual coping skills or abilities are overwhelmed by workplace demands, either psychological or physical. Over recent decades, workplace stress has been a highly researched topic, with many authors attempting to provide clarity regarding workplace aspects that contribute most to the development of occupational stress. Generally, the literature suggests that analyzing and identifying all elements that may represent etiological factors for workplace stress has proven to be a difficult task (Elovainio, Kivimäki, Steen, et al., 2000; Ettner and Grzywacz, 2001).

One of the primary justifications for the difficulty in identifying pure explanatory variables for the development of workplace stress is found in worker individual characteristics. That is, personality traits, coping strategies, world views, and perceptions about job demands and stressors all impact individual interpretation of workplace events. However, despite individual variation, aspects of the workplace environment that have consistently been demonstrated as creating workplace stress include a mismatch between competency and responsibility, insecurity, ambiguity, and psychological or physical overload.

Stress

Stress is a ubiquitous construct. It percolates nearly every aspect of our lives, is a strong motivator for action, and is a potent determinant of health outcomes. Over the past century, the word stress has slowly become a common, everyday household term. Many individuals would contend that, at an implicit level, they have an idea of the meaning of stress. However, in scientific research, the term stress must be precisely defined and placed into operational terms that can be identified and measured. At its most fundamental level, stress is composed of two dimensions—the physical and the psychological. The physical dimension involves a cascade of biological processes that results from bodily challenge, while the psychological dimension involves the cognitive perception of an event as exceeding resources for coping (Lovallo, 2005). Several popular models have been postulated that have advanced our understanding of stress and its consequences.

Stress can be conceptualized in three different ways. Many individuals consider stress to be a biological response, such as "I must be under a great deal of stress because my heart is racing and my palms are sweating." Other people refer to stress as a stimulus in the environment, such as "writing financial reports really stresses me out." Still others view stress as a process arising through an interaction between person and environment. For example, "I become stressed whenever John gives me a report to complete after 3:00 pm without any prior notice but I am fine if he gives me advanced warning earlier in the day."

A scientist by the name of Hans Selye began studying the concept of stress in the 1930s and continued with this research until his death in 1982. Selye originally conceptualized stress to be a stimulus, but changed his focus in the 1950s to conceptualize stress as a response made by the organism. He was the first researcher to use the term stressor to refer to the stimulus, and the term stress to mean the process. In addition, Selye is famous for conceptualizing stress as the General Adaptation Syndrome (GAS; Selye 1976, 1982). The GAS is a three-stage process characterizing the body's attempt to defend itself against stressful agents. During the first phase, the *alarm phase*, the threat is recognized and the body's defenses against a stressor are mobilized. This results in activation of the autonomic nervous system and the production of various hormones such as cortisol. These physical reactions are adaptive during short-term emergency situations but pose problems during prolonged exposure to stress. Unfortunately, many modern-day stress situations involve prolonged stress that cannot be modulated through a physical response.

The second phase of the GAS, the *resistance phase*, is characterized by an individual's adaptation to the stressor. The individual gives the outward appearance of normality while continuing stress results in pathological internal functioning of the body typified by heightened neurological and hormonal activation. The duration of the resistance phase depends on the severity of the stressor and the organism's reserve capacity for adjusting to insults. The demands of the resistance stage create wear and tear on the body such that if the organism cannot successfully overcome the stressor, prolonged resistance will lower the body's immune system and can lead to disease.

The final stage of the GAS is the exhaustion stage. Every organism has a finite energy reserve to aid in adapting to stress. Once this energy reserve is depleted, the organism begins to break down. The sympathetic nervous system becomes over-activated and the organism falls prey to exhaustion, depression, or even death. The GAS is a useful model to conceptualize the physical dimension of stress as a response, but fails to acknowledge individual variability in the perception and interpretation of stressful experiences.

Richard Lazarus was one of the first theorists to elucidate a model of stress as a process. He believed that stress is a result of the interaction between a person and their environment (Lazarus, 1966, 1984 and 1993). According to Lazarus, the effects of stress are determined by the perception of the stressor as threatening, vulnerability to stress, and the resources available to cope. This model has great utility because it defines stress differently for each individual. For example, losing a business account may be extremely stressful for a young employee with few accounts, but may not be stressful for the seasoned employee who holds numerous accounts.

According to Lazarus, the stress process involves three types of appraisals of the situation—primary appraisal, secondary appraisal, and reappraisal (Lazarus and Folkman, 1984). Primary appraisals are the first appraisals used when an individual first encounters an event. Primary appraisals are used to determine how an event, situation, or opportunity impinges on well-being. The event being appraised can be viewed as irrelevant, positive, or stressful. If the event is appraised as stressful it can be viewed as harmful (that is, an assessment of damage that has already been done), threatening (that is, the expectation of future harm), or challenging (that is, providing an opportunity to grow or profit). These appraisals generate different emotions; harm produces emotions such as anger and sadness, threat produces emotions such as worry and fear, and challenge produces emotions such as excitement or anticipation (Lazarus, 1993). Importantly, individuals are more likely to evaluate a situation as stressful if they are vulnerable to stress—if the situation is judged to be of personal importance, and/or the individual experiences physical or social deficits.

Once the initial appraisal has been made, the individual must assess available coping resources. This assessment is called secondary appraisal and involves determining the available options, and the likelihood of success given these options. Secondary appraisals can be used to alleviate or exacerbate the initial stressful appraisal. In cases of adequate resources or belief that one's actions will make a difference (that is, feelings of self-efficacy and control), stress is typically reduced. Finally, individuals continually engage in acts of reappraisal as new information becomes available. Thus, the perception of stress always has the potential to be altered.

Finally, among the most popular theorists to conceptualize stress as a stimulus were the psychiatrists Thomas Holmes and Richard Rahe who examined the medical records of over 5,000 patients to determine whether stressful events cause illnesses (Holmes and Rahe, 1967). These researchers believed that generic stimuli (in their case, social events) would create a stress response that was approximately equivalent in any patient experiencing a similar stimulus. They developed the Social Readjustment Rating Scale (SRRS) by having participants quantify the level of readjustment that would be required following 43 life events (for example, marriage, trouble with boss, change in residence, divorce, being fired from work, and so on). Thus, the SRRS captures stress as a stimulus resulting from social events. However, despite its wide use in research, this view ignores individual variability in interpretation of stressful events, resulting in a serious weakness of the model.

Costs

As is often the case, one of the primary drivers for interest in the field of occupational stress is the clear evidence for the overwhelming related costs. Overall costs of workplace stress have previously been estimated at $20–$30 billion US annually (Tillman and Beard, 2001) and such costs are described as created by workplace aspects such as absenteeism, employee turnover, accidents, unsafe work practices, impaired performance, reduced productivity, employment-related discipline, loss of trained workers, cost of training new employees, and other indirect costs such as loss of morale (Burton, Chen, Conti, et al., 2005; DeFrank and Ivancevich, 1998; Goetzel, Ozimkowski, Sederer, et al., 2002; Leontaridi and Ward, 2002; Noonan and Wagner, 2010; WHO, 2010). According to the Australian Government Safety, Rehabilitation and Compensation Commission (Comcare, 2009), between 2004 and 2009 mental stress claims accounted for 9 per cent of all claims. Interestingly, mental stress claims were associated with the greatest payout in terms of total claim costs. Mental stress claims represented 34 per cent of the total claims costs, with an average total cost per claim of approximately $149,000. Similarly, within Canada it has been said that "stress is part of an explosion in workplace mental health issues now costing the Canadian economy an estimated 33 billion a year in lost productivity, as well as billions more in medical costs" (MacQueen, Patriquin, and Intini, 2007, p. 2); further, the recent Canadian General Social Survey suggested that 27 per cent of workers are "extremely" or "quite a bit" stressed, and another 46 per cent are "a bit" stressed (Crompton, 2011). Other staggering statistics suggest that mental health and stress-related claims are the fastest-growing category of disability insurance claims in Canada, that occupational stress and healthcare costs account for a majority of occupationally related physician visits, and that workplace stress is a driver for nearly 20 per cent of Canadian healthcare costs (Manning, Jackson, and Fusilier, 1996; Sutherland, 1991; MacQueen, Patriquin, and Intini, 2007). Recently, a Canadian study found that individuals in high-stress jobs had a 26 per cent increase in healthcare visits, to both general practitioners and specialists (Azagba and

Sharaf, 2011). According to the National Institute for Occupational Health and Safety (1999) work-related stress is more strongly predictive of health complaints than other forms of reported stress (that is, financial, family, and so on).

Contributing to the high cost of occupational stress are the health conditions that result from ongoing exposure to high-stress environments. According to Selye's stress adaptation model, our bodies are designed to withstand short-term exposure to environmental stressors. However, when environmental stressors are experienced on a longer-term basis, our well functioning adaptive systems move into the stage of exhaustion, at which point stress related illness is likely to become evident. Stress-related illness may manifest in a variety of forms including somatic complaints such as headaches, stomach aches, low back or other musculoskeletal complaints, as a well as a variety of other potential somatic symptoms. Stress-related symptoms may also result in psychological symptoms including such things as depression, anxiety, and/or substance misuse. Given the complexity of the interaction between environmental, individual, and physical factors, diagnosis and intervention for stress-related illness proves to be difficult. This difficulty is presumed to often result in alternate explanations for symptoms that could be better explained through the evaluation of work-related stress. As a result, the assumed cost of workplace stress is likely an underestimate of the true price tag attached to unattainable workplace psychological or physical demands.

Physiology of Stress

The physiological processes involved in stress are complex and a thorough understanding is beyond the scope of this chapter. However, basic understanding into the physiology of stress is important and so a simplified version will be presented here. Prolonged stress can deleteriously impact nearly every system in the body including the nervous system, the endocrine system, the cardiovascular system, and the immune system.

STRESS AND THE NERVOUS SYSTEM

The quickest and easiest way for your brain to tell the rest of your body what to do is to send messages through nerves that branch from the brain to the spinal cord and out to the periphery. The primary facet of the nervous system involved in regulating stress responses is the autonomic nervous system. It is called autonomic because it acts to regulate the body outside of conscious awareness. It is the system that ensures air is being breathed and stomach muscles are undergoing peristalsis. The autonomic nervous system is divided into two complementary branches. One branch is responsible for vigilance, arousal, and the mobilization of resources during times of stress or danger. This branch is called the sympathetic nervous system and is essential for coordinating the "fight-or-flight" response.

Autonomic balance is shifted towards sympathetic dominance when there is real or perceived threat. Activation of the sympathetic nervous system results in the release of epinephrine and norepinephrine from the sympathetic nerve endings located throughout the body. Epinephrine and norepinephrine are chemical messengers that arouse various organs throughout the body and stimulate muscle contraction. Release of epinephrine and norepinephrine increases heart rate, increases vascular tone and consequently blood pressure, stimulates the release of glucose from energy stores, and diverts blood flow to the skeletal muscles.

The second branch of the autonomic nervous system is the parasympathetic nervous system which is the vegetative branch. This branch is responsible for slowing down the body to promote rest, relaxation, regeneration, and the conservation of energy when there is no impending threat or stress on the organism. Thus, the two branches of the autonomic nervous system work in an antagonistic manner to regulate physiological responses to stress. The sympathetic branch increases heart rate, respiration rate, and blood pressure while the parasympathetic branch acts to slow these down. Similarly, the sympathetic branch diverts blood supplies to the muscles while the parasympathetic branch redirects blood flow to digestion.

STRESS AND THE HPA-AXIS

It should come as no surprise that the neuroendocrine system is also involved in the stress response. The experience of threat or stress results in the release of a cascade of hormones from the hypothalamus and pituitary. These hormones linger in the body for several hours and may explain why the effects of stress are so pronounced. One of the most well-documented neuroendocrine stress response systems is the hypothalamic-pituitary-adrenal-corticoid axis (HPA-Axis). The HPA-Axis is a regulatory system involving the hypothalamus (located near the base of the brain), the pituitary (a pea-shaped structure located below the hypothalamus), and the adrenal gland (located atop the kidneys). The hypothalamus is the control center for most hormones in the body. During times of stress, the hypothalamus releases corticotrophin releasing factor

(CRF) which binds to receptors on the pituitary and stimulates the release of adrenocorticotropic hormone (ACTH). ACTH then travels through the body to the adrenal glands where it stimulates the release of cortisol. Cortisol then forms a negative feedback loop with the hypothalamus. When there is a sufficient concentration of cortisol in the blood stream, the hypothalamus will inhibit the production of CRF, halting the production of cortisol. Interestingly, epinephrine and norepinepherine are also released by the adrenal gland, stimulate the release of CRF from the hypothalamus, and act as a positive feedback loop.

The release of cortisol into circulation has a number of effects on the body such as elevating blood glucose for use in times of elevated metabolic demand. In addition, cortisol suppresses immune system responses by preventing the release of immunotransmitters.

STRESS AND THE CARDIOVASCULAR SYSTEM

The cardiovascular system is responsible for pumping blood throughout the body to deliver a supply of oxygen to cells in the body and ensuring that carbon dioxide is safely removed. Initially, the blood supply travels through larger blood vessels such as the aorta and gradually branches into smaller and smaller vessels and capillaries. The heart is basically a pump attached to arteries, veins, and capillaries, the essential blood-transmitting tubing.

Stress alters the dynamics of the cardiovascular system, causing the heart to beat faster, pumping more blood throughout the system. This increase in heart rate results in an increase in blood pressure. Stress also results in the constriction of veins that further elevates blood pressure by increasing total peripheral resistance. In other words, more pressure is generated by constricting the size of the opening at the end of the line. Chronic elevation in blood pressure resulting from chronic stress can cause damage at branch points in arteries throughout the body. High-velocity blood flow crashes into the funneling walls as veins gradually merge to capillaries and can damage the smooth inner lining of the vessels. Damage to this lining causes an inflammatory response—immune system cells aggregate at the site of injury. This aggregate of cells can clot and cause atherosclerotic plaques. As if this was not bad enough, the sympathetic nervous system makes blood more viscous and epinephrine promotes platelet clotting which exacerbates the risk for developing atherosclerotic plaques. Thus, chronic stress can result in an elevated heart rate, increased blood pressure, and a heightened propensity to develop atherosclerotic plaques (Kamarck, Muldoon, Shiffman, et al., 2004).

Chronic stress increases the risk of experiencing cardiac complications. The INTERHEART study was a large-scale study that assessed the association between psychosocial risk factors and the risk of acute cardiac events among 11,119 patients with a first myocardial infarction and 13,648 age matched control (Rosengren, Hawken, Ounpuu, et al., 2004). Participants were recruited from 52 countries including Asia, Europe, Middle East, Africa, Australia, North America, and South America. Results indicated that individuals with stress were nearly two-fold more likely to experience a cardiac event than individuals who were not stressed. Permanent stress at work raised the risk of myocardial infarction by 2.14 times while several periods of stress at work raised the risk by 1.38 times. Similarly, permanent stress at home raised the risk of myocardial infarction by 2.12 times while several periods of stress at work raised the risk by 1.52 times. Interestingly, the risk of cardiac event accountable to stress was greater than that accountable to depression. Individuals who were highly stressed in general were 2.17 times more likely to experience a myocardial infarction, while individuals with 5 or more depressive symptoms were only 1.44 times more likely.

As will be discussed in greater detail, lacking control can be very stressful and have negative health consequences. People who have little or no control over their work environments are more likely to experience a heart attack or other health problems (Bosma, Marmot, Hemingway, et al., 1997; Cheng, Kawachi, Coakley, et al., 2000; Fried, Laurence, Shirom, et al., 2013). For example, men who have low perceived control over scheduling or changing their work activities have higher levels of atherosclerotic plaques (Kamarck, Muldoon, Shiffman, et al., 2007). Similarly, employees with high job demands and low control are twice as likely to die from a cardiovascular related cause (Kivimaki, Leino-Arjas, Luukkonen, et al., 2002). Finally, recent research has demonstrated some linked between job stress and obesity and absent-mindedness (Elfering, Grebner, and Boillat, 2013; Han, Trinkoff, Storr, et al., 2012; Sliter, Sliter, Withrow, et al., 2012).

STRESS AND THE IMMUNE SYSTEM

The primary function of the immune system is to fight off infectious agents and defend the body from disease. In order to accomplish this lofty goal, the body must distinguish between normal body cells and infectious agents. Luckily, the body has many immune defenses that are up for such a task. White blood cells (lymphocytes and monocytes) represent the body's first line of defense against foreign invaders. Two types of lymphocytes are important in mounting a successful immune response—T cells and B cells. While they both originate in the bone marrow, T-cells migrate to the thymus to mature, while B-cells mature in bone marrow.

The immune responses mounted by T and B cells vary somewhat. T cells facilitate cell-mediated immunity. Infectious agents are identified by macrophages (a type of monocyte) which call upon a certain type of T cell called a T helper cell. The T helper cell acts to sound a metaphorical alarm that facilitates proliferation of surrounding T cells in response to the infectious agent. This proliferation results in the activation and proliferation of cytotoxic killer cells that destroy the infectious agent. The B cells, in contrast, cause antibody-mediated immunity. Once a foreign agent has been identified, T helper cells will stimulate B cell proliferation. B cells then differentiate and generate antibodies that are specifically suited to attack one specific foreign antigen in a manner that is analogous to a lock and key. The specificity is crucial, for once the antibodies bind to the specific feature they immobilize the foreign agent and target it for destruction.

Stress has been found to compromise immune system functioning. A meta-analytic review analyzed more than 300 empirical articles describing the relationship between psychological stress and immune system functioning and concluded that the effects of stress on immune function are complex and time specific (Sergerstrom and Miller, 2004). Acute time-limited stress such as public speaking actually increased immune system functioning by increasing adaptive upregulation of natural immunity (particularly natural killer cells and lymphocytes), and suppressing specific immunity. Further, brief natural stressors such as preparing for an examination were found to alter cytokine production away from cellular immunity and towards humoral immunity. This should not come as a surprise given that the body has adapted to prepare the organism to effectively manage short-term stressors. During brief stress, the body appears to be preparing the natural immune system for infections that arise due to challenges to the integrity of the organism. These changes are the most efficient and conserve the largest amount of energy. Consistent with Selye's GAS, stress dampens immune system functioning and proves problematic when it is chronic in nature. Sergerstrom and Miller (2004) found that chronic stressors such as unemployment have negative effects on almost every functional measure of the immune system. From T helper cells to B cells, and natural killer cells, both natural and specific immunity were suppressed during stress of a chronic nature. Importantly, these effects persisted across all ages and individuals of every demographic, suggesting that no one is safe from the adverse effects of chronic stress.

Occupational Stress Prevalence

The prevalence of stress in the workplace is of interest to both employers and government. Stress is a markedly common phenomenon. According to the 2010 nationally representative General Social Survey (GSS), 27 per cent of Canadian workers reported their lives on most days as "quite a bit" or "extremely" stressful (Crompton, 2011). This equates to approximately 3.7 million Canadians who find their lives very stressful from day to day. A total of 62 per cent of these 3.7 million Canadians who live very stressful lives reported that work was their main source of stress. This equates to 16.75 per cent, or 2.3 million Canadian workers who are very stressed most days due to work related concerns. Those with lower annual income (less than \$40,000), and poor mental health were more likely to report greater stress.

MODELS OF WORKPLACE STRESS

Demand-Control model

Karasek's (1979) oft-cited Demand-Control model is arguably the most well-known and well-studied model of workplace stress. In Karasek's original model, he postulated that workplace environments with high demand combined with low control would result in greater degrees of workplace psychological strain (Bonn and Bonn, 2000; Karasek, 1979; Kristensen, 1995). In this case, job demand referred to the psychological load required by the respective job tasks in combination with work-related competing demands, including expectations, work rate, and other occupational pressures. Job control, on the other hand, was intended to reflect the amount of control an individual worker held over job tasks, job demands, and so on. In the Job Demand-Control (JDC) model the interaction of excessive job demand combined with lack of job control was presumed to result in the creation of Karasek's well-described concept of job strain. Although the combination of high demand and low control provided the primary mechanism whereby this theorist felt job strain was created, subsequent discussions regarding his model suggested alternate combinations may also prove to predict workplace outcomes. Specifically, in situations of high demand and high control, Karasek and Theorell (1990) felt that employees would be motivated to rise to the occasion so that increased demands combined with the ability to control their own environment would result in a heightened motivation, engagement, and desire to learn. Alternately, the same authors talked about low-demand, low-control jobs as creating an environment in which employee motivation and engagement would be reduced, resulting in feelings of resignation regarding empowerment in the workplace.

Despite its popularity, the JDC model has not been immune to criticism. Given use and interest in the JDC model for ongoing investigation of occupational stress, several authors have questioned whether discussions of this model intended for job demand and job control as interacting in a synergistic fashion. That is, questions have been raised about whether the combination of high job demand and low job control together create more job strain than either variable would create independently. A secondary area of criticism on the JDC model is the lack of recognition for other types of distributions that may explain the relationship between demand and control. For example, some researchers have discussed the potential value in a U-shaped explanatory model, whereby interactions between high demand and high control may be beneficial up to a certain point, at which point the benefit turns to detriment. That is, even in situations of high demand and high control, employees may experience resignation and lack of engagement, if the demands are outside of individual competency. A final criticism of the JDC model was brought to light when Johnson and others (1996) discussed the value of social support as an additional predictor in the evaluation of workplace stress. In an attempt to increase the predictive value of the JDC model, in the early 1990s Karasek and Theorell revised their original job-demand-control model to become the Job-Demand-Control-Social Support model (JDCS). According to the more recent and currently most often cited model, the greatest levels of job strain will occur in situations of a high-demand, low-control, low social support environment.

One of the primary contributions of the more recent JDCS model is its contention that the strain-related impacts of high demand and low control may be to some degree mediated in situations with high social support. In general, the JDCS model has received ample support as a useful and meaningful model in the explanation of workplace stress. Through decades of research, it has maintained its status as a primary leader in workplace stress theory.

The JDCS model continues to hold a primary position in occupational stress literature. Recent research has provided ongoing evidence for the application of this model, but also contributes to the understanding of complexity for occupational stress research. Specifically authors such as Bakker, Veldhoven and Xanthopoulou (2010) have completed research demonstrating the additional contribution of workplace aspects such as resources. Other authors have recently suggested improvements to this model that include individual variables such as person characteristics or personality (Gyorkos, Becker, Massoudi, et al., 2012; Rubino, Jansen Perry, Milam, et al., 2012). Other recent research has supported the impact of additional variables such as managerial leadership as important independent of the contribution of demand, control, and support (Westerlund, Nyberg, Bernin, et al., 2010) and that population and societal contexts influence the link between health and the prominent model (Netterstrom, Kristensen, Jensen, et al., 2010).

Effort-reward Imbalance model

The Effort-Reward Imbalance model was proposed by Siegrist (1996; 2001; Siegrist, Siegrist and Weber, 1986) and the essential components of this model suggest that occupational stress can be predicted through the balance of effort and the results of the respective effort. In reference to the workplace, this model often discusses the demands placed upon the worker and the motivational level of the worker, compared with work-related rewards such as remuneration, status, security, and so on. Fundamental tenants of this model suggest that effort and reward are placed upon a continual balance beam whereby the level of effort and reward must be complementary. In situations where effort is exceedingly high in relation to the resulting reward, the worker may feel undervalued and have minimal motivation to complete requested work tasks. In contrast, if work tasks are over-rewarded in relation to the amount of required effort, this too may impact the amount of effort and the amount of reward must be both matched and appropriate to the requested work demands.

Previous research has suggested the Effort-Reward Imbalance model may be particularly useful when completing work stress research with particular occupational groups. For example, human service professions where the effort output could often be considered intense, in combination with poor social status, and often low levels of pay may be particularly appropriate for explanation according to this model. Other research has suggested that a high degree of job strain related to such imbalance has been found to result in negative health outcomes for workers (Van Vegchel, de Jonge, Bosma, et al., 2005).

Similar to the JDC model, authors have discussed potential weaknesses of the Effort-Reward Imbalance model. Specifically, some discussion has been written about the potential lack of applicability for the ERI model across various occupational groups (de Jonge and Dorman, 2003). As well, Van Vegchel et al. (2005) highlighted the difficulty with using balance versus imbalance as dichotomous variables in complex relationships that included complicated variables such as worker perception and workplace stress. Further, other authors have criticized the ERI model for its focus on physical effort and time pressure as the primary sources of effort (Melamed, Kushnie, and Meir, 1991; Van Der Doef and Maes, 1999).

The Effort-Reward Imbalance model has recently received more attention as a useful contributor to understanding occupational stress. Specifically, degree or balance between effort and reward has been linked to several workplace factors including work ability (Bethge and Radoschewski, 2010), job performance (Feuerhahn, Kuhnel, and Kudielka, 2012), occupational well-being (Feldt, Huhtala, Kinnunen, et al., 2013), and work-related over-commitment (Birgit, Gunnevi, and Ann, 2013). Alternately, Allisey, Rodwell and Noblet (2012) completed a study with 897 police officers and found no interaction effects of over-commitment with effort or reward. In addition to workplace variables, the Effort-Reward Imbalance model has also been linked to health outcomes including vagal withdrawal (Eller, Bond, Nielson, et al., 2011), salivary cortisol (Eller, Nielson, Blond, et al., 2012), musculoskeletal symptoms (Lapointe, Dionne, Brisson, et al., 2013), cardiovascular disease (Aboa-Eboule, Brisson, Maunsell, et al., 2011; Siegrist, 2011), stress-related disorders in men (Nakata and Takahashi, 2011), emotional exhaustion (Feuerhahn, Kuhnel, and Kudielka, 2012), and hypertension (Gilber-Ouimet, Brisson, Vezina, et al., 2012).

Person-Environment Fit model

The Person-Environment Fit (PE Fit) model was developed out of the University of Michigan in the 1970s (Harrison, 1978, 1985). This model posits that one of the primary drivers for workplace stress exists in the fit between the occupational environment and the individual characteristics of the worker (for example, skill, personality, and so on). Further, the model suggests that this form of fit is bi-directional, and that ideally workplace fit requires the characteristics of the individual to fit the needs of the workplace and, similarly, the characteristics of the workplace are required to fit the needs of the worker. One of the primary strengths of this model is its consideration of individual characteristics as predictors of workplace stress. Both the effort-reward imbalance and the JDCS model essentially dismiss individual characteristics as predictors of worker outcome. However, despite the helpful addition of including individual characteristics as a predictor for occupational stress, the inclusion of individual characteristics in the Person-Environment Fit model may also be this model's greatest weakness. That is, the Person-Environment Fit model tends to negate the importance of many workplace environmental factors such as the social context within which the worker is working.

Since the original model was proposed in 1970, several follow-up models to the Person-Environment Fit model have been proposed. Specifically, the Supplies-Values Fit (SV Fit; French, Caplan, and Harrison, 1982) model, the Demands-Abilities Fit (DA Fit; Edwards, 1996) model, and the Isometric Theory

of Stress (ITS; Quick, Nelson, Quick, et al., 2001) models have all been discussed as specific renditions of the more general original model. Specifically, the SV Fit model suggests that the primary characteristic required to reduce workplace strain can be found in an appropriate match between individual values and characteristics of the worksite. In particular, this model proposes that high levels of workplace stress will be found in situations where an individual is required to compromise one's own values in order to meet the demands of the workplace.

The DA Fit model suggests that workplace stress is most likely predicted by a lack of fit between the demands of the workplace and the worker's perception about one's own abilities to meet those demands. While the Person-Environment Fit, SV Fit, and DA Fit models all propose two-dimensional models, the Isometric model proposes a multidimensional model. This model postulated that stress is multifaceted and that workplace stress is a function of the individual, the work environment, and additional variables such as control, uncertainty, and interpersonal relationships. Essentially, the Isomorphic Theory of Stress proposes that workplace strain will occur in situations where fit between the individual, environment, and other workplace and individual variables cannot be found.

Recent research employing the Person-Environment Fit model for has been less abundant than the more prominent JDCS and ERI models. Despite the relative lack of recent research applying the model, important relationships have been demonstrated. Specifically, Lambert and colleagues (Lambert, Altheimer, Hogan, et al., 2011) found that for correctional staff whose values were consistent with the organizational context, roll stress, work-family conflict, life satisfaction, and moral commitment were increased. Similarly, Ford (2012) reported a relationship between person-environment fit and improved job satisfaction, perceived support, and depression. Finally, Miles and Perrewé (2011) found that person-environment fit was a mediator between training satisfaction and job satisfaction, and between work area design and job-induced tension.

Transactional model

The essential tenant of the Transactional model of stress is based upon Lazarus' (1966) transactional theory which posits that all relationships are interpreted through a dynamic cognitive evaluation of the environment. That is, an employee's experience of the workplace and related workplace stress cannot be measured solely by objective stressors and related capabilities, but must also take into consideration individual personal characteristics, personal resources, and personal ways of perceiving the world. In particular, this model is novel in that it requires consideration of a cognitive appraisal related to the demand resource relationship prior to estimating the degree of strain that will be experienced.

The primary value in this relationship is the recognition that workplace events and worker characteristics do not occur in a vacuum, but rather are always interpreted through the lens of the individual worker. In this way, this model is useful for considering workplace stress as a phenomenon that is relative to the individual; for asking the question of why some workers interpret workplaces as very stressful while others do not. This strength in the Transactional model can also be interpreted as a weakness. That is, in its efforts to include the cognitive appraisal of the individual worker as an important predictor in the interpretation of workplace events, this model risks the potential lack of recognition for meaningful workplace variables such as overarching organizational stressors.

Little recent research has specifically employed the Transactional model in occupational stress research. However, Cash and Gardner and found that for New Zealand employees (n = 297), "higher levels of hardiness were associated with more positive appraisals and more coping responses" (Cash and Gardner, 2011, p. 646).

Assessment of Stress

Workplace stress as a disability category is a misunderstood and unclear concept. The primary message that can be relayed here is that stress is not currently a diagnosable mental illness, nor is it typically included as a disability code for most standardized disability benefit or categorization definitions. As discussed in other chapters in this text, diagnosable psychopathology is dictated by the current version of the Diagnostic and Statistical Manual (American Psychiatric Association, 2013). Although this manual is interpreted by many types of professionals, typically in North American society a recognized diagnosis according to the DSM requires assessment by a physician, psychiatrist, or psychologist. Under DSM diagnoses, work-related stress must be reflected in the development of a subsequent mental health diagnosis. For example, as highlighted earlier in this chapter, work-related stress may result in development of depression, anxiety, adjustment disorders, substance misuse, and so on. If occupational stress has resulted in any of these types of diagnosable disorders, the identified issue will typically be compensated under some type of disability claim. If, however, occupational stress is the primary complaint, with no accompanying diagnosable DSM category, compensation for work-related disability will be less likely.

Recent changes to worker's compensation legislation in some jurisdictions (for example, Bill 14 in British Columbia, Canada; Government of BC, 2011) have increased coverage so that a mental illness resulting from a "cumulative series of significant work related stresses" may now be compensable. Previously, a compensable worker's compensation claim required an identifiable incident to which the mental health issue could be linked. For example, a bank teller who experienced a bank robbery while at work would likely have a successful compensation claim for post-traumatic stress disorder related to the robbery. However, other types of cumulative stress issues such as depression or anxiety due to workplace harassment, or regular exposure to traumatic events in the workplace would not be covered by workers' compensation. Illnesses related to these types of less definable incidents required disability insurance for which direct linkage to the workplace was not necessary (for example, short-term or long-term disability insurance). Despite the fact that the present changes in the legislative environment for some jurisdictions will allow more recipients of benefits for workers' compensation as a result of mental health issues related to workplace stress, a diagnosable DSM disorder remains the primary criteria upon which this type of claim will be evaluated. Regardless of type of compensation requested, in most cases a mental health assessment completed by a physician, psychiatrist, or psychologist will remain the central method of determining eligibility for coverage.

Many employers feel confused by the lack of clarity regarding the evaluation and determination of workplace stress-related illness. As discussed above, research shows that positive stress in the workplace can increase employee motivation, productivity, and engagement. Therefore, employers should not be seeking the absolute removal of workplace stress as the most desirable outcome. However, when job requirements or other workplace characteristics become unbalanced with the capabilities of the individual worker, negative occupational stress can result, ultimately leading to subsequent illness. When subsequent illness occurs and an employee is requesting disability benefits due to stress-related physical or psychological impacts, often employers and/or disability providers will request documentation of such impacts prior to providing benefits. Regardless of the nature of the resulting complaint, either physical or psychological, assessment of workplace stress-related illness requires the assessment professional to consider several primary factors in their evaluation. In order to adequately address the work-related nature of a physiological or psychological complaint, an assessment professional should be seeking information about personal factors such as personality, coping skills, previous injuries and illnesses, and so on; work-related factors such as job satisfaction, job demand, job control, performance issues, and rate of remuneration; social factors such as family issues, financial issues, and social support in the workplace; organizational factors such as organizational culture and structure; environmental factors such as jobless rate and social acceptance of disability; as well as any other physical or psychosocial variables that may help to explain the individual's present disability status. Each of these factors has been strongly supported as important to consider when evaluating workplace stress, both by long-standing theories of occupational stress, as well as by subsequent research evaluating these ideas.

Psychological Variables

Psychological variables that may contribute to the development of workplace stress fall into the categories of cognitive, emotional/motivational, and personality. Cognitive variables are usually described as aspects of the individual related to their understanding of the world. Such cognitive variables will often include individual aspects such as intellectual aptitude for a particular job demand, as well as more generalized capabilities such as attention, memory, and executive functioning (scheduling/planning and so on). Individual variables such as intellect may contribute to workplace stress through various mechanisms. In particular, the Person-Environment Fit model, and more specifically the Demands-Abilities Fit model, may be especially useful for understanding the potential impact of intellectual capability on the development of workplace stress. If the intellectual or neuropsychological requirements of a particular occupational position are beyond the intellectual capacity of a respective worker, there may be limited fit between the individual and workplace characteristics. For example, if an individual has difficulty with quickly shifting focus and has chosen a career as a lawyer, there may be limited fit between individual abilities and typical courtroom activities.

Personality variables may also contribute to workplace stress and some research has investigated the value of personality as a predictor for related aspects such as vocational success and workplace resilience. Many theories of personality are currently available, with three of the most well known including Costa and McCrae's Five Factor model (1985, 1992a, 1992b, 1992c), Cattell's 16PF (Cattell and Krug, 1986), and Eysenck's Three Factor model

(Eysenck and Eysenck, 1975). The FFM is based upon lexical descriptions of behavior that followed five major dimensions meant to describe consistent traits (extroversion, neuroticism, openness to experience, agreeableness, and conscientiousness). This model approaches measurement of personality on scale descriptions anchored by opposites (for example, extroversion-introversion; agreeableness-antagonism). The FFM posits that personality characteristics are stable, lifelong and measurable. Eysenck's Three Factor model is similar to the FFM in that it discusses broad dimensions intended to reflect a group of specific traits. However, instead of five domains of personality as described by the FFM, the Three Factor model uses extroversion, neuroticism, and psychoticism as its three primary factors. Finally, Cattell's 16PF uses factor analytic techniques to provide a pictorial representation of individual personality according to a personality profile created from 16 dimensions. Specifically, these dimensions include cool-warm, concrete thinking-abstract thinking, affected by feelings-emotionally stable, submissive-dominant, sober-enthusiastic, expedient-conscientious, shy-bold, tough-minded-tender, trusting-suspicious, practical-imaginative, forthright-shrewd, self-assured-apprehensive, conservative-experimenting-group orientated-self-sufficient, undisciplined self conflict-following self image, and relaxed-tense (Cattell and Krug, 1986).

Recent research regarding the impact of personality on occupational stress is limited. Further, the literature on personality as a predictor for workplace stress varies in terms of its theoretical orientation, so that an overall general summation of available research on this topic is difficult to create. However, according to the second author's general read of the research in this area, several consistent themes seem to persist. These themes can be summarized to suggest that the characteristics agreeableness, extraversion, and openness to experience appear to create generalized workplace resilience, and assist in the prevention of workplace stress. In contrast, the individual characteristic neuroticism seems consistently to result in negative impacts on workplace outcomes (for example, Liu, Wang, Zhan, et al., 2009; Meng, Chen, Li, et al., 2009).

Using our workplace models to help explain the influence of personality on workplace stress, the most appropriate model once again seems to be Person-Environment Fit. Ideally, individual personality will interact in a complementary way with the demands of the worksite. For example, the hospitality industry often requires individuals with outgoing, happy and extroverted personalities. If a neurotic, introverted individual chose employment as a children's entertainer at a family-focused hotel, that individual would likely feel significant stress about the lack of fit between his/her inherent tendencies and the outgoing, friendly requirements of the position.

The final psychological variable to be discussed here is that of emotional and/ or motivational variables. Although often lumped in as a form of personality variables, emotional and motivational variables can often be differentiated from conventionally described personality variables by their relatively transient nature. Whereas traditionally described personality variables are typically considered to be enduring characteristics that influence behavior across a variety of contexts, emotional and motivational variables tend to be described as more transitory and situation-specific. These types of variables include factors such as individual approaches to mood, coping style, locus of control, self-efficacy, resilience, and so on. Aspects of mood that could be included as an emotional variable impacting the workplace could be feelings of depression or sadness that could have a negative impact on employee level of productivity or relationships with co-workers and supervisors. Alternately, a personal situation with no relationship to the workplace (for example, a new relationship) may create a feeling of sociability and happiness for a particular worker, potentially increasing productivity and improving workplace relationships. Coping style has also been linked to workplace stress such that individuals with a problem-focused coping style have been found to cope more effectively with workplace stress (for example, Wallace, Lee, and Lee, 2010). In contrast, individuals who tend to approach difficulties with emotion-focused coping styles (for example, distancing) seem to experience increased levels of occupational strain. Similarly, individuals with an internal locus of control, greater self-efficacy, and more abundant resilience will tend to have greater capacity to deal with workplace demands.

The impact of emotional and/or motivational variables seems to fit well with several of our workplace stress models. Specifically, the Person-Environment Fit model may be applicable for emotional and motivational variables, for similar reasons as those described above with respect to personality characteristics. However, the Supplies-Values Fit model may be particularly applicable for these variables. That is, if an individual is highly motivated toward a certain value set, a workplace that shared a similar set of values may be particularly motivating and emotionally fulfilling. Similarly, the Effort-Reward Imbalance model may also be applicable for these variables for related reasons. Individuals who are highly motivated by, or emotionally attached to, a particular environment may feel that ample effort is justified in exchange for the rewarding fulfillment of the workplace. Finally, the transactional theory of stress may be applicable to emotional and motivational variables. If the worksite is motivating and emotionally fulfilling for a respective worker, this will be the lens through which all other cognitive appraisals of workplace characteristics will take place. Regardless of the model chosen through which to interpret emotional and motivational variables, examples of individual worker behavior remain similar. For example, workers who choose religious and/or social service work often opt to participate in this highly demanding and often comparatively poorly remunerated field in exchange for the potential fulfillment provided by the motivational and emotional reward.

Physical Variables

Physical factors such as weight, nutrition status, exercise status, sleep status, and access to healthcare have also been investigated as potential contributors to workplace stress. Research regarding nutrition and exercise status suggests that workers with better nutritional and exercise habits are healthier overall and, consequently, more likely to be capable of coping with workplace demands. Nutrition plays a role in ability to focus, as well as one's bodily health (for example, Stancil and Hicks, 2009). Similarly, regular exercise is vital to increased physical function and also plays a significant role in improving psychological functioning through aspects such as improved self-esteem and stress reduction (for example, Nishida and Otomo, 2010). Weight has also been investigated as a potential contributor to workplace stress, although the bulk of literature considering weight as a workplace predictor has considered the impact of overweight status as a predictor of disability (for example, Duijts, Kant, Swaen, et al., 2007). Generally, overweight or obese status could contribute to workplace stress through the function of increased risk of physical injury, increased physical demands created by additional weight, as well as psychological consequences of overweight or obese status (for example, reduced self-esteem).

Sleep status and access to healthcare may be related to workplace stress in manners similar to those discussed above. That is, ample sleep is required for optimum physiological and psychological functioning. Without positive sleep status, a worker may find the physical demands of the workplace overwhelm the energy level available in an overtired state. Furthermore, a lack of adequate sleep often leads to psychological consequences such as decreased focus and irritability, both of which may impact an individual's ability to complete workplace tasks and get along in the workplace social environment. Access to healthcare may be alike in its relationship to workplace stress in that inadequate care of one's health may be a strong predictor of difficulty meeting workplace demands. Untreated physical illness may result in an inability to meet the physical demands of the workplace and may also interfere with psychological functioning as described for other physical symptoms.

From the perspective of workplace stress theory, physical variables may be most adequately explained by using the Person-Environment Fit model, specifically the Demands-Abilities Fit model, or the Effort-Reward Imbalance model. From the perspective of the Demands-Abilities Fit model, individual level of physical functioning would be required to fit with the physical demands of the worksite. Similarly, the Effort-Reward Imbalance model would suggest that the physical demands of the worksite must be consistent with the level of remuneration provided in exchange. For example, in a physically demanding job such as construction worker, a fit would be required between the necessity of carrying heavy construction materials, and the inherent physical capabilities of the worker (for example, strength). In addition, construction work requires regular involvement in highly demanding physical tasks, often completed in unfavorable weather. Consequently, according to the Effort-Reward Imbalance model, construction work would require suitable wage, working hours, benefits, job satisfaction, or other variables to compensate for the required physical demands.

Social Variables

Social variables that may impact workplace stress include factors at the organizational, supervisory, co-worker, and personal level. Organizational culture has been strongly supported as a factor in prediction of workplace stress and related disability (for example, Shim, 2010). Organizational culture may include contributors to workplace stress such as lack of fairness and equity in the workplace, negative perceptions of illness and disability, reorganizational stress, managerial involvement (too much or too little), and benefit levels. Other organizational factors that may be predictive of workplace stress include job flexibility, access to accommodations, and overall organizational value placed on workers.

At the supervisory level, research has suggested that the front-line supervisor is one of the most important predictors of workplace adjustment (for example, Sterner, 2009). A direct supervisor who lacks strong supervisory skills or who harasses or belittles employees certainly has the potential to contribute to workplace stress. At the co-worker level, stress may be induced by interpersonal conflict, lack of fairness in completion of job tasks, noninclusive social groupings, and other group-related dynamics. Workplace social variables as a predictor for occupational stress may be most clearly explained through use of the Transactional or Job-Demand-Control-Support models. That is, individuals who feel supported in their workplace are more likely to have coping resources necessary to meet the demands of employment. If a worker feels highly supported at work, occupational demands will be seen through a positive lens regarding social support in the workplace. With respect to other important factors, organizational and supervisory climate will have an intimate impact on worker control and demand in the workplace. For example, an emergency room nurse who is required to regularly cope with traumatic human suffering, but who has several other co-workers from whom she can access help and support, may find the demands of her workplace entirely manageable. However, this same nurse may continue to feel workplace stress despite the support of her co-workers, because she feels that her supervisors and managers do not understand the truly difficult nature of her job.

Although social support in the workplace is an important factor in the prediction of workplace stress, personal social support also plays a role in the maintenance of psychological well-being and related stress prevention. Research suggests that strong personal support available via romantic relationships, family relationships, friendships, group-related relationships (for example, religious-based organizations), and other forms of social support increase individual capacity to cope with a variety of stressful situations, including workplace stress (Jimmieson, McKimmie, Hannam, et al., 2010). In the same way that workplace social support fits well with the Transactional and Job-Demand-Control-Support models, personal social support can be regarded using the same models; that is to say, personal social support may help mediate workplace stress directly, and also may create a positive perception through which workplace demands are viewed. For example, the same nurse who feels frustration about not being supported by her supervisors and managers may have a very strong romantic partner who is willing to listen and provide empathy regarding her workplace frustrations. As a result, her personal social relationship helps to mediate her overall level of workplace stress.

Societal/Environmental Variables

Societal and environmental variables as predictors of work stress are overarching influences that may be largely beyond the control of the worker, employer, or organization. Some such variables include the social acceptance of stress as a disability according to the present values of the respective society. These types of values may then be directed into practice through political ideologies and legislative choices. Access to compensation for stress-related disability will fluctuate according to the political and social climate of the times. Further, social factors such as acceptance of diversity (for example, gender, religious, or cultural factors) may impact the level of workplace stress experienced by traditional minority groups. Finally, social and environmental factors will dictate work stress as it relates to job climate. In times of reduced economic prosperity, greater likelihood of layoffs, downsizing, and so on, in combination with increased likelihood of unemployment, may create ample opportunity for occupational stress.

From the perspective of our models, the only model that seems to fit with the overarching nature of social and environmental variables is the Transactional model. Namely, the Transactional model allows for cognitive appraisal of the environment to impact individual interpretation of the workplace situation. For example, an Islamic salesperson that depends on a good economy to make his sales could experience substantial work-related stress if he is working many hours but not making any sales. Also, if the company he works for is based in a geographic region with less influence of human rights requirements, he may be considered the most expendable employee because of his minority status. In this case, the worker may actually report limited workplace stress in order to reconcile his working situation and the environmental factors that may make him place high value on his current position.

Job Factors as Predictors of Disability

Recently a comprehensive synthesis of systematic reviews was completed in British Columbia (White, Wagner, Schultz, et al., 2012). Although the synthesis was focused on predictors of disability as opposed to predictors of workplace stress specifically, ample research suggests that psychosocial factors such as workplace stress are important predictors in most forms of disability. Consequently, the succinct findings of this review may provide useful advice for employers attempting to reduce disability costs as a result of workplace stress factors.

Evidence from the synthesis was divided into four categories: workplace factors (modifiable and non-modifiable) and worker factors (modifiable and non-modifiable). For modifiable workplace factors, strong evidence was available to suggest that lack of social support, increased job strain, increased physical demands, low job satisfaction, lack of supervisory support, increased psychological demands, and lack of worker control were related to increased rates of disability. In addition, moderate-level evidence was available for a link between disability status and non-full-time work, poor quality leadership, lack of job control, lack of fairness in the workplace, and lack of managerial involvement. Weak-level evidence was available for increased absenteeism tolerance, reorganizational stress, and increased time to treatment.

For non-modifiable workplace factors, only moderate-level evidence was available for the link between disability status and predictive factors. The specific predictive factors identified through the synthesis included lower occupational level, existence of a workers' compensation claim, and decreased length of employment.

At the level of the worker, strong evidence was available for the modifiable variables emotional distress, increased depressive symptoms, negative injuring psychological characteristics (for example, neuroticism), negative health and disability perceptions, decreased activity levels, lack of family support, poor general health, increased functional disability factors, increased pain, increased fatigue, and lack of encouragement for earlier return to work. Moderate-level evidence was available for the modifiable worker factors sleep difficulties and substance use; whereas, only weak-level evidence was available for the factor lack of non-work physical activity.

For the relationship between non-modifiable worker factors and disability, strong evidence was found for older age, poor personal functioning, increased psychological symptoms, increased clinical factors, decreased physical functioning, increased sick leave history, lower educational involvement, overweight status, and increased emotional distress. Moderate evidence was found for non-married status, female gender (only for rheumatoid arthritis and low back pain), and presence of respiratory conditions. Weak evidence was found for the relationship between disability and rural residence, negative injuring psychological characteristics, medication use, and the discriminatory impacts of non-white ethnic status.

Although the level of evidence provided is entirely dependent on the available literature, factors with strong and/or moderate-level evidence provided well-supported avenues for interventions regarding workplace stress. Although factors not currently supported as strong or moderate evidence may subsequently move into these categories as more research is completed, employers would be well advised to consider the currently substantiated categories as important places to start when attempting to reduce occupational stress and related disability costs. In particular, modifiable workplace variables such as workplace social support and job-related physical and/or psychological demands may be the easiest and most meaningful initial starting points.

Interventions

A comprehensive coverage of stress management interventions is beyond the scope of this chapter and the interested reader is referred to books by Biron, Karanika-Murray and Cooper (2012) and Weinberg, Sutherland and Cooper (2010). In brief, workplace stress management interventions can be conceptualized by adopting a tripartite model. Primary-level stress management interventions use organizational-level strategies that are geared towards preventing work stress by targeting the stressor. Secondary-level stress management interventions target the individual employee and are response-driven; they aim to develop stress resistance and coping skills through education and training. Tertiary-level stress management interventions are symptom directed and aim to cure and rehabilitate stressed and distressed employees.

Primary (stressor directed) strategies can focus on the macro-environment (for example, organizational culture, workload, safety climate), the micro-environment (for example, task redesign, alternate work arrangements, communication exercises), or employee perceived control.

The macro-environment includes organizational culture and policies that are amenable to change. For example, stress at work can be reduced by designing and building an organizational culture that is open, supportive, compassionate to employee concerns, and places high value on workplace personnel. A review of more than 70 studies indicated that work organizations governed by fairness, supervisory support, organizational rewards, and favorable job conditions were associated with employee positive mood, job satisfaction, affective commitment, and higher performance (Rhoades and Eisenberger, 2002).

Training courses offering management coaching and coping can also be implemented to reduce employee stress and improve well-being. For example, a case-control intervention in the UK suggests that coaching decreased psychological strain among managers, and improved personal development among staff (Weinberg, 2008). Further, a meta-analysis of 18 studies reported that organizational coaching interventions improved employee performance, well-being, coping, work attitudes, and self-regulation with effects ranging between $g = .43$ and $g = .74$ (Theeboom, Beersma and van Vianen, 2013).

Employees are often required to work long hours (for example, > 50 hours each week), potentially resulting in occupational strain. A study of 936 call centre employees reported that work overload was associated with musculoskeletal disorders and that this association was mediated by job strain (Sprigg et al., 2007). Reducing work overload and increasing flexibility in scheduling are effective methods for lowering employee stress due to work overload. Other methods of altering the macro-environment to reduce work stress include: 1) minimizing the impact of working in dangerous or hazardous conditions; 2) preventing employee demotivation, frustration, and feelings of injustice by instating career development programs and favourable psychological contracts (for example, provision of realistic and honest job description, reduction of uncertainty by appraisal interview; Turnley and Feldman, 2000; Warr, 2007); and 3) preventing and managing workplace bullying (see Chapter 8 for additional information on workplace bullying).

The micro-environment consists of altering work systems and practices (that is, job design) in order to prevent stress. It is well known that jobs characterized by high demand and low control are strongly associated with employee stress and illness. Redesigning or enriching a job to increase worker skill and autonomy and providing opportunities for decision-making can be used to prevent employee stress. One source of employee stress is work-family conflict. A meta-analysis of work family-conflict examined 427 effect sizes and reported that work-family conflict was negatively associated with numerous employee performance and well-being indices with small to moderate effects (Amstad, Meier, Fasel, et al., 2011). Some methods for redesigning the workplace include creating a family-friendly work environment, offering flexible work hours, and providing supervisors and management skill development in offering work-family support. Family-friendly work environments can improve organizational profitability (Kinnunen, Mauno, Geurts, et al., 2005) and decrease tardiness, sickness absence, and turnover (Baltes, Briggs, Huff, et al., 1999; Dalton and Mesch, 1990; Kauffeld, Jonas, and Frey, 2004). Further, a meta-analysis of 85 studies comprising over 70,000 employees reported that supervisory and organizational work-family support (that is, support for the employees ability to jointly manage work and family relationships) was instrumental in reducing work-family conflict (Kossek, Baltes and Matthews, 2011).

Role ambiguity is another source of workplace stress that can be managed using job redesign. For example, an intervention designed to reduce role stress by facilitating balance in clinical and administrative workloads among nurses in the UK reported that reducing role stress improved performance, staff development functions, and organizational culture (Randall, Cox, and

Griffiths, 2007). Similarly, tweaking job characteristics to improving perceptions of worker control and worker participation in decision-making can effectively reduce work stress, anxiety, and depression (see review by Egan, Bambra, Thomas, et al., 2007). Strategies to minimize role ambiguity typical involve fostering employee autonomy and may include developing semi-autonomous work groups, implementing safety improvement programs, or providing health circles. For example, reinstituting a policy that allowed the rail transport managers to address faults with station equipment increased employee satisfaction and well-being (Randall, Griffiths, and Cox, 2005). Similarly, training employees to rectify machine faults reportedly increased production time by 6 percent and output by $125,000 (Leach, Jackson and Wall, 2001), while increasing employee job related knowledge reduced psychological strain (Leach, Jackson and Wall, 2003).

Secondary (that is, response-driven) stress management interventions focus on techniques to help the individual employee manage and cope with stress. Such techniques may include: skills training/education and wellness programs. Organizations can reduce employee stress by providing classes offering techniques that can be added to an employee's stress management toolbox (for example, social skills training, assertiveness training, cognitive coping strategies, time management, relaxation training, anger management). For example, six 5-hour social skills training classes (for example, clarifying misunderstandings, providing constructive feedback, and asking others for help) enhanced mental health and job satisfaction among a sample of 785 employees (Heaney et al., 1995). In another intervention among 166 financial service agents, teaching employees workplace-adapted cognitive behavioral techniques improved job satisfaction, self-esteem, and productivity while reducing psychological distress (Proudfoot, Corr, Guest, et al., 2009). Further, clear direction, planning, and prioritizing were the most important predictors of perceived work effectiveness among university staff and students (Kearns and Gardiner, 2007), suggesting the importance of time management in reducing stress (see review by Richards, 1987). Furthermore, relaxation therapy was reported to reduce work stress and improve life satisfaction among a sample of high school teachers (Kaspereen, 2012) and a recovery training program that included relaxation training reportedly increased employee recovery from job stress (Hahn et al., 2011). There is some evidence that cognitive behavioral skill development may be particularly effective for minimizing employee stress. A review of meta-analyses for managing stress at work reported that cognitive coping skill development was more effective at reducing employee strain, anxiety, and depression than other secondary stress management strategies (Bhui, Dinos, Stansfeld, et al., 2012). Skills and education awareness training may confer additional physiological benefits such as reductions in cortisol (Theorell, Emdad, Arnetz, et al., 2001), blood pressure, and heart rate (Murphy, 1996).

Many organizations have instituted wellness programs to help employees maintain optimal health by choosing healthy behaviors (for example, healthy weight, avoidance of substance use, and good sleep hygiene). These programs have been somewhat successful. A large-scale intervention covering 10,000 employees of 32 organizations in nine English regions provided well-being initiatives focused on physical activity, sport and recreation, nutrition, alcohol consumption, smoking cessation, and health checks (Bull, Adams, Hooper, et al., 2008). The initiative was found to reduce employee absenteeism by 20 per cent.

Tertiary stress management interventions are designed to assist employees who have been exposed to significant stress or strain in recovery. These intervention techniques are reactive rather than proactive. Strained or stressed employees have been found to benefit from a number of options. One intervention is the use of psychological counseling services. While their effectiveness has been debated, research evidence suggests that counseling services in the workplace tend to benefit individual employees (for example, McLeod, 2008, 2010) and organizations, with accompanying significant reductions in sick absences of approximately 60 per cent (Masi and Jacobson, 2003). It is worth noting that employees can often gain access to short-term independent services (for example, counseling) through the use of employee assistance programs. Another option is to offer training in basic counseling skills to supervisors and managers. Finally, employees may benefit from social support on the job as well as a short-term respite from work (that is, career sabbaticals).

While particularly beneficial for individual outcomes (Bhui, Dinos, Stansfeld, et al., 2012), the effects of individual-level stress management interventions appear to be generally short-lived and decline over time. Evidence suggests that the effects of organizational-level stress management interventions last longer than those of individual-level interventions (Giga, Noblet, Faragher, et al., 2003). However, it must be recognized that stress-related problems are multifaceted and best managed by organizations and individual employees working in a collegial manner. Research suggests that integrating individual- and organizational-level stress management interventions have effects that are stronger and more enduring than either level of intervention offered in isolation (Awa, Plaumann and Walter, 2010).

Concluding Remarks

As the present chapter demonstrates, prevention of workplace stress requires participation at the individual, job, supervisory, organizational, and social/environmental levels. Although it is not entirely clear which specific factors must be altered in order to prevent workplace stress, what is clear is that without cooperation at all levels, workplace stress will not be managed. An individual with perfect personal coping mechanisms cannot be immune to the stressful impacts of a highly disorganized, conflict-driven or unsupported workplace. Alternately, an individual with minimal personal coping mechanisms may experience significant and impairing occupational stress even in organizational environments with high levels of support, ideal interactions between job demands and control, and no threat of reorganization or downsizing. Consequently, a multidimensional approach to occupational stress management, one that attempts to mitigate all manageable distress-inducing factors, provides the best approach for prevention of stress in the workplace and should be model of choice for employers.

More information can be found at the following sources;

http://www.helpguide.org/mental/work_stress_management.htm

http://www.apa.org/helpcenter/work-stress.aspx

http://www.ccohs.ca/oshanswers/psychosocial/stress.html

References

Aboa-Eboule, C., Brisson, C., Maunsell, E., Bourbonnais, R., Milot, A., and Dagenais, G. (2011). Effort-reward imbalance at work and re-current coronary heart disease events: a four year prospective study of post-myocardial infarction patients. *Psychosomatic Medicine*, 73(6), 436–47.

Allisey, A., Rodwell, J., and Noblet, A. (2012). Personality and the effort-reward imbalance model of stress: individual differences in reward sensitivity. *Work and Stress*, 26(3), 230–251.

American Psychiatric Associaton. (2013). Diagnostic and statistical manual of mental disorders (5th ed.). Washington, DC: APA.

American Psychiatric Associaton. (2004). *Diagnostic and Statistical Manual of Mental Disorders (4th ed.) Text Revision*. Washington, DC: APA.

Amstad, F.T., Meier, L.L., Fasel, U., Elfering, A., and Semmer, N.K. (2011). A meta-analysis of work–family conflict and various outcomes with a special emphasis on cross-domain versus matching-domain relations. *Journal of Occupational Health Psychology*, 16(2), 151.

Awa, W.L., Plaumann, M., and Walter, U. (2010). Burnout prevention: a review of intervention programs. *Patient Education and Counseling*, 78(2), 184–90.

Azagba, S. and Sharaf, M.F. (2011). Psychosocial working conditions and the utilization of health care services. *BMC Public Health*, 11, 642 (Open Access).

Bakker, A.B., van Veldhoven, M., and Xanthopoulou, D. (2010). Beyond the demand-control model: thriving on high job demands and resources. *Journal of Personnel Psychology*, 9(1), 3–16.

Baltes, B.B., Briggs, T.E., Huff, J.W., Wright, J.A., and Neuman, G.A. (1999). Flexible and compressed workweek schedules: A meta-analysis of their effects on work-related criteria. *Journal of Applied Psychology*, 84(4), 496.

Bethge, M. and Radoschewski, F.M. (2012). Adverse effects of effort-reward imbalance on workability: longitudinal findings from the German socio-medical panel of employees. *International Journal of Public Health*, 57(5), 797–805.

Bhui, K.S., Dinos, S., Stansfeld, S.A., and White, P.D. (2012). A synthesis of the evidence for managing stress at work: a review of the reviews reporting on anxiety, depression, and absenteeism. *Journal of Environmental and Public Health*, 2012.

Birgit, E., Gunnevi, S., and Ann, O. (2013). Work experiences among nurses and physicians in the beginning of their professional careers: analyses using the effort-reward imbalance model. *Scandinavian Journal of Caring Sciences*, 27(1), 36–43.

Biron, C., Karanika-Murray, M. and Cooper, C. (2012). *Improving Organizational Interventions for Stress and Well-being: Addressing Process and Context.* New York, NY: Routledge.

Bonn, D. and Bonn, J. (2000). Workplace and related stress: can it be a thing of the past? *Lancet*, 355, 124.

Bosma, H., Marmot, M.G., Hemingway, H., Nicholson, A.C., Brunner, E., and Stansfeld, S.A. (1997). Low job control and risk of coronary heart disease in Whitehall II (prospective cohort) study. *BMJ*, 314(7080), 558–65.

Bull, F.C., Adams, E.J., Hooper, P.L., and Jones, C.A. (2008). Well@ Work: A summary report and calls to action. British Heart Foundation, London.

Burton, W., Chen, C., Conti, D., Schultz, A., Pransky, G., and Edington, D. (2005). The association of health risks with on-the-job productivity. *Journal of Occupational and Environmental Medicine*, 47(8), 769–77.

Cash, M. and Gardner, D. (2011). Cognitive hardiness, appraisal and coping: comparing two transactional models. *Journal of Managerial Psychology*, 26(8), 646–64.

Cattell, R.B. and Krug, S.E. (1986). The number of factors in the 16 PF: a review of the evidence with special emphasis on methodological problems. *Educational and Psychological Measurement*, 46, 509–22.

Cheng, Y., Kawachi, I., Coakley, E.H., Schwartz, J., and Colditz, G. (2000). Association between psychosocial work characteristics and health functioning in American women: prospective study. *BMJ*, 320(7247), 1432–6.

Comcare, ABN. (2009). *Compendium of OHS and Workers' Compensation Statistics*. Retrieved from: http://www.srcc.gov.au/__data/assets/pdf_file/0003/57333/00524_SRCC_Compendium_v17.pdf.

Costa, P.T. and McCrae, R.R. (1985). *The NEO Personality Inventory Manual*. Odessa, Fla: Psychological Assessment Resources.

Costa, P.T. and McCrae, R.R. (1992a). Four ways five factors are basic. *Personality and Individual Differences*, 13, 653–65.

Costa, P.T. and McCrae, R.R. (1992b). "Four ways five factors are *not* basic": reply. *Personality and Individual Differences*, 13, 861–5.

Costa, P.T., Jr. and McCrae, R.R. (1992c). *Revised NEO Personality Inventory (NEO-PI-R) and the NEO Five-Factor Inventory (NEO-FFI) Professional Manual*. Odessa, Fla: Psychological Assessment Resources.

Crompton, S. (Oct., 2011). What's Stressing the Stressed: Main Sources of Stress among Workers. Component of Statistics Canada Catalogue no. 11-008-X Canadian Social Trends. Retrieved from: http://www.statcan.gc.ca/pub/11-008-x/2011002/article/11562-eng.pdf, October 12, 2012.

Dalton, D.R. and Mesch, D.J. (1990). The impact of flexible scheduling on employee attendance and turnover. *Administrative Science Quarterly*, 370–387.

DeFrank, R.S. and Ivancevich, J.M. (1998). Stress on the job: an executive update. *Academy of Management Executive*, 12(3), 55–66.

Duijts, S.F., Kant, I., Swaen, G.M., van den Brandt, P.A., and Zeegers, M.P. (2007). A meta-analysis of observational studies identifies predictors of sickness absence. *Journal of Clinical Epidemiology*, 60(11), 1105–15.

Jonge, J. de and Dormann, C. (2003). The DISC Model: Demand-Induced Strain Compensation Mechanisms in Job Stress. In: M.F. Dollard, A.H. Winefield, & H.R. Winefield (eds), *Occupational Stress in the Service Professions* (pp. 43–74). London: Taylor & Francis.

Edwards, J.E. (1996). An examination of competing versions of the person-environment fit approach to stress. *Academy of Management Journal*, 39(2), 292–339.

Egan, M., Bambra, C., Thomas, S., Petticrew, M., Whitehead, M., and Thomson, H. (2007). The psychosocial and health effects of workplace reorganisation. 1. A systematic review of organisational-level interventions that aim to increase employee control. *Journal of Epidemiology and Community Health*, 61(11), 945–54.

Elfering, A., Grebner, S., and Boillat, C. (2013). Busy at work and absent-minded at home: mental workload, cognitive failure, and domestic falls. *Swiss Journal of Psychology*, 72(4), 219–28.

Eller, N., Blond, M., Nielsen, M., Kristiansen, J., and Netterstrom, B. (2011). Effort reward imbalance is associated with vagal withdrawal in Danish public sector employees . *International Journal of Psychophysiology*, 81(3), 218–24.

Eller, N., Nielsen, S., Blond, M., Nielsen, M., Hansen, A., and Netterstrom, B. (2012). Effort reward imbalance, and salivary cortisol in the morning. *Biological Psychology*, 89(2), 342–8.

Elovainio, M., Kivimäki, M., Steen, N., and Kalliomäki-Levanto, T. (2000). Organizational and individual factors affecting mental health and job satisfaction: a multilevel analysis of job control and personality. *Journal of Occupational Health Psychology*, 5, 269–77.

Ettner, S.L. and Grzywacz, J.G. (2001). Workers' perceptions of how jobs affect health: a social ecological perspective. *Journal of Occupational Health Psychology*, 6(2), 101–13.

Eysenck, H.J. and Eysenck, S.B.G. (1975). *Manual of the Eysenck Personality Questionnaire*. San Diego: Edits.

Feldt, T., Huhtala, M., Kinnunen, U., Hyvonen, K., Makikangas, A., and Sonnentag, S. (2013). Long-term patterns of effort-reward imbalance and over-commitment: investigating occupational well-being and recovery experiences as outcomes. *Work and Stress*, 27(1), 64–87.

Feuerhahn, N., Kuhnel, J., and Kudielka, B. (2012). Interaction effects of effort-reward imbalance and over commitment on emotional exhaustion and job performance. *International Journal of Stress Management*, 19(2), 105–31.

Ford, M. (2012). Job-occupation misfit as an occupational stressor. *Journal of Vocational Behavior*, 80(2), 412–21.

French, J.R.P., Jr, Caplan, R.D., and Harrison, R.V. (1982). *The Mechanisms of Job Stress and Strain*. New York: Wiley.

Fried, Y., Laurence, G.A., Shirom, A., Melamed, S., Toker, S., Berliner, S., et al. (2013). The relationship between job enrichment and abdominal obesity: a longitudinal field study of apparently healthy individuals. *Journal of Occupational Health Psychology*, 18(4), 458–68.

Giga, S.I., Noblet, A.J., Faragher, B., and Cooper, C.L. (2003). The UK perspective: a review of research on organisational stress management interventions. *Australian Psychologist*, 38(2), 158–64.

Gilber-Ouimet, M., Brisson, C., Vezina, M., Milot, A., and Blanchette, C. (2012). Repeated exposure to effort-reward imbalance, increased blood pressure, and hypertension incidence among white-collar workers: effort reward imbalance and blood pressure. *Journal of Psychosomatic Research*, 72(1), 26–32.

Goetzel, R., Ozminkowski, R., Sederer, L., and Mark, T. (2002). The Business Case for Quality Mental Health Services: Why Employers Should Care About the Mental Health and Well-Being of Their Employees. *Journal of Occupational & Environmental Medicine*, 44(4), 320–330.

Gyorkos, C., Becker, J., Massoudi, K., de Bruin, G.P., and Rossier, J. (2012). The impact of personality and culture on the job demands-control model of job stress. *Swiss Journal of Psychology*, 71(1), 21–8.

Government of British Columbia. *Bill 14–2011: Workers Compensation Amendment Act*. Available at: http://www.leg.bc.ca/39th4th/1st_read/gov14-1.htm, October 6, 2012.

Hahn, V.C., Binnewies, C., Sonnentag, S., and Mojza, E.J. (2011). Learning how to recover from job stress: Effects of a recovery training program on recovery, recovery-related self-efficacy, and well-being. *Journal of Occupational Health Psychology*, 16(2), 202.

Han, K., Trinkoff, A., Storr, C., Geiger-Brown, J., Johnson, K., and Park, S. (2012, August). Comparison of job stress and obesity in nurses with favorable and unfavorable work schedules. *Journal of Occupational and Environmental Medicine*, 54(8), 928–32.

Harrison, R.V. (1978). Person-environment fit in job stress. In C.L. Cooper and R. Payne (eds), *Stress at Work* (pp. 23–52). New York: Wiley.

Harrison, R.V. (1985). The person-environment fit model and the study of job stress. In T.A. Beehr and R.S. Bhagart (eds), *Human Stress and Cognition in Organizations: An Integrated Perspective* (pp. 23–52). New York: Wiley.

Holmes, T.H. and Rahe, R.H. (1967). The Social Readjustment Rating Scale. *J Psychosom Res*, 11(2), 213–8.

Jimmieson, N.L., McKimmie, B.M., Hannam, R.L., and Gallagher, J. (2010). An investigation of the stress-buffering effects of social support in the occupational stress process as a function of team identification. *Group Dynamics: Theory, Research, and Practice*, 14(4), 350–367.

Johnson, J.V., Stewart, W., Hall, E.M., Fredlund, P., and Theorell, T. (1996). Long-term psychosocial work environment and cardiovascular mortality among Swedish men. *American Journal of Public Health March*, 86(3), 324–31. DOI: 10.2105/AJPH.86.3.324.

Kamarck, T.W., Muldoon, M.F., Shiffman, S.S., and Sutton-Tyrrell, K. (2007). Experiences of demand and control during daily life are predictors of carotid atherosclerotic progression among healthy men. *Health Psychol*, 26(3), 324–32. DOI: 10.1037/0278-6133.26.3.324.

Kamarck, T.W., Muldoon, M.F., Shiffman, S., Sutton-Tyrrell, K., Gwaltney, C., and Janicki, D.L. (2004). Experiences of demand and control in daily life as correlates of subclinical carotid atherosclerosis in a healthy older sample. *Health Psychol*, 23(1), 24–32. DOI: 10.1037/0278-6133.23.1.24.

Karasek, R. (1979). Job demands, job decision latitude, and mental strain: implications for job redesign. *Administrative Science Quarterly*, 24, 285–306.

Karasek, R. and Theorell, T. (1990). *Healthy Work: Stress, Productivity, and the Reconstruction of Working Life*. New York: Basic Books.

Kaspereen, D. (2012). Relaxation intervention for stress reduction among teachers and staff. *International Journal of Stress Management*, 19(3), 238.

Kauffeld, S., Jonas, E., and Frey, D. (2004). Effects of a flexible work-time design on employee-and company-related aims. *European Journal of Work and Organizational Psychology*, 13(1), 79–100.

Kearns, H. and Gardiner, M. (2007). Is it time well spent? The relationship between time management behaviours, perceived effectiveness and work-related morale and distress in a university context. *High Education Research & Development*, 26(2), 235–47.

Kinnunen U, Mauno S, Geurts S., and Dikkers J (2005) Work-family culture in organizations: theoretical and empirical approaches. In Poelmans SAY (ed.) *Work and family: an international research perspective*. Lawrence Erlbaum, Mahwah NJ, pp 87–120.

Kivimaki, M., Leino-Arjas, P., Luukkonen, R., Riihimaki, H., Vahtera, J., and Kirjonen, J. (2002). Work stress and risk of cardiovascular mortality: prospective cohort study of industrial employees. *BMJ*, 325(7369), 857.

Kossek, E. E. Balter, B. B., & Matthews, R. A., 2011). Focal article. how work-family research can finally have an impact in the workplace. *Industrial and Organizational Psychology: Perspectives on Science and Practice*, 4, 352–369.

Kristensen, T.S. (1995). The demand-control-support model: methodological challenges for future research. *Stress Medicine*, 11, 17–26.

Lambert, E.G., Altheimer, I., Hogan, N., and Barton-Bellessa, S.M. (2011). Correlated of correctional orientation in a treatment-oriented prison: a partial test of person-environment fit theory. *Criminal Justice and Behavior*, 38(5), 453–70.

Lapointe, J., Dionne, C., Brisson, C., and Montreuil, S. (2013). Effort-reward imbalance and video display unit's factors interact in women on incidence of musculoskeletal symptoms. *Work. Journal of Prevention, Assessment and Rehabilitation*, 44(2), 133–43.

Lazarus, R.S. (1966). *Psychological Stress and the Coping Process*. New York: McGraw-Hill.

Lazarus, R.S. (1993). From psychological stress to the emotions: a history of changing outlooks. *Annu Rev Psychol*, 44, 1–21. DOI: 10.1146/annurev.ps.44.020193.000245.

Lazarus, R.S. and Folkman, S. (1984). *Stress, Appraisal, and Coping*. New York, NY: Springer.

Leach, D.J., Wall, T.D., and Jackson, P.R. (2003). The effect of empowerment on job knowledge: an empirical test involving operators of complex technology. *Journal of Occupational and Organizational Psychology*, 76(1), 27–52.

Leach, D.J., Jackson, P.R., and Wall, T.D. (2001). Realizing the potential of empowerment: the impact of a feedback intervention on the performance of complex technology. *Ergonomics*, 44(9), 870–886.

Leontaridi, R. and Ward, M. (2002). "Work-related stress, quitting intentions and absenteeism." IZA Discussion Papers 493, Institute for the Study of Labor (IZA), 1–26.

Liu, S., Wang, M., Zhan, Y., and Shi, J. (2009). Daily work stress and alcohol use: Testing the cross-level moderation effects of neuroticism and job involvement. *Personnel Psychology*, 62(3), 575–97.

Lovallo, W.R. (2005). *Stress and Health: Biological and Psychological Interactions* (2nd ed.). Thousand Oaks, CA: Sage.

MacQueen, K., Patriquin, M., and Intini, J. (2007, October 15). Workplace Stress Costs the Economy Billions. MacLean's Magazine. Retrieved March 12, 2009 from http://www.thecanadianencyclopedia.com/index.cfm?PgNm=TCE&Params=M1ARTM0013158.

Manning, M.R., Jackson, C.N., and Fusilier, M.R. (1996). Occupational stress and health care use. *Journal of Occupational Health Psychology*, 1(1), 100–109.

Masi, D.A. and Jacobson, J.M. (2003). Outcome measurements of an integrated employee assistance and work-life program. *Research on Social Work Practice*, 13(4), 451–67.

McLeod, J. (2010). The effectiveness of workplace counselling: a systematic review. *Counselling and Psychotherapy Research*, 10(4), 238–48.

McLeod, J. (2008). *Counselling in the Workplace: A Comprehensive Review of the Research Evidence*. British Association for Counselling & Psychotherapy.

Melamed, S., Kushnie, T., and Meir, E. (1991). Attentuating the impact of job demands: added is an interactive effects of perceived control and social support. *Journal of Vocational Behavior*, 39, 40–53.

Meng, H., Chen, Y., Li, Y, and Xiong, M. (2009). The relationship of personality with job stress and burnout – Evidence from a sample of teachers. *Psychological Science (China)*, 32(4), 846–9.

Miles, A. and Perrewe, P. (2011). The relationship between person-environment fit, control, and strain: the role of a ergonomic work design and training. *Journal of Applied Social Psychology*, 41(4), 729–72.

Murphy, L.R. (1996). Stress management in work settings: a critical review of the health effects. *American Journal of Health Promotion*, 11(2), 112–15.

Nakata, A. and Takahashi, M. (2011). Effort-reward imbalance, over commitment, and cellular immune measures among white-collar employees. *Biological Psychology*, 88(2–3), 270–279.

Netterstrom, B., Kristensen, T.S., Jensen, G., and Schnor, P. (2010). Is the demand-control model still a useful tool to assess work-related psychosocial risk for ischemic heart disease? Results from 14 year follow-up in the Copenhagen city heart study. *International Journal of Occupational Medicine and Environmental Health*, 23(3), 217–24.

Nishida, J. and Otomo, S. (2010). Influence of exercise and physical activity on the mental health of elementary and junior high school teachers: Individual characteristics and experiences with stress. *Japanese Journal of Educational Psychology*, 58(3), 285–97.

National Institute for Occupational Health and Safety. (1999). Stress at Work. DHHS (NIOSH) Publication No. 99–101. Retrieved on October 10, 2005 from http://www.cdc.gov/niosh/stresswk.html.

Noonan, J. and Wagner, S.L. (2010). Workplace stress: theory and recommendations. *Journal of Vocational Evaluation and Work Adjustment*, 37(1), 1–10.

Proudfoot, J.G., Corr, P.J., Guest, D.E., and Dunn, G. (2009). Cognitive-behavioural training to change attributional style improves employee well-being, job satisfaction, productivity, and turnover. *Personality and Individual Differences*, 46(2), 147–53.

Quick, J.C., Nelson, D.L., Quick, J.D., and Orman, D.K. (2001). An isomorphic theory of stress: The dynamics of person-environment fit. *Stress and Health*, 17, 147–57.

Randall, R., Cox, T., and Griffiths, A. (2007). Participants' accounts of a stress management intervention. *Human Relations*, 60(8), 1181–209.

Randall, R., Griffiths, A., and Cox, T. (2005). Evaluating organizational stress management interventions using adapted study designs. *European Journal of Work and Organizational Psychology*, 14(1), 23–41.

Rhoades, L. and Eisenberger, R. (2002). Perceived organizational support: a review of the literature. *Journal of Applied Psychology*, 87(4), 698.

Richards, J.H. (1987). Time management – a review. *Work & Stress*, 1(1), 73–8.

Rosengren, A., Hawken, S., Ounpuu, S., Sliwa, K., Zubaid, M., Almahmeed, W.A. … investigators, Interheart. (2004). Association of psychosocial risk factors with risk of acute myocardial infarction in 11,119 cases and 13,648 controls from 52 countries (the INTERHEART study): case-control study. *Lancet*, 364(9438), 953–62. DOI: 10.1016/S0140-6736(04)17019-0.

Rubino, C., Jansen Perry, S., Milam, A.C., Spitzmueller, C., and Zapt, D. (2012). Demand-control-person: integrating the demand-control and conservation of resources models to test an expanded stressor-strain model. *Journal of Occupational Health Psychology*, 17(4), 456–72.

Segerstrom, S.C. and Miller, G.E. (2004). Psychological stress and the human immune system: a meta-analytic study of 30 years of inquiry. *Psychological Bulletin*, 130(4), 601–30. DOI: 10.1037/0033-2909.130.4.601.

Selye, H. (1976). *Stress in Health and Disease*. Reading, MA: Butterworth-Heinemann.

Selye, H. (1982). History and present status of the stress response. In L. Goldberger and S. Breznitz (eds), *Handbook of Stress: Theoretical and Clinical Aspects*. New York, NY: Free Press.

Shim, M. (2010). Factors influencing child welfare employee's turnover: Focusing on organizational culture and climate. *Children and Youth Services Review*, 32(6), 847–56.

Siegrist, J. (1996). Adverse health effects of high effort/low reward positions. *Journal of Occupational Health Psychology*, 1(1), 27–41. DOI: 10.1037/1076-8998.1.1.27.

Siegrist, J. (2001). A theory of occupational stress. In I.J. (ed.), *Stress in the Workplace: Past, Present and Future*. London: Whurr Publishers.

Siegrist, J. (2011). Perceived rewards at work and cardiovascular health. *Psychosomatic Medicine*, 73(6), 434–5.

Siegrist, J., Siegrist, K., and Webers, I. (1986). Sociological concepts in the etiology of chronic disease: the case of ischemic heart disease. *Social Science and Medicine*, 20, 247–53.

Sliter, K., Sliter, M., Withrow, S., and Jex, S. (2012, October). Employee adiposity and incivility: establishing a link and identifying demographic moderators and negative consequences. *Journal of Occupational Health Psychology*, 17(4), 409–24.

Sprigg, C.A., Stride, C.B., Wall, T.D., Holman, D.J., and Smith, P.R (2007). Work characteristics, musculoskeletal disorders, and mediating role of psychological strain: A study of call center employees. *Journal of Applied Psychology*, 92(50, 1456.

Stancil, A.N. and Hickes, L.H. (2009). Glyconutrients and perception, cognition, and memory. *Perceptual Motor Skills*, 108(1), 259–70.

Sterner, W.R. (2009). Influence of the supervisory working alliance on supervisee work satisfaction and work-related stress. *Journal of Mental Health Counseling*, 31(3), 249–63.

Sutherland, J.E. (1991). The link between stress and illness. Do our coping mechanisms influence our health? *Postgraduate Medicine*, 89(1), 159–64.

Theeboom, T., Beersma, B., and van Vianen, A.E. (2013). Does coaching work? A meta-analysis on the effects of coaching on individual level outcomes in an organizational context. *The Journal of Positive Psychology* (ahead-of-print), 1–18.

Theorell, T., Emdad, R., Arnetz, B., and Weingarten, A.M. (2001). Employee effects of an educational program for managers at an insurance company. *Psychosomatic Medicine*, 63(5), 724–33.

Tilmann, J.N. and Beard, M.T. (2001). Manager's healthy lifestyles, coping strategies, job stressors, and performance: an occupational stress model. *The Journal of Theory Construction and Testing*, 5(1), 7–11.

Turnley, W.H. and Feldman, D.C. (2000). Re-examining the effects of psychological contract violations: unmet expectations and job dissatisfaction as mediators. *Journal of Organizational Behavior*, 21(1), 25–42.

Van Der Doef, M. and Maes, S. (1999). The job demands-control-support model and psychological well-being: a review of 20 years of empirical research. *Work and Stress*, 13(2), 87–114.

Van Vegchel, N., de Jonge, J., Bosma, H., and Schaufeli, W. (2005). Reviewing the effort-reward imbalance model: drawing up the balance of 45 empirical studies. *Social Science and Medicine*, 60, 1117–31.

Wallace, S., Lee, Y., and Lee, S. (2010). Job stress, coping strategies, and burnout among abuse-specific counselors. *Journal of Employment Counseling*, 47(3), 111–22.

Warr, P. (2007). *Work, Happiness, and Unhappiness*. Mahwah, New Jersey: Lawrence Erlbaum Associates, Inc..

Weinberg, A. (2008). Management Coaching Initiative Final Report. July, University of Salford.

Weinberg, A., Sutherland, V.J., and Cooper, C. (2010). *Organizational Stress Management: A Strategic Approach*. New York, NY: Palgrave Macmillan.

Westerlund, H., Nyberg, A., Bernin, P., Hyde, M., Oxenstierna, G., Jappinen, P., et al. (2010). Managerial leadership is associated with employee stress, health, and sickness absence independently of the demand-control-support model. *Work*, 37, 71–9.

White, M.I., Wagner, S.L., Schultz, I. Iverson, R., Kaczorowski, J., Hsu, V., et al. (June 1, 2012). A stakeholder-centred synthesis of systematic reviews on risk and protective factors for work absences across common health conditions: Final Report to WorkSafeBC Stakeholders.

World Health Organization. (2010). Depression. Retrieved on January 20, 2010 from http://www.who.int/mental_health/management/depression/definition/en/.

Chapter 7

Post-traumatic Stress in the Workplace

Courage is endurance for one moment more ...
Unknown Marine Second Lieutenant in Vietnam

Introduction

Exposure to traumatic events in the workplace has recently become a pressing issue for occupational stress researchers. The concern regarding workplace traumatic stress is especially important for workers who are employed in careers considered to be traditionally at high risk for regular exposure to human pain and suffering. Specifically, emergency service workers, emergency medical staff, military, corrections, bank employees, and transportation employees are considered among those at greatest risk for traumatic exposure in the workplace. Although, as discussed in the chapter on general workplace stress, the workplace environment is changing in its treatment of mental health symptoms related to traumatic stress, compensation for traumatic stress claims typically continue to require an appropriate diagnosis from the most current edition of Diagnostic and Statistical Manual of Mental Disorders, most commonly Acute Stress Disorder or Post-traumatic Stress Disorder.

ACUTE STRESS DISORDER (ASD)

Diagnosis. As described in the DSM-IV-TR, diagnosis of ASD requires an individual to display symptoms in eight different categories (Criteria A–H). Criterion A requires the individual to have "experienced, witnessed, or have been confronted with an event or events that involved actual or threatened death or serious injury, or a threat to the physical integrity of self or others" and to have felt a response that "involved intense fear, helplessness, or horror" (American Psychiatric Association, 2000, p. 471). Criterion B describes dissociative features, of which the individual must endorse three or more. The dissociative features required include a sense of numbing, detachment or emotional unresponsiveness; a lack of connectedness with one's surroundings; derealization; depersonalization; and/or dissociative amnesia. Criterion C addresses symptoms related to re-experiencing the event including recurrent images, thoughts, dreams, illusions, flashback episodes, a sense of reliving the experience, and/or distress related to reminders of the event. Criterion D describes symptoms connected to avoidance of things related to the traumatic experience, and Criterion E describes increased symptoms of anxiety or arousal. In addition to symptoms as described by Criterion A through E, Criterion F through H also require that the symptoms create clinically significant distress or impairment, that the disturbance lasts for a minimum of two days and a maximum of four weeks (within four weeks of the traumatic event), and that the disturbance is not due to a physiological condition or substance.

According to the DSM-IV-TR, the prevalence of ASD in the general population is unknown; however, rates among individuals exposed to intense traumatic events are estimated to fall somewhere between 14 and 33 percent. In addition, prevalence may be complicated by cultural differences in coping reactions to traumatic events. For example, dissociative features or hallucinatory experiences may have cultural appropriateness within some environments. Some evidence also suggests that psychosocial variables such as social supports, family history, childhood experiences, pre-existing mental health status, and personality may influence susceptibility to the onset of ASD. However, in situations where stressors are particularly traumatic, symptoms may develop even in individuals that would typically be considered at low risk for mental health symptomatology.

Considerations for differential diagnosis in ASD include general medical and substance use explanations for related behaviors (for example, hyperarousal). ASD must also be distinguished from a previously existing mental disorder with increased or changed symptom presentation, and from situations where briefly experienced psychotic symptoms are a result of a severely traumatic event, in which case Brief Psychotic Disorder should be used as a diagnosis in place of ASD. Similarly, Adjustment Disorder may be appropriate in situations where full symptom criteria are not met for ASD, but the individual under consideration continues to struggle. Depressive symptoms may also be evident in ASD diagnosis, and must be carefully considered to determine whether such symptoms are an aspect of ASD, or, alternately, whether a comorbid diagnosis of Major Depressive Episode is also appropriate. Finally, in cases where financial remuneration or benefits may be a potential outcome of diagnosis, malingering should be a consideration of the diagnostic process (American Psychiatric Association, 2000).

The release of the DSM-V in May 2013 led to some revisions in the diagnostic criteria for ASD with the most important among them that both ASD and PTSD (see below) have moved from the category of Anxiety Disorders to a new designation of Trauma and Stressor-Related Disorders. Another significant change was the requirement for explicit recognition of whether the traumatic event was experienced directly, witnessed, or experienced indirectly and the removal of Criterion A2 regarding the subjective response as described above. Finally, the previous three clusters were divided into four clusters including the previous intrusions, avoidance, and hyperarousal (now alterations in arousal and reactivity) and a new cluster called negative alterations in cognitions and mood (American Psychiatric Association, 2013).

POST-TRAUMATIC STRESS DISORDER (PTSD)

Diagnosis. According to the diagnostic criteria listed in the DSM-IV-TR, a defining characteristic between ASD and PTSD is length of symptom experience. ASD requires that symptom onset is required within four weeks of the traumatic incident, and that symptoms are resolved within four weeks of onset. In contrast, the description of PTSD does not speak to a specified amount of time between the incident and the onset of symptoms. Instead, the timing criterion for PTSD is found in Criterion E which states that the duration of symptoms must be more than one month. Qualitative descriptors are also provided such that symptoms of less than three months' duration are specified as acute, and symptoms of longer than three months' duration are specified as chronic. In addition, if onset of symptoms occurs at more than six months post-event, the specifier "with delayed onset" would be applied.

In place of the eight categories required for diagnosis of ASD, the DSM-IV-TR provides only six categories (A–F) for evaluating PTSD. Criterion A remains the same in both diagnoses, with exposure to a traumatic event and a personal response of helplessness, fear or horror as the primary criteria. The remaining core criteria for diagnosis of PTSD include symptoms of intrusions, avoidance, and hyperarousal. Specifically, Criterion B (intrusions) requires the individual to experience one or more of recurrent and intrusive recollections, distressing dreams, acting or feeling as if the event were recurring, and/or intense psychological or physiological reactivity to reminders of the event. Criterion C (avoidance) requires the individual to experience three or more of: avoidance of thoughts, feelings or conversations associated with the event; efforts to avoid activities, places, or people associated with the event; inability to recall important trauma-related information; loss of interest or pleasure; feelings of detachment or estrangement; restricted range of affect; and/or sense of foreshortened future. Criterion D (hyperarousal) requires the individual to experience two or more of: sleep disturbance, irritability/anger, difficulty concentrating, hypervigilance, and/or exaggerated startle reflex. Similar to the criteria for ASD, experienced symptoms must create clinically significant impairment in one or more areas of functioning.

Unlike with ASD, general population prevalence estimates for PTSD are available and place the disorder at 8 percent of the adult population. (USA statistics). Among those exposed to severe traumatic events, prevalence is estimated at much higher rates, perhaps somewhere between one-third and one-half of victims. According to the DSM-IV-TR, those most at risk for the development of PTSD include survivors of rape, military combat, captivity, and internment or genocide with ethnic or political motives.

The course of PTSD may be highly unpredictable, with about 50 percent of cases demonstrating complete recovery from symptoms within a three-month timeframe. For the other half, symptom presentation may occur with a waxing and waning presentation, often persisting for more than 12 months. Increased symptomatology may be related to reminders of the traumatic event, experience of new traumatic events, or general life stressors. Similar to ASD, PTSD may be more likely in individuals with predisposing factors, but the greatest predictive factor for the development of PTSD remains the severity, duration, and proximity of the traumatic event.

Differential diagnosis of PTSD shares many characteristics with differential diagnosis for ASD. That is, PTSD can be distinguished from Adjustment Disorder by level of severity for both the stressor and the response, and consideration for malingering must be taken into account in cases of potential financial remuneration. As well, diagnosis of post-traumatic symptoms that do not meet the criteria for PTSD should be considered for other forms of mood or anxiety disorders. A diagnosis of PTSD also requires distinction from Obsessive Compulsive Disorder, in which the intrusive thoughts are not related to experienced trauma, and other psychotic disorders (for example, Schizophrenia, Mood Disorder with Psychotic Features, and so on).

The DSM-V changes for PTSD are parallel to those as described above for ASD. It should be noted, however, that there are now two additional subtypes for PTSD, "dissociative subtype", intended to describe individuals who meet PTSD criteria and also experience symptoms of depersonalization and derealization, and "preschool subtype", intended to provide separate diagnostic criteria for children six years old and younger. Alterations were also made to allow for lower diagnostic thresholds for children and adolescents with the intent of making the diagnostic criteria more developmentally sensitive (American Psychiatric Association, 2103).

History

The historical roots for the description of PTSD are often found in military literature, although other reports suggest that early descriptions of trauma-related symptoms were described in early religious and literary text. In military-based descriptions of post-traumatic symptoms, the terms "shellshocked", "soldier's heart," "combat exhaustion," and others were used to describe the anxiety-type symptoms that many soldiers demonstrated, having returned from active combat. For the mental health community, the first description of such a syndrome was provided by the DSM-I (APA, 1952) under the name of Stress Response Syndrome. In the subsequent version of the DSM, Stress Response Syndrome was lumped in with a group of disorders called Situational Disorders. Finally, during the time of the Vietnam conflict, much research on post-traumatic symptomatology was completed and led to the inclusion of PTSD as a diagnosis in the DSM-III (APA, 1980). This description of PTSD was the first time that stress-related symptoms attached to a particular traumatic event were considered as potentially chronic symptoms in place of simply short-term adjustment. Both the DSM-III and the DSM-IIIR defined a traumatic event in an objective way, essentially negating the contribution of individual perception of or reaction to the event. Specifically the DSM-III required that the traumatic event could be considered to have caused significant symptoms of distress in almost anyone, and the DSM-IIIR required that the event be outside of the range of normal human experience. Since then, the revisions completed during the writing of the DSM-IV provided for the inclusion of individual perception and response. As described above, the present criteria for PTSD requires that the individual felt intense fear, helplessness, or horror during the event.

At the time of writing, the DSM-V continues to be debated prior to its eventual publication and implementation. McNally (2009), an advisor to the APA committee for PTSD, has suggested sweeping changes are required to the diagnostic criteria for PTSD in order to restore scientific credibility to the field of traumatic stress studies. He argues that the requirement for physical presence at the scene of a traumatic event should be considered an essential component of the diagnosis, and that sufferers of traumatic stress symptoms related to an indirect source should be provided with either an alternate anxiety-related diagnosis, or that an additional diagnostic category should be created. This promoter also advocates for removal of the Criterion C symptom, inability to recall an important aspect of the event. He argues for removal of this symptom based on the ambiguity found in its inability to distinguish between encoding failure and retrieval failure. In general, McNally suggests that revisions to the diagnostic criteria should hold, as their basic principle, movement for PTSD diagnostic criteria from a pop culture diagnosis to one based on research and scientific evidence. Other researchers have supported McNally's claim that PTSD diagnostic criteria need revision. Specifically, Kubany, Ralston, and Hill (2010) suggest that for Criterion A, individual reaction should include all three of the potential descriptors, intense fear, helplessness, and horror. Other researchers working from a large national survey (US) have also found substantial overlap between PTSD symptoms and symptoms related to other mood and anxiety disorders. These results create some confusion about the construct validity of PTSD as an independent construct (Elhai, Grubaugh, Kashdan, et al., 2008). Researchers as well as advisers and advocates are currently debating the value of each of these types of perspectives. Only upon the publication of the DSM-V will the dominance of each position become clear for practitioners working in the field of mental health diagnosis.

Interventions

Interventions for ASD/PTSD have resembled interventions for mental health generally. That is, essentially interventions for traumatic stress fall either into the category of personal or group interventions, or medication therapy. While not considered a treatment for PTSD, arguably the most common form of workplace intervention to prevent the development of post-traumatic symptomatology is the Critical Incident Stress Debriefing (CISD). Although the CISD is intended to be provided only within the context of the complete model called Critical Incident Stress Management (CISM), many workplaces appear to employ the CISD in isolation.

CISD is a seven-stage debriefing process intended to occur within three days of a traumatic event as a method of reducing the impact of the trauma through an opportunity for cognitive framing, emotional release, and social support. Development of the model is attributed to a firefighter turned psychologist,

Jeffery Mitchell, who was interested in providing peer support to firefighters exposed to traumatic events in the line of duty. Essentially, he proposed his model as a method of facilitating recovery from traumatic events, by preventing the development of post-traumatic symptoms through promoting the CISM as a method for enhancing return to previous level of functioning and as an early screening tool (Mitchell and Everly, 1995).

CISD has been both highly praised and highly criticized in the literature. For example, some authors suggest that this short-term intervention neither significantly reduces traumatic stress reactions, nor improves individual ability to cope (for example, Harris, Baloglu, and Stacks, 2002). In general, available data on the use of the CISD seems to suggest that use of this intervention in the workplace should be completed with caution, and that if any benefit is to be available, application with emergency service groups would be the only recommended usage. Further, employers of emergency service organizations would be well advised to apply use of the CISD only within the context of a complete CISM stress management model. For employers of other types of organizations, use of the CISD, especially as a standalone intervention, is not currently supported by available research.

Other forms of psychotherapy often employed in PTSD cases include cognitive therapy, behavior therapy (for example, exposure therapy, anxiety management skills), or a combination of the two, termed cognitive behavior therapy (CBT). Cognitive therapy, described by Beck (1979), focuses on altering maladaptive patterns of emotional responses, thinking, and/or responding. The patient is challenged to reframe unhelpful thought patterns that are impeding growth and change, or creating distress. For example, a client may seek therapy for feelings of depression and be encouraged to reframe perpetually negative interpretations of the world. Cognitive therapy is generally considered a therapy driven by the interaction between individual thought and the environment.

Behavior therapy, first described by Thorndike (1911), is focused on changing behavior in order to interrupt the antecedent, behavior, consequent (ABC) pattern. Behavior therapists work on the principle that behavior is initiated by an environmental trigger (antecedent), which then perpetuates the undesirable behavior (behavior), and then, finally, the unwanted consequences (consequent). In order to change behavior, behavior management techniques suggested that the antecedent, behavior, consequent chain must be broken. For example, an individual who is attempting to quit smoking may seek the advice of the behavior therapist and participate in a process of identifying their individual ABC chain. From this analysis, the patient and therapist decide that the patient's first cigarette of the day is triggered by pouring a cup of coffee. In order to interrupt the ABC chain, the therapist might encourage the patient to refrain from drinking their morning java. In comparison to the thought-based changes required by cognitive therapy, behavior therapy interprets behavior as a result of the relationship between an individual's behavior and the environment.

Cognitive behavioral therapy (CBT) is typically thought to be a therapy that brings together the positive aspects of both cognitive therapy and behavior therapy. For example, for the client described above who was experiencing depressive thoughts, cognitive therapeutic techniques such as reframing negative interpretations may be included in therapy, but the cognitive techniques would also be complemented by behavioral interventions such as avoidance of caffeine intended to improve sleep. In this case, intake of caffeine acts as the antecedent, not getting enough sleep as the behavior, and depressive feelings related to sleep withdrawal as the consequent. Research on CBT has suggested a combination of cognitive and behavioral techniques as an important form of intervention in PTSD cases (Bryant, 2011).

Two of the most well-known CBT techniques used in treatment of PTSD include exposure therapy and anxiety management training. Exposure therapy directly, or indirectly, exposes an individual to the traumatic material in a graduated fashion, while teaching cognitive and behavioral relaxation techniques to reduce anxiety related to the exposure. For example, while treating the victim of a violent assault, a therapist may start with graded imagination exercises within the therapy office. The therapist would train the patient in relaxation techniques, and then slowly introduce traumatic material over a series of sessions. Slowly, as the patient's competency at handling the material improves, the therapist may choose to complete some in-vivo exposures and may actually take the patient back to the scene of the crime. Bolton et al. (2004) suggest that exposure therapy is a valuable form of intervention for PTSD and that this type of therapy has been demonstrated as successful in reducing symptoms such as nightmares, intrusive thoughts, and hyperarousal. However, he also states that this type of therapy may be less successful at addressing symptoms of irritability and anger.

Anxiety management training essentially amounts to providing a variety of skills intended to give the PTSD sufferer a "toolbox" of skills that can be used in situations where PTSD symptoms become problematic. Such skills include abilities such as biofeedback, relaxation training, assertiveness training, healthy living, challenging worrisome thoughts, and so on. For example, a patient who comes in to see a therapist with minor post-traumatic symptoms regarding a recent death in the family, might be encouraged to use distraction to keep from concentrating on the loss, deep breathing in times when the anxiety becomes unbearable, as well as to avoid caffeine and other potentially anxiety-provoking substances. As less evidence is available to support anxiety management training as a treatment for PTSD, some authors suggest that this intervention type should likely be used in combination with other types of treatments (Bolton, Holohan, King, et al., 2004).

Medication therapy, the other most-used form of PTSD intervention, is sometimes used independently, and other times in combination with one of the psychotherapeutic treatments discussed above. Psychopharmacological options used for treatment of PTSD include anxiolytic medication, antidepressants, and antipsychotics (MacDonald, Colotla, Flamer, et al., 2003). Positive effects of medication therapy are often reported to include reduction in post-traumatic symptoms such as intrusive thoughts, hypervigilance, increased arousal, avoidance, sleep disturbances, depression, and re-experiencing of traumatic events (Bolton, Holohan, King, et al., 2004). Negative impacts of medication therapy must also be considered and can include decreased arousal, attentiveness, and libido (MacDonald, Colotla, Flamer, et al., 2003). Medication therapy has also been criticized for issues with medication adherence and for providing a "Band-Aid" solution to the underlying traumatic stress issues.

Often, because PTSD often has occupational, social, interpersonal, and health consequences, treatments require multifaceted approaches, driven by the needs of the individual patient. This multidimensional approach frequently means that treatment of PTSD requires both personal and medication therapy. Medication therapy may provide reduced symptoms so that the affected individual can adequately cope with the demands of psychotherapeutic intervention. As individual competence with psychotherapeutic techniques increases, reliance on medication may be reduced.

In general, research suggests that treatment knowledge regarding best evidence interventions for PTSD remains inadequate. Interventions with too-short durations, delayed effects that occur after final data collection, and compensation programs fashioned after treatment of physical injury have all been suggested as possible reasons for lack of clarity for treatment effectiveness. In addition, treatment of PTSD inherently requires a process of increasing anxiety at certain points in the therapeutic process. As a consequence, outcome studies with inappropriate measurement cycles may inadvertently introduce bias by choosing data collection patterns that do not take this wax and wane pattern into account (Bolton, Holohan, King, et al., 2004; Brunello, Davidson, Deahl, et al., 2001; MacDonald, Colotla, Flamer, et al., 2003).

Measurement of PTSD

Impact of Events Scale/Impact of Events Scale–Revised. The Impact of Events Scale (IES; Horowitz, Wilner, and Alvarez, 1979) is a 15-item scale measuring the original core criteria for traumatic stress, intrusions (seven items) and avoidance (eight items). The IES was one of the earliest measures of PTSD and has been widely used in traumatic stress research. This tool asks respondents to score each of the items on a five-point scale, reflecting experiences of post-traumatic symptoms over the past seven days. Although primarily intended for research, not clinical purposes, a score of 26 has been proposed as an appropriate clinical cutoff (Chemtob, Tomas, Las, et al., 1997). The IES has demonstrated good internal consistency, test-retest reliability, sensitivity over time, and detection for differences between groups (Horowitz, Wilner, and Alvarez, 1979; Schwarzwald, Solomon, Weisenber, et al., 1987; Thewes, Meiser, and Hickie, 2001; Zakowski, Valdimarsdottir, Bovbjerg, et al., 1997; Zilberg, Weiss, and Horowitz, 1982).

In 1977, Weiss and Marmar revised the original IES to provide more consistency with the DSM-IV criteria. Specifically, these researchers altered the scale so that it now reflects the core criteria of intrusions (eight items), avoidance (eight items), and the newer items measuring hyperarousal (six items). Similar to its predecessor, the IES-R was demonstrated as having adequate internal consistency and test-retest reliability (Beck, Grant, Read, et al., 2008; Creamer, Bell, and Failla, 2003; Weiss and Marmar, 1997). The IES-R has been found to correlate moderately to highly with other accepted measures of post-traumatic stress disorder (Creamer, Bell, and Failla, 2003; Beck, Grant, Read, et al., 2008), and to provide similar levels of reliability and internal consistency for translated versions (Asukai, Kato, Kawamura, et al., 2002; Creamer, Bell, and Failla, 2003). Some debate continues to exist regarding the IES-R underlying construct structure. Specifically, although the IES-R was designed with the intent of measuring the three core components of PTSD as described in the DSM-IV and some researchers have found support for this factor structure (Beck, Grant, Read, et al., 2008; Brunet, St-Hillaire, Jehel, et al., 2003), others report avoidance as an independent subscale, and the hyperarousal and intrusions subscales as a single construct (Asukai, Kato, Kawamura, et al., 2002; Creamer, Bell, and Failla, 2003).

Mississippi Scale for Combat-Related PTSD (M-PTSD). The M-PTSD is a 35-item scale designed to reflect the DSM-III criteria for PTSD as well as some additional symptoms including substance use, suicidality, and depression. This scale was developed for use with veteran populations and validated with Vietnam War veterans (Keane, Caddell, and Taylor, 1988). However, it has also been suggested as a possible method of detecting war-related, but noncombat stress in veterans (Sloan, Arsenault, Hilsenroth, et al., 1995). Similar to the IES scales, the M-PTSD is scored on a five-point Likert scale, with cutoff scores between 91 and 121 suggested (Engdahl, Eberly, and Blake, 1996; Keane, Caddell, and Taylor, 1988; Lyons and Keane, 1992). Although the M-PTSD has been shown to have high test-retest reliability and internal consistency, sensitivity and specificity estimates have suggested highly variable hit rates (Engdahl, Eberly, and Blake, 1996; Keane Caddell, and Taylor, 1988; Lyons, Caddell, Pittman, et al., 1994; McFall, Smith, MacKay, et al., 1990).

Civilian Mississippi Scale (CMS or C-Mississippi) and Revised CMS (R-CMS). The Civilian Mississippi Scale (CMS) is a 39-item revision of the veteran version, modified for civilian populations. Twenty-four items were maintained as in the veteran version, with other items altered to remove military context. The modification also included four new items intended to evaluate re-experiencing, psychogenic amnesia, hypervigilance, and additional symptomatology (Lauterbach, Vranna, King, et al., 1997). Generally, the original CMS demonstrated less than ideal psychometric properties, with issues such as reduced internal consistency, inconsistent factor structure, issues with reverse-worded items, and lack of correlation with other accepted measures of PTSD (Bourque and Shen, 2005; Lauterbach, Vranna, King, et al., 1997; Vreven, Gudanowski, King, et al., 1995).

In 1996, Norris and Perilla modified the CMS to become a 30-item tool revised to reduce redundancy, and remove overly general items or items irrelevant to civilian experience. These authors also added two intrusions items and anchored the first 18 items to a specific event. The revised version was considered to have good-to-adequate internal consistency and test-retest reliability, and was seen as providing information about PTSD symptoms as aligned in the DSM-IV (Norris and Perilla, 1996; Shapinsky, Rapport, Henderson, et al., 2005).

Mississippi Scale—Police Version. In 2003, an additional version of the Mississippi Scale was created by changing references to "military" in the original version to "police service". This 35-item police-service-related scale demonstrated high internal consistency and good convergent validity with other validated measures of PTSD (Pole, Neylan, Best, et al., 2003).

Post-traumatic Symptoms Scale (PTSS). The original version of the PTSS (PTSS-10) had 10 items and was translated into English from the Norwegian version in 1989 (Holen, Sund, and Weisaeth, 1983; Raphael, Lundin, and Weisaeth, 1989). In 1993, the 12-item version (PTSS-12) was also translated into English (Holen, 1990; Holen, 1993). This scale was originally developed for screening traumatic stress symptoms related to disasters and was not intended to map onto DSM criteria for PTSD. Symptoms considered by this scale include sleep problems, nightmares, depression, startle reflex, withdrawal, irritability, mood swings, guilt, fear, tension, and impaired memory and concentration (last two for PTSS-12 only). Both the PTSS-10 and the PTSS-12 can be scored either as a yes/no answer or as a rating on a seven-point Likert scale. Either form of response has generated adequate internal consistency and test-retest reliability properties (Eid, Thayer, and Johnsen, 1999; Holen, 1990; Mehlum ad Weisaeth, 2002; Schuffel, Chade, and Schunk, n.d.).

Post-traumatic Diagnostic Scale (PDS or PTDS). The PDS is arguably one of the most influential post-traumatic stress scales. This scale is a revised version of the PSS-SR (Foa, Riggs, Dancu, et al., 1993; Foa, Cashman, Jaycox, et al., 1997) which measures recent (past 30 days) PTSD symptoms according to the DSM-IV criteria. An important difference in this scale as compared to other scales is its inclusion of items related to Criterion A1 and A2 from the DSM-IV. The scale is divided into four parts with the first and second assessing experience of a traumatic event, the third assessing PTSD symptoms, and that last section assessing related functional impairment. The PDS has demonstrated adequate-to-good levels of internal consistency and reliability, even for translated versions (Foa, Riggs, Dancu, et al., 1997; Griesel, Wessa, and Flor, 2006; Odenwald, Lingenfelder, Schauer, et al., 2007; Powell and Rosner, 2005). One criticism of the PDS has been its higher agreement with measures of depression and anxiety than with highly specific PTSD measures such as structured clinical interviews (Ehring, Kleim, Clark, et al., 2007; Foa, Riggs, Dancu, et al., 1997; Griffin, Uhlamnsiek, Resick, et al, 2004; Sheeran and Zimmerman, 2002).

Post-traumatic Stress Disorder Checklist (PCL). This scale is a 17-item measure developed out of the National Center for PTSD (Weathers, Litz, Herman, et al., 1993) that is intended to parallel the DSM-IV PTSD criteria. Each item is ranked on a five-point scale, indicating level of symptoms over the past 30 days. The PCL has been modified to civilian (PCL-C) and specific trauma (PCL-S) versions by removing military references and/or referring to a particular stressful experience. Psychometric research on the specific scales has demonstrated strong internal consistency, reliability, and concurrent validity for the PCL-M (Blanchare, Jones-Alexander, Buckley, et al., 1996; Cook, Elhai, and Arean, 2005; Forbes, Creamer, and Biddle, 2001; Ruggiero, Del Ben, Scotti, et al., 2003; Smith, Redd, DuHamel, et al., 1999; Weathers, Litz, Herman, et al., 1993; Ventureya, Yao, Cottraux, et al., 2002), the PCL-S (Blanchard, Jones-Alexander, Buckley, et al., 1996), and the PCL-C (Dobie, Kivlahan, Maynard, et al., 2002; Lang, Laffaye, Satz, et al., 2003).

Other Self-Report Measures. Additional self-report measures of PTSD include the Davidson Trauma Scale (DTS), Disaster-Related Psychological Screening Test (DRPST), Los Angeles Symptoms Checklist (LASC), Primary Care PTSD Screen (PC-PTSD), and Trauma Screening Questioner (TSQ). With the exception of the TSQ, each of these self-report measures has items that map onto the DSM-IV criteria for PTSD. The DTS (Davidson, Book, Colket, et al., 1997) is a 17-item scale designed to be used in situations where the respondent has a history of trauma and its primary purposes were to measure symptom severity and frequency as well as response to treatment. The LASC (King, King, Leskin, et al., 1995) is a 43-item measure, with 17 of the items corresponding to DSM criteria for PTSD and the remaining items asking about general psychological distress. This scale provides three subscale scores, the first a categorical PTSD diagnosis, the second a PTSD severity score, and the third reflecting overall distress. For each of the subscales, the LASC does not specify the timing of symptom experience (Orsillo, 2001). Next, the PC-PTSD (Prins, Quimette, Kimerling, et al., 2004) screens for evidence of PTSD symptoms through use of four items corresponding to primary components of PTSD including re-experiencing, avoidance, hyperarousal, and numbing. This screening tool was originally intended for and validated with primary care veterans and endorsement of two or more items is seen to reflect the possibility of PTSD (Prins, Quimette, Kimerling, et al., 2004; Quimette, Wade, Prins, et al., 2008). Finally, the TSQ (Brewin, Rose, Andrews, et al., 2002) is a 10-item screening questionnaire evaluating re-experiencing and arousal symptoms experienced a minimum of twice within the past seven days, with six or more items considered to suggest possible presence of PTSD.

Structured Clinical Interview for DSM-IV Axis I Disorders (SCID-I). The SCID-I is a structured clinical interview intended to be completed by a trained mental health professional that covers all primary forms of Axis 1 psychopathology. For PTSD specifically, a particular section of the anxiety disorders interview is applicable (Ventura, Liberman, Green, et al., 1998).

Clinician-Administered PTSD Scale (CAPS). Considered the gold standard in PTSD assessment (Blake, Weathers, Nagy, et al., 1995; Foa and Tolin, 2000) the CAPS uses a structured clinical interview to assess endorsement of the 17 DSM-IV PTSD symptoms (Orsillo, 2001; Weathers, Keane, and Davidson, 2001). Strengths of the CAPS include flexibility to assess all PTSD diagnostic criteria, symptom severity, and flexibility in terms of identification for timeline symptoms (week, month, lifetime; Weathers, Keane, and Davidson, 2001). The CAPS is generally considered the gold standard in PTSD assessments due to its strong psychometric properties across a variety of environments and populations (for example, Charney and Keane, 2007; Foa and Tolin, 2000; Gearson, Bellack, and Tenhula, 2004; Griffin, Uhlmansiek, Resick, et al., 2004; Hinton, Chhean, Pich, et al., 2006; Mueser, Salyers, Rosenberg, et al., 2001; Weathers, Keane, and Davidson, 2001).

PTSD in High-risk Occupational Groups

MILITARY

Prevalence of PTSD in military populations has been suggested as ranging from approximately 4 to 19.9 percent after deployment, with higher rates among veterans who had been injured (38 percent), and combat veterans seeking treatment (40.2 percent; Hoge, Terhakopian, Castro, et al., 2007; Jakupcak, Conybeare, Phelps, et al., 2007). Some authors have suggested that although previous veteran populations have contributed immensely to our understanding of PTSD (Rick, Perryman, Young, et al., 1998), currently accepted prevalence rates may be subject to selection and recall bias (Hotopf, Hull, Fear, et al., 2006). Additionally, veterans involved in current conflicts (for example, Iraq and Afghanistan) may have experiences different than older cohorts and can provide long-term and current sources of potential new information in the PTSD field (Cabrera, Hoge, Bliese, et al., 2007; Hoge, Terhakopian, Castro, et al., 2004; Jakupcak, Conybeare, Phelps, et al., 2007; Reeves, 2007). Evidence suggesting that prevalence rates in more recent cohorts may differ from previous older groups of veterans can be found in two studies completed by Hoge and colleagues (Hoge, Terhakopian, Castro, et al., 2004; 2007). The results of these two pieces of research found that, compared to soldiers deployed to Afghanistan and other locations, army and marine soldiers sent to Iraq displayed higher rates of PTSD. Interestingly, some international research has found no increased risk of PTSD for deployed military members (Engelhard, van den Hout, Weerts, et al., 2007; Hotopf, Hull, Fear, et al., 2006; Hacker Hughes, Cameron, Eldridge, et al., 2005).

Differences in PTSD rates may be partially explainable through factors both related to, and not related to, military experience. Engelhard et al. (2007) completed a longitudinal study and found that evidence of traumatic stress symptoms pre-deployment, previous traumatic life events, post-deployment vulnerability measures, and number of negative events during deployment were all related to PTSD symptoms. Lapierre, Schwegler, and LaBauve (2007) completed a cross-sectional analysis that suggested being an officer and being unmarried were related to lower experience of post-traumatic symptomatology. Using similar methodology, Cabrera and colleagues (Cabrera, Hoge, Bliese, et al., 2007) found that more adverse childhood experiences were predictive of increased PTSD. Other factors found to be related to experience of post-traumatic symptomatology include more time on the front-line, inconsistency between training and experience, threat of dying, witnessing trauma to others, and poor deployment morale (Iverson, Fear, Ehlers, et al., 2008). Interestingly, while in one study combat duties were associated with increased PTSD (Hotopf, Hull, Fear, et al., 2006), another study found no such relationship (Iverson, Fear, Ehlers, et al., 2008).

PTSD has also been supported as a predictor for negative health outcomes in military workers. Specifically, workers with greater levels of post-traumatic symptoms report poorer self-rated health, more sick call visits, increased feelings of anger/hostility, more need for counseling and increased time off work (Hoge, Terhakopian, Castro, et al., 2007; Jakupcak, Conybeare, Phelps, et al., 2007; Lapierre, Schwegler, and LaBauve, 2007).

EMERGENCY SERVICE WORKERS

Emergency service workers (ESW) may include ambulance personnel, firefighters, police, and emergency room personnel, among others. Although it can be argued that the bulk of literature in the disaster field has focused on victims of disaster, an increasingly impressive body of literature now speaks to the potential traumatic stress impacts for workers (Weiss, Marmar, Metzler, et al., 1995).

Literature regarding prevalence rates of PTSD among ambulance workers, including paramedics and emergency medical technicians, is limited. Research from Sweden reported prevalence of PTSD among ambulance workers at between 12 and 20 percent (Jonsson and Segesten, 2003, 2004). Similar prevalence rates were reported for British EMTs and paramedics (Bennett, Williams, Page, et al., 2004; Clohessy and Ehlers, 1999) as well as experiences and junior US ambulance workers (Grevin, 1996). Lower rates have been reported for Dutch ambulance workers (van der Ploeg and Kleber, 2003) and Australian paramedic students (Lowery and Stokes, 2005); however, for both of these lower rate studies, parameters of the research differed from those used for the high-rate studies reported for other regions.

Positive predictors for post-traumatic stress symptoms in ambulance workers have been suggested to include longer job tenure, increased age, increased physical or psychological workload, organizational stress, response volume, and incident-related dissociation (Jonsson and Segesten, 2003; Bennett, Williams, Page, 2004). In contrast, Clohessy and Ehlers (1999) did not find that age, gender, or work tenure were predictive of PTSD, but instead reported wishful thinking and responses to intrusions as related to the experience of PTSD. Other authors have also considered the relationship between personal factors and post-traumatic symptomatology in this population. Specifically, lower sense of coherence (Jonsson and Segesten, 2003) was seen to be positively associated with traumatic stress symptoms, while Grevin (1996) found that for experienced paramedics, denial was negatively associated with PTSD. Other predictive factors with some support in the literature include dysfunctional peer social support (Lowery and Stokes, 2005), identification with victims, feelings of shame and guilt (Jonsson and Segesten, 2003; 2004), as well as high emotional demands and poor communication in the workplace (van der Ploeg and Kleber, 2003).

Firefighters represent an occupational group separate from, but similar to, emergency medical workers. Over the past several decades, fire service work has changed from responsibility for traditional fire suppression activities only to including all types of emergency response, including emergency medical response. Some research has looked specifically at prevalence rates of PTSD in fire service members and has generally reported rates similar to those found with ambulance workers. Specifically, looking at Canadian and US professional firefighters, Corneil et al. (1999) reported rates between 17 and 22 percent. Similar rates have been reported for Japanese (17.7 percent) and German (18.2 percent) career firefighters, while trainee firefighters were reported to have slightly lower rates of traumatic stress (16.3 percent; Heinrichs, Wagner, Schoch, et al., 2005; Mitani, Fujita, Nakata, et al., 2006; Wagner, Heinrichs, and Ehlert, 1998). Other authors have reported lower rates for Australian professional, volunteer, and trainee firefighters (7 and 12 percent, respectively; Bryant and Guthrie, 2007; Wagner, McFee, and Martin, 2010).

Several variables have been investigated as possibly related to PTSD in firefighters. Positive predictive factors have been suggested to include years of service, cognitive behavioral avoidance and numbing, volume of traumatic incidents, work strain, prior help seeking behavior, and relational capacity (that is, alienation, insecurity, social incompetence) (Beaton, Murphy, Johnson, et al., 1999, Chen, Chen, Chou, et al., 2007; Corneil, Beaton, Murphy, et al., 1999; Regehr, Hill, Glancy, 2000; Regehr, Hemsworth, and Hill, 2001; Wagner, Heinrichs, and Ehlert, 1998). An interesting study completed by Heinrich et al. (2005) found existence of low self-efficacy and high hostility prior to entry into the fire services was significantly predictive of PTSD symptomatology at two years follow-up. Within the two-year timeframe, firefighters with both characteristics demonstrated a steady climb in post-traumatic and other mental health symptoms; in contrast, firefighters without these characteristics demonstrated no evidence of increased psychopathology. Bryant and Guthrie (2005, 2007) also made significant contributions to this field with their findings that negative cognitive appraisals, especially negative thoughts about self (assessed during training), were predictive of PTSD symptoms after six months and three to four years of active service. Importantly, these authors reported that neither number of incidents experienced nor severity rating of worst incident, were predictive of PTSD.

Health impacts of traumatic stress symptoms with firefighters have also been investigated. In cases of increased reports of PTSD, firefighters also reported more somatic symptoms, depressed mood, increase substance misuse, lower quality of life, and burnout (Chen, Chen, Chou, et al., 2007; Mitani, Fujita, Nakata, et al., 2006; Wagner, Heinrichs, and Ehlert, 1998).

Likely the most studied emergency response group, the police service has received considerable attention as a source of potential work-related trauma (Abdollahi, 2002). Evidence of the attention paid to this occupational grouping can be found in the variety of measures developed for use with police populations, including the Scale for Traumatic Incidents in Police Work (PLES; Brunet, Weiss, Metzler, et al., 2001). Prevalence estimates of PTSD in policing personnel are suggested to be similar to other emergency service populations, perhaps somewhere between 7 and 20 per cent, with higher rates reported for police members working in conflict ridden areas (Carlier, Lamberts, and Gersons, 1997; Harvey-Lintz and Tidwell, 1997; Kopel and Friedman, 1997; Maia, Marmar, Metzler, et al., 2007 Peltzer, 2001).

Factors suggested as possible contributors to the development of PTSD in police members include greater presence of peritraumatic distress/dissociation, problem-focused coping, routine work stress, lack of social support, physiologic response, elevated startle reflex, lower waking cortisol, and alexithymia

(Marmar, Weiss, Metzler, et al., 1996; Stephens and Long, 2000; Stephens, Long, and Miller, 1997; Pole, Neylan, Best, et al., 2003; Neylan, Brunet, Pole, et al., 2005; Guthrie and Bryant, 2005; McCaslin, Inslicht, Neylan, et al., 2006a; McCaslin, Metzler, Best, et al., 2006b). However, it should be noted that for each of these factors, the amount of support varies and some potentially related factors (for example, alexithymia) seem to be supported by only a single cross-sectional study.

In a longitudinal study, Carlier and colleagues (1997) found that short-term PTSD symptoms could be predicted by introversion, emotional exhaustion during trauma, lack of organizational support, job insecurity, and insufficient time for resolution. Longer-term PTSD symptoms were associated with different predictors that included lack of hobbies, job dissatisfaction, work-related brooding, lack of social support, subsequent experience of trauma, and hyperarousal. These authors and others (for example, Galea, Nandi, and Vlahov, 2005) suggest that such findings may suggest that contributing factors related to acute and chronic PTSD differ. In another longitudinal study, Hodgins et al. (2001) found the PTSD symptoms were most strongly predicted by peritraumatic dissociation, initial adjustment and severity of exposure.

Recent studies that have considered the health impacts of post-traumatic stress on police have continued to find negative outcomes related to the experience of traumatic stress symptoms. Specifically, police with higher rates of PTSD symptoms were found to have abnormal serum composition, increased medical visit rate, greater lifetime suicidal ideation, and a subclinical biomarker for cardiovascular disease (Maia, Marmar, Metzler, et al., 2007; Violanti, Andrew, and Burchfiel, 2006).

Emergency room personnel are another category of emergency service workers requiring additional research regarding experience of PTSD. Emergency room personnel (ERP) have received little attention in the traumatic stress research literature, perhaps because ERPs tends not to be at the same physical risk as fire, ambulance, and police workers. However, ERPs remain at risk for witnessing human trauma and suffering, as well as threats to personal safety, including potential physical assault from patients (Laposa and Alden, 2003). Incidents described by emergency room personnel as highly traumatic include death of a child, caring for a traumatized family member of a patient, caring for a personal family member or someone who resembles a family member, traumatic injuries (for example, dismemberment, massive bleeding), cardiac arrest, unsuccessful resuscitation, miscarriage, florid psychiatric conditions, and physical assault on self (Beavan and Stephens, 1999; Jonsson and Halabi, 2006;

Laposa and Alden, 2003; Laposa, Alden, and Fullerton, 2003). Differences between ER nurses and nurses in other departments have been suggested with respect to peritraumatic dissociation, depression and anxiety (Kerasiotis and Motta, 2004). Additionally, experienced physical assault for ER nurses has been demonstrated as a predictor for reduced job satisfaction, patient-related fear, and reduced job performance (Crilly, Chaboyer, and Creedy, 2004; Fernandes, Bouthillette, Raboud, et al., 1999).

Few studies have looked at correlates of PTSD in ERP. Only two research groups seem to have attempted to address this question. Laposa and colleagues (Laposa and Alden, 2003; Laposa, Alden, and Fullerton, 2003) used the cognitive model of PTSD proposed by Ehlers and Clark (2000; discussed above) to attempt to describe cognitive contributors to PTSD symptoms in ER nurses. This research group found that PTSD symptom severity was most closely associated with negative cognitions, negative responsiveness, and peritraumatic dissociation. Kerasiotia and Motta (2004) also looked at this question and, contrary to Laposa's group, found no relationship between PTSD and peritraumatic dissociation. However, both research groups agreed that PTSD was unrelated to years of service in the emergency room.

While acknowledging the important contributions of currently available studies, the paucity of research regarding PTSD and ERPs suggests that much work has yet to be completed in this area. Few conclusions can currently be drawn, other than perhaps that years of service in the emergency room appears to be an unrelated factor.

Critical care and other non-emergency room nurses that experience patient pain and suffering, and work in environments with intense patient morbidity and mortality, may also be at risk for post-traumatic symptomatology (Mealer, Shelton, Berg, et al., 2007). The bulk of research on these workers has focused on violence in the workplace, in particular risk factors and prevalence rates (for example, Mendonca, 1991; Whittington and Wykes, 1994). A few studies have considered the psychological consequences of violence on nursing employees, but in most cases this research may not be comparable to other work in the traumatic stress field due to lack of consistency with DSM-IV Criterion A1 and A2 (Hogh and Viitasara, 2005; Rick, Perryman, Young, et al., 1998). Only two studies could be found that specifically assessed post-traumatic symptoms for non-ER nurses. The first, also discussed in the ER nurse section, compared emergency room nurses with nurses working in intensive care (ICU) or on general floor (GF). This study found that all groups had PTSD scores well below the clinically significant range (Kerasiotis and Motta, 2004). In a separate study, ICU nurses were found to have similar levels of PTSD with GF nurses, but higher levels of anxiety and depressive symptoms (Mealer, Shelton, Berg, et al., 2007).

A final category of disaster response workers for which little research is available on are individuals who choose humanitarian aid work as an occupation. Little discussion occurs regarding humanitarian aid workers in the post-traumatic literature, likely because humanitarian aid is often considered to occur in the aftermath of disaster missions (Robbins, 1999). Despite its less dramatic underpinnings, humanitarian aid is often provided in politically unstable environments where regular exposure to human pain and suffering, as well as potential personal risk may be daily occurrences (Palmer, 2005; Schaefer, Blazer, Carr, et al., 2007). In addition, increasing requirements for complex humanitarian missions suggests that traumatic workplace exposure in this occupation will likely become more common (Cardozo, Holtz, Kaiser, et al., 2005; Erikson, Kemp, Gorsuch, et al., 2001). In one of few studies addressing this issue, Schaefer et al. (2007) reported that depression, subjective experience of the trauma, functional impairments, and number of traumatic events (greatest predictor) were positively related to reported post-traumatic stress. In a separate study, Eriksson et al. (2001) found that both personal and vicarious exposure to traumatic events was related to severity of PTSD for humanitarian aid workers. These authors also noted an interaction with social support such that for workers with high levels of exposure, PTSD severity was lessened in situations of high perceived social support.

TRANSPORTATION WORKERS

Research regarding post-traumatic symptoms and transportation workers has looked at employees from all modes of transport including air, rail (including mass transit systems), road, and water. Although typically not given as much recognition in popular culture as PTSD with military and emergency responders, there is little doubt that traumatic exposure for transportation workers is a serious concern.

Air incidents are typically assumed to include mid-flight incidents, takeoff and landing incidents, as well as hijack/hostage incidents. Due to the tendency for high rates of mortality in the case of an air incident, traumatic stress research seems to focus on residents living near the site who are exposed to the disaster (for example, Chung, Easthope, Chung, et al., 1999) or involved rescue workers (for example, Huizink, Slottje, Whitteveen, et al., 2006; Schooler, Dougall, and Baum, 1999), rather than on the airline employees. As a result, research investigating post-traumatic symptoms in airline employees is limited.

In contrast to the paucity of literature regarding airline workers, railway workers have been a more-studied group, especially with respect to railway crashes and suicide. According to Vatshelle and Moen (1999) workplace traumatic stress exposure for Norwegian train drivers was reported by nearly half of the drivers who responded to a survey; further, those drivers who reported having experienced a workplace trauma also reported decreased mental, musculoskeletal, and gastrointestinal health. Similarly, Malt et al. (1993) found that during an approximately two-year timeframe, 5.1 percent of drivers working for the Swedish State Railways and 2.2 percent of drivers working for the Norwegian State Railways had experienced a work-related accident causing major injury or death.

Prevalence estimates of PTSD in this population are highly variable depending on when the measurement was collected as well as the type of incident. For example, a French study (Cothereau et al., 2004) estimated post-incident PTSD as just over 1 per cent at three-month follow-up, and a Korean study (Yum, Roh, Ryu, et al., 2006) estimated anytime-in-career PTSD prevalence as 64.6 percent for drivers having experienced person-under-train incidents. Many other studies found prevalence rates somewhere in between this range (for example, Tang, 1994; Malt, Karlehagen, Hoff, et al., 1993). The apparent increased prevalence of PTSD for person-under-train incidents has been attributed to the uncontrollability of the event, potential exposure to severely mutilated bodies, and possible guilt about the accident (Karlehagen, Malt, Hoff, et al., 1993; Theorell, Leymann, Jodko, et al., 1992).

Due to the lack of consistency and resulting lack of comparability among studies regarding railway workers, general conclusions about prevalence and risk and protective factors for train drivers are difficult. In general, available studies appear to suggest that for the proportion of drivers who have experienced a serious workplace incident the rates of PTSD are significant (8–17 percent; Malt, Karlehagen, Hoff, et al., 1993; Karlehagen, Malt, Hoff, et al., 1993; Tranah and Farmer, 1994) and are higher than for non-exposed drivers (Cothereau, de Beaurepaire, Payan, et al., 2004; Limosin, Loze, Cothereau, et al., 2006). However, the pattern of results also seems to suggest that although many will experience PTSD symptoms early after the incident, only a few will have ongoing post-traumatic symptoms.

Similar to airline incidents, post-traumatic stress research regarding road accidents tends to focus on survivors, rather than employees. However, bus drivers are one occupational grouping that has received some attention regarding workplace traumatic events, including violent assaults. Specifically, bus drivers have been found to have slightly higher lifetime exposure to traumatic events, with work-related events including receiving a personal threat, being physically assaulted, or having been involved in a serious accident (Kessler, Sonnega, Bromet, et al., 1995). Similar to other occupational groups, prevalence rates for bus drivers who have experienced traumatic stress at work are varied. One study found a 10.7 percent prevalence of PTSD for bus drivers who had experienced a workplace traumatic event (Boyer and Brunet, 1996), while another study found that London bus drivers assaulted at work had a prevalence rate of approximately 22 percent for long-term PTSD (18 months) symptoms (Fisher and Jacoby, 1992). In relationship to health outcomes, Vedantham et al (2001) found that for a group of Canadian bus drivers, drivers meeting the diagnostic criteria for lifetime PTSD expressed significantly more health complaints, used more health services, and ranked their health more poorly than non-exposed drivers, or drivers without clinical symptoms.

Water comprises the final category of transportation, and maritime workers are another relatively understudied group. Similar to air and road disasters, maritime disaster research tends to focus on passengers, rather than employees (for example, Gregg, Medley, Fowler-Dixon, et al., 1996; Joseph, Dalgleish, Thrasher, et al., 1996). Contributing to the literature in this poorly studied area, Dixon and colleagues (Dixon, 1991; Dixon, Rehling, and Shiwach, 1993) completed two studies and found that PTSD symptoms were evident following maritime accidents, even for ferry crew members who had no direct contact with the disaster, either as survivors or as helpers.

BANK EMPLOYEES

Groups of employees most at risk for violence include those working with cash and those involved in service sectors. Workers in these groups may be especially vulnerable to acts of malevolence which may influence the interpretation of the event, and change the experience of post-traumatic reactions (Kamphuis and Emmelkamp, 1998). Several international studies have looked at the frequency of bank robberies and have suggested that for the banking industry, traumatic exposure in the form of robbery should be considered a relatively frequent occurrence (for example, Borzychi, 2003; Miller-Burke, Attridge, and Fass, 1999). Further, Kamphuis and Emmelkamp (1998) found that robbery victims were more psychologically distressed than non-victims, and that post-traumatic symptomatology was negatively related to time since the event. Miller-Burke et al. (1999) found that PTSD symptoms were more likely in situations where the victim had close proximity to the robber, had greater perceived threat to personal safety, and when the robbery involved a weapon.

OTHER OCCUPATIONAL GROUPS POTENTIALLY AT RISK

Other occupational groups that have received some limited research attention regarding post-traumatic stress include journalists, mountain guides, and forensic pathologists. Specifically, some research has suggested that current and lifetime prevalence for war journalists fell at 10.7 percent and 28.6 percent, respectively; these rates were in stark contrast to the 4.3 percent prevalence for non-war newspaper journalists, suggesting that war journalists may be at particular risk for post-traumatic stress symptomatology, especially for intrusive symptoms (Feinstein, Owen, and Blair, 2002).

Mountain guides may be at risk of post-traumatic symptoms if in addition to their mountaineering skills they are also called upon to participate in search and rescue or recovery efforts. Workers in this field report that traumatic aspects of their work may include unexpected confrontation with multiple victims, severely mutilated bodies, victims known to the rescuer, or technically difficult operations in risky environments. Although aspects of trauma were described, the only available studies suggested that prevalence of PTSD for this group was low (2.7 percent; Sommer and Ehlert, 2004).

Three studies looked at traumatic stress symptoms in forensic workers. The first found that for forensic technicians, intrusion symptoms were related with perceived severity of previous personal or work-related traumatic exposures (Hyman, 2004). The second study suggested that number of attendances at forensic events possibly involving aggressive perpetrators predicted self-reported post-traumatic symptomatology (van der Ploeg and Dorresteign, 2003). The final study in this group found that dentists completing postmortem identification had higher symptoms of intrusions and total score on the Impact of Events of Scale. For those dentists who completed the identifications, younger age, less experience, and less spousal and work support were related with greater self-reported distress (McCarroll, Fullerton, Ursano, et al., 1996).

Concluding Remarks

Post-traumatic stress disorder is a mental health concern typically considered to be among those mental disorders most clearly tied to workplace etiology. Although PTSD is a risk in all employment settings, some occupations are typically considered at higher risk for traumatic exposure in the workplace. Further, conceptualizations of workplace traumatic exposure are broadening such that cumulative exposure to human suffering (for example, child welfare work) is also now often included as a possible workplace contributor to post-traumatic symptomatology. Research provides information about assessment and prevention of workplace traumatic stress and employers would be well advised to implement interventions intended to address PTSD risk factors.

More information can be found at the following sources:

http://www.psychologytools.org/ptsd.htmlhttp://www.ptsd.va.gov/

http://www.mentalhealth.com/icd/p22-an06.html

http://www.who.int/mediacentre/news/releases/2013/trauma_mental_health_20130806/en/

References

Abdollahi, K. (2002). Understanding police stress research. *Journal of Forensic Psychology Practice, 2*, 1–24.

American Psychiatric Association. (1952). Diagnostic and statistical manual of mental disorders. Washington, DC: APA.

American Psychiatric Association. (1968). Diagnostic and statistical manual of mental disorders (2nd ed.). Washington, DC: APA.

American Psychiatric Association. (1980). Diagnostic and statistical manual of mental disorders (3rd ed.). Washington, DC: APA.

American Psychiatric Association. (2000). Diagnostic and statistical manual of mental disorders (4th ed., text rev.). Washington, DC: APA.

American Psychiatric Association. (2013). Diagnostic and statistical manual of mental disorders (5th ed.). Washington, DC: APA.

Asukai, N., Kato, H., Kawamura, N., Kim, Y., Yamamoto, K., Kishimoto, J., et al. (2002). Reliability and validity of the Japanese-language version of the Impact of Event Scale-Revised (IES-R-J): four studies of different traumatic events. *Journal of Nervous and Mental Disease, 190*, 175–82.

Beaton, R., Murphy, S., and Johnson, C. (1999). Coping responses and posttraumatic stress symptomatology in urban fire service personnel. *Journal of Traumatic Stress, 12*, 293–308.

Beavan, V. and Stephens, C. (1999). The characteristics of traumatic events experienced by nurses on the accident and emergency ward. *Nursing Praxis in New Zealand, 14*, 12–21.

Beck, A.T., Rush, A.J., Shaw, B.F., and Emery, G. (1979). *Cognitive Therapy of Depression*. New York: The Guilford Press. p. 11. ISBN 0-89862-919-5.

Beck, J., Grant, D., Read, J., Clapp, J., Coffey, S., Miller, L., et al. (2008). The Impact of Event Scale–Revised: psychometric properties in a sample of motor vehicle accident survivors. *Anxiety Disorders*, 22, 187–98.

Bennett, P., Williams, Y., Page, N., Hood, K., and Woollard, M. (2004). Levels of mental health problems among UK emergency ambulance workers. *Emergency Medical Journal*, 21, 235–6.

Blake, D., Weathers, F., Nagy, L., Kaloupek, D., Gusman, F., Charney, D., and Keane, T. (1995). The development of a Clinician-Administered PTSD Scale. *Journal of Traumatic Stress*, 8, 75–90.

Blanchard, E., Jones-Alexander, J., Buckley, T., and Forneris, C. (1996). Psychometric properties of the PTSD Checklist (PCL). *Behaviour Research and Therapy*, 34, 669–73.

Bolton, E., Holohan, D.R., King, L.A., and King, D.W. (2004). Acute and post-traumatic stress disorder. In J.C. Thomas and M. Hersen (eds), *Psychopathology in the Workplace: Recognition and Adaptation* (pp. 119–31). New York: Bruner-Routledge.

Borzycki, M. (2003). Bank robbery in Australia. In *Trends and Issues in Crime and Criminal Justice, No. 253*. Canberra, Australia: Australian Institute of Criminology. Retrieved January 16, 2008, from http://www.aic.gov.au/publications/tandi2/tandi253.pdf.

Bourque, L. and Shen, H. (2005). Psychometric characteristics of Spanish and English versions of the Civilian Mississippi Scale. *Journal of Traumatic Stress*, 18, 719–728.

Boyer, R. and Brunet, A. (1996). Prevalence of post-traumatic stress disorder in bus drivers. *Santé Mentale au Québec*, 21, 189–208.

Brewin, C., Rose, S., Andrews, B., Green, J., Tata, P., McEvedy, C., et al. (2002). Brief screening instrument for post-traumatic stress disorder. *British Journal of Psychiatry*, 181, 158–62.

Brunello, N., Davidson, J.R.T., Deahl, M., Kessler, R.C., Mendlewicz, J., Racagni, G., Shalec, A.Y., and Zohar, J. (2001). Post-traumatic stress disorder: Diagnosis and epidemiology, comorbidity, and social consequences, biology and treatment. *Neuropsychobiology*, 43, 150–162.

Brunet, A., St-Hillaire, A., Jehel, L.,and King, S. (2003). Validation of a French version of the Impact of Event Scale-Revised. *Canadian Journal of Psychiatry*, 48, 56–61.

Brunet, A., Weiss, D, Metzler, T., Best, S., Neylan, T., Rogers, C., et al. (2001). The Peritraumatic Distress Inventory: a proposed measure of PTSD criterion A2. *American Journal of Psychiatry*, 158, 1480–1485.

Bryant, R. (2011). Psychological interventions for trauma exposure and PTSD. In D. Stein, M. Friedman, and C. Blanco (eds), *Post-traumatic Stress Disorder* (pp. 171–202). USA: Wiley Blackwell. DOI 978-0-470-68897-7.

Bryant, R. and Guthrie, R. (2005). Maladaptive appraisals as a risk factor for posttraumatic stress: a study of trainee firefighters. *Psychological Science*, 16, 749–52.

Bryant, R. and Guthrie, R. (2007). Maladaptive self-appraisals before trauma exposure predict posttraumatic stress disorder. *Journal of Consulting and Clinical Psychology*, 27, 812–5.

Cabrera, O., Hoge, C., Bliese, P., Castro, C., and Messer, S. (2007). Childhood adversity and combat as predictors of depression and post-traumatic stress in deployed troops. *American Journal of Preventive Medicine*, 33, 77–82.

Cardozo, B., Holtz, T., Kaiser, R., Gotway, C., Ghitis, F., Toomey, E., and Salama, P. (2005). The mental health of expatriate and Kosovar Albanian humanitarian aid workers. *Disasters*, 29, 152–70.

Carlier, I., Lamberts, R., and Gersons, B. (1997). Risk factors for posttraumatic stress symptomatology in police officers: a prospective analysis. *Journal of Nervous and Mental Disease*, 185, 498–506.

Chemtob, C., Tomas, S., Law, W., and Cremniter, D. (1997). Postdisaster psychosocial intervention: a field study of the impact of debriefing on psychological distress. *American Journal of Psychiatry*, 154, 415–7.

Chen, Y., Chen, M., Chou, F., Sun, F., Chen, P., Tsai, K., et al. (2007). The relationship between quality of life and posttraumatic stress disorder or major depression for firefighters in Kaohsiung, Taiwan. *Quality of Life Research*, 16, 1289–97.

Clohessy, S. and Ehlers, A. (1999). PTSD symptoms, response to intrusive memories and coping in ambulance service workers. *British Journal of Clinical Psychology*, 38, 251–65.

Charney, M. and Keane, T. (2007). Psychometric analyses of the Clinician-Administered PTSD Scale (CAPS)—Bosnian translation. *Cultural Diversity and Ethnic Minority Psychology*, 13, 161–8.

Chung, M., Easthope, Y., Chung, C., and Clark-Carter, D. (1999). The relationship between trauma and personality in victims of the boeing 737-2D6C crash in Coventry. *Journal of Clinical Psychology*, 55, 617–29.

Cook, J., Elhai, J., and Areán, P. (2005). Psychometric properties of the PTSD Checklist with older primary care patients. *Journal of Traumatic Stress*, 18, 371–6.

Corneil, W., Beaton, R., Murphy, S., Johnson, C., and Pike, K. (1999). Exposure to traumatic incidents and prevalence of posttraumatic stress symptomatology in urban firefighters in two countries. *Journal of Occupational Health Psychology*, 4, 131–41.

Cothereau, C., de Beaurepaire, C., Payan, C., Cambou, J., and Conso, F. (2004). Professional and medical outcomes for French train drivers after "person under train" accidents: three year follow up study. *Occupational and Environmental Medicine*, 61, 488–94.

Creamer, M., Bell, R., and Failla, S. (2003). Psychometric properties of the Impact of Event Scale—Revised. *Behaviour Research and Therapy*, 41, 1489–946.

Crilly, J., Chaboyer, W., and Creedy, D. (2004). Violence towards emergency department nurses by patients. *Accident and Emergency Nursing*, 12, 67–73.

Davidson, J., Book, S., Colket, J., Tupler, L., Roth, S., David, D., et al. (1997). Assessment of a new self-rating scale for posttraumatic stress disorder. *Psychological Medicine*, 27, 153–60.

Dixon, P. (1991). Vicarious victims of a maritime disaster. *British Journal of Guidance & Counselling*, 19, 8–12.

Dixon, P., Rehling, C., and Shiwach, R. (1993). Peripheral victims of the Herald of Free Enterprise disaster. *British Journal of Medical Psychology*, 66, 193–202.

Dobie, D., Kivlahan, D., Maynard, C., Bush, K., McFall, M., Epler, A., et al. (2002). Screening for post-traumatic stress disorder in female Veteran's Affairs patients: validation of the PTSD Checklist. *General Hospital Psychiatry*, 24, 367–74.

Ehlers, A. and Clark, D. (2000). A cognitive model of posttraumatic stress disorder. *Behaviour Research and Therapy*, 38, 319–45.

Ehring, T., Kleim, B., Clark, D., Foa, E., and Ehlers, A. (2007). Screening for posttraumatic stress disorder. What combination of symptoms predicts best? *Journal of Nervous and Mental Disease*, 195, 1004–12.

Eid, J., Thayer, J., and Johnsen, B. (1999). Measuring post-traumatic stress: a psychometric evaluation of symptom- and coping questionnaires based on a Norwegian sample. *Scandinavian Journal of Psychology*, 40, 101–8.

Elhai, J.D., Grubaugh, A.L., Kashdan, T.B., and Frueh, B.C. (2008). Emperical examination of a proposed refinement to DSM-IV Posttraumatic Stress Disorder symtom using the national Co-morbidity Survery Replication Data. *Journal of Clinical Psychiatry*, 1–6.

Engdahl, B., Eberly, R., and Blake, J. (1996). Assessment of posttraumatic stress disorder in World War II veterans. *Psychological Assessment: A Journal of Consulting and Clinical Psychology*, 8, 445–9.

Engelhard, I., van den Hout, M., Weerts, J., Arntz, A., Hox, J., and McNally, R. (2007b). Deployment-related stress and trauma in Dutch soldiers returning from Iraq: prospective study. *British Journal of Psychiatry*, 191, 140–145.

Eriksson, C., Kemp, H., Gorsuch, R., Hoke, S., and Foy, D. (2001). Trauma exposure and PTSD symptoms in international relief and development personnel. *Journal of Trauma Stress*, 14, 205–11.

Feinstein, A., Owen, J., and Blair, N. (2002). A hazardous profession: war, journalists, and psychopathology. *American Journal of Psychiatry*, 159, 1570–1575.

Fernandes, C., Bouthillette, F., Raboud, J., Bullock, L., Moore, C., Christenson, J., et al. (1999). *Canadian Medical Association Journal*, 161, 1245–48.

Fisher, N. and Jacoby, R. (1992). Psychiatric morbidity in bus crews following violent assault: a follow-up study. *Psychological Medicine*, 22, 685–93.

Foa, E., Cashman, L., Jaycox, L., and Perry, K. (1997). The validation of a self-report measure of PTSD: The Posttraumatic Diagnostic Scale. *Psychological Assessment*, 9, 445–51.

Foa. E.B., Riggs, D.S., Dancu, C., and Rothbaum, B.O. (1993). Reliability and validity of a brief instrument for assessing post-traumatic stress disorder. *Journal of Traumatic Stress*, 6, 459–73.

Foa, E. and Tolin, D. (2000). Comparison of the PTSD Symptom Scale-Interview Version and the Clinician-Administered PTSD Scale. *Journal of Traumatic Stress*, 13, 181–91.

Forbes, D., Creamer, M., and Biddle, D. (2001). The validity of the PTSD checklist as a measure of symptomatic change in combat-related PTSD. *Behaviour Research and Therapy*, 39, 977–86.

Galea, S., Nandi, A., and Vlahov, D. (2005). The epidemiology of post-traumatic stress disorder after disasters. *Epidemiologic Reviews*, 27, 78–91.

Gearson, J., Bellack, A., and Tenhula, W. (2004). Preliminary reliability and validity of the Clinician-Administered PTSD Scale for schizophrenia. *Journal of Consulting and Clinical Psychology*, 72, 121–5.

Gregg, W., Medley, I., Fowler-Dixon, R., Curran, P., Loughrey, G., Bell, P., et al. (1996). Psychological consequences of the Kegworth air disaster. *British Journal of Psychiatry*, 167, 812–7.

Grevin, F. (1996). Posttraumatic stress disorder, ego defense mechanisms, and empathy among urban paramedics. *Psychological Reports*, 79, 483–95.

Griesel, D., Wessa, M., and Flor, H. (2006). Psychometric qualities of the German version of the Posttraumatic Diagnostic Scale (PTSD). *Psychological Assessment*, 18, 262–8.

Griffin, M., Uhlmansiek, M., Resick, P., and Mechanic, M. (2004). Comparison of the posttraumatic stress disorder scale versus the clinician-administered posttraumatic stress disorder scale in domestic violence survivors. *Journal of Traumatic Stress*, 17, 497–503.

Guthrie, R. and Bryant, R. (2005). Auditory startle response in firefighters before and after trauma exposure. *American Journal of Psychiatry*, 162, 283–90.

Hacker Hughes, J., Cameron, F., Eldridge, R., Devon, M., Wessely, S., and Greenberg, N. (2005). Going to war does not have to hurt: preliminary findings from the British deployment to Iraq. *British Journal of Psychiatry*, 186, 538–9.

Harris, M.B., Baloğlu, M., and Stacks, J.R. (2002). Mental health of trauma-exposed firefighters and critical incident stress debriefing. *Journal of Loss and Trauma*, 7, 223–38.

Harvey-Lintz, T. and Tidwell, R. (1997). Effects of the 1992 Los Angeles civil unrest: post traumatic stress disorder symptomatology among law enforcement officers. *Social Science Journal*, 34, 171–83.

Heinrichs, M., Wagner, D., Schoch, W., Soravia, L., Hellhammer, D., and Ehlert, U. (2005). Predicting posttraumatic stress symptoms from pretraumatic risk factors: a 2-year prospective follow-up study in firefighters. *American Journal of Psychiatry*, 162, 2276–86.

Hinton, D., Chhean, D., Pich, V., Pollack, M., Orr, S., and Pitman, R. (2006). Assessment of posttraumatic stress disorder in Cambodian refugees using the Clinician-Administered PTSD Scale: psychometric properties and symptom severity. *Journal of Traumatic Stress*, 19, 405–9.

Hodgins, G., Creamer, M., and Bell, R. (2001). Risk factors for post trauma reactions in police officers: a longitudinal study. *Journal of Nervous Mental Disease*, 189, 541–7.

Hoge, C., Castro, C., Messer, S., McGurk, D., Cotting, D., and Koffman, R. (2004). Combat duty in Iraq and Afghanistan, mental health problems, and barriers to care. *New England Journal of Medicine*, 351, 13–22.

Hoge, C., Terhakopian, A., Castro, C., Messer, S., and Engel, C. (2007). Association of posttraumatic stress disorder with somatic symptoms, health care visits, and absenteeism among Iraq war veterans. *American Journal of Psychiatry*, 164, 150–153.

Hogh, A. and Viitasara, E. (2005). A systematic review of longitudinal studies of nonfatal workplace violence. *European Journal of Work and Organizational Psychology*, 14, 291–313.

Holen, A. (1990). *A Long-term Outcome Study of Survivors from a Disaster*. Oslo, Norway: University of Oslo Press.

Holen, A. (1993). The North Sea Oil Rig Disaster. In J. Wilson and B. Raphael (eds), *International Handbook of Traumatic Stress Syndromes* (pp. 471–8). New York: Plenum Press.

Holen, A., Sund, A., and Weisæth, L. (1983). Alexander L. Kielland—katastronfen 27. mars 1980 [The Alexander L. Kielland disaster March 27, 1980]. Division for Disaster Psychiatry, University of Olso, Norway.

Horowitz, M., Wilner, N., and Alvarez, W. (1979). Impact of Event Scale: a measure of subjective distress. *Psychosomatic Medicine*, 41, 208–18.

Hotopf, M., Hull, L., Fear, N., Browne, T., Iversen, A., Jones, M., et al. (2006). The health of UK military personnel who deployed to the 2003 Iraq war: a cohort study. *Lancet*, 367, 1731–41.

Huizink, A., Slottje, P., Whitteveen, A., Bijlsma, J., Twisk, J., Smidt, N., et al. (2006). Long term health complaints following the Amsterdam Air Disaster in police officers and fire-fighters. *Occupational and Environmental Medicine*, 63, 657–62.

Hyman, O. (2004). Perceived social support and secondary traumatic stress symptoms in emergency responders. *Journal of Traumatic Stress*, 17, 149–56.

Iverson, A., Fear, N., Ehlers, A., Hughes, H., Hull, L., Earnshaw, M., et al. (2008). Risk factors for post-traumatic stress disorder among UK Armed Forces personnel. *Psychological Medicine*, 38, 511–22.

Lversen, A., Chalder, T., and Wessely, S. (2007). Gulf War Illness: Lessons from medically unexplained symptoms. *Clinical Psychology Review*, 27, 842–54 [PubMed].

Jakupcak, M., Conybeare, D., Phelps, L., Hunt, S., Holmes, H., Felker, B., et al. (2007). Anger, hostility, and aggression among Iraq and Afghanistan war veterans reporting PTSD and threshold PTSD. *Journal of Traumatic Stress*, 20, 945–54.

Jonsson, A. and Halabi, J. (2006). Work related post-traumatic stress as described by Jordanian emergency nurses. *Accident and Emergency Nursing*, 14, 89–96.

Jonsson, A. and Segesten, K. (2003). The meaning of traumatic events as described by nurses in ambulance service. *Accident and Emergency Nursing*, 11, 141–52.

Jonsson, A. and Segesten, K. (2004). Guilt, shame and need for a container: a study of post-traumatic stress among ambulance personnel. *Accident and Emergency Nursing*, 12, 215–23.

Joseph, S., Dalgleish, T., Thrasher, S., Yule, W., Williams, R., and Hodgkinson, P. (1996). Chronic emotional processing in survivors of the Herald of Free Enterprise disaster: the relationship of intrusion and avoidance at 3 years to distress at 5 years. *Behavior Research and Therapy*, 34, 357–60.

Kamphuis, J.H. and Emmelkamp, P.M.G. (1998). Crime-related trauma: psychological distress in victims of bankrobbery. *Journal of Anxiety Disorders*, 12, 199–208.

Karlehagen, S. Malt, U., Hoff, H., Tibell, E., Herrstromer, U., Hildingson, K., et al. (1993). The effect of major railway accidents on the psychological health of train drivers--II. A longitudinal study of the one-year outcome after the accident. *Journal of Psychosomatic Research*, 37, 807–17.

Keane, M., Caddell, J., and Taylor, K. (1988). Mississippi Scale for Combat-Related Posttraumatic Stress Disorder: three studies in reliability and validity. *Journal of Consulting and Clinical Psychology*, 56, 85–90.

Kessler, R., Sonnega, A., Bromet, E., Hughes, M., and Nelson, C. (1995). Posttraumatic stress disorder in the National Co-morbidity Survey. *Archives of General Psychiatry*, 52, 1048–60.

Kerasiotis, B. and Motta, R. (2004). Assessment of PTSD symptoms in emergency room, intensive care unit, and general floor nurses. *International Journal of Emergency Mental Health*, 6, 121–33.

King, L., King, D., Leskin, G., and Foy, D. (1995). The Los Angeles Symptom Checklist: a self-report measure of posttraumatic stress disorder. *Assessment*, 2, 1–17.

Kopel, H. and Friedman, M. (1997). Posttraumatic symptoms in South African police exposed to violence. *Journal of Traumatic Stress*, 10, 307–16.

Kubany, E.S., Ralston, T.C., and Hill, E.E. (2010). Intense fear, helplessness, "and" horror? An empirical investigation of DSM-IV PTSD Criterion A2. *Psychological Trauma: Theory, Research, Practice, and Policy*, 2(2), 77–82. DOI: 10.1037/a0019185.

Lang, A., Laffaye, C., Satz, L., Dresselhaus, T., and Stein, M. (2003). Sensitivity and specificity of the PTSD Checklist in detecting PTSD in female veterans in primary care. *Journal of Traumatic Stress*, 16, 257–64.

Lapierre, C., Schwegler, A., and LaBauve, B. (2007). Posttraumatic stress and depression symptoms in soldiers returning from combat operations in Iraq and Afghanistan. *Journal of Traumatic Stress*, 20, 933–43.

Laposa, J. and Alden, L. (2003). Posttraumatic stress disorder in the emergency room: exploration of a cognitive model. *Behavior Research and Therapy*, 41, 49–65.

Laposa, J., Alden, L., and Fullerton, L. (2003). Work stress and posttraumatic stress disorder in ED nurses/personnel. *Journal of Emergency Nursing*, 29, 23–8.

Lauterbach, D., Vranna, S., King, D., and King, L. (1997). Psychometric properties of the civilian version of the Mississippi PTSD Scale. *Journal of Traumatic Stress*, 10, 499–513.

Limosin, F., Loze, J., Cothereau, C., de Beaurepaire, C., Payan, C., Conso, F., et al. (2006). A prospective study of the psychological effects of "person under train" incidents on drivers. *Journal of Psychiatric Research*, 40, 755–761.

Lowery, K. and Stokes, M. (2005). Role of peer support and emotional expression on posttraumatic stress disorder in student paramedics. *Journal of Traumatic Stress*, 18, 171–9.

Lyons, J. and Keane, T. (1992). Keane PTSD scale: MMPI and MMPI-2 update. *Journal of Traumatic Stress*, 5, 111–7.

Lyons, J., Caddell, J., Pittman, R., Rawls, R., and Perrin, S. (1994). The potential for faking on the Mississippi Scale for Combat-Related PTSD. *Journal of Traumatic Stress*, 7, 441–5.

MacDonald, H.A., Colotla, V., Flamer, S., and Karlinsky, H. (2003). Post-traumatic stress disorder (PSTD) in the workplace: A descriptive study of workers experiencing PSTD resulting from work injury. *Journal of Occupational Rehabilitation*, 13(2), 63–77.

Maia, D., Marmar, C., Metzler, T., Nóbrega, A., Berger, W., Mendlowicz, M., et al. (2007). Post-traumatic stress symptoms in an elite unit of Brazilian police officers: prevalence and impact on psychosocial functioning and on physical and mental health. *Journal Affective Disorders*, 97, 241–5.

Malt, U., Karlehagen, S., Hoff, H., Herrstromer, U., Hildingson, K., Tibell, E., et al. (1993). The effect of major railway accidents on the psychological health of train drivers--I. Acute psychological responses to accident. *Journal of Psychosomatic Research*, 37, 793–805.

Marmar, C., Weiss, D., Metzler, T., Ronfeldt, H., and Foreman, C. (1996). Stress responses of emergency services personnel to the Loma Prieta earthquake Interstate 880 freeway collapse and control traumatic incidents. *Journal of Traumatic Stress*, 9, 63–85.

Mealer, M., Shelton, A., Berg, B., Rothbaum, B. and Moss, M. (2007). Increased prevalence of post-traumatic stress disorder symptoms in critical care nurses. *American Journal of Respiratory and Critical Care Medicine*, 175, 693–7.

Mendonca, C. (1991). A prospective study of patient assaults on nurses in a provincial psychiatric hospital in Canada. *Acta Psychiatrica Scandinavica*, 84, 163–6.

McCarroll, J., Fullerton, C., Ursano, R., and Hermsen, J. (1996). Posttraumatic stress symptoms following forensic dental identification: Mt. Carmel, Waco, Texas. *American Journal of Psychiatry*, 153, 778–82.

McCaslin, S., Inslicht, S., Neylan, T., Metzler, T., Otte, C., Lenoci, M., et al. (2006a). Association between alexithymia and neuroendocrine response to psychological stress in police academy recruits. *Annals of the New York Academy of Sciences*, 1071, 425–7.

McCaslin, S., Metzler, T., Best, S., Liberman, A., Weiss, D., Fagan, J., et al. (2006b). Alexithymia and PTSD symptoms in urban police officers: cross-sectional and prospective findings. *Journal of Traumatic Stress*, 19, 361–73.

McFall, M., Smith, D., Mackay, P., and Tarver, D. (1990). Reliability and validity of Mississippi Scale for Combat-Related Posttraumatic Stress Disorder. *Psychological Assessment: A Journal of Consulting and Clinical Psychology*, 2, 114–21.

McNally, R. (2009). Can we fix PTSD in DSM-V? *Depression and Anxiety*, 26, 597–600.

Mehlum, L. and Weisæth, L. (2002). Predictors of posttraumatic stress reactions in Norwegian UN peacekeepers 7 years after service. *Journal of Traumatic Stress*, 15, 17–26.

Miller-Burke, J., Attridge, M., and Fass, P. (1999). Impact of traumatic events and organizational response: a study of bank robberies. *Journal of Occupational and Environmental Medicine*, 41, 73–83.

Mitani, S., Fujita, M., Nakata, K., and Shirakawa, T. (2006). Impact of post-traumatic stress disorder and job-related stress on burnout: a study of fire service workers. *Journal of Emergency Medicine*, 31, 7–11.

Mitchell, J.T. and Everly, G.S. Jr (1995). Critical incident stress debriefing (CISD) and the prevention of work-related stress among high risk occupational groups. In J.T. Mitchell and G.S. Everly (eds), *Psychotramatology* (pp. 267–80). New York, NY: Plenum.

Mueser, K., Salyers, M., Rosenberg, S., Ford, J., Fox, L., and Carty, P. (2001). Psychometric evaluation of trauma and post-traumatic stress disorder assessments in persons with severe mental illness. *Psychological Assessment*, 13, 110–117.

Neylan, T., Brunet, A., Pole, N., Best, S., Metzler, T., Yehuda, R., et al. (2005). PTSD symptoms predict waking salivary cortisol levels in police officers. *Psychoneuroendocrinology*, 30, 373–81.

Norris, F. and Perilla, J. (1996). The revised Civilian Mississippi Scale for PTSD: reliability, validity, and cross-language stability. *Journal of Traumatic Stress*, 9, 285–98.

Odenwald, M., Lingenfelder, B., Schauer, M., Neuner, F., Rockstroh, B., Hinkel, H., and Elbert, T. (2007). Screening for posttraumatic stress disorder among Somali ex-combatants: a validation study. *Conflict and Health*, 1(10)

Orsillo, S. (2001). Measures for acute stress disorder and posttraumatic stress disorder. In M. Anthony and S. Orsillo (eds), *Practitioner's Guide to Empirically Based Measures of Anxiety* (pp. 255–307). New York: Kluwer Academic/Plenum. Retrieved on: February 7, 2008, from http://www.ncptsd.va.gov/ncmain/nc_archives/nc_artics/id24368.pdf.

Palmer, I. (2005). ABC of conflict and disaster. Psychological aspects of providing medical humanitarian aid. *British Medical Journal*, 331, 152–4.

Peltzer, K. (2001). Stress and traumatic symptoms among police officers at a South African police station. *Acta Criminologica*, 14, 52–6.

Pole, N., Neylan, T., Best, S., Orr, S., and Marmar, C. (2003). Fear-potentiated startle and posttraumatic stress symptoms in urban police officers. *Journal of Traumatic Stress*, 16, 471–9.

Powell, S. and Rosner, R. (2005). The Bosnian version of the international self-report measure of posttraumatic stress disorder, the Posttraumatic Stress Diagnostic Scale, is reliable and valid in a variety of different adult samples affected by war. *BMC Psychiatry*, 5(11).

Prins, A., Quimette, P., Kimerling, R., Camerson, R., Hugelshofer, D., Shaw-Hegwer, J., et al. (2004). The primary care PTSD screen (PC-PTSD): development and operating characteristics. *Primary Care Psychiatry*, 9, 9–14.

Quimette, P., Wade, M., Prins, A., and Schohn, M. (2008). Identifying PTSD in primary care: comparison of the Primary Care-PTSD Screen (PC-PTSD) and the General Health Questionnaire-12 (GHQ). *Anxiety Disorders*, 22, 337–43.

Raphael, B., Lundin, T., and Weisæth, L. (1989). A research method for the study of psychological and psychiatric aspects of disaster. *Acta Psychiatrica Scandinavia*, 80, Suppl. 353, 1–75.

Reeves, R. (2007). Diagnosis and management of post-traumatic stress disorder in returning veterans. *Journal of the American Osteopathic Association*, 107, 181–9.

Regehr, C., Hill, J., and Glancy, G. (2000). Individual predictors of traumatic reactions in firefighters. *Journal of Nervous and Mental Disease*, 188, 333–9.

Regehr, C., Hemsworth, D., and Hill, J. (2001). Individual predictors of posttraumatic distress: a structural equation model. *Canadian Journal of Psychiatry*, 46, 156–61.

Rick, J., Perryman, S., Young, K., Guppy, A., and Hillage, J. (1998). *Workplace Trauma and Its Management: Review of the Literature*. Colgate, Norwich: Her Majesty's Stationery Office. Retrieved on: January 5, 2008, from www.hse.gov.uk/research/crr_pdf/1998/crr98170.pdf.

Robbins, I. (1999). The psychological impact of working in emergencies and the role of debriefing. *Journal of Critical Nursing*, 8, 263–8.

Ruggiero, K., Del Ben, K., Scotti, J., and Rabalais, A. (2003). Psychometric properties of the PTSD Checklist-Civilian Version. *Journal of Traumatic Stress*, 16, 495–502.

Ruggiero, K.J., Del Ben, K., Scotti, J.R., and Rabalais, A.E. (2003). Psychometric properties of the PTSD Checklist-Civilian Version. *Journal of Traumatic Stress*, 16, 495–502.

Schaefer, F., Blazer, D., Carr, K., Conner, K., Burchett, B., Schaefer, C., et al. (2007). Traumatic events and posttraumatic stress in cross-cultural mission assignments. *Journal of Traumatic Stress*, 20, 529–39.

Schooler, T., Dougall, A., and Baum, A. (1999). Cues, frequency, and the disturbing nature of intrusive thoughts: patterns seen in rescue workers after the crash of Flight 427. *Journal of Traumatic Stress*, 12, 571–85.

Schüffel, W., Schade, B., and Schunk, T. (n.d.). A brief inventory to investigate stress reactions: Posttraumatic Symptom Scale, 10 Items (PTSS-10) by Raphael, Lundin & Weisæth. Retrieved on: March 20, 2008, from http://psydok.sulb.uni-saarland.de/volltexte/2004/437/pdf/artikel.pdf.

Schwarzwald, J., Solomon, Z., Weisenberg, M., and Mikulincer, M. (1987). Validation of the Impact of Event Scale for psychological sequelae of combat. *Journal of Consulting and Clinical Psychology*, 55, 251–6.

Shapinsky, A., Rapport, L., Henderson, M., and Axelrod, B. (2005). Civilian PTSD Scales. Relationship with trait characteristics and everyday distress. *Assessment*, 12, 220–230.

Sheeran, T. and Zimmerman, M. (2002). Screening for posttraumatic stress disorder in a general psychiatric outpatient setting. *Journal of Consulting and Clinical Psychology*, 70, 961–6.

Sloan, P., Arsenault, L., Hilsenroth, M., and Havill, L. (1995). Use of the Mississippi Scale for Combat-Related PTSD in detecting war-related, non-combat stress symptomatology. *Journal of Clinical Psychology*, 51, 799–801.

Smith, M., Redd, W., DuHamel, K., Vickberg, S., and Ricketts, P. (1999). Validation of the PTSD Checklist-Civilian Version in survivors of bone marrow transplantation. *Journal of Traumatic Stress*, 12, 485–99.

Sommer, I. and Ehlert, U. (2004). Adjustment to trauma exposure. Prevalence and predictors of posttraumatic stress disorder symptoms in mountain guides. *Journal of Psychosomatic Research*, 57, 329–35.

Stephens, C. and Long, N. (2000). Communication with police supervisors and peers as a buffer of work-related traumatic stress. *Journal of Organizational Behavior*, 21, 407–24.

Tang, D. (1994). Psychotherapy for train drivers after railway suicide. *Social Science Medicine*, 38, 477–8.

Thewes, B., Meiser, B., and Hickie, I. (2001). Psychometric properties of the Impact of Event Scale amongst women at increased risk for hereditary breast cancer. *Psycho-Oncology*, 10, 459–68.

Theorell, T., Leymann, H., Jodko, M., Konarski, K., Norbeck, H., and Eneroth, P. (1992). "Person under train" incidents: medical consequences for subway drivers. *Psychosomatic Medicine*, 54, 480–488.

Thorndike, E.L. (1911). Provisional laws of acquired behavior or learning (Chapter 4), *Animal Intelligence*. New York: The McMillian Company.

Tranah, T. and Farmer, R. (1994). Effects on train drivers: psychological reactions of drivers to railway suicide. *Social Science Medicine*, 38, 459–69.

van der Ploeg, E. and Dorresteijn, S. (2003). Critical incidents and chronic stressors at work: their impact on forensic doctors. *Journal of Occupational Health Psychology*, 8, 157–66.

Vatshelle, Å. and Moen, B. (1999). Serious on-the-track accidents experienced by train drivers: psychological reactions and long-term health effects. *Journal of Psychosomatic Research*, 42, 43–52.

Vedantham, K., Brunet, A., and Boyer, R. (2001). Posttraumatic stress disorder, trauma exposure and the current health of Canadian bus drivers. *Canadian Journal of Psychiatry*, 46, 149–55.

Ventura J., Liberman R.P., Green M.F., Shaner A., and Mintz, J. (1998). Training and quality assurance with the structured clinical interview for DSM-IV (SCID-I/P). *Psychiatric Research*, 79(2), 163–73.

Ventureyra, V., Yao, S., Cottraux, J., Note, I., and De Mey-Guillard, C. (2002). The validation of the Posttraumatic Stress Disorder Checklist Scale in posttraumatic stress disorder and nonclinical subjects. *Psychotherapy and Psychosomatics*, 71, 47–53.

Violanti, J., Andrew, M., and Burchfiel, C.M. (2006). Posttraumatic stress symptoms and subclinical cardiovascular disease in police officers. *International Journal of Stress Management*, 13, 541–54.

Vreven, D., Gudanowski, D., King., L., and King, D. (1995). The civilian version of the Mississippi PTSD Scale: a psychometric evaluation. *Journal of Traumatic Stress*, 8, 91–109.

Wagner, D., Heinrichs, M., and Ehlert, U. (1998). Prevalence and symptoms of posttraumatic stress disorder in German professional firefighters. *American Journal of Psychiatry*, 155, 1727–32.

Wagner, S.L., McFee, J.A., and Martin, C.A. (2010). Mental Health Implications of Fire Service Membership. *Traumatology*, 16(2), 26–32.

Weathers, F., Keane, T., and Davidson, J. (2001). Clinician-Administered PTSD Scale: a review of the first ten years of research. *Depression and Anxiety*, 13, 132–56.

Weathers, F., Litz, B., Herman, D., and Keane, T. (1993, October). *The PTSD Checklist: Reliability, Validity and Diagnostic Utility*. Paper presented at the Annual Meeting of the International Society for Traumatic Stress Studies, San Antonio, TX.

Weiss, D., and Marmar, C. (1997). The Impact of Event Scale–Revised. In J. Wilson and T. Keane (eds), *Assessing Psychological Trauma and PTSD* (pp. 399–411). New York: Guildford.

Weiss, D., Marmar, C., Metzler, T., and Ronfeldt, H. (1995). Predicting symptomatic distress in emergency services personnel. *Journal of Consulting and Clinical Psychology*, 63, 361–8.

Whittington, R. and Wykes, T. (1994). Violence in psychiatric hospitals: are certain staff prone to being assaulted? *Journal of Advanced Nursing*, 19, 219–25.

Yum, B., Roh, J., Ryu, J., Won, J., Kim, C., Lee, J., et al. (2006). Symptoms of PTSD according to individual and work environment characteristics of Korean railroad drivers with experience of person-under-train accidents. *Journal of Psychosomatic Research*, 61, 691–7.

Zakowski, S., Valdimarsdottir, H., Bovbjerg, D., Borgen, P., Holland, J., Kash, K., et al. (1997). Predictors of intrusive thoughts and avoidance in women with family histories of breast cancer. *Annals of Behavioral Medicine*, 19, 362–9.

Zilberg, N., Weiss, D., and Horowitz, M. (1982). Impact of Event Scale: a cross-validation study and some empirical evidence supporting a conceptual model of stress response syndromes. *Journal of Consulting and Clinical Psychology*, 50, 407–14.

Chapter 8
Toxic Work Environment

Bullying consists of the least competent most aggressive employee projecting their incompetence on to the least aggressive most competent employee and winning.

Tim Field

Introduction

In the last two decades there has been an increase in awareness that work climate, organizational practices, and employee relations have a profound impact on employee retention, productivity, and well-being.

The present chapter is divided into two sections. The first section discusses the elements that make a work environment toxic. The second section outlines toxic employee relations such as workplace bullying and mobbing and their associated costs.

The Toxic Work Environment

Toxicity is synonymous with poisonous. Toxins are agents that act to produce serious injury or death once inside the system. Applying this definition of toxicity to the workplace, toxic work environments are environments that negatively impact the long-term viability of an organization. It is reasonable to conclude that an organization can be considered toxic if it is ineffective as well as destructive to its employees (Appelbaum and Roy-Girard, 2007). But just what elements make a workplace toxic?

A potential caveat should be mentioned before proceeding. Not every toxic element outlined in this chapter will cause dramatic poisonous effects once inside the system. Rather, like living systems, organizational systems operate within a range of toxicity that can be tolerated before aspects of the system begin to suffer and shut down. Perhaps a simple analogy will make this point more clear. Take the element selenium for example. Selenium is an essential micronutrient in humans that plays an important role in the functioning of the thyroid gland. Humans tolerate and even require selenium in small quantities. This is because small amounts of selenium are required in order for the thyroid to activate hormones and their metabolites. However, selenium is toxic when taken in large doses and even a concentration larger than 800 micrograms per day can become poisonous. Large doses can result in symptoms such as: hair loss, fatigue, neurological damage, cirrhosis of the liver, and death. The organizational climate is no different with respect to its tolerance of toxic elements. While having employees work longer hours, accomplish additional work tasks, and sign a daunting contract might not appear toxic when considered in isolation, when taken together these elements can prove poisonous. It is not until toxic elements accumulate in the workplace that the effects become noticeably crippling. Without further interruption, let us turn our attention to the characteristics that make a workplace toxic.

As can be seen in Figure 8.1, workplace toxicity ultimately arises when employees experience a breach in their psychological contract and bring negative emotions into the workplace. The elements that lead to a breach in the psychological contract and exacerbate workplace toxicity can be placed into the

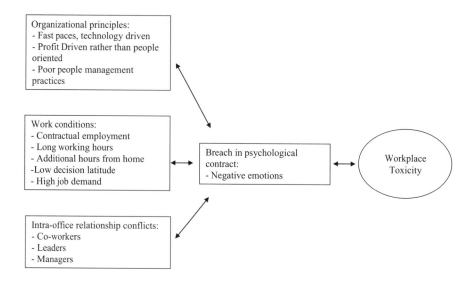

Figure 8.1   Elements of workplace toxicity

three general categories: organizational principles, work conditions, and intra-office relationship conflicts. Each element of Figure 8.1 will be discussed in turn starting with the psychological contract.

BREACH IN PSYCHOLOGICAL CONTRACT

Toxicity occurs when an employee suffers a breach in their psychological contract. The psychological contract refers to an employee's unwritten perceptions of what they feel they owe their employer and what their employer owes them (Robinson, 1996). This contract is inherently perceptual and it should be recognized that one person's understanding will not necessarily be shared by other parties. This means that a breach in the psychological contract can occur because of a 'real' breach (for example, an employer promises an employee a raise and then rescinds the offer) or a 'perceived' breach (for example, an employee does not receive a promotion that management suggested the employee was a strong candidate for).

The psychological contract is created during the recruitment and hiring process and is continually refined throughout the term of employment. Contracts of this nature are developed through an employee's interactions with organization members and with the organization's culture. Thus, psychological contracts are shaped by both overt actions as well as through vicarious learning and organization norms. Most psychological contracts are governed by morality and the rules of fair exchange and would endorse such expectations as: fair and respectful treatment, compensation for overtime, to be a valued member in the organization, and to have the opportunity for additional training and advancement. The best way to maintain and develop a clear psychological contract is to make business practices and role expectations as explicit as possible at the outset of employment.

Research has shown that there are two basic types of psychological contract violations—reneging and incongruence. Reneging occurs when an organization knowingly breaks a promise given to an employee. For example, due to unforeseen circumstances a company is no longer able to give their employee a management promotion that had previously been promised. The second type of violation—incongruence—occurs when there is a discrepancy between the views of the organization and those of the employee. For example, an employee may hold the belief that there should be additional compensation for work performed at home while the employer may view such work as an inherent aspect of the job. Regardless of whether the perceptions held are accurate, the negative effects arising from a breach in the psychological contract are very real and severe. Sandra Robinson from the University of British Columbia along with her colleagues have shown that a breach in psychological contract results in reduced employee trust, job satisfaction, intent to stay with the organization, sense of obligation, and work performance. These are toxic effects which introduce negative emotions such as contempt, anger, and disgust into the organizational culture which leads to poor work performance and intra-office relationship conflicts. Sometimes it is the organization's governing principles that increase the risk of violating employee psychological contracts and resulting in workplace toxicity.

Toxic Organization Principles

In many situations it is the fundamental principles governing an organization that lead to workplace toxicity and ultimately to decay in the organization and burgeoning mental illness. Toxic organizations operate in a fast-paced and technologically driven manner, are profit-driven rather than people-oriented, and have poor people management practices. Today's work environment is unlike any before. The ease and accessibility of the internet and technology makes the sharing of information increasingly easy. Employers now demand that their employees acquire vast amounts of knowledge, become proficient in a number of new technologies, and work increasingly long hours. These changes are making the work environment increasingly fast-paced, technologically driven, and toxic.

The manner by which work environments are changing to fast-paced, technology-driven enterprises is leading to the deterioration of employee psychological work conditions (Landsbergis, 2003). Employees in the 21st century are often required to work long hours and choose a work-life imbalance that favors work. Let us consider the advent of mobile phones as one key example. Mobile phones are one of the most commonly found commodities in the world. According to the International Telecommunication Union (ITU, 2010), 77 percent of the world and 94.1 percent of North Americans currently own mobile phones. Mobile phones are great for allowing people to stay connected anywhere in the world and to be contacted at any time during the day. Most people would agree that this is good for their personal life but it proves problematic when navigating work needs. Whether employees realize it or not, owning a mobile phone places employees in contact with their employers 24 hours a day through phone or e-mail and creates an unwritten expectation that employers should be able to contact the employee as required. This unwritten availability makes it increasingly difficult for many employees to relax and wind down as they feel the continual pressure of work bearing down upon them. Being in constant contact with work violates a psychological contract that most employees have about maintaining a work-life balance and introduces harmful negative emotions into the system which can spur forth mental illness.

All employees look for employment that has a balance between work life and personal life. In 1999 Gemini Consulting conducted an international poll of work needs among 10,339 employees from some 13 countries. Findings from this poll indicated that there are universal qualities that are desirable in the workplace. The five most desirable qualities were:

1. the ability to balance work and personal life

2. work that is truly enjoyable

3. job security for the future

4. a fair wage or salary

5. co-workers who are enjoyable to be around.

Healthy organizations are employee-oriented while toxic organizations are profit-driven. Toxic organizations focus on the bottom line rather than employee health and well-being. The fundamental principles of such organizations are not based on reciprocity, mutual respect, and care but rather on controlling employees, handing out additional assignments, generating profit, and perpetuating a "company comes first" attitude. Organizations operating in such a manner view employees as a cost of production or an expense rather than their most valuable assets. Viewing employees as an expense rather than an asset is considered a poor people management practice because it sends the message that employees are expendable and not valued. Recall from Chapters 4 and 5, creating an unpredictable work environment without the feeling of job-security, where employees are devalued and belittled can result in the development of anxiety or depression. Such practices are highly toxic and can end up costing employers some 18 percent in terms of productivity and profitability (Patterson, West, Lawthom, et al., 1997).

It must be recognized that being obsessed with success is not synonymous with toxicity. Rather, toxicity occurs when an obsession for success and capital gain leads to negative/counterproductive emotions. Successful companies demand a great deal from their employees but they bend, compromise, reward, and give back to their employees in return. Successful companies avoid creating a culture of toxicity by building people management practices into the structure and integrity of their organization. This includes having clear and universally accepted business policies and aims, having better training, offering appraisals, allowing for job variety, fostering job responsibility, and endorsing teamwork and communication. Such practices pay dividends in the long run.

Implementing good people management practices can be highly profitable for an organization. Companies with high people management practices consistently and reliably outperform companies with low people management practices (Rishardson and Thompson, 1999; Dyck and Roithmayer, 2001). Some evidence suggests that effective human resource practices can raise shareholder value (that is, stock market value) by between $20,000 and $40,000 per employee (Pfeffer, 1998). It seems that businesses receive above average returns if they adopt a broader range of human resources practices for more employees and integrate these practices into their infrastructure (Huselid and Becker, 1996).

Toxic Work Conditions

Work conditions have a pronounced influence on workplace toxicity and employee mental health. Poor work conditions such as contractual employment, increasingly long working hours, and high job demand with low job control create an atmosphere in which the employee feels devalued, stressed, and disrespected. Organizations that promote poor work conditions in turn promote the decay of employee psychological well-being and increase the likelihood of mental illness in the workplace.

One element that has proven particularly toxic is the employee contract. Forcing employees on their first day of work to sign at-will a contract giving the employer the right to fire the employee for any reason sends the wrong kind of message. Much like being in a relationship, what happens on the first day at work sets the precedence for the rest of that working relationship. Forcing employees to sign a contract sends the message on day one that the employee does not have a permanent employment relationship but rather a contractual relationship. Such contractual relationships remove job security, create stress, result in unpredictability at work, and deter feelings of loyalty and trust (Grazier, 1999; Pfeffer, 1998). Perhaps a quick analogy would be of use. If you were on a blind date with a potential attractive mate would you inform this person that as soon as they "misbehave" you will terminate the relationship in search of a more suitable mate? Most people would agree that such a response would not win over too many second dates. Work relationships bear many similarities with social and romantic relationships in that they are founded in a common understanding of respect, trust, and reciprocity, all of which can be defeated by the initial contract. Thus, it is crucial that employers take care and attention to carefully draft an inviting contract.

Moving towards a fast-paced and technologically driven workforce, employees work longer hours in order to learn, master, and stay at the forefront of an evolving labor market that requires an increasingly large skill-set. For example, not only does the average worker now have to master their mobile phone but they must learn how to tether the device to their iPad, sync the device to their automobile, and download and manage applications to track weekly sales. Working increasingly long hours is a toxic element that is nowhere more evident than in the United States. Americans work longer hours than workers in most European and Asian countries (Pfeffer, 2010; Yang, Schnall, Jauregui, et al., 2006). A good body of research now suggests that long working hours are impacting the physical health of Americans, resulting in hypertension, depression, anxiety, and substance abuse among other disorders (Frone, 2000; Frone, Russell, and Barnes, 1996). A main reason why long working hours have toxic effects is because they place stress on the family unit by disequilibrating the work-life balance in favor of work. Research has supported this conclusion, finding that employees with a significant amount of work-family conflict are some 2 to 30 times more likely to suffer from a mental illness (Frone, 2000).

Not only are employees working longer hours, more employees are finding it necessary to bring their office work home at night. According to a poll conducted by the National Sleep Foundation (2008), Americans working full time spend 9.5 hours a day at the office and an additional 4.5 hours per week working from home. Most of us do not like these additional working hours to take away from our leisure time so instead we compromise on the amount of sleep that we get each night. This is exactly what was found in the poll conducted by the National Sleep Foundation. Only 21 percent of full-time employees reported that they slept for 8 hours per night. Further, the relationship between hours worked and sleep attained was dose-dependent such that as the number of working hours increased the number of sleeping hours decreased. By now most employers should be aware that stress reduces sleep and that lethargic employees are less productive on the job, yet in many occupations long working hours is still the norm.

Two other work conditions that are highly toxic when taken together are low decision latitude combined with high job demand. Recall from Chapter 6 that occupations with high job demands combined with low decision-making control are associated with extremely high levels of stress that are accompanied by rampant physical and mental health concerns. For this chapter it is only important to know that a stressful job with high demand and low decision latitude is toxic to employee mental and physical health. The interested reader can revisit Chapter 6 for a more thorough consideration of this issue.

Warning Signs of the Toxic Environment

As was mentioned earlier in this chapter, organizations can operate and thrive within a range of workplace toxicity. So how do we know when workplace toxicity has crossed the threshold of toxicity into the realm of poisonous? Luckily several warning signs have been identified which may suggest that the workplace has reached its toxicity threshold. Warning signs include:

- High absenteeism or turnover: Workers are not showing up to work or are leaving the job because of discomfort with the organization climate.

- Poorly performed work: Employees feel devalued and it shows in the work effort that they are providing.

- High customer complaints: Customers can easily recognize a negative organizational environment and, having nothing to lose, are not afraid to file complaints.

- Turf wars between employees: Turf wars indicate that the overall atmosphere is not one of team work but rather one of competition and production.

- Complaints of verbal or physical intimidation, sexist or racist comments, or excessive foul language: Utterances of threats and profanities shows that the atmosphere has turned from one of positive citizenry to one riddled with negative emotions and contempt.

- Increased worker compensation claims: Employees are looking for a way out of the organization because they can no longer handle the daily stressors.

- Poor turnouts during social functions: A clear indicator that the personality of employees clash.

- Repeated refusal/avoidance of overtime that would normally have been accepted: Employees no longer see the company as a beneficial place to spend their time and are in need of a better family-work life balance.

- Decline in workplace mental health: The stress at work has reached a critical boiling point.

As a general rule of thumb, the greater the number of signs that the work environment is toxic the more likely it is that the organization has exceeded its threshold of workplace toxicity.

Toxic Employee Relations

Humans are inherently social beings. All of us engage in a plethora of social interactions each and every day as we navigate our way through the world. Some of these interpersonal interactions are with friends, some with family, and others are with co-workers or even strangers. Some of these interactions carry with them the weight of the world (for example, interviewing for a career) while others occur seemingly unnoticed (for example, paying courtesy to the stranger holding open the door). Most social interactions are positive and rewarding however sometimes they can be unpleasant and negative. There are those social interactions that we decide to engage in and those that we are forced to engage in. Social interactions between co-workers—employee relations—can prove particularly difficult because they are obligatory in nature. Employees are expected to maintain a civilized and cordial working relationship within an organization. Most employees adhere to such practices but there are some employees who do not get along with others. Organizations are often large and diverse, resulting in a melting pot of personalities, some that are bound to clash from time to time. When addressed immediately and properly, negative employee relations are effectively neutralized with no further repercussions. However, toxic workplaces tolerate, endorse, and sometimes promote negative employee relations, leading to negative interactions such as workplace bullying.

The toxic workplace is fast-paced and profit-driven with poor people management practices. These organizations rarely have systems in place to resolve co-worker disputes and overlook the warning signs of harmful office communication. In fact, toxic work conditions and toxic organization practices introduce negative emotions into the workplace which stimulate or exacerbate toxic employee relations. For example, workplace bullying has been found to result from dissatisfaction with management, role conflicts, low decision latitude, and monotonous or unchallenging work environments (Einarsen, Raknes and Matthiesen, 1994). In the case of workplace bullying the negative emotions of one employee arising from toxic work conditions are transferred onto other unsuspecting and innocent employees who become the targets of unsolicited physical and psychological abuse.

At the lowest level, toxic employee relations begin as indirect, discrete, and often unnoticed behavior. These lower level behaviors include acts of verbal aggression, victimization, and incivility. Acts of verbal aggression encompass all forms of name calling, malicious jokes, discrimination, threats, prejudice, humiliation, and the like. Victimization includes acts that exploit other co-workers such as: taking undue credit for the work of other employees, stealing the ideas and property of co-workers, making false accusations, and placing undeserved blame onto others. Finally, acts of incivility are those actions that ostracize or socially isolate co-workers such as socially excluding co-workers or spreading rumors.

Toxic employee relations often begin when one or more difficult employees who are overly critical, judgmental, or demanding identify a co-worker that they view as different, submissive, or privileged. Difficult employees will often precipitate a negative workplace relationship by identifying a flaw in a potential victim and playing a game of cat and mouse where they methodically use, manipulate, and expose that flaw, leaving the employee defenseless. Stated alternatively, difficult employees engage in negative social interactions with employees in an attempt to judge whether or not the employee has the capacity to fight back and defend themselves. If an employee is unable to defend himself then the difficult employee increases the frequency and intensity of their attacks. These attacks are performed in an attempt to gain an advantage over the target. Perhaps an example will clarify how this vicious cycle can be perpetuated.

Consider Slim and Jim who both work on the assembly production line for the local automobile company. This automobile company is a volume retailer and keeps a fast-paced work environment to ensure that supply can meet demand. Slim is a highly competitive employee who is negative, critical, and fault-finding in the performance of other co-workers. Jim on the other hand is a more laid back and carefree employee, but a hard worker nonetheless. Slim has troubles with his wife at home and comes into work in a negative mood. Slim begins criticizing Jim on the speed with which he uses hand tools and the craftsmanship of his work. Although upset by these comments, Jim realizes that he is not as quick as Slim when it comes to assembly so he ignores his banter and quietly continues to work. This exchange allows Slim to realize that he can disrespect and mock Jim with no repercussion. Slim then decides to test this theory further by making the attack more personal in identifying a characteristic weakness of Jim, in this case his large ears. Slim says to Jim, "What are you deaf? Are you not going to respond? With ears that big you would think that you could hear better?" This scenario highlights the ease with which negative office communications can occur and worsen. An effective organization with good people management practices would realize that Slim is upset because he is having problems at home and would likely inform Slim that work is not the place for these issues by sending him home for the day. A toxic organization, on the other hand, would reinforce this behavior by ignoring it or agreeing with Slim and informing Jim that he could work a little more efficiently. Toxic behaviors such as this create a perceived power imbalance, favoring Slim. This power imbalance is an important point that we will return to when we discuss workplace bullying.

Employees who are perpetrators of toxic employee relations have been found to display certain personality characteristics. Workplace bullies are usually critical, negative perfectionists who are fault-finding, aggressive, and have little trouble distorting the truth (Speedy, 2006). Other toxic characteristics portrayed by bullies include: insincerity, arrogance, insensitivity, remorselessness, impatience, erratic behavior, unreliability, and a general lack of personal and professional ethics. Workplace bullies often are impulsive, locking onto ideas like a guided missile. They view the path to success as one achieved through ruthless, cutthroat business tactics in which other employees are expendable and the bottom line is all that matters. Interestingly, some of the same characteristics that make a good office bully also make a manager who is effective at using employees to generate maximum results.

Toxic work relationships are not only perpetuated by co-workers but are also, and more commonly, perpetuated by organization leaders and management. In a nationally representative survey, perpetrators of workplace bullying were managers or leaders in 72 percent of reported cases (Namie, 2007). A leader is considered toxic when they negatively affect work climate, lack concern for others, and are motivated purely by self interest (Appelbaum and Roy-Girard, 2007). Toxic leaders find glory in "turf protection", fighting and control. They have difficulty relinquishing control over any aspect of the organization. Their sense of control is maintained through quickly passing blame when problems arise and by failing to accept blame or personal responsibility for their decisions. In essence, toxic leaders create an unpredictable work environment where trust is not built and solutions are not sought out due to a fear of negative repercussions. In this sense, toxic leaders are not good at managing their staff because they have not learned to use positive reinforcement or a token economy but rather implement a totalitarian regime.

Toxic managers are a special case of toxic leaders who degrade the work environment internally through their poor people management practices. The toxic manager creates a negative work atmosphere by destroying morale, impairing retention, interfering with cooperation and information sharing, and by being unpredictable and disrespectful to staff (Appelbaum and Roy-Girard, 2007). They see staff as expendable commodities and are narrowly focused on immediate goals that satisfy a fast-paced, budget-driven business. Such treatment of staff increases turnover, absenteeism, and presenteeism, as well as physiological and stress-related disorders. The need for an organization to be in the black (in profit) encourages the existence of the toxic manager who may achieve short-term budgetary goals but fails to plan long-term organization agendas.

As will be illustrated in the next session on workplace bullying, the profitability and human capital related costs of toxic employee relations is both real and severe. Not only do harmful office relationships decrease company profitability and employee productivity, but such relationships create wear and tear on employee mental and physical well-being.

Workplace Bullying

Workplace bullying is a poisonous event that is surprisingly common among today's workforce. A systematic review conducted on more than 86 independent samples suggests that workplace bullying occurs in 14.8 percent of the workforce (Nielsen, Matthiesen, and Einarsen, 2010). Worse yet, the negative impacts of workplace bullying permeate through the entire organization. It is as if some individuals never truly get to escape high school.

You might be asking yourself, how do I know if bullying is occurring in my workplace? Before we answer this question with a definition of workplace bullying, you should know that bullying likely is occurring in your workplace but has been overlooked or unnoticed. Definitions of bullying incorporate frequency, intensity, duration, and power disparity (Leymann, 1990; Einarsen, 1999). First, bullying is more than an isolated negative behavior, but rather consists of persistent negative acts that occur regularly, usually defined as weekly or more frequently (Mikkelsen, 2001; Mikkelsen and Einarsen, 2002). Second, bullying is marked by intense negative behaviors meaning that bullying encompasses a wide range of negative acts (Leymann, 1990; Agervold, 2007; Einarsen, Hoel and Notelaers, 2009). As such, isolated or rare negative acts constitute lesser forms of subordinate behaviors rather than workplace bullying itself. Third, the negative effects must persist for a minimum duration of six months (Einarsen, 2000; Hoel, Cooper and Faragher, 2001). Finally, some form of real or perceived power difference must exist between the bully and the target. The power difference between the victim and the bully is crucial as it indicates that the victim has become compromised and represents a highly vulnerable target incapable of changing their own circumstance. This might be the reason why employees in lower organizational positions are at an increased risk of being bullied; lower status workers are simply more vulnerable (Hodson, Roscigno, and Lopez, 2006).

Thus, bullying at work can be defined as a "social interaction in which the sender uses verbal and/or nonverbal communication regularly, weekly and for a period of at least six-months that is characterized by negative or aggressive elements directed towards the personality and self-esteem of the receiver" (Agervold, 2007, p. 165). To add to this definition, the aggressor's acts need be intentional and the target must perceive the acts as threatening or damaging.

Bullying at work may be particularly difficult to notice because it evolves gradually over a four-stage process. First, the perpetrator directs subtle aggressive outlets towards employees. These subtle aggressive outlets consist of less severe negative acts that are often overlooked or ignored. Second, it becomes apparent that a co-worker cannot adequately defend himself from the bully, leading to an increase in the frequency and intensity of subtle aggressive outlets directed against the target. Third, after a while, bullying begins to place a negative social stigma on the target. The social stigma placed on the target highlights the targets personality flaws and results in intra-office prejudice against the target. Finally, prejudices having been formed towards the target because of bullying cause the organization to treat the target rather than the bully as the problem. The organization tends to view the target as a function of its own misfortune. In addition to this, co-workers or managers may perceive the situation as fair treatment of a difficult person.

A work-environment hypothesis has been put forward suggesting that bullying arises because of the work environment. Research in support of this hypothesis has found that bullying at work occurs most often if employees are dissatisfied with management, experience role conflicts, have low decision latitude, or find work monotonous and unchallenging (Einarsen, Raknes and Matthiesen, 1994). This research suggests that employees will begin to bully co-workers if they are dissatisfied and bored with their jobs and have no clear role or decision-making power at work. Essentially, workplace bullying may be the result of employees redirecting unmet needs or frustrations onto another innocent co-worker.

Strandmark and Hallberg (2007) postulated a model of the origins of workplace bullying that can be viewed in Figure 8.2a, with a model using more familiar terms from this chapter being seen in Figure 8.2b. According to this model, workplace bullying begins with potential arenas of conflict and personal strengths or vulnerabilities. Potential arenas of conflict represent organizational characteristics such as job reorganization, poor leadership, and unclear roles that violate the psychological contract. Personal strengths or vulnerabilities refer to personality characteristics of the victim that make them a high-profile target. Such personality characteristics can be strengths (for example, being strong, driven, motivated or engaged) or vulnerabilities (for example, emotionally unstable, neurotic, easily upset, shy, depressed, low self-esteem, or lacking social competence). The basic premise behind this model is that unstable work characteristics can create potential arenas for conflict that arise because several employees hold differing personal and professional values. A power struggle emerges when two or more employees engage in a conflict over personal or professional values. As neither party wishes to show weakness or back down they will flex their "occupational muscle" so to speak and try to prove that they are the office alpha employee by demeaning, belittling, and bullying an employee who has personal strengths or vulnerabilities that can be exploited (that is, an employee who sticks out their neck or goes against the "office norms"). This is the basic premise of the model postulated by Strandmark and Hallberg to which we have added one important feature. We have shrouded this model of workplace bullying by personality characteristics of the perpetrator. Not every dispute or conflict results in workplace bullying. Workplace bullying will only occur when a particular type of employee is engaged in an intra-office dispute. These are the

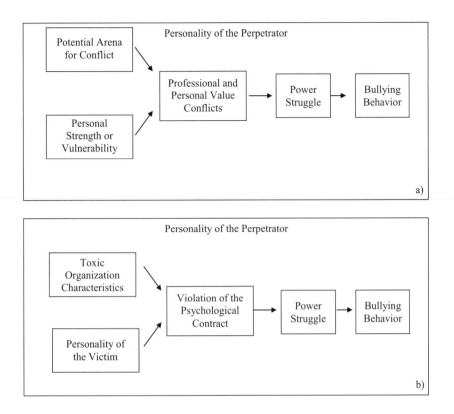

Figure 8.2   Etiology of Workplace Bullying

insincere, arrogant, impulsive, impatient, remorseless employees who view the path of success as one achieved through ruthless, cutthroat business tactics. In certain circumstances, workplace bullying can be viewed as a means of adaptation and survival in the toxic workplace.

ECONOMIC BURDEN OF WORKPLACE BULLYING: DEVELOPMENT OF AN ROI EQUATION

The proceeding sections outline the costs associated with workplace bullying. The most reliable and representative costs are used to calculate an ROI equation that is presented in Appendix C, along with instructions on how to use this equation to estimate the cost savings that organizations can anticipate from addressing workplace bullying.

Prevalence

Workplace bullying is more than four times as prevalent as workplace harassment, with an estimated 37 percent or 54 million Americans reporting being bullied at some point during their working lives. Estimates on the lifetime prevalence of workplace bullying are highly varied ranging between 17 and 43 percent of employees. This wide range in prevalence is due to a variety of definitions from which researchers derive their estimates. In 2007, Pamela Lutgen-Sandvik, working out of the University of New Mexico, and her colleagues, from the University of Arizona, surveyed 469 American employees, determining that the prevalence of workplace bullying varies depending on the operational definition used by the researcher. These researchers found that workplace bullying impacts 9.4 percent of employees when subjective reports were used and 28 percent of employees when exposure to bullying behavior was reported. Interestingly, all employees who subjectively reported being targets of bullying reported a higher occurrence of negative acts than did non-bullied participants. This suggests that identifying targets of bullying through negative acts captures the same employees who self-report being bullied as well as those employees who do not wish to self-identify as targets.

Results from the research of Lutgen-Sandvik and others highlight two important features on workplace bullying. First, employees are reluctant to self-report being bullied and as a result bullying at work is commonly underestimated. This reluctance to self-report bullying is probably a result of the stigma attached to being viewed as a weak employee who cannot defend themselves from the attacks of a bully in the workplace. Second, bullying in the workplace is best captured through behavioral measures meaning that workplace bullying is best identified by asking employees to list their exposure to behaviors characteristic of bullying. Examples of behaviors of workplace bullying include, spreading gossip or rumours, making insults or offensive remarks, withholding information that effects another person's performance, forcing someone to work below their level of competence, ignoring someone, persistent criticism, or being exposed to an unmanageable workload.

The best estimate on the prevalence of workplace bullying comes from a meta-analysis conducted by Nielsen, Mathiesen and Einarsen in 2010. In common research practice the experimenter will obtain information from a sample (for example, say of 3,000 employees from a particular company) and devise a prevalence rate based upon that sample (for example, 450 out of the 3,000 employees show signs of characteristic x). This process is illustrated in Equation 10.1. A meta-analysis goes one step beyond this typical practice and uses the results of published studies as the sample rather than individual employees. For example, where typical research would obtain information from 3,000 employees a meta-analysis would obtain prevalence estimates from 3,000 separate experiments and use these prevalence estimates as the unit of analysis. The meta-analysis conducted by Nielson and colleagues examined the prevalence of workplace bullying through an examination of 102 prevalence estimates of bullying from 86 independent samples. Therefore, this meta-analysis is examining 102 estimates that were derived from 103,973 employees. The prevalence of workplace bullying obtained using behavioral measures (remember we determined behavioral measures to be the best method for measuring workplace bullying) was found to be 14.8 percent—a prevalence estimate which will be used to calculate our return on investment equation for workplace bullying.

Equation 10.1   Prevalence = $\dfrac{\text{sample with characteristic}}{\text{Total sample (n)}} \times \dfrac{\text{450 employees with signs}}{\text{3,000 employees assessed}}$

Impact of Workplace Bullying—Effects on the Organization

Workplace bullying is a serious issue that bears a great financial cost on employees, organizations, and society in general. In terms of direct financial costs, workplace bullying has been found to cost the Australian economy an estimated $13 billion per annum in increased absenteeism, presenteeism, recruitment costs, payouts, and legal fees (Speedy, 2006). The average cost of workplace bullying in non-litigated cases is approximately $20,000 when absenteeism, sick leave, counseling and rehiring are included. Some American estimates place the total costs of workplace bullying between $US 30,000 and $US 100,000 for each employee subjected to bullying in the workplace (Sheehan, 1999). These figures represent rough estimates into the direct costs of workplace bullying. This chapter takes a highly conservative approach in calculating the costs of workplace bullying using the best evidence currently available.

One of the negative impacts of workplace bullying is an increase in employee absenteeism. Targets of workplace bullying take additional time off work using sick days, family days, and mental health days in order to gain respite from the toxic work environment. Victims of bullying take, on average, seven additional days off work per annum than do their non-bullied counterparts (Hoel and Cooper, 2000). This equates to 56 hours of lost work a year; 4.67 lost working hours each month.

Not only do victims of workplace bullying miss more work days each year but their time spent while at work is far less productive. Presenteeism was examined in order to gain traction on employee productivity while at work. Presenteeism is a measure of time spent at work where the employee is not being productive. Victims of workplace bullying self-rate their level of productivity 7 percent lower than do non-victims (Hoel and Cooper, 2000). Assuming a 40 hour work week, a 7 percent reduction of productivity equates in 2.8 unproductive working hours each week (40 hours per week * 7%) or 11.2 unproductive hours spent at work each month.

Perhaps the largest cost of workplace bullying comes from employee retention. Victims of workplace bullying often view the only solution to their problems is to leave the organization and find employment elsewhere. Independent estimates indicate that 25 percent of victims leave their job as a result of workplace bullying (Rayner, 1997, 2000). Victims of workplace bullying do not leave their jobs immediately; however the best available evidence indicates that victims of workplace bullying are likely to leave the organization within the first three years of bullying. We can therefore place the yearly estimate of employee resignation due to workplace bullying at 8 percent (25 percent/three years). Employee turnover is a costly affair in terms of direct costs (recruitment, loss of experienced staff, overtime pay to cover shifts, testing and training new hires) and indirect costs (decreased morale, insufficient staffing, loss of social networks). The average estimate of replacing an $8/hr employee is $9,444.47 (Sasha-Corporation, January 2007).

Impact of Workplace Bullying—Effects on the Target's Health

Beyond the direct financial costs, workplace bullying wreaks havoc on the target, resulting in severe mental and physical health complications. Workplace bullying damages the target's self-esteem, cognitive health, physical health, and emotional health. These damages occur both directly as a result of bullying and indirectly as a result of poor coping mechanisms. Most individuals suffering from workplace abuse turn to avoidant coping strategies in which they typically engage in negative behaviors such as excessive smoking, excessive drinking, drug taking, and overeating (Shannon, Rospenda, and Richman, 2007). Indeed, abused employees are at an increase risk of developing depression, post-traumatic stress disorder, alcohol abuse, stress disorder, hypertension, or committing suicide (Lutgen-Sandvik, Tracy and Alberts, 2007).

Workplace bullying can directly lead to a host of adverse physiological, psychological, organizational and clinical symptoms. The physiological effects of bullying include: migraine, sweating, palpitations, nausea, stomach/ bowel disorder, elevated blood pressure, disrupted sleep patterns, and a reduction in energy. The psychological effects resulting from workplace bullying include: suffering a nervous breakdown, panic attacks, depression, loss in confidence and self-esteem, reduced concentration, and burnout. The organization impacts of workplace bullying include: moodiness, exacerbating toxic work conditions, bad co-worker relations, loss of respect for the organization, increased presenteeism, absenteeism, resignation, damaged reputation, litigation fees, and a loss of clientele. Finally, workplace bullying is a significant source of workplace social stress leading to a variety of clinical symptoms including: stress-related disorder, depression, anxiety, social isolation, psychosomatic illnesses, despair and compulsions (Leymann, 1990). One study found workplace bullying to be moderately associated with an increase in stress ($r = .34$) and strongly associated with a decline in job satisfaction ($r = -.59$). In essence, job satisfaction declines and employees become increasingly on edge and distressed as harmful workplace behaviors increase to the level of bullying.

A 2002 study examined the relationship between workplace bullying and psychosomatic complaints among 240 Danish factory workers after using statistical methods to control for the effects of negative emotions and self-efficacy (Mikkelsen and Einarsen, 2002). Eight percent of employees were found to suffer at least one act of bullying weekly over a six-month timeframe and were considered victims of bullying. Exposure to workplace bullying showed a strong association with psychological health complaints ($r = .52$) and a moderate association with psychosomatic complaints ($r = .32$) and the propensity with which employees experience negative emotions ($r = .41$). After controlling for negative emotions, bullying accounted for 27 percent of the variance in psychological health complaints (for example, reports of depression, anxiety, somatic complaints). Bullying accounted for a further 10 percent of the variance in psychosomatic complaints (for example, dizziness, stomach ache, chest pains). This study was one of the first of its kind to reveal that a distinct and direct relationship exists between workplace bullying and the development of adverse physical and psychological outcomes on behalf of the target.

Using the aforementioned study we can begin to examine the cost of workplace bullying on the target's mental and physical health. First, bullying accounts for approximately 27 percent of the variance in reported mental health symptoms and also 10–20 percent of the adverse effects of stress. Furthermore, 23 percent of psychosomatic symptoms among victims can be explained by exposure to bullying. However, eradicating bullying will not alleviate its total effect on ill-health because the effects of bullying are cumulative and pervasive. Therefore, employing conservative estimates, it is reasonable for employers to anticipate lower ROIs in the way of 15 percent of mental and physical healthcare premiums among victims of bullying. This translates to a per employee savings of 2.25 percent for mental and physical healthcare (prevalence of workplace bullying 14.8 percent * the estimate of averted healthcare claims of 15 percent). Now that we have used inductive logic to determine the relative proportion of health insurance claims that are attributable to workplace bullying we can multiply this number by the average yearly employer expenditure on health insurance.

2011 statistics released from the United States Bureau of Labor Statistics (BLS) (ftp://ftp.bls.gov/pub/special.requests/ocwc/ect/ececrse.pdf; http://www.bls.gov/news.release/ecec.nr0.htm) indicate that employers spent on average $2.87 on health insurance and medicare per employee, per hour worked. This means that the average employer pays $114.80 each week for the health insurance of a full-time employee (cost of health insurance per hour $2.87 * hours worked per week 40). These costs include both mental and physical healthcare claims. If we can assume that our previous calculation into the relative proportion of health insurance claims that are attributable to workplace bullying is correct then employers who address the issue can expect to save approximately $2.58 (money spent on health insurance per employee per week $114.80 * proportion of claims attributable to bullying 2.25 percent) on health insurance payouts per week per employee. This equates to a savings of $12.04 per employee per month.

Impact of Workplace Bullying—Effects on Co-workers

The negative consequences of workplace bullying extend beyond the immediate target, creating a wake of collateral damage that consumes the organization and co-workers. Acts of bullying create secondary victims (that is, the witnesses) or employees who were not violated but whose perceptions, fears, and expectations changed as a result of vicarious exposure to workplace bullying. Bullying makes the work environment for non-targets worse by increasing office tension and stress while reducing group cohesion, morale, and functioning (Agervold, 2007). The effects of bullying percolate throughout the office environment making it more toxic and combative. Group cohesion is thwarted as negative emotions squash the positive work atmosphere and breed further contempt. It has been estimated that 11 percent of employees witness workplace bullying to a degree that is considered harmful (Lutgen-Sandvik, Tracy and Alberts, 2007). Productivity in those vicariously exposed to workplace bullying is reduced by approximately 2 percent (Hoel and Cooper, 2000).

Like a stone tossed into a pond, the effects of bullying ripple throughout the entire organization. Employees who bear witness to workplace violence suffer great duress, stress, and even mental illness. Lutgen-Sandvik et al. (2007) examined the workplace impact of bullying, finding that the negative effects of bullying exist on a gradient. Research has shown that employee stress level and psychosomatic complaints steadily increase as bullying moves from non-bullied employees to witnesses to targets of bullying. This suggests that employees working in an environment in which they see others being abused also experience heightened levels of negativity and distress. This idea is congruent with the finding that an audience of co-workers suffer, live in fear of becoming the next target, and report higher levels of stress and intent to resign than do non-exposed employees (Vartia, 2001). Bullying must then be considered a dangerous problem for the entire organization and not just for the individual target. Sometimes bullying is not the result of malevolent actions of a single individual but rather the malevolent actions of a group of employees.

Workplace Mobbing: When Bullying Becomes a Group Phenomenon

Workplace mobbing is like workplace bullying in that it involves: i) targeting self-esteem and creating social exclusion, ii) attacks made against the social relationships of the target, iii) attacks on reputation, iv) attacks on professional qualifications and life situation, and v) attacks on health (Leymann, 1990). Like bullying, workers who are the target of mobbing are subject to permanent criticism, detrimental comments, malicious gossip, attacks on their attitudes or beliefs, threats, or acts of violence. The difference between workplace mobbing and workplace bullying is that workplace mobbing is a more severe form of bullying in which the perpetrator is a group of individuals rather than a single individual.

Workplace mobbing can be defined as an abusive group behavior seeking to exclude, punish, and humiliate targets in order to drive them from the workplace (Speedy, 2006). Mobbing requires an increasingly toxic work atmosphere in which abusive behavior and social ostracizing has become the norm rather than the exception. The occurrences of such acts require a workplace tolerant of verbal and abusive behavior in which competition is encouraged and standout performances are shunned. Managers and leaders offer the best protection and intervention for workplace mobbing because mobbing is most likely the result of work colleagues rather than the manager (Hoel and Beale, 2006).

One study examining 406 employees in Spain for mobbing at work discovered that 111 employees (28 percent) met the criteria of suffering from two mobbing behaviors at least once per week for a period of six months (de Pedro, Sanchez, Navarro et al., 2008). The victims of mobbing were more susceptible to stress and reported many more psychosomatic symptoms. In fact, mobbing accounted for 27 percent of the variance in psychosomatic complaints reported. The targets of mobbing suffer clear and evident adverse effects and become increasingly susceptible to work stress and mental illness.

The targets of workplace mobbing are generally perceived as weak individuals who have personality flaws, do not fit in well with other, do not perform well at work, and cannot adequately defend themselves. Once it has begun, mobbing is a very difficult problem to address and correct because it is a group phenomenon that requires organizational change. It is the toxic organization climate that has become tolerant of conflicts that allows workplace mobbing to occur, indicating that it is the underlying company policies that must be changed to address the issue.

WORKPLACE BULLYING/MOBBING: PREVENTION AND TREATMENT STRATEGIES

In order to effectively deal with workplace bullying companies must tackle bullying and office disputes at every layer. Bullying prevention and reduction programs should address the enabling structures, the motivating structures, and the precipitating processes that lead to workplace bullying (Salin, 2003). At the front end, employers need to address the enabling conditions that make workplace bullying viable. Enabling conditions include the power imbalance, low perceived costs associated with bullying, as well as dissatisfaction and low decision latitude at work.

The most efficient way to reduce enabling conditions is through clear company rules and policies. Companies need to have a zero tolerance policy for bullying, coupled with a method for filing and evaluating complaints, and a system of internal communication. This will alleviate the power imbalance between management and employees, and create an environment of equal accountability. A strict zero tolerance policy for bullying that is adequately enforced and common knowledge to all employees will greatly increase the perceived costs associated with workplace bullying. Furthermore, company infrastructure that promotes whistle-blowing and other means of reporting intra-office conflicts will also reduce bullying/mobbing. It is recommended that complaint filing systems accept anonymous complaints to encourage targets to come forward. Keep in mind however that anonymous complaint systems require an investigative team to conduct follow-up analysis to verify the accuracy of such claims. Finally, employers can work to decrease employee dissatisfaction and increase decision latitude by performing regular reviews where the employee and management co-discuss job demands, job skills and the viability of additional training.

Motivating structures of workplace bullying include internal competition, reward systems that facilitate competition, and the perceived benefits of bullying an employee (Salin, 2003). Organizations can remove internal competition, reward systems, and perceived benefits by promoting teamwork and office civility rather than cutthroat business practices. Office teamwork and civility can be gained by making pay grades and promotions the decision of a management panel who judge the office conduct as well as performance markers for employees who are up for promotion. Organizations should also set clear expectations regarding acceptable and preferred office behavior while encouraging feedback to ensure that such expectations are being followed (Pearson, Andersson and Porath, 2000). Finally, organizations would be wise to acknowledge, praise, and reward exemplary office behavior.

Precipitating processes are events that are likely to result in workplace bullying. These processes are usually office crises such as restructuring, downsizing, implementing cost-cutting measures, demotions, or general staff turnover. The result of office crises are threat, pressure, stress, tension, and expressions of hostility and obstructionism (Baron and Neuman, 1996; Sheehan, 1999; Hoel and Cooper, 2000). The best way to deal with precipitating processes is to realize that they are associated with higher occurrences of problematic office behavior and plan for them well in advance. Staff should be notified of any large-scale changes well in advance of such changes. Employees should also have a chance to give their opinions about the changes. Finally, companies would be wise to encourage stressed or abused employees to seek relaxation training, keep fit, and to eat healthily so that stress does not become unhealthy and add to workplace toxicity.

Concluding Remarks

The modern workplace is a dynamic, fast-paced, and profit-driven environment where proper employee management practices often take a back seat to the bottom line of a company. The message being sent is that employees are expendable commodities rather than indispensable assets. To make matters worse, modern organizations are often riddled with toxic elements, such as demanding jobs, daunting employee contracts, long work hours, 24-hour availability, and low job security. Unsurprisingly, toxic workplace elements have a negative impact on employee health and well-being. The results can be an elevation in work absences, turnover, co-worker strife, and a decrease in workplace mental health. Fast-paced, profit-driven companies often promote employees with fault-finding, judgmental, and perfectionist qualities. By doing so, these companies are implicitly advocating for such tendencies in their employees. While more likely to maximize profit, such employees are less likely to manage employee relations in an egalitarian manner and are more likely to promote an environment conducive to co-worker strife, bullying, and aggression. Workplace bullying is surprisingly common among employees and results in negative effects that permeate throughout the entire organization. Victims of workplace bullying take more sick days, have more workplace absences, are less productive while they are at work, and are more likely to suffer from mental illness. Similar effects can also be observed in co-workers who bear witness to workplace bullying. It is in the best interests of an organization and its employees to implement strategies to effectively manage toxic workplace elements and bullying before serious problems emerge. This can often be accomplished by assessing organization practices and targeting enabling conditions.

More information can be found at the following sources:

Workplace bullying resources at http://www.workplacebullying.org/ or http://www.psa.org.nz/Campaignsandissues/WorkplaceBullying. aspx

Preventing and responding to workplace bullying at http://www.worksafe. vic.gov.au/forms-and-publications/forms-and-publications/ preventing-and-responding-to-bullying-at-work or http://www. stopbullyingsa.com.au

References

Agervold, M. (2007). Bullying at work: a discussion of definitions and prevalence, based on an empirical study. *Scandinavian Journal of Psychology*, 48(2), 161–72.

Appelbaum, S.H. and Roy-Girard, D. (2007). Toxins in the workplace: affect on organizations and employees. *Corporate Governance*, 7(1), 11.

Baron, R.A. and Neuman, J.H. (1996). Workplace violence and workplace aggression: evidence on their relative frequency and potential causes. *Aggressive Behavior*, 22(3), 161–73.

Bureau of Labor Statistics (2011). National Compensation Survey. Washington, DC: United States Department of Labor. Available at: ftp://ftp.bls.gov/pub/special.requests/ocwc/ect/ececrse.pdf.

de Pedro, M.M., Sanchez, M.I.S., Navarro, M.C.S., et al. (2008). Workplace mobbing and effects on workers' health. *Spanish Journal of Psychology*, 11(1), 219–27.

Dyck, D. and Roithmayer, T. (2001). The toxic workplace: is your organization making workers sick? *Benefits Canada*, 25(3), 52.

Einarsen, S. (1999). The nature and causes of bullying at work. *International Journal of Manpower*, 20(1–2), 16–27.

Einarsen, S. (2000). Harassment and bullying at work: a review of the Scandinavian approach. *Aggression and Violent Behavior*, 5(4), 379–401.

Einarsen, S., Hoel, H., and Notelaers, G. (2009). Measuring exposure to bullying and harassment at work: Validity, factor structure and psychometric properties of the Negative Acts Questionnaire-Revised. *Work and Stress*, 23(1), 24–44.

Einarsen, S., Raknes, B.B., and Matthiessen, B . (1994). Gullying and harassment at work and their relationship to work environment quality: an exploratory study. *European Journal of Work and Organizational Psychology*, 4(4), 381–401.

Frone, M.R. (2000). Work-family conflict and employee psychiatric disorders: the national comorbidity survey. *Journal of Applied Psychology*, 85(6), 888–95.

Frone, M.R., Russell, M., and Barnes, G.M. (1996). Work-family conflict, gender. and health-related outcomes: a study of employed parents in two community samples. *Journal of Occupational Health Psychology*, 1(1), 57–69.

Gemini Consulting (1998) *International Workforce Management Study: Capitalising on the Workforce*. London: Gemini Consulting.

Grazier, P.B. (1999). The toxic workplace. Retrieved June 12, 2009, from http://www.teambuildinginc.com/article_toxic.htm.

Hodson, R., Roscigno, V.J., and Lopez, S.H. (2006). Chaos and the abuse of power: workplace bullying in organizational and interactional context. *Work and Occupations*, 33(4), 382–416.

Hoel, H. and Beale, D. (2006). Workplace bullying, psychological perspectives and industrial relations: Towards a contextualized and interdisciplinary approach. *British Journal of Industrial Relations*, 44(2), 239–62.

Hoel, A. and Cooper, C.L. (2000). *Destructive Conflict and Bullying at Work*. Manchester, UK, University of Manchester Institute of Science and Technology.

Hoel, H., Cooper, C.L., and Faragher, B. (2001). The experience of bullying in Great Britain: the impact of organizational status. *European Journal of Work and Organizational Psychology*, 10(4), 443–65.

Huselid, M.A. and Becker, B.E. (1996). Methodological issues in cross-sectional and panel estimates of the human resource-firm performance link. *Industrial Relations*, 35(3), 400–422.

ITU, International Telecommunications Union (2010). Mobile phone use statistics. Available at: http://www.itu.int/newsroom/press_releases/2010/06.html.

Landsbergis, P.A. (2003). The changing organization of work and the safety and health of working people: a commentary. *J Occup Environ Med*, 45(1), 61–72.

Leymann, H. (1990). Mobbing and psychological terror at workplaces. *Violence Vict*, 5(2), 119–26.

Lutgen-Sandvik, P., Tracy, S.J., and Alberts, J.K. (2007). Burned by bullying in the american workplace: prevalence, perception, degree and impact. *Journal of Management Studies*, 44(6), 837–62.

Namie, G. (2007). The Workplace Bullying Institute 2007 US Workplace Bullying Survey. Available at: http://bullyinginstitute.org/wbi-zogby2.html.

National Sleep Foundation (2008). 2008 Sleep in America poll: Summary of findings. Washington, DC: National Sleep Foundation. Available at: http://www.sleepfoundation.org/atf/cf/%7Bf6bf2668-a1b4-4fe8-8d1a-a5d39340d9cb%7D/2008%20POLL%20SOF.PDF.

Nielsen, M.B., Matthiesen, S.B., and Einarsen, S. (2010). The impact of methodological moderators on prevalence rates of workplace bullying: a meta-analysis. *Journal of Occupational and Organizational Psychology*, 83, 955–79.

Mikkelsen, E.G. (2001). Workplace bullying: Why and for whom is bullying such a strain. *Nordisk Psykologi*, 53(2), 109–31.

Mikkelsen, E.G. and Einarsen, S. (2002). Relationships between exposure to bullying at work and psychological and psychosomatic health complaints: the role of state negative affectivity and generalized self-efficacy. *Scandinavian Journal of Psychology*, 43(5), 397–405.

Patterson, M.G., West, M.A., Lawthom, R., and Nickell, S. (1997). Impact of people management practices on business performance. *Issues in People Management*. London, Institute of Personell and Development, 39.

Pearson, C.M., Andersson, L.M., and Porath, C.L. (2000). Assessing and attacking workplace incivility. *Organizational Dynamics*, 29(2), 123–37.

Pfeffer, J. (1998). *The Human Equation: Building Profits by Putting People First.* Boston, MA, Harvard Business School Press.

Pfeffer, J. (2010). Building sustainable organizations: the human factor. *The Academy of Management Perspectives*, 24(1), 24–35.

Rayner, C. (1997). The incidence of workplace bullying. *Journal of Community & Applied Social Psychology*, 7(3), 199–208.

Rayner, C. (2000). *Building a Business Case for Tackling Bullying in the Workplace: Beyond a Basic Cost-benefit Approach.* Transcending Boundaries, Griffith University, Brisbane, Australia.

Rishardson, R. and Thompson, M. (1999). *The Impact of People Management Practices on Business Performance: A Literature Review.* London, CIPD.

Robinson, S.L. (1996). Turst and breach of the psychological contract. *Administrative Science Quarterly*, 41(4), 574–99.

Salin, D. (2003). Ways of explaining workplace bullying: a review of enabling, motivating and precipitating structures and processes in the work environment. *Human Relations*, 56(10), 1213–32.

Shannon, C.A., Rospenda, K.M., and Richman, J.A. (2007). Workplace harassment patterning, gender, and utilization of professional services: findings from a US national study. *Soc Sci Med*, 64(6), 1178–91.

Sasha-Corporation. (January 2007). Compilation of turnover cost studies. Retrieved July 15, 2009, from http://www.sashacorp.com/turnframe.html.

Sheehan, M. (1999). Workplace bullying: responding with some emotional intelligence. *International Journal of Manpower*, 20(1–2), 57–69.

Speedy, S. (2006). Workplace violence: the dark side of organisational life. *Contemp Nurse*, 21(2), 239–50.

Strandmark, M. and Hallberg, L.R. (2007). The origin of workplace bullying: experiences from the perspective of bully victims in the public service sector. *J Nurs Manag*, 15(3), 332–41.

Vartia, M.A.L. (2001). Consequences of workplace bullying with respect to the well-being of its targets and the observers of bullying. *Scandinavian Journal of Work Environment & Health*, 27(1), 63–9.

Yang, H., Schnall, P.L., Jauregui, M., Su, T., and Baker, D. (2006). Work hours and self-reported hypertension among working people in California. *Hypertension*, 48, 744–50.

Chapter 9

Worksite Reactions and Interactions with Mental Health

An organizational culture that values autonomy and individual initiative would allow more decision latitude at the individual level, which, in turn, would be associated with improved mental health. (Gauthier et al., 2012)

Introduction

In previous chapters we have covered mental health and mental illness at the level of statistics and impacts. This chapter will provide more detail on the interactions of mental health in the workplace and how mental health is either supported or sabotaged. All types of mental illness are likely present in the workplace. However, mental health problems that are most common in the workplace are stress, depression, and anxiety. These three Common Mental Health Problems (CMHPs) can have negative and lasting impacts on an individual's quality of life, social functioning, and ability to work (Nielsen, Rugulies, Hjortkjaer, et al., 2013). The statistics make for a powerful case for us to be alarmed. Mental illness rates for major depressive episodes in Canadians (age 15 and over) are estimated to have been 4.8 percent in 2002, while that for experiencing symptoms of anxiety was estimated to be 4.7 percent. In general, higher rates of mood and anxiety disorders are found among the 30–69 age range in a sample of Canadians in 2009 (Gadalla, 2009). The Canadian Mental Health Association estimates that one in five Canadians will at some time in their life experience some form of mental health issue (CMHA, 2011). For these reasons alone, consideration must be given to how this information is interpreted, how it is dealt with in society and in particular how worksites can effectively deal with these issues.

More startling data reveals that by 2020, mental illness is expected to be the leading cause of disability in the workplace in Canada (Hatchard, Henderson, and Stanton, 2012). The growing concern over economic burdens is only multiplied by the concern for supports needed in society and for those returning to work after an episode of acute mental illness. These individuals may face complex challenges and barriers to their re-entry into the world and into the workplace and, as such, organizations need to be prepared with the appropriate tools and services to offer. With the statistics above and the economic burden below, there is no time to waste in addressing mental illness in the workplace.

As mentioned in Chapter 3, the economic cost to the Canadian economy of mental illness was found to be approximately $51 billion in 2003 (Canadian Mental Health Association, 2011), which is quite a heavy burden. Despite this huge negative economic impact, it is alarming to note that individuals with mental illness may still come across adverse reactions to their disabilities within the workplace from co-workers and supervisors alike. While recent years have seen the need to bring mental illness education into the workplace, much work still needs to be done. Education about the negative impacts that an individual with mental illness faces in the workplace needs attention. The achieving of mental health literacy is a goal that everyone in society needs to set for themselves and certainly should be a goal of every workplace. Then by being knowledgeable and aware we can address these issues with foresight and accommodation. Specific items for employers and co-workers to consider when reflecting on mental illness are:

1.   How an individual's social relationships at work are impacted;

2.   Are they being treated fairly or differently because their illness is common knowledge?;

3.   Are career opportunities being diminished due to others' preconceptions of their abilities?;

4.   Finally, are they at increased risk for work loss due to their mental illness? (Nielsen, Rugulies, Hjortkjaer, et al., 2013).

With these questions in mind, it is possible to begin to investigate attitudes in the workplace and to begin a change process that will culminate with persons with mental illness being welcomed into society and the workforce.

Organizational Attitudes toward Mental Health

Industrialized countries face the ever-growing issue of lost time days, presenteeism and absenteeism due to factors related to mental health issues. A silent but unimpeachable truth is that mental health problems are one of the main causes of lost time at work. For example, research focusing on the impacts of mental illness in the workplace has noted that individuals suffering from depression experience a negative impact upon their educational attainment and productivity at work (Gadalla, 2009). These impacts are felt far beyond the individual as they also adversely affect the whole population in regards to a reduced Gross Domestic Production (GDP) resulting from lost productivity due to lost time days, and reduced productivity due to presenteeism. It is long past time that this issue is addressed.

One barrier to effectively addressing mental as well as physical illness in the workplace is that interventions trying to address these issues mostly target the individual as opposed to the whole organization. This results in many one-off solutions which are of little benefit to the whole organization. Organizations benefit most from well-organized, strategic programs that are designed with the specific workforce and specific production requirements in mind. Policies and procedures need to be in place long before they are actually needed. Employee morale is boosted when they know in advance that they will be well treated if they sustain an injury or if the experience a mental illness. When this is followed up it is a win-win solution for everyone involved. Dextras-Gauthier et al. (2012) suggest that the best way to address this is to incorporate the organizational component with the group culture that naturally develops in the workplace. In other words, build on the strengths of the organization. When mental health and supporting recovery and return to work become an integral part of the organizational culture, individuals and the corporation are working towards a common goal. That common goal is to ensure everyone has an equal opportunity to succeed and to enjoy their work.

ATTITUDES AND BEHAVIOURS

The organization (workplace) is essentially a social system wherein employees and employers are both agents and subjects. Within an organization there exist values which are assumptions about right and wrong, good and bad, held by those in the workplace. These assumptions, these belief systems are internalized by members of the group. As a result of the internalization of these values, a set of perceptions is created, thought processes and unconscious feelings occur, and all together they regulate relationships and exchanges within an organization

(Dextras-Gauthier, Marchand, and Haines III, 2012). This is how stigma is created and also how stigma can be undone. The values of an organization shape the attitudes and behaviors of the actors in the organization which in turn influence the functioning of the organization. As attitudes and behaviors can have a direct impact on successful functioning of an organization, it stands to reason that they also play a major role with respect to employee health and well-being within an organization (Dextras-Gauthier, Marchand, and Haines III, 2012).

Pinto-Foltz et al. (2011) found that a program specifically addressing mental health literacy directly related to stereotypical thinking about mental illness was shown to have positive effects on literacy after 4–8 weeks. Unfortunately, the intervention they used did not make an impact on the stigma component of attitudes toward mental illness. The authors explain this effect in terms of emotions and logic. Stereotypes and stigmas are easily associated with an emotional response from individuals, more so than the logical thinking part of mental illness. The emotional barrier is difficult to break down because it is often implicit, not logical. This simply identifies the need to aggressively address these emotional barriers.

NEGATIVE

Honey (2003) notes that individuals who have a mental illness report that as a result of their disability stressors that are present in the workplace may have more of a negative impact on them than on others. They point to difficulties in the ability to make decisions, to think clearly, to having little or no energy, to behaving and making decisions based on symptoms being experienced, and other physical discomforts that come with medication side-effects. These attitudes are not only felt by the individual with the mental illness but according to Russinova et al. (2011), co-workers and managers in the workplace also start describing a person's actions based on their mental illness. This creates a belief system in which an employee's actions are attributed to their mental illness, rather than situational circumstances, such as having a bad day. All of these factors feed into negative attitudes, defeat the self-confidence of the individual, and incite feelings that mental illness reduces the individual's work performance (Honey, 2002).

From a more subtle perspective, Russinova et al. (2011) note prejudicial practices that often go unchecked or uncorrected in the workplace. As noted above, the first is using the mental illness to describe an employee's behaviour at work—in other words, an individual with a mental illness has their actions defined by their illness and cannot simply be having a bad day. The second practice that may go uncorrected is the patronizing form in which an employer selects inappropriate times to ask an employee about their mental health or treatment. It is imperative for employers to ensure that workplaces are accommodating without falling into these subtle prejudicial practices. These prejudicial traps can be alleviated through mental health literacy and the development of mental health initiatives.

POSITIVE

It is important to note that recent work investigating public perceptions of mental illness have revealed that individuals who have suffered from a mental illness themselves at some point in time or knew of someone with a mental illness were less likely to hold negative stereotypes and to have a positive outlook on recovery and outcomes for persons with mental illness (Kobau, DiIorio, and Chapman, 2010). Findings such as these suggest that potential exists for stigma and negative perceptions to be reduced in the workplace by increasing contact with mental illness through anti-stigma campaigns. The general population having more contact with people with mental illness in the workplace has been shown to have a positive impact on perceptions of mental illness. This interaction reduces the likelihood that an individual will continue to be defined by their disability but rather be a valued asset in the workplace. Organizations that value autonomy and the initiative of individuals also enjoy improved mental health which is also co-related with an increase in decisional latitude (Dextras-Gauthier, Marchand, and Haines III, 2012). In other words, workers who know what they are expected to do, who are rewarded for doing it, and who have some independence and flexibility to go about their tasks are happier and more productive workers. Providing this level of empowerment to those with a mental illness is an invaluable component of a healthy organizational culture.

Joachim and Acorn (2000) discuss how understanding invisible and visible conditions can support nursing staff to better address the needs of their patients. It is not a great stretch to see that the same is true in accommodating persons with mental illness in the workplace. Understanding the needs and realizing the potential impacts of work and return to work policies are beginning to show a trend in Canadian workplaces towards supporting persons with mental illness to make their own decisions, set goals, and manage the steps they take in their recovery process (Hatchard, Henderson, and Stanton, 2012). Those who do successfully stay at work or return to work note some key factors in successfully reintegrating into the workplace:

- Solid partnerships

- Communication with co-workers and supervisor

- Positive co-worker and supervisor relationships

- Resources and supports at the individual level

- Long-term investment from healthcare providers

- Workplace structures to prevent mental illness

- (Hatchard, Henderson, and Stanton, 2012).

Mental Illness in the Workplace

At this point we no longer need to address the economic impacts of mental illness in the workplace. Rather, it is time to look into how mental illness exists in the workplace from a psychosocial perspective. Within psychosocial considerations there exist interpersonal relations, stigma, distress, job quality, job strain, and discussions on effort-reward arrangements. These topics are directly linked to productivity on the job and overall job satisfaction. Beyond these indicators of productivity and satisfaction in the workplace, it must also be considered how the workplace can impact an individual with mental illness.

Research on outcomes for persons with mental illness reveals employment to be a major component of the recovery process due to the many additional benefits that come with it. Employment for persons with mental illness provides a means to self-esteem, self-worth (Szeto and Dobson, 2013), and empowerment. That said, these positive outcomes are dependent upon the workplace and the level of stress perceived by employees who have a mental illness. In situations where a job is deemed as stressful, findings have shown increased mental disorders also occur (Szeto and Dobson, 2013). As an example, individuals who rate their jobs as extremely stressful were more likely to be treated for emotional or mental health issues (in the last 12 months) than individuals who did not report as much stress or no stress at all. Additionally, those in stressful jobs were 2.4 times more likely to have been diagnosed with a mental health issue by a professional for either an anxiety disorder or a mood disorder (Szeto and Dobson, 2013).

The interesting thing about Szeto and Dobson's findings in 2013 is that they are highly similar to research findings completed with 2002 and 2003 data in 2006 by Wang on 'Perceived Work Stress, imbalance between work and family/personal lives, and mental disorders'. This observation is a clear indication that much work still needs to be done by workplaces, by industry, by organizations, and by employers to address how mental illness interacts with stressors in the workplace.

STIGMA

> *The fact is that people experiencing mental health problems are systematically subjected to societal exclusion and discrimination in most areas of their lives. The effect of stigma on the individual is pervasive, and can potentially have devastating consequences ...*
> *(Bezborodovs and Thornicroft, 2013)*

The main barrier between employees with mental disabilities and the workplace is that of stigmatization. The most common setting where persons with mental illness report experiencing stigma is in the workplace. Persons with mental illness who return to work have been noted to experience harassment, intimidation, and teasing to the point of having to resign or be dismissed from their job. Even the fear of the prospect of these types of behaviours happening prevents individuals with mental illness from even taking the step towards applying for a job (Bezborodovs and Thornicroft, 2013).

In the 1980s Jones and colleagues noted six dimensions of stigma that may provide more insight into how this social function develops. These dimensions impact interpersonal relations between those who are not and those who are stigmatized. The first of these dimensions is concealability—to what degree is the condition (whether it be mental or physical) visible to the general population? This is the first of the dimensions for good reason as many of our social attitudes and perceptions of others are built on the foundation of visibility and can incite 'negative social reactions' immediately. The second dimension is the course of the condition over time—does it change or remain the same? Thirdly, the strain a condition places on interpersonal relations is the next dimension—sadly, a condition may be focused on more than the interpersonal give and take that occurs in social situations. A fourth dimension looks at aesthetic qualities and while this may come off as shallow or excessively negative, there are situations in which a condition can affect the appearance (thus the perception of) a person. Of course we can't discuss mental conditions without discussing cause, which is the fifth dimension Jones et al. (1984) discussed—is the condition acquired over time or is it congenital? Finally, the sixth dimension is that of peril—this of course considers the dangers that become associated with stigmatized people as a result of disclosure of their mental illness (Joachim and Acorn, 2000). While admittedly hard to discuss, these dimensions need to be addressed in order for full disclosure to occur, as understanding and progress can be made in accommodating persons with mental illness in the workplace.

Stigma is the result of knowledge (ignorance or misinformation), attitudes (prejudice), and behaviour (discrimination) that targets the feelings and attitudes of the person being singled out (Thornicroft, Brohan, Rose, et al., 2009). Stigma influences an individual's help-seeking behavior in that many mental illnesses go unchecked and undertreated. A major factor influencing the decision to not seek out support for mental illness is the perceived lack of social support many individuals with mental illness have (Gadalla, 2009). The mere presence of stigma, whether blatant or subtle, marginalizes individuals and creates a barrier to full work integration (Krupa, Kirsh, Cockburn, et al., 2009). These negative responses are a hurdle for individuals when it comes to achieving a better quality of life and recovery by undermining the chance to achieve self-esteem (Wahl, 1999). However, stigmatization is not only externally imposed. Stigmatization can also be self-imposed by the person with a mental illness.

Beyond the occurrence of external expressions of stigma and the fear of stigma is the potential for an individual to take on self-stigma when it comes to mental illness. Living among stereotypes and witnessed accounts of mental illness stigma may cause an individual to eventually internalize those feelings and see their illness as a personal failure which in turn destroys their self-esteem, self-efficacy, and motivation to participate in social interactions (Stuart, 2004).

Entry and re-entry into the workforce for individuals with mental illness is a complex transition in regards to social stereotyping and stigmatization. Society often relies on the media and past experience regarding information pertaining to persons with mental illness. These representations can be negative and misleading. In some instances, the individual may not directly face stigmas; however, the fear of facing them remains and can be as debilitating for self-esteem and motivation in the workplace:

> *The serious stigma attached to mental illness in general is one of the most recognized hurdles facing their diagnosis and treatment. (Gadalla, 2009)*

Such prejudice and discrimination impede recovery from mental illness by preventing the regaining of self-esteem, sense of purpose, and quality of life (Russinova, Griffin, Bloch, et al., 2011). Thornicroft et al. (2007) call for a change in the approach employers use in regards to the hiring of those with mental illness. Instead of assessing stigmatization, research should be directed towards investigating discrimination by assessing whether employers actually do hire individuals with mental illness disabilities (Thornicroft, Rose, Kassam, et al., 2007). Beyond hiring, employers should be receptive to bringing those with mental illness back into the workplace post incident. With the ability to look beyond stigma, organizations will recognize the economic impact of losing employees with mental illness from the workplace and the repercussions of not having a willingness to accommodate persons with mental illness disabilities. Ultimately, anxiety and mood disorders account for a major negative economic impact in regards to lost productivity and elevated claims for disability insurance (Gadalla, 2009). Change and accommodation can only improve the situation for both the persons with mental illness and workplace outcomes.

BARRIERS EXACERBATING MENTAL ILLNESS

> *Stigmatization can foster a climate that exacerbates stress, and may trigger or worsen the person's condition. It may also mean that someone who has a problem and needs help may not seek it, for fear of being labeled. (Ontario Human Rights Commission, 2009)*

Extending what is known about stigma and the effects it has on individuals with mental illness disabilities, it should be noted that stigma itself is a major contributor to one of the most tragic barriers in recovering from mental illness—that of help seeking. In Canada we enjoy universal health coverage of physical and other hospital services, however this is not enough. In 2002 it was found that 44 percent of Canadian women who had experienced a major depressive episode did not seek help for their symptoms. Even more alarming, 60 percent did not seek any kind of health professional when symptoms of anxiety were present (Statistics Canada, 2002 as cited in Gadalla, 2009). This only adds to the many barriers individuals face when recovering from an episode of mental illness.

For people with mental illness, the medications they are prescribed are often a barrier to moving forward in their employment opportunities. Many medications can affect job performance by reducing abilities to think clearly, creating a lack of energy, making interactions with others difficult, creating issues with co-workers, as well as the various physical side-effects (Honey, 2003). This is an experience that is often missed in discussions surrounding employing persons with mental illness and is also often not understood or accessed by researchers. A focus on the Duty to Accommodate from both a legal and moral ground provides insight into an individual's right to work regardless of a mental illness being present. Positive outcomes of employment for persons with mental illness are increased self-esteem, less social disability, and more control over psychiatric symptoms (Campbell, Bond, and Drake, 2011).

DISCLOSURE

Disclosure or self-disclosure can be defined as the process of communicating information about oneself verbally to another person. (Brohan, Henderson, Wheat, et al., 2012)

As if having a mental illness were not barrier enough to being involved in the workplace and enjoying a satisfying quality of life, many persons with mental illness face the issue of needing to disclose their condition. Disclosure is a barrier to persons with mental illness due to the concern it creates over whether it will or will not change an employment situation or relationship with supervisor or co-workers. Mental illness is a condition that does often have the dilemma of whether to disclose or not as the illness/disability maybe relatively invisible. The person with the mental illness then wonders if they can continue to keep it covert or if it will become overt through disclosure. Unlike most other illnesses, mental illness can often be concealed and then revealed at a time of one's choosing. This dilemma arises as a direct result of the stigma attached to mental illness. Disclosure about a mental illness can severely impact on the social identity of the individual, their work environment, and especially relationships with others. Further, mental illness ranks at the top when it comes to "discreditable identities" (Brohan, Henderson, Wheat, et al., 2012), and while persons with mental illness may not know the data behind this fact, they almost immediately feel the consequences in a very real way. From the worksites' point of view and from the view of colleagues and friends an individual can go from appearing perfectly competent to an easily identifiable person with a mental illness who is now debased because of the illness they have disclosed. They have come out of the closet as it were.

According to Brohan et al., disclosure can be viewed along four dimensions:

1. Voluntary or involuntary: does an individual have the choice to disclose or is their illness visible and disclosed through their inability to conceal it?

2.   Full or partial disclosure: what parts of an illness are disclosed? Some illnesses have different aspects, some of which may be concealable.

3.   Selectiveness: who does the person with a mental illness (PWMI) disclose to? A person with a mental illness may choose to only reveal their illness to certain people.

4.   Timing of disclosure: at what point does a PWMI decide to disclose their illness? The decision can be made to disclose before or after an employment opportunity (Brohan, Henderson, Wheat, et al., 2012).

With these dimensions in mind we can begin exploring pathways towards creating a healthy workplace including healthy interactions between employers, employees, and those who may experience mental illness.

Ingredients for Healthy Interactions in the Workplace

THE EMPLOYEE AND THE WORKPLACE

As noted above, employees with mental illness are forced to decide whether to disclose their illness to their employers and co-workers and risk the almost certain possibility of stigmatization. This very real fear leading to reluctance to disclose makes employment difficult to retain due to the stress surrounding the fear of being discovered or the pressures of performing as if a mental illness does not exist. As an example, individuals with schizophrenia tend to have poorer employment outcomes. This may be due to many factors including the result of being placed in entry level jobs with high turnover, the desire to avoid stress, the effects of medication, and depression resulting from the impact of mental illness on life (Honey, 2003). In order to relieve these extra stressors that exist for people with mental illness, it is imperative that organizations engage in developing mental health education and awareness programs, employing the group culture present in the workplace.

The workplace is a highly social environment and with the appropriate values and beliefs being injected into the organization it can provide social support, foster human relations, and act as an arena for interpersonal exchange. When a group culture is purposely developed within an organization, the workplace can be a friendly and safe environment for people to spend time. Those who are leaders in such an organization are seen as mentors who can be approached for social and emotional support (Dextras-Gauthier, Marchand, and Haines III, 2012). As such, the workplace takes on values of teamwork that recognize and develop mutual trust, feedback streams, and recognition for work completed.

According the Dextras-Gauthier et al. (2012) this opens the doors to higher employee participation in:

- Suggesting how to improve their work and performance

- Gaining empowerment over their working conditions

- Perceiving higher autonomy in their work decisions

- Recognizing the meaning behind their work

When these options are available to those with mental illness in the workplace, these individuals become a part of the team and may partake in career development once again. However, it is important to recognize that recent investigations into organizational culture note that there are other ways towards integration beyond group culture. Developmental, rational, and hierarchical organizational frameworks also can provide balance in the workplace. The developmental workplace is innovative and geared towards change and flexibility, while the rational workplace is built upon results, rivalry, and productivity in which inherent benefits are decision-making power and rewards for end-results. Finally, the hierarchical culture offers stability, formalism, and control which offer security for employees, but tends to limit decision-making by employees. It is important to note the need to balance these four cultural frameworks in the workplace in order to achieve a healthy workplace inclusive of mental health illness (Dextras-Gauthier, Marchand, and Haines III, 2012).

HIRING AND RETAINING PERSONS WITH MENTAL ILLNESS DISABILITY

The culture of a workplace greatly influences the hiring and retaining of employees with mental illness. Startling statistics out of the United Kingdom based on a pole of employers who were hiring (n = 109) showed that approximately half would not or would only occasionally hire someone who is unwell. The percentage dropped to 28 percent when the scenario was changed to hiring someone who was "previously ill." It appears that these statistics are similar around the world (Bezborodovs and Thornicroft, 2013). These findings would appear to run counter to the prevailing management rhetoric around inclusive workplaces as well as the expressed desires of public policy. This belief and attending policy indicates that employers will be more successful when the culture of the workplace is able to accommodate persons with various needs, including mental illness, so that everyone can actively and successfully participate in the workforce.

As noted in Chapter 3, negative stereotypes have deep roots in human society and only further marginalize and delegitimize individuals with mental illness (Russinova, 2011). While there are many mental illnesses present in society and in the workforce, those most commonly identified are schizophrenia, alcoholism, and drug dependence (Crisp et al., 2010 as cited in Kobau, DiIorio, and Chapman, 2010). Szeto and Dobson (2013) stress that there is still much to be done on the part of employers when it comes to addressing how mental health in the workplace can easily be impacted by stress. The interactions of mental health and the workplace require further attention to properly address the continuing issues being faced by Canadian employees with mental illness.

The Canadian Manufacturers & Exporters (CME) have developed a human resources tool directly aimed at hiring and retaining persons with mental illness that covers a comprehensive set of topics, issues, and solutions for industry. Highlighting the positive, the CME has a set of benefits an organization can look forward to when hiring or retaining employees with disabilities such as:

- A creative work environment—employee teams will enjoy a diverse work team with increased innovative and creative thinking;

- Broader base of experience—different perspectives approaching organisational problems and business strategies;

- Fresh perspective for decision-making—individuals with disabilities can bring unique life experience to decision-making processes that may challenge and stimulate a "higher level of critical analysis";

- Assist in using technology in new ways—productivity and efficiency can enjoy a healthy increase;

- Development of new products and services—employees with disabilities can drive innovation with their insight into the needs of a broad spread of customers and assist in products or services being appealing to diverse customers (Canadian Manufacturers & Exporters, 2011.

FURTHER READING FOR MANAGERS AND EMPLOYERS

Developing a healthy workplace can be a rewarding experience especially when the goal is the re-organization of the workplace so that a vibrant, healthy, and inclusive workplace culture can thrive. Within every workplace there is a group of people who work together on a regular basis. This group forms a culture and this workplace culture influences how the workplace functions. Within group culture there are three significant features to be mindful of: social support, teamwork, and employee participation.

Having a culture of social support within a workplace is fostered by leaders who are mentors and by an organization that highly values interpersonal relations between employees. The true worth of such a culture lies in the emotional support that people can provide for each other, especially in times of difficulty. Another feature of a positive workplace culture is teamwork which embraces the values of cooperation, and mutual trust. Teamwork values often provide pathways for more feedback and recognition pertaining to work. Finally, active employee participation in the workplace is key feature that allows people to have a say in their work tasks and the work culture and then to suggest ways to improve their overall performance. This final feature brings a sense of empowerment and meaning to work for employees that is invaluable (Dextras-Gauthier, Marchand, and Haines III, 2012).

Managers and employers can benefit from return to work (RTW) initiatives that support their employees in resuming their work life. However, the dilemmas involved in RTW are not often understood and deserve more attention if organizations are to be successful in retaining employees and reducing their production and eventual economic losses. Some individuals are able to RTW with few barriers or difficulties, but with that said there are some who may face issues with their self-image or concerns about returning to employment that may have caused the mental illness in the first place. With psychological support alongside employer support persons with mental illness may be able to discover their true self and determine their healing process on their journey back to work (Nielsen, Rugulies, Hjortkjaer, et al., 2013).

Employee Wellness: Disability in the Workplace

The duty to accommodate is a legal obligation that requires employers to identify and eliminate barriers to participation in the workplace, including barriers to persons with disabilities. Accommodation measures for employees with disabilities can include changes to work duties or hours of work, as well as the provision of specialized equipment or support services. (Treasury Board of Canada Secretariat, 2011)

In each and every Canadian workplace there is a legal obligation for employers to identify and eliminate any barriers that may prevent persons with mental illness from participating in the workplace. The message here clearly states that healthy workplaces are in the best interest for everyone involved and that due attention is required to address the needs of all workers (Treasury Board of Canada Secretariat, 2011). For this reason, return to work is an incredibly important process to focus on for persons with mental illness who are considering employment or coming back after a period of absence. Surprisingly little work has been done on RTW from a qualitative research perspective as much of the research focuses on enumerating physical disabilities or other musculoskeletal issues. However, those that do consider the stories of RTW find some commonalities in the experience persons with mental illness have with this transition in their lives. These stories reveal experiences of emotional crises such as breakdowns, feelings of powerlessness, being overwhelmed, and exhausted. These feelings can lead to a decision to leave work rather than persevering in the face of such adversity.

The decision to leave work due to mental illness is not an easy one. Upon leaving work, or not returning to work, persons with mental illness often report negative impacts upon self-esteem and self-image while also experiencing the burden of what Neilsen et al. (2013) call a double identity crisis. A double identity crisis arises when a person begins to negotiate their social identity with the identity that has arisen due to their mental illness. Furthermore, this double identity is exacerbated by the concern the person with mental illness has of becoming a burden to others as a result of their illness. When considering maintaining persons with mental illness in the workforce or helping them return to the workforce it is important to remember that these pressures, along with others that almost everyone experiences, may be more present in persons with mental illness than in others and will likely require additional attention (Nielsen, Rugulies, Hjortkjaer, et al., 2013).

Concluding Remarks

Lessons to take away from this chapter center upon the interactions between mental illness and the workplace. Persons with mental illness face a multitude of struggles in regards to applying for jobs, fear of stigmatization and associated behaviours, institutional barriers to employment, and possibly returning to a job that caused the initial mental health issue. Mental health literacy can encourage and rise to the next level where understanding the needs of employees with mental illness in the workplace, the needs of the employer, and the requirements of taking on the challenge actually are a focus of the organization. We have tried to present a positive perspective on hiring and retaining persons with mental illness and the additional benefits they can bring to the workplace. This is a crucial undertaking at a time when industry and organizations are becoming more diverse need to keep their highly skilled workers employed. For many of the reasons we have mentioned, persons with mental health disabilities are often overlooked when considering sources of labour.

The task ahead for the workplace is to look beyond mental illness and instead consider the person behind the label. Such action will serve to remove stigmatizing barriers and rather facilitate involvement in the workplace for individuals with mental illness. Much of the difficulty encountered in this endeavor is due to the ignorance of society in general and worksites in particular. Efforts to foster mental health literacy need to be increased and this needs to be coupled with the development of policies and procedures that make accommodating persons with mental illness issues possible.

Openness to changing conditions in the workplace will function to support employers to move beyond the status quo of the workplace and to enter into a domain of inclusion and diversity. The more individuals with mental illness disabilities are given the support and boost they need in the workplace, the more workplaces will enjoy a boost in their productivity and satisfaction of their employees.

More information can be found at the following sources:

SafeAbility—Safe and Able to Work at www.safeability.ca

Institute for Work & Health at www.iwh.on.ca

Treasury Board of Canada Secretariat. Disability Management: Employee Wellness Resources at http://www.tbs-sct.gc.ca/hrh/dmi-igi/fundamentals-fondements/ewr-rme-eng.asp

References

Bezborodovs, N. and Thornicroft, G. (2013). Stigmatisation of mental illness in the workplace: evidence and consequences. *Die Psychiatrie*, 2, 1–6.

Brohan, E., Henderson, C., Wheat, K., Malcolm, E., Clement, S., Barley, E.A., Slade, M., and Thornicroft, G. (2012). Systematic review of beliefs, behaviours and influencing factors associated with disclosure of a mental health problem in the workplace. *BioMed Central Psychiatry*, 12(11), 1–14.

Campbell, K., Bond, G.R., and Drake, R.E. (2011). Who benefits from supported employment: a meta-analytic study. *Schizophrenia Bulletin*, 37(2), 370–380.

Canadian Mental Health Association (2011). Integrating Needs for Mental Well-Being into Human Resource Planning: Summary Final Report. Retrieved from: http://www.cmha.ca/public_policy/project-in4m-integrating-needs-for-mental-well-being-into-human-resource-planning/ on September 5th, 2013.

Canadian Manufacturers & Exporters (2011). Taking Action: An HR Guide—Hiring and Retaining Employees with Disabilities. Retrieved from: http://on.cme-mec.ca/download.php?file=h6z1z1ea.pdf on September 5th, 2013.

Dextras-Gauthier, J., Marchand, A., and Haines III, V. (2012). Organizational Culture, Work Organization Conditions, and Mental Health: A Proposed Integration. *International Journal of Stress Management*, 19(2), 81–104. DOI: 10.1037/a0028164.

Gadalla, T.M. (2009). Association between mood and anxiety disorders and self-reported disability: results from a nationally representative sample of Canadians. *Journal of Mental Health*, 18(6), 495–503. DOI: 10.3109/09638230903111106.

Gauthier, J., Marchand, A., and Haines, V. (2012). Organizational culture, work conditions and mental health: A proposed integration. *International Journal of Stress Management*, 19(2), 81–104.

Hatchard, K., Henderson, J., and Stanton, S. (2012). Workers' perspectives on self-directing mainstream return to work following acute mental illness: reflections of partnerships. *Work*, 43(1), 43–52. DOI: 10.3233/WOR-2012-1446.

Honey, A. (2003). The impact of mental illness on employment: consumers' perspectives. *Work*, 20, 267–76.

Joachim, G. and Acorn, S. (2000). Stigma of visible and invisible chronic conditions. *Journal of Advanced Nursing*, 32(1), 243–8.

Jones, E.E. (1984). *Social Stigma: The Psychology of Marked Relationships: A Series of Books in Psychology*. WH Freeman Limited.

Kobau, R., DiIorio, C., Chapman, D., and Delvecchio, P. (2010). Attitudes about mental illness and its treatment: validation of a generic scale for public health surveillance of mental illness associated stigma. *Community Mental Health Journal*, 46, 164–76.

Krupa, T., Kirsh, B., Cockburn, L., and Gewurtz, R. (2009). Understanding the stigma of mental illness in employment. *Work*, 33, 413–25.

Nielsen, M.B.D., Rugulies, R., Hjortkjaer, C., Bultmann, U., and Christensen, U. (2013). Healing a vulnerable self: exploring return to work for women with mental health problems. *Qualitative Health Research*, 23, 302–14. DOI: 10.1177/1049732312468252.

Ontario Human Rights Commission (2009). Policy and guidelines on disability and the duty to accommodate. Retrieved on: August 14th, 2012 at http://www.ohrc.on.ca.

Pinto-Foltz, M.D., Logsdon, M.C., and Myers, J.A. (2011). Feasibility, acceptability, and initial efficacy of a knowledge-contact program to reduce mental illness stigma and improve mental health literacy in adolescents. *Social Science & Medicine*, 72, 2011–19.

Russinova, Z., Griffin, S., Bloch, P., Wewiorski, N.J. and Rosoklija, I. (2011). Workplace prejudice and discrimination toward individuals with mental illness. *Journal of Vocational Rehabilitation*, 35, 227–41. DOI: 10.3233/JVR-2011-0574.

Stuart, H. (2004). Stigma and work. *Healthcare Papers*, 5(2), 100–111.

Szeto, A.C.H. and Dobson, K.S. (2013). Mental disorders and their association with perceived work stress: an investigation on the 2010 Canadian community health survey. *Journal of Occupational Health Psychology*, 18(2), 191–7. DOI: 10.1037/a0031806.

Thornicroft, G., Brohan, E., Rose, D., Sartorius, N., and Leese, M. (2009). Global pattern of experienced and anticipated discrimination against people with schizophrenia: a cross-sectional survey. *Lancet*, 373, 408–15.

Thornicroft, G., Rose, D., Kassam, A., and Sartorius, N. (2007). Stigma: ignorance, prejudice or discrimination? *The British Journal of Psychiatry*, 190, 192–3.

Treasury Board of Canada Secretariat (2011). Disability Management: Employee Wellness Resources. Available at: http://www.tbs-sct.gc.ca/hrh/dmi-igi/fundamentals-fondements/ewr-rme-eng.asp.

Wahl, O. (1999) Mental health consumers' experience of stigma. *Schizophrenia Bulletin*, 25(3), 467–78.

Wang, J.L. (2006). Perceived work stress, imbalance between work and family/personal lives, and mental disorders. *Social Psychiatry and Psychiatric Epidemiology*, 41, 541–8. DOI: 10.1007/s00127-006-0058-y.

Chapter 10

Psychological Assessment
for the Workplace

*People with high assurance in their capabilities approach difficult tasks
as challenges to be mastered rather than as threats to be avoided.*

Albert Bandura

Introduction

Psychological assessment is an assessment completed for the purpose of diagnostic clarification regarding the enduring symptoms of a psychological or psychiatric disorder. Psychological assessment can be completed by either a psychologist or a psychiatrist, depending on the type of questions being asked. Psychological assessment is important from the workplace perspective because much of the literature suggests psychosocial factors as primary predictors in both the development of independent workplace illness, as well as a contributor to extended workplace absence for physical illness (van den Heuvel, Geuskens, Hooftman, et al., 2010). Psychological assessment is also important to the workplace because mental health and related disorders tend to be among the most daunting and confusing for employers from the perspective of intervention and accommodation. The most common purpose for having an employee complete a psychological assessment would be to attain information necessary such that accommodations within the workplace intended to mitigate the complications of the mental health disorder could be put into place. Specific accommodations are described in detail in Chapter 12 (Accommodations in the Workplace).

WHO CAN COMPLETE A PSYCHOLOGICAL ASSESSMENT?

Psychological assessment can be completed by either a psychologist or a psychiatrist, depending on the question being asked. It is often the case that workplace stakeholders are unsure whether a referral should be made to a psychologist or psychiatrist, perhaps because they are unsure of the true differences between the two professions. The differences are as follows. Psychologists are primarily experts in human behavior. They receive extended training in mental health and other related disorders, human behavior, assessment, and intervention. Psychologists are not medical doctors, but instead have advanced degrees related to the interaction of brain and behavior, human health, child development, social psychology, neuropsychology, or a variety of other areas of specialization. Given that psychologists are broadly trained in human behavior, they have much to contribute in terms of behavioral interventions for many types of mental health issues. Psychologists will typically provide guidance regarding environmental, personal, or behavioral variables that can be altered in order to provide intervention. Because psychologists are not medical doctors, in cases where need for psychopharmacology is recommended, a psychologist will refer for a psychiatric assessment. A request for psychiatric assessment from a psychologist would be similar to the same process of referral completed by a workplace stakeholder seeking pharmacotherapy for an employee. That is, typically psychiatric referrals are initiated by the individual's family doctor.

In contrast to the educational background of a psychologist, psychiatrists receive very different training during their academic and clinical training career. Specifically, psychiatrists are first and foremost medical doctors. Psychiatrists are trained initially as medical doctors and receive a medical degree, which they then follow up with an area of specialization; this specialized training is where they received their training as a psychiatrist. Psychiatrists are trained specifically in mental health, and provide the highest level of specialization with respect to psychopharmacology. In situations where medication is considered to be the primary avenue of intervention for a particular employee, psychiatric intervention should be the first consideration.

Confusion regarding psychologists and psychiatrists may often result from the fact that both professions are trained and often actively engaged in therapeutic intervention. That is, both psychiatrists and psychologists are trained and competent to provide personal counseling. It should be clear however, that for both professions provision of therapeutic intervention in the form of personal counseling is considered a professional choice. That is to say, although both psychiatrists and psychologists are actively trained in providing therapeutic intervention, this may or may not be a professional activity they choose to engage in. Both professions provide many clinical services, and some professionals will make choices to refine their clinical expertise. For example, many psychologists work primarily within the area of psychological assessment, and become experts in providing diagnostic clarity; but, upon the provision of a diagnosis, do not provide intervention as an aspect of clinical practice. Similarly, psychiatric providers may provide therapy, but may also choose to work primarily in the field of diagnostic assessment and psychopharmacology. These types of professional choices are often dictated by community need. For example, in highly underserved communities, psychiatric diagnosis and psychopharmacology would be in great demand and likely would be all-absorbing of the practitioner's time. Personal therapy requires more time and resources, something underserved areas tend to lack in terms of professional services. With respect to psychologists, many psychologists also make a choice about practice area based on preference, as there are many different facets in the psychological profession. Specifically, psychologists often will self-identify primarily as therapists, assessors, behavioral consultants, and so on.

What Should I Expect from a Psychological Assessment?

As stated above, distinct differences exist between an assessment completed by a psychiatrist, and those completed by a psychologist. So, when should a workplace stakeholder make a referral to which type of professional? In cases where mental health is the primary concern, severe behaviors would influence psychological scores, medication is presumed to be the primary avenue of presumed need, the services of a medical doctor are considered paramount (for example, in cases where there may be need to invoke legislation such as the adult guardianship act), and sometimes in cases where governmental coverage of the service is necessary, psychiatric assessment should be the assessment of choice. In contrast, psychological assessment would be specifically indicated in situations where there is a desire to have psychometric scores regarding cognitive abilities, neuropsychological capabilities, mental health, achievement, and so on. It should be noted that psychological assessment, in most jurisdictions, will not be covered by government medical services plans, and, consequently, financial considerations must also be taken into account when contemplating a psychological assessment. In summary, psychological assessment will answer different questions than those that will be answered by a psychiatric assessment; however, both forms of assessment are equally important and should be used as complimentary, according to the type of information desired. However, given the recent increase in psychological testing as a function of workplace activities, combined with the apparent lack of clarity regarding the aspects and outcome of a psychological assessment, the focus of this chapter will be on the specifics of psychological, not psychiatric, assessment.

What Does a Psychological Assessment Include?

In the experience of the authors, psychological assessment is often suggested; however, the suggestion for assessment is accompanied by a lack of clarity about what exactly the assessment could, or should provide. In general, psychological assessments provide information about cognitive aptitude, neuropsychological profile, achievement scores, and mental health. In addition, for workplace specific types of referrals, psychological assessment will often include a small component regarding vocational interests. This section would typically only be included if the individual was initially considering employment, or was considering a change in employment area due to workplace illness or injury.

What Kinds of Issues Require a Referral for Psychological Assessment?

Workplace stakeholders often consider psychological assessment, but seem unsure of when the expense of an assessment would be justified. Some of the very common reasons why psychological assessment is recommended would include changes in behavior in the workplace, concerns for an employee, or a need for further information in order to provide accommodation. Other, more specific situations for which psychological assessment is often recommended would include concern regarding:

- learning disabilities

- mental health issues

- acquired brain injury (ABI)

- autism spectrum disorder (ASD)

- developmental delay (DD)

- neuropsychological issues (for example issues with attention, memory, executive functioning and so on)

- adult attention deficit hyperactivity disorder (ADHD)

- personality disorder (PD)

- fetal alcohol spectrum disorder (FASD; note: requires multidisciplinary assessment, including a physician)

WHAT IS COGNITIVE APTITUDE?

Cognitive aptitude refers to an individual's basic capabilities in a variety of important areas. Generally, traditional views of cognitive aptitude have considered a variety of intellectual domains, with the most common including capacities in verbal comprehension, spatial skills, memory, and processing speed. Other domains sometimes evaluated by tests of cognitive aptitude include sequential processing skills, sustained and/or divided attention, general knowledge, and so on. Cognitive aptitude tests are generally based on one of the primary theories of intelligence. Specifically, theories of intelligence typically have followed the perspectives of Alfred Binet, David Weschler, and Jean Piaget, or have fallen into the theoretical orientations provided by factor analysis or information processing. In the late 1800s, Alfred Binet approached intellectual assessment from the perspective of complex measurement. Binet argued that intellectual capability can only be measured through distinct processes given that multiple cognitive abilities may be necessary for a variety of intellectual tasks (Binet and Henri, 1895a, 1895b, 1895c). Similar to the perspective of Binet, Weschler described intelligence as being made up of qualitatively distinct abilities which could be differentiated through quantitative measurement. In particular, Weschler described verbal and performance domains of intelligence. In contrast to Binet, Weschler focused more on a global capacity for intellectual ability (Weschler, 1958, 1974). Different than either Binet or Weschler, Piaget saw intelligence as an ongoing interaction between biological maturation and environment. This theorist saw intelligence as the culmination of developmental stages that created cognitive organization or reorganization through experience (Piaget, 1954, 1971). Factor analytic theories of intelligence have been supported through the use of factor analysis, a group of statistical techniques used to determine factors or constructs determined by data. Prominent factor analytic theories of intelligence have included Spearman's two factor theory of intelligence (Spearman, 1927), Thurstone's seven "primary abilities" (Thurstone, 1938), Gardner's theory of multiple intelligences (Gardner, 1983), and Carroll's three-stratum theory of cognitive abilities (Carroll, 1997). Finally, information processing theory derives from Russian neuropsychologist and theorist Aleksandr Luria (Luria, 1966a, 1966b). Luria saw intelligence primarily as a function of *how* information is processed, rather than *what* is processed. In particular, this theorist saw a distinction between simultaneous/parallel and successive/sequential processing.

Although measures of cognitive aptitude include both those that have existed for many, many years, as well as those that are considered to be less established, newer tasks (for example, Comprehensive Test of Nonverbal Intelligence [CTONI; CTONI-2]), arguably the two most well-used, and well-known tests of cognitive aptitude, include the Weschler tests of intelligence, and the Stanford-Binet tests of intelligence. Current versions of the Weschler tests of intelligence include the Weschler Preschool and Primary Scale of Intelligence—Third Edition (WPPSI-III), the Weschler Intelligence Scale for Children—Fourth Edition (WISC-IV), and the Weschler Adult Intelligence Scale—Fourth Edition (WAIS-IV). Current versions of the Stanford-Binet intelligence scale include the Stanford-Binet Intelligence Scales for Early Childhood—Fifth Edition (Early SB-5) and the Stanford-Binet Intelligence Scale—Fifth Edition (SB-5). When assessing an adult working population, use of the WAIS-IV or SB-5 would be very common as the chosen method to assess intellectual capacity.

NEUROPSYCHOLOGICAL ASSESSMENT

On the face of it, from the perspective of workplace practitioners, one of the most confusing areas of psychological assessment is the area of the neuropsychological assessment. It seems that many workplace stakeholders are unclear about when a neuropsychological assessment is indicated. In short, the neuropsychological assessment would be completed in cases where assessment of cognitive aptitude does not provide enough specificity with respect to the function of specific psychological capacities. That is, areas including spatial reasoning, language, memory, attention, and executive functioning can be considered more fully and with a greater level of specificity when a neuropsychological assessment is completed.

Neuropsychological assessment would often be indicated in situations where concerns regarding a particular individual involved, for example, issues with memory and attention. Although the previously described tests of cognitive aptitude will often establish cognitive capability for memory and attention, broadly defined, tests such as the WAIS-IV and the SB-V are not capable of providing specific information regarding particular aspects of memory and attention at the level which can be completed via neuropsychological methods. For example, in general the WAIS-IV working memory domain tends to be primarily focused on verbal memory. Therefore, it would be difficult for an assessor to use this cognitive aptitude test only, and then discuss an individual's capability with respect to nonverbal memory. Further, cognitive aptitude tests tend to provide more information in certain areas (for example, perceptual reasoning), but little information about an individual's capacity in other domains (for example, sustained attention, and/or executive functioning). Even more so, specifics within these other domains tend to be neglected. For example, attention includes many specific aspects such as attention to verbal information, attention to nonverbal information, divided attention, and so on. Only through the use of neuropsychological assessment tools can this level of specificity be obtained.

Neuropsychological assessment is a complex and continually developing area. In addition, there are significant controversies within this area, including discussions regarding use of neuropsychological batteries versus use of single domain approaches. Publishers of neuropsychological tests have gone back and forth between the publication of overall batteries, intended to provide a single avenue for comprehensive neuropsychological assessment, and providing tests focused on a particular area of the neuropsychological assessment (for example, executive functioning). For example, the Neuropsychological Assessment Battery (NAB) is a comprehensive neuropsychological battery that provides tools for assessment of attention, memory, language, special, and executive functioning components. In contrast, assessment tools such as the Delis-Kaplan Executive Function System (D-KEFS) only consider specific neuropsychological domains such as executive functions within verbal and spatial domains. The choice of neuropsychological instruments will be dependent on the knowledge, experience, and training of the individual assessment professional. Consequently, it is difficult to provide workplace stakeholders with advice about which neuropsychological tests can be expected on a psychological assessment report. When considering neuropsychological testing, the domain of interest (for example, attention, memory, and so on) should be considered of more importance than the particular test used to assess capacity.

ACHIEVEMENT TESTING

In addition to cognitive aptitude and neuropsychological testing, a typical psychological assessment would include some aspect of achievement testing. Achievement testing typically considers where an individual is functioning relative to academic grade standards. Achievement testing in combination with achievement history and cognitive aptitude make up the primary diagnostic tools for an evaluation of specific learning disability. According to the DSM-IV (American Psychiatric Association, 2000), the diagnostic criteria for a learning disability requires achievement scores significantly below that which would be expected given an individual's cognitive profile, in combination with a history of achievement inconsistent with that which would be expected given the individual's overall measured intellectual functioning.

Verbal learning disabilities are typically described as a disorder in one or more of the three most common achievement areas, reading, writing, and/or math. Specifically, an individual might be diagnosed with Reading Disorder, Disorder of Written Expression, or Mathematics Disorder. In addition, a furthercategory of learning disability, Learning Disorder—Not Otherwise Specified (NOS), can also be used if an individual has learning difficulties that are less defined than those typically seen within a single domain. For example, this category could be used to describe an individual with reading and writing ability substantially below expected levels, but not consistent with the clinical criteria for independent diagnoses of both Reading Disorder and Disorder of Written Expression. In this case, a diagnosis of Learning Disorder—NOS might be used to describe the fact that the individual has significant difficulties in two primary domains of achievement; however, even though achievement difficulties in these domains would certainly influence overall achievement level, full diagnostic criteria for a specific learning disability have not been met.

Typically, achievement testing consists of tasks that look very similar to those which would be seen within a school setting. Tasks on achievement tests generally increase incrementally, as would be expected as an individual moves through grade level schooling. In addition, achievement tests often provide scores suggestive of a particular grade level. These grade level equivalency scores are considered to be among the least valid of psychological scores, and they should be used only as a general indication of grade equivalency. However, despite the weaknesses in grade equivalencies as psychometric scores, grade equivalency scores can be helpful in terms of intervention. For example, grade scores may provide indications regarding literacy, requirements for additional support, competency for some adult level tasks (for example, completion of contracts), and so on.

At present, some of the more commonly used achievement tests include the Weschler Individual Achievement Test-Second Edition (WIAT-II), the Woodcock-Johnson-III (WJ-III), and the Kaufman Test of Educational Achievement-Second Edition (KTEA-II).

MENTAL HEALTH

Mental health assessment should be considered to be one of the most complex types of diagnostic assessment. The complexity in mental health diagnoses exists as a result of the construct-based evaluation that is completed in an effort to define mental illness. Diagnosis of mental illness is dictated by descriptions provided in the DSM-IV and/or DSM-V, as appropriate (Diagnostic and Statistical Manual for Mental Disorders-Fourth Edition; Diagnostic and Statistical Manual for Mental Disorders-Fifth Edition). The DSMs are extremely useful guides for understanding, describing, and categorizing mental illness. However, existing deficiencies in our understanding and description of mental illness, combined with the inability to use the DSM-IV to describe a spectrum-based approach, is reflected in the weaknesses of the DSM. That is, diagnosis of mental illness is often fraught with environmental, social, and personal variables, as well as complexities regarding differential diagnoses. In addition, diagnosis of mental disorder requires self and/or third-party reporting as a primary method of achieving information. There is no objective measurement tool for mental illness and, consequently, accurate diagnosis of mental illness depends on competency of the clinician.

Mental health diagnosis is the area shared most completely by psychologists and psychiatrists; both psychologists and psychiatrists are fully competent to complete mental health assessment, provide recommendations, and follow up with interventions if necessary. As discussed above, the primary distinction in the approach of these professionals is that psychologists would tend to rely primarily on behavioral interventions, whereas typically psychopharmacology would be the selected domain of psychiatrists.

In assessing mental health, both psychologists and psychiatrists would approach assessment in a similar manner. Mental health is typically assessed using a combination of a clinical interview with complementary self- and/or third-party reports about symptoms and behavior. The distinction between the use of self- and third-party reports for mental health diagnoses would typically be driven by the competency of the individual being assessed. If an individual is entirely competent, articulate, self-aware and forthright about their mental health symptoms, the use of a self-report clinical interview and/ or questionnaires may be fully appropriate. In contrast, if the individual has diminished capabilities for any reason—for example, is a member of a vulnerable population (for example, developmentally delayed, demented adults etc.)—third-party reporting regarding mental health symptoms would be indicated. Both self-report and third-party report of mental health issues will focus on both internalizing and externalizing indicators of mental illness. In particular, assessment will request information about positive symptoms of mental illness (for example, panic attacks), as well as negative symptoms of mental illness (for example, lack of interest). Typically, an indication of symptoms through either clinical interview or questionnaire-based reporting (self- or third-party), would be followed up by inquiry regarding behavioral examples of the type of symptoms described.

The clinical interview is considered to be one of the most important aspects of a mental health assessment. A clinical interview is a discussion between an experienced diagnostic clinician and the client (or representative), focused on evaluating the individual's level of mental health symptomatology. Several options are currently available for guiding the clinical interview; these options are provided by publishers who print structured clinical interviews specifically intended to help the clinician investigate all possible areas of mental illness, as well as to guide the practitioner through evaluating possibilities for differential diagnoses. Some of the more commonly used structured clinical interviews would include the Structure Clinical Interview for DSM Disorders—Axis 1 (SCID-I), the Schedule for Affective Disorders and Schizophrenia (SADS), and the Structured Interview of Reported Symptoms (SIRS).

To support the conclusions of the clinical interview, clinicians will typically also ask clients to complete one or more questionnaire-based measures of mental health. Several advantages are provided by these standardized tools, including access to validity scales available in commercially produced self-report questionnaires, a secondary check on the clinician's impressions created during the clinical interview, an opportunity for the individual to express additional symptoms that he or she may have neglected to express directly to the clinician during the clinical interview, and standardized data to which comparison can be made. Arguably some of the most commonly used and most well-validated scales for this task include the Personality Assessment Inventory (PAI), the Minnesota Multiphasic Personality Inventory (MMPI), and the Symptoms Checklist 90 (SCL-90).

FUNCTIONAL ADAPTIVE SKILLS

Assessment of functional adaptive skills considers the independent living skills of the individual being assessed. Normally assessment in this domain would involve a detailed interview or questionnaire completed with a third-party respondent who is familiar with the client's functioning within the social/communicative, self-care, community living, and motor skills areas. Functional adaptive skills are important for intervention planning in that individuals with weaknesses in functional domains typically required significantly more support than their age peers. In addition, assessment of functional skills will always be a primary component of an assessment for developmental delay, and will often comprise an important aspect for many other types of neurodevelopmental disorders such as Autism Spectrum Disorder, Fetal Alcohol Spectrum Disorder, Traumatic Brain Injury, and so on. The most commonly used methods of collecting information in this domain include the Scales of Independent Behavior-Revised (SIB-R), Adaptive Behavior Assessment System-Second Edition (ABAS-II), and the Vineland Adaptive Behavior Scales-Second Edition (Vineland-II).

VOCATIONAL INTERESTS

When completing a psychological assessment, the final component of the assessment may include a short evaluation of vocational interests. This section of the psychological assessment would be driven by the referral question, as well as the current needs of the referred employee. Although some psychologists have expertise in vocational assessment, this is not typically an area of expertise that would be provided during a psychological assessment specifically. In addition, vocational assessment can be provided by individuals with specialization in this area, who typically can provide their services at fees lower than that required by a psychologist. Therefore, in cases where only a vocational assessment is required and/or a great deal of specificity is required within the vocational area, it would be recommended to access an individual whose primary role is to provide vocational assessment, rather than the services of psychologist.

Given the availability of vocational assessment experts, one may question why a psychologist would complete vocational assessment at all. Completion of vocational interest inventories would be indicated during a psychological assessment if the individual has been referred specifically for psychological reasons, but is not currently engaged in an ongoing and durable workplace environment. In particular, for an individual who has been referred to the psychologist for the primary purpose of evaluating the need for accommodations required for securing employment, or returning to school in order to access a new vocational field, a short evaluation of vocational interest should be considered important. Although a psychologist typically would not provide a wide, extensive evaluation of vocational interests and aptitudes, having some indication of vocational interest should be considered important to round-out the overall message that can be garnered from the psychological assessment. The collection of this information allows the psychologist to determine whether consistency exists between the vocational interests and the general capability of the individual, as suggested by the attained psychometric profile. For example, if an individual has very strong skills in the areas of verbal comprehension and writing, and has vocational interests consistent with the clerical field, the psychologist could suggest an overall picture of consistency between aptitude and interest. In contrast, if the individual is interested in the clerical field but has a psychometric profile suggestive of Reading Disorder, Disorder of Written Expression, and poor communication skills, a lack of fit between aptitude, achievement, and vocational interest would be suggested.

The field of vocational interest is overwhelmed by potential analyses that could be completed in order to determine the fit between an individual's vocational interests and respective workplace environments. Although it is beyond the scope of this chapter to discuss all of the aspects of vocational assessment, we believe that three of the most commonly used vocational interest inventories used by psychologists include the Canadian Work Preference Inventory (CWPI), the Reading Free Vocational Interest Inventory-Second Edition (RFVII-2), and the Self-Directed Search (SDS).

What Type of Assessment Should I Request?

When deciding to go ahead with a psychological assessment, it is often the case that workplace stakeholders struggle with the question of what type of assessment should be requested. Different types of psychological assessment are described in specific ways, but often refer to a similar process. Essentially psychological assessment comes in three different types, and the specifics of that type are primarily driven by the referral question.

The most involved, most expensive, and most explanatory type of psychological assessment would be a comprehensive psychological assessment that included all six primary aspects described previously. These aspects include cognitive aptitude, neuropsychological profile, achievement profile, mental health evaluation, functional adaptive skills, and a short indication of vocational interests. Referral for a comprehensive assessment would be suggested in cases where the individual being referred is considered to be highly complex, there is little knowledge regarding the individual's profile, and/or there is a desire to collect as much information as possible in order to clarify the particular situation. In the experience of the authors, the comprehensive assessment is often the most useful type of assessment. This type of assessment allows for the clinician to evaluate all possible diagnostic avenues, and, as a result, to provide the most information in terms of diagnostic clarity and differential diagnoses. A comprehensive assessment will allow the clinician to provide recommendations about all aspects of an individual's psychometric profile and eliminate the risk that, by evaluating only one domain, the primary area of concern has been neglected in the evaluation. In a comprehensive evaluation, the first five primary areas of evaluation are required; however, as stated previously, vocational interest may or may not be indicated, depending on the referral question and the unique needs of the client.

In some cases, assessors are provided with specific referral questions for evaluation of learning disability. A learning disability assessment would typically only include an assessment of cognitive aptitude and achievement profile. In the case of a learning disability assessment, a referral for this type of consideration should be made only in situations where all other concerns have either been addressed via another avenue (for example, psychiatric assessment), or where the possibility of learning disability is the one and only concern. For example, a learning disability specific assessment may be appropriate in the situation where an individual has no struggles with respect to attention, memory, mental health, and so on, but has only had very specific difficulties within one domain of their achievement history (for example, mathematics). The need for a learning disability assessment should be evaluated carefully, as a simple request for learning disability assessment can result in incomplete information about an individual's psychometric profile. Consequently, many ongoing questions regarding other difficulties may remain unanswered.

Referrals will also often come in the form of a psycho-educational and/ or psycho-vocational assessment request. These types of assessments are typically fall somewhere between the limited nature of a learning disability assessment and a fully comprehensive assessment. Depending on the referral question, and the skills of the assessor, a psycho-educational assessment may range from a basic review of cognitive aptitude and achievement profile, right through to an entirely comprehensive assessment as described previously. In the case of the psycho-vocational assessment, a similar type of approach would be taken, however a psycho-vocational review would include all aspects of an educational assessment, with the referral question and resulting intervention/recommendations more directed toward vocational, rather than educational pursuits. When receiving these types of requests, experienced clinicians will more often than not weigh more closely to the comprehensive type of assessment. Approaching all assessments as comprehensives increases the probability that all information pertinent to the most appropriate diagnosis will be obtained.

The final type of general referral category is a mental health specific assessment. A referral for mental health assessment only would typically occur in situations where mental illness was considered to be the primary concern for the individual. A referral for mental health assessment only would also be indicated in situations where the individual's mental health symptoms may impact his or her ability to complete the testing process involved in a full psychometric assessment. Mental health diagnoses can be completed by either a psychologist or psychiatrist, and, as previously described, would typically involve only a clinical interview and accompanying self- and/or third-party report questionnaires. Mental health only assessments are often completed as a first step, in an attempt to provide the individual with interventions to stabilize their level of functioning. It is often the case that, once mental health symptoms are well controlled, a comprehensive psychological assessment is indicated in order to provide additional information about how mental health and other aspects of the individual's psychological profile may be inter-related.

What Can I Expect in the Report?

Reports resulting from psychological assessment tend to follow a similar structure; however, the content and style of the report will be specific to the individual assessor. In general, a psychological report would typically include a description of the reason for referral. In the reason for referral, comments will often be made about how the reason for referral was addressed. Second to the reason for referral, professional credentials of the individual assessor will usually be discussed. This section of the report is sometimes overlooked as a formality. However, the credentials of the individual completing the assessment are a very important aspect of the quality of the assessment, and should not be taken lightly. Individuals completing psychological assessment should be recognized by their governing body (for example, College of Psychologists) as a registered professional in the field, and have particular expertise in the area of psychological assessment. Following the professional credentials of the individual assessor, a record of observations from the assessment process will often be provided. In this section, the assessor will provide subjective impressions about the individual's qualitative behavior during the assessment, a summary statement about the perceived validity of the current scores, as well as other comments that may impact the overall interpretive nature or usefulness of the assessment.

Following observations from the observations section, a report will typically review the individual's social history. The length of this section will depend on the amount of information available to the assessor, the nature of the assessment, as well as the environment in which the assessment is taking place. For example, in situations where the assessment is part of a multidisciplinary team assessment, the social history would often be fully described in the report of a social worker, and would typically include only a short review in the psychological assessment. In addition to the social history, the social history section will sometimes include either information about a self-report history and/or a report from a third party respondent (for example, parent, adult sibling, and so on). Often times, in this section there is an indication of concerns, strengths, and weaknesses as identified by the individual or the third-party respondent.

The next section of the report will often be composed of the psychometric interpretation. This is the section where the psychologist will provide an interpretation for each section of the evaluation. Typically, the psychometric interpretation section will provide substantial detail about interpretation of each aspect of the individual's functioning, including strengths and weaknesses within the cognitive domain, issues with any aspect of neuropsychological functioning, an evaluation of reading, writing, and mathematics, a description of the findings from the clinical interview and other mental health evaluations, as well as vocational interests if collected. After the full description of each independent aspect of the psychological assessment has been completed in the psychometric interpretation section, a summary and recommendations section will typically pull all of the information together in a short summative statement about the overall conclusions from the assessment. In the case of a workplace referral, as is the focus of this book, the summary and recommendations section will typically include clear recommendations for suggested interventions, as well as clear recommendations for workplace accommodation requirements.

Concluding Remarks

Psychological assessment can provide valuable information required by employers for the purpose of adequately addressing employees' accommodation needs. However, it seems that it is often unclear which type of assessment should be requested in a given situation. Using information such as that presented in this chapter will assist employers toward becoming knowledgeable about which type of professional and which type of assessment will best suit the needs of workplace stakeholders when attempting to best help employees remain at or return to work.

More information can be found at the following sources:

http://www.icdl.com/graduate/documents/Chapter18.pdf

http://www.springerpub.com/samples/9780826144713_chapter.pdf

References

American Psychiatric Association. (2000). *Diagnostic and Statistical Manual of Mental Disorders (Fourth Edition Text Revision).* Washington: American Psychiatric Association.

American Psychiatric Association. (2013). *Diagnostic and Statistical Manual of Mental Disorders (Fifth Edition).* Washington: American Psychiatric Association.

Binet, A. and Henri, V. (1895a). La mémoire des mots. *L'Année Psychologique,* 1, 1–23.

Binet, A. and Henri, V. (1895b). La mémorie des phrases. *L'Année Psychologique,* 1, 24–59.

Binet, A. and Henri, V. (1895c). La psychologie individuelle. *L'Année Psychologique,* 2, 411–65.

Carroll, J.B. (1997b). The three-stratum theory of cognitive abilities. In D.P. Flanagan, J.L. Genshaft and P.L. Harrison (eds), *Contemporary Intellectual Assessment: Theories, Tests, and Issues* (pp. 122–130). New York: The Guilford Press.

Gardner, H. (1983). *Frames of Mind: the Theory of Multiple Intelligences.* New York: Basic Books.

Luria, A.R. (1966b). *Higher Cortical Functions in Man.* New York: Basic Books.

Luria, A.R. (1966a). *Human Brain and Psychological Processes.* New York: Harper & Row.

Piaget, J. (1971). *Biology and Knowledge.* Chicago: University of Chicago Press.

Piaget, J. (1954). *The Construction of Reality and the Child.* New York: Basic Books.

Spearman, C. (1927). *The Abilities of Man: Their Nature and Measurement.* New York: MacMillan.

Thurstone, L.L. (1938). *Primary Mental Abilities (Psychometric Monographs, No 1).* Chicago: University of Chicago Press.

van den Heuvel, S.G., Geuskens, G.A., Hooftman, W.E., Koppes, L.L., and van den Bossche, S.N. (2010). Productivity loss at work; health-related and work-related factors. *Journal of Occupational Rehabilitation*, 20, 331–9.

Weschler, D. (1974). *Manual for the Weschler Intelligence Scale for Children-Revised*. New York: Psychological Corporation.

Weschler, D. (1958). *The Measurement and Appraisal of Adult Intelligence* (4th ed.). Baltimore: Williams & Wilkins.

Chapter 11

How to Create a
Healthy Workplace

*Significant, successful implementation of health and safety programs
requires employers and employees to work towards a common goal,
namely, creating a healthier, safer workplace. Changes must be realistic,
achievable goals for all parties. One important goal is to clearly define the
employer's responsibility toward its employees. (Olafsdottir, 2004, p. 29)*

Introduction

In previous chapters we began exploring mental illness and disability
management from multiple perspectives and through diverging frameworks.
We investigated mental illness from the perspective of the person with a mental
illness and the employer, barriers to staying at work and returning to work
(including discrimination and stigmatization), and the costs of mental illness
for the individual and the organization. In this chapter we examine how we can
create a mentally healthy workplace. A healthy workplace is mutually beneficial
for the individual and the organization for many reasons. Workplaces that have
instilled health as a primary goal for their organization can enjoy healthier and
happier employees and employees can enjoy higher satisfaction from their
employment. With these two benefits working in tandem, organizations can
enjoy higher productivity and relevance to their customer base as persons with
a mental illness contribute solutions and opinions to improve the performance
of the organization.

Grawitch, et al. (2006) provide four guiding principles for creating a
healthier workplace:

1.   Organizational health exists on a continuum from mortality to vibrant health in that it is a move towards abundant life.

2.   Organizational health is a continuous process that constantly needs to be maintained.

3.   Organizational health is a mixture of interrelated factors which means that an organization can only be healthy if all the components of the workplace are free of threats and vulnerabilities.

4.   Organizational health is dependent upon fulfilling relationships with "constant communication, collaboration, and relationship building."

Let's look at each of these. In order to create a healthy workplace there has to be a commitment by the employer to making improvements that support health for employees. Workplaces are uniquely positioned to enhance the health and well-being of their employees when you consider that most employed people spend a large portion of their lives in the workplace (Michaels and Greene, 2013). Offering programs such as: employee assistance, flexible benefits and working conditions, treating employees fairly, employee development, health and safety, and prevention of work stress all have the potential to improve health outcomes for organizations (Kelloway and Day, 2005). It is also important to note that individuals already possess many of the resources necessary to promote health such as optimism and resilience which have been linked to better psychological health in the workplace (Boudrais, Desrumaux, Gaudreau, et al., 2011). These two factors in particular can support employees to develop coping skills for occasions when job demands cause stress.

It is very important to understand what we mean by health. In 1946 the World Health Organization defined health as "a state of complete physical, mental, and social well-being and not merely the absence of disease of infirmity" (WHO as cited in Boudrias, Desrumaux, Gaudreau, et al., 2011). This definition illustrates that health is not a simple continuum where absence of illness lies at one end of the spectrum while illness or disease lies at the other. Stepping away from this disease model makes it possible to more readily address mental illness issues that often do not fit at either ends of the spectrum but rather fall somewhere in-between. Not thinking of the disease model with its attending medical solutions makes it possible to consider other types of interventions such as prevention and education often referred to as health promotion.

Even though health promotion programs have been increasing in numbers in recent years, due largely to an increasing awareness of the importance of employee health (Aldana and Pronk, 2001) there is still much work to be done. While there clearly is a moral imperative for employers to provide healthy workplaces, the financial burden of not doing so should provide sufficient motivation for taking action.

Depression, sadness, and mental illness are the top contributors to medical costs, absence, short-term disability, and presenteeism. These are estimated to cost $348/year for eligible employees (Goetzel, Long, Ozminkowski, et al., 2004). An extreme example of stress-related absenteeism provided by Ecnotech (2008, in Idris, Dollard, Coward et al., 2012) illustrates the current picture in Australia in which costs have been estimated to be $14.8 billion a year. Michaels and Greene (2013) discuss Workplace Health Promotion (WHP) programs in the context of beneficiaries, benefits, and reasons behind the move towards implementing WHP. As has been mentioned previously, the beneficiaries of WHP are not simply the employees receiving the programming but rather also the employer, the employee's families, the community, and stakeholders in a company. Still resistance is all too frequent. Some reasons for this resistance include fear of liability, ignorance about benefits, accommodation difficulties, lack of trained personnel, and of course a lack of funding (Michaels and Greene, 2013).

Reasons for resisting change in the workplace include common barriers noted by Graham Lowe in 2004 such as: organizational inertia, difficulties surrounding the mobilization of people around a new vision for the workplace, and the tendency to substitute rhetoric for action. Another barrier of note is viewing the intervention movement as more of a novelty in the workplace instead of truly implementing it as an organizational value (DeJoy and Wilson, 2010). A possible solution to increasing the interest in workplace health promotion programs is to turn to the employees themselves. Self-Determination Theory defines three basic psychological needs people require in order to achieve their full potential and to avoid ill-health. These needs are: the innate inclination to achieve autonomy, competence, and relatedness. Autonomy refers to the need to have a sense of volition and ownership of behavior while competence refers to a person's sense of their own efficiency and mastering of the environment. Finally, relatedness serves to cover the component of human need to have close relationships and a sense of belonging. When these exist, a person is capable of psychological growth and being healthy in the sense that self-esteem, well-being, and vigor can be achieved (Boudrais, Desrumaux, Gaudreau, et al., 2011). These basic needs among other organizational supports influence healthy workplaces and should all be considered when developing programs designed to positively influence health.

Other protective factors of note when addressing workplace stressors that impact health are the resilience and hardiness of employees. These are individual characteristics that play an important role in decreasing the experience of distress in the workplace. Resilience is essentially the ability of a person to bounce back from an experience of a stressor. Coupled with optimism noted earlier, an individual can be equipped with the personal strength required to flourish in a workplace by being more active and autonomous employees (Boudrais, Desrumaux, Gaudreau, et al., 2011).

In order to gain a better understanding of antecedents and consequences of healthy workplaces, Kelloway and Day, (2005) developed a simple diagram to arrange existing research on the topic. We present this diagram to clearly show the level complexity that is present when rearranging a workplace into a healthier focus.

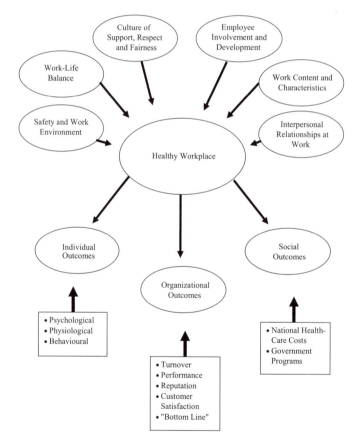

Figure 11.1   Antecedents and outcomes of healthy workplaces (Kelloway and Day, 2005, p. 229)

Ten-Step Process to a Healthier Workplace

There is research to suggest that workplaces need to focus on more than the mere absence of ill-health and begin to take an intervention approach. Also of note is that workplace changes in job design, workplace culture, organizational systems, and management practices are imperative for any increase in employee health to occur (Lowe, 2004). Intervention approaches can improve personal growth and engagement, and positively affect well-being for employees. Focusing on positive changes that can be implemented allows for programming that achieves healthier individual outcomes (satisfaction and healthy lifestyles) and subsequently healthy organizational outcomes in the long run (Kelloway and Day, 2005). These positive outcomes are a result of promoting well-being at work and need further investigation in future research (Neilsen, Randall, Holten, et al., 2010).

Also apparent in the research is that work-life benefits along with a more supportive environment helps workplaces retain workers and has been linked to job satisfaction, motivation, and the reduction of stress (O'Neill, Harrison, Cleveland, et al., 2009). Adjustments within the workplace focused on keeping employees healthy can notably improve worker well-being (Blustein, 2008). Leadership is critical if such changes are to take place. Providing training on transformational leadership for example may improve the approaches taken by workplace leaders so that they engage employees in the process (Neilson, Randall, Holten, et al., 2010).

STEP 1: OBTAIN ORGANIZATIONAL COMMITMENT

It is important to differentiate between commitment to the organization and commitment of the organization. Organizational buy-in and organizational commitment both have significant roles to play in psychologically healthy workplaces. For example, although employees who are committed to the organization are commonly presumed to be less likely to exhibit absenteeism; multiple research studies have found no direct link between absenteeism and organizational commitment (Price, 1997; Schalk, 2010). On the other hand, organizational buy-in, a fundamentally different concept, has been shown to be a particularly important factor in health promotion initiatives. A study looking at workplace weight loss interventions found that the majority of participants indicated that the most important factor leading to the success of previous health initiatives was leadership support and participation (Wilson, et al., 2007).

Employees may be reluctant to utilize benefits provided by the organization unless they perceive that their supervisor or the organization as a whole is supporting the use of the benefits (O'Neill, Harrison, Cleveland, et al., 2009). Many studies have found that employees are reluctant to use family-friendly benefits. In particular employees are reluctant to use family-friendly benefits if they perceive that in doing so they may harm their careers (Butler, Gasser, and Smart, 2004). Given that we are well off this concern it would be wise to conduct a readiness check and assess if a workplace is ready to accept such initiatives. It is at this stage that concerns can be addressed that may sabotage a new initiative such as a health promotion program.

Organizational audit

One way of beginning to address mental health issues is to conduct a mental health/wellness audit. Workplaces are very familiar with conducting safety audits which are designed to protect the physiological safety of their workers. Why not use this same practice but focus it on mental wellness? We are not aware of any specific audit tools available at this time but this is an area that consultants are beginning to work in. A lesson may be taken by assessing psychosocial risk factors such as: psychological support, organizational culture, clear leadership and expectations, civility and respect, psychological job fit, growth and development, recognition and rewards, involvement and influence, workload management, engagement, balance, and psychological protection. Questionnaires could be designed that examine these factors and determine the amount of risk or exposure a worksite has in these areas.

STEP 2: ASSEMBLE A TEAM/COMMITTEE

Participation of all stakeholders is critical to the success of all health-related programming. New ways of thinking and looking for solutions is critical. The tenets of transformational leadership are particularly useful here. Members of committees or teams dedicated to improving the health of an organization should take into consideration the attributes of individuals. Those who have transformational attributes should be considered as they have been associated with psychological well-being in regards to feeling motivated, cheerful, enthusiastic, lively, joyful, and energetic. Together with these factors, transformational leadership has also been shown to be associated with the cultivation of meaningful work environments (Arnold, Turner, Barling, et al., 2007). These findings suggest that teams built to take on healthy initiatives in the workplace should be made up of individuals possessing these attributes in order to research/ design/and implement a strong plan for the organization.

Ensuring this committee is reflective of the diversity in the workplace will be of great benefit. Members should include gender equality, individuals from different business backgrounds, and individuals from the target population for the WHP program (Michaels and Greene, 2013).

STEP 3: GATHER INFORMATION ON EMPLOYEES' PERCEPTION OF NEEDS AND WISHES

Before beginning any form of intervention it is imperative to understand pre-existing plans in place within the organization. This step is taken in order to explore the possibility of building upon or modifying what is already present in the organization as opposed to starting from scratch. An excellent resource on steps an organization can take to enhance psychological health in the workplace is "Guarding Minds at Work," commissioned by the Mental Health Commission of Canada.

A possible employee survey tool could consist of 10 steps:

1. Inform Staff: let them know early on that you intend to perform a survey, communicate management support for the undertaking, be open about the goals of the survey, welcome employees to give feedback and ask questions prior to beginning the survey, and arrange for meetings and/or e-mail contact with staff to provide continuous communication;

2. Clearly communicate the purpose of the survey: be prepared to answer questions regarding why the survey is being performed, how it will benefit employees, and how will the results be used and communicated to staff;

3. Address employee questions: consider having a person responsible for answering questions that arise;

4. Ensure confidentiality;

5. List key dates and activities: survey start date, distribution of survey, deadline for survey completion (is it optional?), compensation for staff (if applicable);

6. Be prepared with reminders;

7.   Consider providing incentives to increase participation;

8.   Ensure employees are appreciated for their time completing the survey: this will enhance continued support by employees when/if programs are initiated as a result of the survey;

9.   Result communication: it is necessary to have successful follow-up participation;

10.   Implement action strategies.

It is critical to know beforehand how you will be collecting data and what sort of information you are looking for. It is also critical to determine in advance who controls/owns the data, where it will be stored, and under what conditions it will be shared (Michaels and Greene, 2013).

STEP 4: ASSESS NEEDS

A successful method that can be employed to assess the existing needs of an organization is focus groups. An example from industry of how this can be done is health circles. Health circles are workplace discussion groups designed to develop methods for reducing potentially harmful working conditions (Aust and Ducki, 2004). These circles are believed to work by allowing employees to participate in decision-making which in turn leads to increased perceptions of control over their environment. It is also believed that employees are particularly well suited to identifying working conditions that present the biggest risk factors. Further, health circles increase communication among employees and supervisors, resulting in a broader understanding of other viewpoints as well as supporting stable social network conditions (Aust and Ducki, 2004).

In a review of the results of 81 health circles it was found that stress was reduced due to better work organization and reduced physical strain resulting from improved equipment. These improvements happened as a result of ideas generated in meeting between 6 and 10 times over a period of several months to discuss problems and complaints identified in employee surveys or a health report. When assessing needs in a workplace it will take some time to ensure that all data has been unearthed. Such data saturation will let an organization know the common experience and perspectives of those being solicited for information and the consequent impact on their health and wellness.

A review of European methods for improving employee health and well-being found that there were seven criteria that were followed, at least in part, by five models of intervention (Neilsen, Randall, Holten, et al., 2010). The five models were:

1.   The Risk Management approach (UK)

2.   The Measurements Standards (UK)

3.   Work Positive (Ireland)

4.   The Prevenlab method (Spain)

5.   Health Circles (Germany)

And the seven criteria were:

1.   Interventions should focus on organizational-level solutions aimed at changing how work is designed, organized, and managed.

2.   A core component of any intervention should be participatory principles.

3.   When conducting an intervention, methods should consider all the phases that will be involved from the initial planning stages to intervention.

4.   Intervention methods should consider how organizational-level occupational health programs may be integrated with existing procedures, organizational cultures, and the management of occupational safety and health within the organization.

5.   Communication and education on raising awareness of the risks posed by work design features, and organization and management should constitute part of the methods.

6.   Methods should take into account the existing experiences an organization has in dealing with psychosocial risk factors.

7.   The selected method should be applicable to small- and medium-sized companies as well.

From commonalities in the five models, Nielsen and colleagues (2010) developed a model of occupational health interventions that has five phases for approaching interventions aimed at improving psychosocial health in the workplace. This model is an ongoing process in which employees are involved with each stage; thus, it is a means of democratizing the workplace by including the voices of the employees in the intervention process. The stages are: preparation, screening, action planning, implementation, and evaluation (see Figure 11.2).

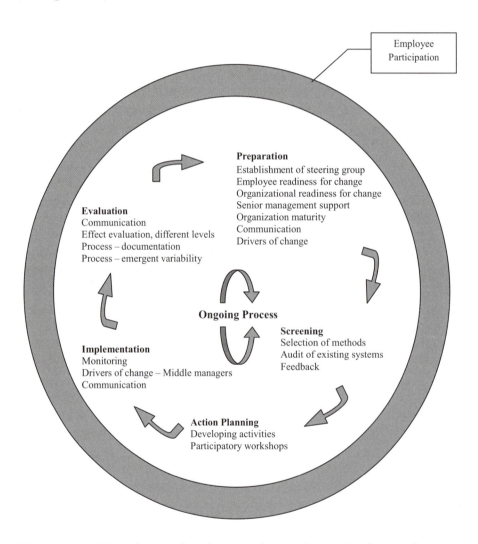

Figure 11.2   Five phases of an intervention and associated core elements, as derived from five major intervention methods. (Source: Neilsen et al., 2010)

STEP 5: DEVELOP A WORKPLACE HEALTH PLAN

This step is based on findings from the psychosocial risk factors audits (or other methods) and can be used to develop a plan of action. Areas of concern can fall into one of four different categories as presented in the Guarding Minds at work program: work environment (norms, values, and practice), training and development, communication, and formal policies and programs. When developing a plan it is important to know what will make a WHP successful. Some tips on ensuring success are:

1. Engage leadership at multiple levels;

2. Align plans with company's identity and aspirations;

3. Make the design broad in scope and high in relevance and quality;

4. Assure accessibility;

5. Create and nurture any internal or external partnerships;

6. Communicate the WHP frequently and clearly (Berry, Mirabito, and Baun, 2010).

STEP 6: DEVELOP INDICATORS TO MEASURE RESULTS

In order to measure results of programs, indicators need to be developed in order to acknowledge success and assess future directions. These indicators can be either general (for example rates of absenteeism) or more specific to certain interventions. Employees could also be asked to rate their work environment in regards to being psychologically safe and healthy.

STEP 7: IMPLEMENT PLAN

In order to maintain the momentum gained during the survey period and retain interest in participation by the employees, an implementation plan needs to be completed in a timely fashion. It is important to maintain employee participation at this stage as it is important for three reasons: 1.) it helps to optimize the fit of an intervention into the culture and context of an organization; 2.) having employee input can be seen as an intervention in and of itself as a process of empowerment; and 3.) their participation can enhance how smoothly an intervention proceeds as exposure is more widespread among organization members (Neilsen, Randall, Holten, et al., 2010).

STEP 8: EVALUATE AND LOOK FOR AREAS TO IMPROVE

Empirical investigation on health circles indicates that participants were generally satisfied with the level of cooperation within the health circles but that reporting back to them was insufficient (Aust and Ducki, 2004). This would indicate that the best way to move forward in the evaluation and improvement stage would be to provide feedback to employees in regards to how effective the intervention has been. Health circles may also be reconvened at this stage in order to review the outcomes of the interventions and assess input from employees. That said it is important to recognize that this is a continuous process that may require further interventions so that improvements can be extended. Although Aust and Ducki (2004) present health circles as a one-off process that takes about 15 months to complete, they could also be used as a part of a consistent and continuous process. Information process in this way would then form the final outcome report used by the organization to assess the success/effectiveness of a program.

STEP 9: IMPLEMENT ANY CHANGES INDICATED BY EVALUATION

The circular renewal process mentioned at the end of Step 9 must be enshrined in the program and supported on an ongoing basis. Employing the input received and ensuring steps are taken to support continuous improvements will lead to a strong flourishing program. This in turn will support improved employee morale and productions as they know that their employer is actively engaging in supporting their ongoing mental health. This will ensure the process does not stall and will foster participation by employees as they continue to see change and efforts being put forth to improve the workplace and their health.

STEP 10: CONCLUSION

Maintaining changes after an intervention is a challenge and should be at the forefront of efforts to improve organizational health. Managers and employees alike need to be mobilized and assembled to continually assess the ongoing process so that tasks can be prioritized and successfully implemented. When a new intervention is implemented, it is important to evaluate it at all levels so that it remains within the organizational goals.

Overarching societal factors will influence the implementation of an intervention and its overall success. Factors such as: workplace justice, removing class distinction, social environment, physical environment, role clarity, job/future security, autonomy, workload and work pace, work schedule, and transformational leadership will continue to profoundly impact workplaces. However, it is critical to remember why an organization engaged in creating WHP in the first place. Re-emphasizing factors such as the need for a change in business conditions, a need for change in managerial personnel, a deficiency in organizational patterns that existed previous to the WHP, as well as technological reasons, psychological reasons, and moving towards alignment with government policies are all critical factors that benefit from periodic reinforcement (Michaels and Greene, 2013).

Healthier Workplaces

Consideration of the health and wellbeing of workers reflects prevailing social attitudes and tends to lag behind periods of significant industrial change. (Harrison, 2012, p. 261)

Employers and managers shape much of the workplace experience for employees under their watchful eye. While attention is devoted to productivity and organization, it should be noted that employers can have a strong impact on the health of their workplace as well. It goes without saying that a huge amount of an individual's life is spent in their workplace and whatever experiences are had in that part of our lives can enter the social and home life. A great question posted by Galbreath (2011) leads a reflection on how we perceive work in our family and friends. How many people have seen others experience the "Sunday afternoon blues", as he calls it? Or what about the dread that some people face when they contemplate their soon approaching return to work? Furthermore, for those who experience a rough work environment, how are they coping when they go home? The ability to leave work at work and engage in a healthy home life is directly linked and can reveal the health of a workplace.

Recently in the United Kingdom, health and safety strategies in workplaces have become a target area of focus to reduce ill-health, support those who are ill, improve work opportunities, and help individuals return to work. This was a 10-year commitment that began in 2000 with the support of the Government Occupational Health Strategy of England. The program recognized the importance of well-being and workplace health and actually used the workplace environment to promote health. This was the answer to the ever increasing amount of people who were experiencing some form of ill-health as a result of the workplace. This reflects a trend in the UK that healthy employment is good for the overall well-being of employees (Harrison, 2012).

But why should mangers be so concerned with the health of their workplace when their initial responsibilities are focused on productivity? Healthy workplaces and productivity are directly linked and those workplaces that employ a healthy workplace policy for their employees also enjoy highly productive employees (Galbreath, 2011). It should go without saying that employees who enjoy their work due to enhanced healthy workplace policy are also less likely to be absent or to leave their job entirely. Stressful workplaces filter down to employee well-being, and when employees are stressed beyond their ability to cope they are not at their most productive. Stressed employees will experience more health problems. The consequences of this are costly to the workplace and are felt through lost time days, presenteeism, and overall lost productivity (Galbreath, 2011).

Finally, beyond absenteeism and high cost to the workplace, the most important reason why for employers to be concerned about the health of their workplace is because of the health of their employees. At the end of the day, productivity, costs to the workplace, and turnover cannot take priority over basic human concern. Workplaces who take a cost-analysis approach are at risk of entering an inescapable cycle of ill-health in the workplace. As Galbreath notes, it would benefit managers and employers to understand the impacts of their workplace beyond the workplace. From an ethical perspective, you want employees to go home happy and healthy and not bringing "spill-over stress and work related health issues" home with them (Galbreath, 2011).

Instructing Future Managers

> ... such programs might lead to reductions in health care costs and thus health insurance premiums. Second, healthier workers might be more productive and miss fewer days of work. These benefits may accrue at least partially to the employer (such as through improved ability to attract workers), even if the primary benefits accrue to the employee. (Baicker, Cutler, and Song, 2013, p. 1)

Galbreath (2011) has developed a course designed specifically for future managers that prepares them for creating healthy workplaces. This course not only teaches future managers about healthy workplaces but it develops a reflective practice for the individual to assess self-health and manage their own stress. The learning objectives of the course are as follows:

1. Describe a Variety of Work Environment Stressors—What stressors have you encountered in the workplace? (Ill-health, Dissatisfaction, Burnout);

2. List Consequences Resulting From Unhealthy Work Environments—What are the consequences you may experience from an unhealthy workplace? (Person-Environment Fit, Social Support, Balance);

3. Discuss Organizational Factors that Modify the Effects of the Work Environment— What variables affect the relationship between workplace and individual? (Hostility, Self-esteem, Locus of Control);

4. Discuss Personal Factors that Modify the Effects of the Work environment—What personal factors impact the effects of work environment? (Stress Audits, Time Management, Leadership Development);

5. Compare Interventions that Create Healthier Work Environment and Healthier Employees—What are some actions that can be taken to improve workplace and employee health?;

6. Describe Influential Stress Theories—Introducing stress theories that have been linked to work stress and work environments;

7. Tips from Experience—Offers students more suggestions on healthy workplaces from the instructors personal experience (Galbreath, 2011).

As you can see from above, much work has been done by Galbreath in addressing workplace health in a preventative manner that is more conducive than the intervention model typically used. The earlier mangers and employers are trained to see these issues, ideally before they arise, the better prepared workplaces will be to ingrain the concept of healthy workplaces into their organizational models.

Conclusion

Studies have shown us that other factors, such as lack of communication, vague work goals, communications conflicts, poorly delegated tasks, and insecurity in the workforce, cause people mental and physical pain. (Olafsdottir, 2004, p. 27)

The idea of organizational level intervention programs brings to light the idea of employee participation in owning such changes in the workplace and addressing problems together. While there is little research looking into the prevalence of employee participation, it does receive support from the authors in that shared responsibility often leads to greater success compared to management-driven models. Neilsen, Randall, Holten, et al. (2010) also note that changes may have a higher likelihood of being sustained within an interdependent employee participation model.

There is an increasing awareness that RTW programs are very successful and remove the financial burden of job absenteeism or leave for other reasons of disability. In addressing RTW further, programs that respond quickly to employees with a specifically trained RTW coordinator are extremely successful. Early recognition of the needs of persons with a mental illness facilitates the necessary communication that must happen between stakeholders that creates the good will within the organization, and between labour and management that creates successful mental illness programs (Lysaght, Fabrigar, Larmour-Trode, et al., 2012). Essentially it all comes down to understanding the needs of employees with mental illness and learning how to increase awareness of work influences on individuals.

Neilson et al. (2008) identify the part employers play regarding the degree to which they have an influence on their employees' perceptions of work and self-reported well-being. Being aware of the influence you have upon employees brings to light the idea of supporting employees in a way that reduces the stress the workplace can inflict upon an individual. Senior management and supervisors can only benefit from understanding the demands of the workplace and the chronic demands that adversely affect health (Idris, Dollard, Coward, et al., 2012). Research has indicated that social support at work reduces adverse health outcomes by buffering psychological stress (O'Neill, Harrison, Cleveland, et al., 2009; Wilkins and Beaudet, 1998). It is important to note and re-emphasize that mental health stressors are the most important influence on overall health (Idris, Dollard, Coward, et al., 2012).

The costs of not committing to healthier workplaces go far beyond individual employee costs. The effects of ill-health in the workplace influence the physical, mental, behavioral, and overall organizational health of a workplace in many different ways (Kelloway and Day, 2005). Employees who experience interventions creating a shift towards healthy workplaces are found to self-rate their health and perceived safety as improved (DeJoy and Wilson, 2010). The benefits of taking such a stance can improve not only individual outcomes but also organizational outcomes (turnover, performance, customer satisfaction, and the bottom line) and societal outcomes such as health care costs (Kelloway and Day, 2005). Important to note, however, is that intervention programs aimed towards improving health for the individual and organization need to be tailored to the history, culture, and market outcomes, and the specific characteristics of the employees and workplace undergoing the changes (Lowe, 2004).

Those programs that are successful from a prevention and education basis also face the challenge of accommodating those employees who have been through a worksite injury or illness. Lysaght, Fabrigar, Larmour-Trode, et al. (2012) send a clear message regarding the level of supervisory skill that is required to be able to recognize the needs and meeting the accommodation required in today's worksites.

RTW programs and WHP programs should be developed within an organization in such a way that they are sustainable, have access to resources and supports over time, and utilize the expertise of rehabilitation and occupational health specialists (Lysaght, Fabrigar, Larmour-Trode, et al., 2012). The first step is for an organization to recognize that needs are not being met for their employees, and then a course for action must be decided upon as laid out within this chapter. Experts and support systems are available to organizations and managers ready and willing to take on the task of RTW and WHP. How those programs will look to a specific work environment is the challenge that must be worked out amongst key players (employees, employer, manager, stakeholder, and so on). From the perspective of the employer, programs that align the goals of the organization with the health of their employees are the ideal and carry many benefits that far outweigh the perceived costs.

More information can be found at the following sources:

Workplace Health, Safety and Compensation Commission at http://www.whscc.nf.ca/publications.whscc

Canadian Human Rights Commission: A Place for All: A Guide to Creating an Inclusive Workplace at http://www.chrc-ccdp.ca/sites/default/files/aplaceforall_1.pdf

Quick, J.C. and Tetrick, L.E. (2003). Handbook of Occupational Health Psychology. Washington, DC: American Psychological Association.

http://www.gwlcentreformentalhealth.com/display.asp?l1=4&l2=43&d=43

References

Aldana, S.G. and Pronk, N.P. (2001). Health promotion programs, modifiable health risks, and employee absenteeism. *Journal of Occupational and Environmental Medicine*, 34(1), 36–46.

Arnold, K.A., Turner, N., Barling, J., Kelloway, K.E., and McKee, M.C. (2007). Transformational leadership and psychological well-being: the mediating role of meaningful work. *Journal of Occupational Health Psychology*, 12(3), 193–203. DOI: 10.1037/1076-8998.12.3.193.

Aust, B. and Ducki, A. (2004). Comprehensive health promotion interventions at the workplace: experiences with health circles in Germany. *Journal of Occupational Health Psychology*, 9(3), 258–70.

Baicker, K., Cutler, D., and Song, Z. (2013). Workplace wellness programs can generate savings. *Health Affairs*, 29(2), 304–11. DOI: 10.1377/hlthaff.2009.0626.

Berry, L.L. Mirabito, M. and Baun, W.B. (2010). What's the hard return on employee wellness programs? *Harvard Business Review*, December 2010, 1–9.

Blustein, D.L. (2008). The role of work in psychological health and well-being: a conceptual, historical, and public policy perspective. *American Psychologist*, 63(4), 228–40. DOI: 10.1037/0003-066X.63.4.228.

Boudrais, J.S., Desrumaux, P., Gaudreau, P., Nelson, K., Brunet, L., and Savoie, A. (2011). Modeling the experience of psychological health at work: the role of personal resources, social-organizational resources, and job demands. *International Journal of Stress Management*, 18(4), 372–95. DOI: 10.1037/a0025353.

Butler, A., Gasser, M., and Smart, L. (2004). A social-cognitive perspective on using family friendly benefits. *Journal of Vocational Behaviour*, 65, 57–70.

DeJoy, D.M. and Wilson, M.G. (2003). Organizational health promotion: broadening the horizon of workplace health promotion. *American Journal of Health Promotion*, 17, 337–41.

Galbreath, B. (2011). Educating managers to create healthy workplaces. *Journal of Management Education*, 36(2), 166–89. DOI: 10.1177/1052562911430206.

Goetzel, R.Z., Long, S.R., Ozminkowski, R.J., Hawkins, K., Wang, S., and Lynch, W. (2004). Health, absence, disability, and presenteeism cost estimates of certain physical and mental health conditions affecting US employers. *Journal of Occupational and Environmental Medicine*, 46(4), 398–412.

Grawitch, M.J., Gottschalk, M., and Munz, D.C. (2006). The path to a healthy workplace. A critical review linking healthy workplace practices, employee well-being, and organizational improvements. *Consulting Psychology Journal: Practice and Research*, 58(3), 129–47.

Guarding Minds at Work: http://www.guardingmindsatwork.ca/info/index.

Harrison, J. (2012). Occupational safety and health in The United Kingdom: securing future workplace health and wellbeing. *Industrial Health*, 50, 261–6.

Idris, M.A., Dollard, M.F., Coward, J., and Dormann, C. (2012). Psychosocial safety climate: conceptual distinctiveness and effect on job demands and worker psychological health. *Safety Science*, 50, 19–28.

Kelloway, E.K. and Day, A.L. (2005). Building healthy workplaces: what we know so far. *Canadian Journal of Behavioural Science*, 37(4), 223–35.

Lowe, G.S. (2004). Healthy Workplace Strategies: Creating Change and Achieving Results. Prepared for the Workplace Health Strategies Bureau, Health Canada. Available at: http://cprn.org/documents/26838_en.pdf.

Lysaght, R., Fabrigar, L., Larmour-Trode, S., Stewart, J., and Frisen, M. (2012). Measuring workplace social support for workers with disability. *Journal of Occupational Rehabilitation*, 22, 376–86. DOI: 10.1007/s10926-012-9357-1.

Michaels, C.N. and Greene, A.M. (2013). Worksite wellness: increasing adoption of workplace health promotion programs. *Health Promotion Practice*, 14, 473–9. DOI: 10.1177/1524839913480800.

Neilsen, K., Randall, R., Holten, A.L., Gonzalez, E.R.(2010). Conducting organizational-level occupational health interventions: What works? *Work & Stress: An International Journal of Work, Health & Organisations*, 24(3), 234–59. DOI: 10.1080/02678373.2010.515393.

Olafsdottir, L. (2004). Prevention, health and safety program in companies provide a more successful and healthier workplace. *Work*, 22, 27–30.

O'Neill, J.W., Harrison, M.M., Cleveland, J., Almeida, D., Stawski, R., and Crouter, A.C. (2009). Work-family climate, organizational commitment, and turnover: multilevel contagion effects of leaders. *Journal of Vocational Behaviour*, 74(1), 18–29.

Price, J.P. (1997). Handbook of organizational measurement. *International Journal of Manpower*, 18(4, 5, 6), pp. 305–558.

Schalk, R. (2010). The influence of organizational commitment and health on sickness absenteeism: a longitudinal study. *Journal of Nursing Management*, 19(5), 596–600. DOI: 10.1111/j.1365-2834.2010.01170.x.

Wilson, M.G., Goetzel, R.Z., Ozminkowski, R.J., DeJoy, D.M., Della, L., Roemer, E.C., Schneider, J., Tully, K.J., White, J.M., and Baase, C.M. (2012). Using formative research to develop environmental and ecological interventions to address overweight and obesity. *Obesity: A Research Journal*, 15(s1), pp. 37s-47s.

Wilkins, K. and Beaudet, M.P. (1998) *Work Stress and Health. Health Reports*. Publications.gc.ca

Chapter 12

Legislation and Accommodation for Mental Health in the Workplace

Obviously, because of my disability, I need assistance. But I have always tried to overcome the limitations of my condition and lead as full a life as possible. I have traveled the world, from the Antarctic to zero gravity.
Stephen Hawking

Introduction

The employment environment has changed significantly over the last few decades. In particular, the responsibilities of workplace stakeholders within the human rights domain have become increasingly more complex and requiring of additional responsibilities to be met by employers, unions and other involved workplace parties. Since the early 1990s, Canada's human rights climate has changed such that the responsibility for employers goes beyond that which previously used to be primarily directed by common law.

Common law provides employers with the ability to negotiate workplace contracts as they see fit, and does not force employers to enter into contracts of employment with any particular individual. The concept of common law provides flexibility in the employment relationship so that an employer cannot be forced to enter into an employment contract with someone for whom the trust relationship cannot be developed, and also provides some protection against contracts of slavery for employees. In the past, the employment relationship was primarily governed by common law and common law continues to hold an important place within the employment relationship. However, common law within the employment relationship is now overshadowed by the quasi-constitutional nature of Canadian human rights legislation. This means that although common law continues to dictate much of the employment relationship, in every case, human rights legislation will override the jurisdiction of common law as it applies to the employer-employee relationship.

Human Rights Legislation in Canada

Human rights legislation in Canada provides protection for all employees against harassment and discrimination that may occur due to membership in one of the protected groups. In general, human rights legislations of various jurisdictions have as their primary purpose to provide quasi-constitutional legislation that is remedial and not punitive in nature, can be broadly and purposefully applied, cannot be contracted out, and prohibits discrimination based on group membership related to race, national or ethnic origin, color, marital status, religion, age, family status, sex, sexual orientation, disability, or conviction for which a pardon has been granted (D'Andrea, Corry, and Forester, 2004; MacNeill, 2003). In Canada, human rights legislation is often adjudicated via human rights tribunals, but may also include any or all of human rights commission/tribunals/boards of inquiry, labor arbitrators, employment standards adjudicators, occupational health and safety adjudicators, Labor Relations boards, and police services boards. Depending on the nature of the employer, Canadian human rights legislation may be governed by federal, provincial, or territorial acts and the jurisdiction of the act will direct the appropriate adjudication of the matter. It is important to note that although jurisdictional jurisprudence is directed by the independent legislations, human rights decisions are dependent on all decisions made at all levels.

In cases of human rights complaints, the relevant resolution process includes: 1) a complaint of human rights violation made by a complainant, or complainant's representative; 2) investigation of the complaint; 3) mediation or settlement of the complaint and/or beginning of adjudication process; 4) if no resolution is reached, complaint moves to level of human rights tribunal or board of inquiry in the complainant's respective jurisdiction; and 5) appeal or judicial review of adjudicator's decision at higher levels of courts, including the Supreme Court of Canada.

Human rights legislation is of intense importance to workplace environments, as this legislation applies strictly in situations of employment, housing, and public services. Within the employment relationship, human rights legislation will provide direction to the employer-employee relationship, union activities, employer organizations, employment agencies, and other agencies or associations serving vocational and professional groups. The single exception for an employment situation in which human rights legislation has no jurisdiction is employment within a private residence. For example, in-home nannies or domestic help are independent of human rights legislation.

History of Human Rights in Canada

The mid-1980s provide three foundational cases for the development of human rights in Canada. Each of the described cases helps to define the development of human rights law in Canada with respect to an aspect of employment.

The first of these cases involved a gentleman named Michael Huck in the case Cineplex Odeon Theaters Limited versus Huck (Canadian Human Rights Reporter, 1985). This case helped direct human rights with respect to the principle of "equality of outcome". In the case of Mr Huck, he was reliant on a motorized wheelchair for transportation mobility. On an occasion when Mr Huck entered a Cineplex theater he was advised that he would be required to transfer to a chair or sit in the very front area of the movie theater in order to watch the show. Mr Huck grieved this treatment and contested it on the principle that he had not received "equality of outcome" because of his disability. Mr Huck contended that although the theater had been willing to provide him with the seat, a seat in the very front of the movie theater made it difficult for him to enjoy the movie due to the closeness to the large screen. The case was taken to the Court of Appeals and there it was decided that equality of outcome required Mr Huck having the opportunity to view the movie from a more appropriate location. This case was considered fundamental to human rights law in Canada because Mr Huck's case demonstrated that identical treatment for everyone did not necessarily constitute equality of outcome.

A second important case in our nation's human rights history is found in the case Ontario Human Rights Commission versus Simpson Sears (Supreme Court of Canada, 1985). In this case Ms O'Malley was a member of the Seventh-Day Adventist church and was required to observe Sabbath from sundown Friday to sundown Saturday. Ms O'Malley's employment at Simpson Sears required that she be able to work Friday evenings and two out of every three Saturdays. Given her religious affiliation, the complainant was unable to work her turn in the rotation and was disciplined as a result. Ms O'Malley contended that she was being unfairly discriminated against due to her religious beliefs and the Supreme Court of Canada recognized and upheld her complaint. The

O'Malley case is considered foundational for human rights development in Canada because the Supreme Court's ruling demonstrated that a violation of human rights did not require intentional or malicious intent in order to be considered discriminatory.

A third important case from the perspective of the workplace in Canada is found in Robichaud versus Canada (Treasury Board) (Supreme Court of Canada, 1987). The Robichaud case is considered particularly important to employers given that this case demonstrated that employers are to be considered responsible for the discriminatory acts of their employees. In the case of Ms Robichaud, her complaint concluded that she was sexually harassed and discriminated against by individuals in her workplace. Apparently the alleged harassment was known in the workplace and, as a result, the Supreme Court of Canada stated that "the discriminatory act practiced by the employee is to be considered discriminatory practice by the employer as well, whether or not authorized or intended by the latter" (Supreme Court of Canada, 1987).

Duty to Accommodate

The duty to accommodate in employment is primarily directed by the Canadian Charter of Rights and Freedoms, provincial and federal human rights legislation, the employment equity act, and applicable case law. Essentially, the duty to accommodate requires that employers provide accommodated workplace situations in order to provide inclusive opportunities for individuals who are members of protected groups. The responsibility for duty to accommodate lies heavily on employers and requires that, similar to the application of human rights, its application is both broad and purposeful.

Although Acts specifically speaking to the duty to accommodate in cases of disability are currently available in the United States, UK, Australia, and Israel, specific legislative Acts to protect persons with disabilities do not currently exist in Canada. The single exception is the accessibility for Ontarians with Disabilities Act of 2005 (Ministry of Community and Social Services, 2005) which replaced the Ontarians with Disabilities Act of 2001. Despite the lack of clear legislation at the federal and most provincial levels in Canada, the responsibility for employers to uphold the duty to accommodate is clear.

Three fundamental cases in Canadian case law have helped provide guidance regarding the application of the duty to accommodate in the Canadian workplace. The first of these included Central Alberta Diary Poole versus

Alberta (Human Rights Commission) (Supreme Court of Canada, 1990). This case helped to define the meaning of undue hardship with respect to safety, financial costs, effect on collective agreements, employee morale, changes in workforce facilities and compensation, and size of employer. In this case, Mr Christie was a member of the Worldwide Church of God which required that he observed his faith and not work on particular days. As a result of his need for a particular day off, Mr Christie was terminated and, subsequently, filed a complaint that he had been discriminated against based on his religious beliefs. Although the employer argued that Monday was an extremely busy day for the business and that all employees were needed for work on that day, the Supreme Court of Canada held that giving Mr Christie the Monday in question as a day off did not create undue hardship for the employer. The decision in this case went beyond that of Mr Christie's particular circumstances and further described the requirement of undue hardship as applied to several aspects of employer operations.

In 1992, the courts went further in describing the breadth of responsibility with respect to the duty to accommodate. In Central Okanagan School District Number 23 versus Renaud (Supreme Court of Canada, 1992), the Supreme Court of Canada ruled that employers have a responsibility for the duty to accommodate even if it violates current contractual obligations as set out in a collective agreement. Mr Renaud worked for the Central Okanagan School District Number 23 as unionized custodial staff. His participation in the Seventh-Day Adventist religion required observance of Sabbath from sundown Friday until sundown Saturday. The terms of the collective agreement included Friday evening shifts and so, on several occasions, Mr Renaud and the school board worked together to have his employment arrangement altered accordingly. Unfortunately, Mr Renaud's union saw this altered shift as a breach in the collective agreement and eventually he was dismissed for failure to attend his Friday evening shifts. Mr Renaud filed a complaint, contending that he had been unfairly discriminated against because of his religious beliefs. The Supreme Court of Canada agreed with Mr Renaud and stated that both the employer and the union share a responsibility to provide accommodations according to Mr Renaud's religious beliefs and that the union's contractual articles could not be sufficiently applied to overrule the requirements of human rights legislation.

A third important case with respect to duty to accommodate includes British Columbia (Superintendent of Motor Vehicles) versus British Columbia (Councils of Human Rights) (Supreme Court of Canada, 1999). This case involved an individual named Terry Grismer who had an eye condition that impacted his peripheral vision on both sides. As a result of his eye condition, Mr Grismer's driver's license had been revoked by the British Columbia Superintendent of Motor Vehicles. The Superintendent of Motor Vehicles contended that Mr Grismer's vision did not meet the minimum field of vision for peripheral vision and although Mr Grismer had passed all aspects of his driver's license excepting the field of vision test, his driver's license was suspended. Mr Grismer's complaint was upheld by the Supreme Court of Canada on the grounds that the motor vehicle branch had failed to provide evidence that the undue hardship approach had been met and that the requirement for 120° peripheral vision was reasonably necessary to carry out the duties of the task. This case was particularly important with respect to the application of the duty to accommodate because it helped to define undue hardship; in particular, that employers would be required to do individual testing in order to meet their duty to accommodate. In addition, this case helped to reveal the responsibility for society to be able to be willing to take on some level of risk in order to provide equality of outcome for individuals with disabilities.

Finally, arguably one of the most important cases with respect to the application of duty to accommodate in Canada includes British Columbia (Public Service Employee Relations Commission) versus BCGSEU (Supreme Court of Canada, 1999). This case, known as the Meiorin case, involved Tawney Meiorin, a female forest firefighter who had been working for the government of British Columbia for approximately three years when she was terminated for failing a single aspect of the minimum firefighter fitness requirement. Ms Meiorin contended that she had successfully acted as a forest firefighter for many years and had demonstrated first hand her ability to do the job. Additionally, she asserted that the requirement for her to complete the minimum fitness requirement was discriminatory against her because women generally have lower aerobic capacity than men. The Supreme Court of Canada ruled that although the intent of the minimum fitness requirement was not to be directly discriminatory, the distinction between direct and adverse discrimination was artificial; consequently, in this decision, the Supreme Court of Canada rejected the previously applied two-pronged approach to discrimination and established what is now known as the unified test, a test that does not differentiate between direct and adverse forms of discrimination. This case also clearly described the requirement that a bona fide occupational requirement cannot be demonstrated lightly, and that individual testing and accommodation will be required prior to the application of a bona fide occupational defense.

The four cases described outline both the breadth and the depth for application of the duty to accommodate. Specifically, these example cases speak to the requirement for individual testing, difficulty in the application of the bona fide occupational requirement defense, requirement for society to accept some responsibility in order to provide equality for individuals in protected groups, responsibility of the employer for all activities occurring in the worksite, and the shared responsibility for the duty to accommodate for all directors of the worksite including employers and unions. From the perspective of applicability to the worksite, D'Andrea et al. (2004) suggest that the scope of the duty to accommodate may include accepting lengthy medical absences without penalty in terms of seniority or job status; obtaining medical evidence regarding the complainant's abilities and modifying his/her duties based on this information; discussing options with the complainant and the union; allowing shorter shifts with lighter duties; hiring extra employees to perform the duties the employee was unable to perform; and/or restructuring of duties and posting the employee to other positions.

From Meiroin, the Supreme Court of Canada (1999) suggested several guidelines with respect to ensuring that duty to accommodate has been considered appropriately. These guidelines include questions such as:

1. Has the employer investigated alternative approaches that do not have a discriminatory effect, such as individual testing against a more individual instance of the standard?

2. If alternative standards were investigated and found to be capable of fulfilling the employer's purpose, why were they not implemented?

3. Is it necessary to have all employees meet a single standard for the employer to accomplish its legitimate purpose or can standards reflective of group or individual differences in capabilities be established?

4. Is there a way to get a job that is less discriminatory while still accomplishing the employer's legitimate purpose?

5. Is the standard properly designed to ensure that the desired qualification is not without placing an undue burden on those to whom the standard applies?

6. The other parties were obliged to assist in the search for possible accommodations to fill their roles?

In addition to the responsibilities described above, additional responsibilities may be added as case law grows and changes with time. What is clear, is that once the employee has provided the information and participated actively in the accommodation process, the onus of providing an accommodating workplace falls in the hands of the employer. In addition, case law has clearly demonstrated that "assumptions, impressionistic evidence, and out of date medical reports are not sufficient evidence of anything" (D'Andrea, Corry, and Forester, 2004). That is, employers will have difficulty demonstrating active participation in duty to accommodate if attempts to sidestep the process are undertaken.

It is strongly recommended that employers actively engage in a responsibility to both human rights and the duty to accommodate. The single best protection for an employer is to embrace their responsibility to provide an accessible and inclusive worksite that provides equal opportunity for individuals with membership in one of the protected groups. Employers are encouraged to actively engage in the process of duty to accommodate, and to document fully their attempts at accommodation in order to provide protection in case of complaint.

However, despite the best efforts of employers, the potential for complaint continues to exist. Questions arising from employers when even best efforts do not prevent a complaint may include:

1.   Who has legislative jurisdiction over human rights disputes?

2.   How does a human rights complaint progress?

3.   What kinds of penalties may exist in cases where a human rights complaint goes forward?

WHO HAS LEGISLATIVE JURISDICTION?

In case of federal government employees, human rights are governed by the Canadian Human Rights Act as well as the Canadian Charter of Rights and Freedoms. Employees falling into this category and covered by these pieces of legislation would include federally regulated employment sites such as airlines, railways, federal government offices, and so on. At the provincial or territorial level, government employees are subject to provincial or territorial human rights acts as well as the Canadian Charter of Rights and Freedoms. Employees in this category would include those working for the provincial government in the criminal system, education, and so on. Private businesses, on the other hand, are subject only to the provincial or territorial legislation that applies within the respective province(s) of business. For example, local pulp mills and other privately owned employers are subject only to the provincial jurisdiction.

WHAT HAPPENS IN THE CASE OF A HUMAN RIGHTS COMPLAINT?

In order for a human rights complaint to be accepted by the applicable administering body, the employee must demonstrate a prima facie case of discrimination. A prima facie case of discrimination requires that the individual demonstrate existence of membership in a particular group, the conduct under complaint is prohibited by the appropriate legislation, the employer's conduct was influenced by the disability, the employer's behavior or policies resulted in a negative impact for the employee, and the employee suffered harm as a result of the action by the employer. It is important to note that, within the employment arena, the meaning of membership also includes perception of membership. That is, if an employee is perceived to be included in membership for a protected group, but does not in fact belong to that group, any discrimination that occurs as a result of the misinformed perception will also be protected under human rights legislation. Also speaking to its breath, the legislation provides protection for perspective as well as present employees (including all pre-employment inquiries), continuance of employment, seniority and promotion, as well as protection against differential wage streams, lower job classifications, and/or impacted terms of employment.

In general, the demonstration of these standards tends to be liberal and once this liberal standard has been met, the onus of defense rests with the employer. In the case of an accepted complaint, the employer will be required to defend their attempts to provide fair treatment to the disadvantaged employee. The process of defense may occur through one of several avenues depending on the nature and environment of the complaint; specifically, human rights complaints may be ameliorated via mediation, arbitration, tribunal, and, ultimately, higher courts.

WHAT ARE THE REMEDIES AVAILABLE UNDER HUMAN RIGHTS LEGISLATION?

The foundational intent of human rights legislation in Canada is to provide a remedial rather than a punitive system. As a result, the requirement for demonstrating a human rights infraction requires the lesser standard based on a balance of probabilities. Similarly, remedies under this legislation are intended to return the individual to the place that they would have been had the human rights contravention not occurred. As a result of this foundational principle of remediation, remedies under human rights legislation include: the employer being required to cease the contravention against human rights, the employer refraining from committing similar types of contraventions in the future, reinstatement of the employee, opportunities returned that were denied as a result of discrimination, compensation for losses incurred as a result of the discrimination, and possible payment for emotional suffering as a result of the discrimination. In cases where the discrimination is seen to be willfully or recklessly in contravention of the intensive human rights legislation, exemplary payments can be required in the form of damages by the guilty party.

Accommodation in the Workplace

In the experience of the authors, employers have become increasingly proficient regarding accommodation for physical illness and injury. Universal design and universal accommodations are commonly seen in both new developments as well as retrofits to previously existing buildings. Where it seems employers are having much more difficulty in terms of knowledge regarding appropriate accommodation is within the domain of mental health. Consequently, the remainder of this chapter will be dedicated to providing some guidance regarding types of accommodation that may be appropriate in particular situations of cognitive or mental health disabilities.

WHAT DO EMPLOYERS CURRENTLY KNOW ABOUT HUMAN RIGHTS AND THE DUTY TO ACCOMMODATE?

Huang, Wagner, and Harder (2011) were interested in the amount of knowledge that Canadian employees and other workplace stakeholders have with respect to knowledge of human rights and duty to accommodate in Canada. To our understanding, these authors provide the only Canadian research available regarding knowledge of these issues in the Canadian context. In general, the work of these authors suggests that knowledge of human rights and the duty to accommodate by Canadian workplace stakeholders is very low. However, these authors also demonstrate that human resource professionals, those who work with this information on a regular basis, had slightly higher knowledge in this area than other workplace stakeholders. This outcome suggests that increased knowledge for the application of these requirements within the workplace may be a useful method of increasing compliance with relevant legislation.

GENERAL RECOMMENDATIONS FOR MENTAL HEALTH IN THE WORKPLACE

Accommodation for mental health within the workplace is often described by employers as one of the most difficult and complex types of accommodation to provide. Mental health is a very broad description for a wide range of conditions as described in the most current form of the Diagnostic and Statistical Manual. In the workplace context, mental health is often used to refer primarily to issues of depression and anxiety; however, this broad description could also be used to describe psychotic disorders, substance use disorders, personality disorders, factitious disorders, dissociative disorders, eating disorders, and so on. Consequently, due to the wide variety of potential types of disabilities that may be required to be accommodated within this context, as well as a limited amount of research regarding the effectiveness of specific types of accommodation within the workplace with respect to mental illness, the complexity and confusion regarding accommodation of mental illness in the workplace is well-founded.

MENTAL HEALTH

Despite the obvious difficulties in providing recommendations regarding effective accommodations for individuals with mental illness issues, some very basic and broadly applicable accommodations can be suggested. For example, individuals with mental illness issues often require ongoing, regular access to appointments related to personal and medication therapy. Consequently, flexible scheduling that allows for attendance at these appointments can often provide a first-line approach to accommodation for mental illness issues. In addition to flexible scheduling-related therapy appointments, flexible scheduling that recognizes some of the inherent difficulties related to mental illness issues may also be an appropriate accommodation. For example, for a worker with major depression, sleep and lethargy may be inherent aspects of the disability. As a result, scheduling that provides for a flexible start time would allow for accommodation regarding sleep difficulties.

Other examples of workplace accommodation might include the availability of tele-work or working from alternate locations. This type of arrangement could be considered very useful for individuals who have anxiety-related disorders. Working from home or alternate sites may provide an individual with severe anxiety an option to continue to work, even in situations where anxiety prevents them from interacting with others and attending the physical workplace. This type of arrangement may also be very useful for individuals who have behaviorally obvious mental illnesses (for example, Tourette's disorder) in cases where the behavioral manifestations of their disability are more severe, making the individual uncomfortable with attending the on-site work environment.

An additional generalized recommendation for workers who are experiencing issues related to mental illness is to negotiate preplanned contingency plans for situations where the disability requires specific needs on the part of the individual. For example, individuals with anxiety disorders may have situations during which the anxiety prevents them from completing required job tasks (for example panic disorder). In situations such as this, the employer and the employee should have a preplanned and pre-negotiated anxiety management plan, such that the individual can remove themselves from the workplace or engage in other types of activities that are suitable to the employer's worksite while at the same time helping the individual manage their anxiety.

Finally, with respect to mental illness accommodation and worksite, a primary avenue of accommodation can be found in ongoing workplace education and training regarding working with individuals with mental illness. It should not be considered necessary to provide any information that could be considered confidential, but rather to provide this training as a standard aspect of the employment environment. By providing training to workplace participants, regarding both mental health and accommodation issues, it is hoped that co-workers will have increased knowledge, and, consequently, will be less prejudiced towards individuals with mental illness issues. As well, an understanding of the employer's duty to accommodate and the rights of employees to engage in a fair and equitable workplace may ease the understanding of co-workers if someone within their workplace has an alternate working arrangement. Ideally, this process of education, accommodation, and intervention can be directed by someone knowledgeable and proficient regarding the application of the respective legislative requirements.

LEARNING DISABILITIES

A learning disability is a specific disability related to reading, writing, and/or mathematics, relative to respective cognitive capacity. For individuals with learning disabilities, employer accommodations are often relatively easy to implement and these easy accommodations will generally provide successful remediation regarding interference with participation in the workplace. Specific accommodations for individuals with learning disabilities include general support for tasks related to the area of disability. For example, in the case of an individual who has mathematics disorder and works as a server in a restaurant, working with the financial side may be an area of substantial struggle. Consequently, the task of taking and making change could possibly be taken over by another individual or could be accommodated through use of technology. For individuals with a reading or writing disorder, similar types of accommodations could be implemented, with the general goal of reducing responsibility for tasks related specifically to their area of disability.

In addition to extra support in areas related to the specific disability, individuals with learning disabilities will often require additional time for any tasks that continue to be required within the domain of their disability. For example, an individual in a clerical job who has been accommodated for a written output disorder may still be required to write the occasional memo or other type of letter. In situations where this requirement continues to exist, the individual should be provided with additional time to complete the task, as well as additional support in determining whether or not the task is been completed adequately (for example, proofreading by a co-worker, and so on).

In the area of specific learning disabilities, technology has significantly improved the ability to provide accommodation. Currently, employers can provide accommodation for individuals with a learning disability through the use of technologies like grammar and spellcheck systems, software intended to assist in numeracy tasks, and talk-to-text software. Similarly, for individuals with a reading disorder, text-to-speech software can be used to provide originally written text in an auditory medium. Technological accommodations for learning disabilities are expanding at an explosive rate and individuals responsible for workplace disability management are encouraged to continue to update their knowledge in this area such that technological accommodations can be used to their full capacity.

Finally, it is often the case that workplace-based evaluations use written exams as a primary method of evaluating competency. For individuals with specific learning disabilities, demonstration of their abilities through mentoring and application is recommended in place of traditional academic-type knowledge exams.

ATTENTION DEFICIT HYPERACTIVITY DISORDER (ADHD)

Attention deficit hyperactivity disorder is typically seen as a childhood disorder. However, it is clear that children with ADHD will become adults with ADHD, and consequently, ADHD should not be overlooked as a possible expanding disorder within the adult population. For individuals with ADHD, hyperactivity is less common with increasing age; consequently, attention deficit may be the primary issue within the workplace environment. For individuals with attention-related disabilities, work environments with as few distractions as possible should be considered an appropriate accommodation. Limited distraction in terms of other co-workers, noise, and patron activity will likely assist the individual in maintaining attention on the task at hand. For individuals with ADHD, workplace co-workers and supervisors should attempt to ensure they have the individual's attention prior to providing instructions about the workplace task. That is, looking directly at the individual, ensuring the individual is both providing and maintaining attention, and, if appropriate, asking the individual to repeat instructions back to ensure they have attended to task are recommended accommodations. Further, it is recommended that for employees with attention difficulties, only one person speak to the individual at one time. If more than one person is speaking to the individual simultaneously, the individual with attention deficit is unlikely to attend to either person providing instructions.

In addition to clearly and simply providing instructions to an individual with ADHD, it is recommended that accommodation include allowance for recording and/or note-taking of instructions; if note-taking is the chosen option, there should be some provision to ensure the information was recorded correctly (for example, having the message sender double-check the notes). Providing a secondary avenue for review of instruction will allow for the individual with ADHD to ensure that the information is available for reference at a later time, even if they were unable to attend to the full set of instructions at the time that they were given.

NEURODEVELOPMENTAL DISORDERS

The category of neurodevelopmental disorders is a broad category that encapsulates a variety of different types of disabilities that involve neuropsychological or developmental difficulties. Examples of types of disabilities that are often included in this category are difficulties with memory and executive functioning, autism spectrum disorder (ASD), traumatic brain injury (TBI), fetal alcohol spectrum disorder (FASD), and developmental delay. Individuals with neurodevelopmental disorders have an extremely wide variety of different needs, often making accommodation within this area intimidating for employers. However, when taken on an individual level, accommodations for neurodevelopmental disorders can be relatively easily instituted. It is

important to note however, that for the potential accommodations listed below, any one individual may require all or none of these types of accommodations. The needs of the individual must be accommodated on an individual basis, according to negotiations between the employer, employee, and other related workplace stakeholders.

Neuropsychological Difficulties

With respect to general neuropsychological difficulties, this category would often include a description of cognitive difficulties within a particular domain that do not necessarily receive a diagnosis as per the DSM-V. That is, individuals who have a particular difficulty with memory and/or executive functioning may have this described through a comprehensive psychological assessment; however, no particular diagnostic category within the DSM-V is available in order to provide a categorical diagnosis for these difficulties. Consequently, for individuals with described difficulties within particular neuropsychological domains, workplace accommodations should be focused directly on attempting to ameliorate difficulties related to that particular skill.

Neuropsychological domains generally include spatial skills, language-related tasks, memory, attention, and executive functioning. In the experience of the authors, the two most likely areas for requested accommodation in the workplace would include memory-related issues and difficulties in the domain of executive functioning. For both memory and executive function, workplace accommodations should be considered relatively easy for a workplace to implement, often inexpensive in nature, and regularly very helpful in reducing barriers for the employee. An example of workplace accommodations that may be useful for individuals with difficulties of memory and/or executive function includes availability of additional reminders for important meetings and or workplace instructions. These additional reminders can take several forms, according to the desires of the workplace and employee. Specifically, recording important conversations and instructions, or, alternately, taking notes about what has been said in the meeting and asking for those notes to be verified may be a useful method of improving employee memory within the workplace. In addition, the use of visual cues, lists and/or other memory reminders in several locations throughout the worksite will likely be helpful to assist an employee in remembering what tasks are to be accomplished and how to go about those tasks. Routine and repetition in the workplace can also be very helpful in terms of accommodating an individual with issues in memory and/or executive functioning. Learning a particular routine and having the opportunity to complete that routine with few changes will likely benefit the employee in terms of success within the workplace.

Individuals with these difficulties often will also benefit from the use of daily planners, scheduling software and other forms of external memory, planning, and scheduling assistance. Essentially, accommodations for these difficulties are intended to reduce the burden of memory, scheduling, and planning for the respective individual. Similar to learning disabilities, technological advances have significantly reduced the potential impact of neuropsychological difficulties on affected individuals. For example, the use of smart phones and other types of recent technology can provide reminders, note-taking functions, voice recorders, and so on, within easy access for the employee.

In addition to basic types of accommodations that can assist an employee in accommodating for issues of memory and attention, the use of additional checks and balances for the individual as well as the mentorship model are recommended as appropriate. That is, for individuals with executive function issues, having a trusted individual to guide them in thinking through problems, understanding consequences and/or seeing the consequences of their action can be very helpful. Also, if appropriate, it may be helpful to have this trusted individual complete routine checks on the accommodated employee's work to ensure that areas of difficulty can be remedied prior to mistakes being made.

ASD/TBI/FASD

Individuals with autism spectrum disorder, traumatic brain injury, and fetal alcohol spectrum disorder suffer from very different types of disorders, with additional wide variation evident within each disorder. However, despite the variation in the disorders, accommodations for each of these disorders take very similar forms. When working with an individual who has a disability in one of these areas, several important job accommodations can significantly reduce the impact of the individual's disability on their ability to actively participate in the workplace. Accommodations in this category can be seen as simple but useful; however, often employers are unsure how to provide a supportive work environment.

Individuals with one of these disorders may or may not be impacted by intellectual deficits; therefore, it is important to distinguish on an individual level what types of accommodations are appropriate to the individual in each independent situation. General recommendations that can be altered as per individual needs include ensuring that job tasks are clearly outlined and that the expectations of the individual are both blatantly described and communicated to the accommodated worker. Disabilities in these areas can lead to communication issues which can impact the individual's ability to understand what is expected of him or her. Consequently, it should be considered very important that communication in a clearly outlined and understandable way is completed with the employee prior to expectations being placed upon that individual. Also with respect to communication, direct, non-subtle expressions of expectations will be very helpful. That is, implications should be avoided, and direct and explicit statements should be used. For example, stating to the employee that "work starts at nine" is much less useful than stating "you should be here at nine o'clock tomorrow morning". Providing detail and leaving nothing open to interpretation should be considered a priority when communicating with individuals who suffer from neurodevelopmental disorders.

Similar to those with memory and executive functioning issues, individuals with other neurological disorders are often impacted by neuropsychological difficulties within particular neuropsychological domains. Consequently, the accommodations discussed in the previous section are also applicable as potentially helpful here. That is, the use of recorders, note-taking, structured schedules, and routine and repetitive tasks may be very helpful for accommodating individuals with ASD, TBI, and/or FASD.

Avoidance of multitask assignments may also be helpful for individuals with these types of difficulties. Allowing the individual to work on a single task until it is completed may help avoid a feeling of becoming overwhelmed by the requirement to multitask or provide attention to a variety of different activities at one time. If you wish, a mentor within the workplace who is understanding of the individual's difficulties and appreciative of their capabilities can also be very helpful in terms of assisting the individual to succeed in the workplace. This mentor can help an individual with these types of disabilities create tools to assist them to function within the workplace. This mentor can also provide advice with respect to appropriate behavior, understanding of more complex social cues, understanding of consequences, and so on.

It is sometimes the case that individuals with these types of disabilities experience highly sensitive reactions to sensory stimuli. Consequently, reduction of distractions and sensory stimuli within the workplace will likely assist the individual to reduce anxiety and maintain workplace-appropriate behavior. It is also sometimes the case that individuals with disabilities in these areas seem younger than their chronological age, and, as a result, individuals with ASD, TBI, or FASD are sometimes at risk of being taken advantage of by others. Consequently, the mentorship position for an individual within the workplace can also provide guidance for these potentially vulnerable workers such that they are supported in negotiating the complex social world of the workplace.

DEVELOPMENTAL DELAY

Accommodation for individuals with developmental delay often looks quite similar to that provided for those with other types of neurodevelopmental disorders. However, in the case of an individual with developmental delay, accommodations are typically a mixture of accommodations as described for all of the previously described areas of disability. That is, individuals with developmental delay will often require flexible scheduling for personal and medication appointments, especially if they are dually diagnosed such that mental health is an additional aspect of their disability. These individuals will likely require additional time on tasks, technological assistance, and demonstration of their abilities in place of traditional academic tasks. For individuals with developmental delay, visual schedules and lists may be very helpful for the individual to maintain attention and to remember tasks and instructions. Use of schedules, routine and repetitive environment, and the mentorship model should also be considered potential areas of accommodation for individuals with developmental delay.

Concluding Remarks

Accommodations for mental health and cognitive disabilities can be both complex and intimidating for employers attempting to adequately meet the needs of their employees. However, as demonstrated in this chapter, compliance with human rights legislation and the duty to accommodate can be readily accomplished through simple, inexpensive, and adaptable accommodations. The bulk of accommodations as described here will mitigate many of the barriers evident for individuals with mental health and cognitive disorders, while at the same time providing simple and easily implemented methods of providing a fair and equitable workplace and meeting duty to accommodate needs of employers.

Additional information can be found at the following sources:

http://askjan.org/

http://www.workink.com/provincial.php?prID=11261&pgID=11263

http://www.mentalhealthworks.ca/employers/faqs/rights-and-responsibilities
    /reasonable-accommodation

References

Canadian Human Rights Reporter (1985). Michael Huck Case. Retrieved on: January 27, 2008, from http://www.cdn-hr-reporter.ca/index.cfm?fuseaction=hrp.disabilityRights.

D'Andrea, J.A., Corry, D.J., and Forester, H.I. (2004). *Illness and Disability in the Workplace: How to Navigate through the Legal Minefield*. Aurora, Ontario: Canada Law Book Inc.

Huang, D., Wagner, S., and Harder, H.G. (2011). Human Rights and Duty to Accommodate in Employment: Perspectives from Canada. In Geisen, T & Harder, H.G. (eds), *Disability Management and Workplace Integration: International Research Findings*, (pp. 71–84). Farnham, UK: Gower Publishing Limited

MacNeill, K.D. (2003). *The Duty to Accommodate in Employment*. Aurora, Ontario: Canada Law Book Inc.

Ministry of Community and Social Services (2005). *Accessibility for Ontarians with Disabilities Act*. Retrieved on: February 11, 2008, from http://www.e-laws.gov.on.ca/html/statutes/english/elaws_statutes_05a11_e.htm.

Supreme Court of Canada (1985). O'Malley Case. Retrieved on: January 27, 2008, from http://scc.lexum.umontreal.ca/en/1985/1985rcs2-536/1985rcs2-536.html.

Supreme Court of Canada (1987). Robichaud Case. Retrieved on: January 27, 2008, from http://scc.lexum.umontreal.ca/en/1987/1987scr2-84/1987scr2-84.html.

Supreme Court of Canada (1990). Christie Case. Retrieved on: January 27, 2008, from http://scc.lexum.umontreal.ca/en/1990/1990rcs2-489/1990rcs2-489.html.

Supreme Court of Canada (1992). Renaud Case. Retrieved on: January 27, 2008, from http://scc.lexum.umontreal.ca/en/1992/1992rcs2-970/1992rcs2-970.html.

Supreme Court of Canada (1999). Meiorin Case. Retrieved on: January 27, 2008, from http://scc.lexum.umontreal.ca/en/1999/1999rcs3-3/1999rcs3-3.html.

Supreme Court of Canada (1999). Grismer Case. Retrieved on: January 27, 2008, from http://scc.lexum.umontreal.ca/en/1999/1999rcs3-868/1999rcs3-868.html.

Chapter 13
Why Positivity Matters

A pessimist sees the difficulty in every opportunity; an optimist sees the opportunity in every difficulty.

Winston Churchill

Introduction

The following chapter will address positivity: how it occurs, its relationship to success in life, and why it should concern researchers, organizations, and society. Positivity, also termed positive affect, exists as a state level mood as well as an enduring personality trait. Individuals with positive personality traits have a propensity to experience positive emotions more frequently, and across a wider range of situations. Many terms have been used to describe positive states and traits, including happiness, positive affect, hopefulness, optimism, cheerfulness, life satisfaction, and emotional vitality (Lyubomirsky, King, and Diener, 2005). In practice, there is considerable overlap between these constructs (Kashdan, Biswas-Diener, and King, 2008). This chapter addresses a broad range of positive affective states and dispositions.

Why Focus on Positivity?

The focus on positivity has grown from the positive psychology movement that occurred in the late 1990s and early 2000s. Martin Seligman began the positive psychology movement with his presidential address to the American Psychological Association (Seligman, 1999). In this address, Seligman argued that the field of Psychology had focused almost exclusively on the negative aspects of human suffering and what is wrong with people (that is, curing mental illness). This focus on mental illness was successful, as at least 14 disorders can be effectively treated (Seligman and Csikszentmihalyi, 2000), however, it completely ignored the pursuit of psychological health (that is, helping people lead more productive, fulfilling lives, and identifying and nurturing high talent). The purpose of the positive psychology movement was to supplement the literature on mental illness and, in so doing, to provide a complete and balanced scientific understanding of the human experience (Seligman, Steen, Park, et al., 2005).

In a mere five years following Seligman's presidential address the field of positive psychology had seen an explosion of interest and scientific literature, including the publication of a journal dedicated to the study of positive psychology, the publication of many books, and the creation of 29 research pods assessing diverse constructs from character traits to positive psychotherapy. This work has subsequently been extended into epidemiology, healthcare, and the workplace where it is becoming clear that positivity is of benefit. The positive psychology movement has led to an exploration of positive organization behavior—a positive approach to developing and managing human resource strengths and psychological capacities for performance improvement in the workplace (Luthans, 2002; Nelson and Cooper, 2007; Wright, 2003). Positive organization behavior attempts to restore balance to the occupational health literature by subverting attention from the dominant negative perspective regarding occupation stress. A survey of the occupational health literature reported a 15:1 negative to positive ratio of studies, respectively (Schaufeli and Salanova, 2007). This chapter will outline the work that has been performed on positivity in hopes of presenting a balanced scientific understanding of mental health in the workplace.

What are Emotions?

In order to understand positivity we must first understand emotions and how they contribute to emotional tone. Emotions are important motivators of human behavior that percolate every situation. No one characteristic can be used to define an emotion. Instead emotions are best conceptualized as multi-component response tendencies that unfold over relatively short periods of time (Fredrickson, 2004). This means that the experience of emotion coordinates the action of multiple systems (for example, cognition, hormone, endocrine, digestion, and so on) in a short period, usually in one quarter of a second. It is believed that the different components of specific emotions (for example, fear, anger, happiness) co-occur, and that each emotion has a distinct set of motivational, behavioral (for example, motor patterns), expression (for example, facial and vocal signs), and physiological (for example, autonomic nervous system) qualities that distinguish it from other emotions (Levenson, 2011).

The emotion process begins when an individual consciously or subconsciously assesses an antecedent event as personally meaningful. The appraisal of the event triggers a cascade of cognitive, physiological, and subjective experiences that ultimately leads to an emotional experience (Fredrickson, 2004). Each emotion leads to the display of unique facial expressions and action tendencies that characterize the emotion. For example, an individual who experiences feelings of fear would display a tendency to flee or remove themselves from the situation (Plutchik, 2001) whereas an individual experiencing gratitude is prompted to perform prosocial actions in the benefit of others (McCullough, Emmons, and Tsang, 2002).

Thus far we have described states of emotional experience as they occur in a discrete period of time. However, people may also exhibit predispositions to experience certain emotions across a wide variety of situations. Individuals with a predisposition towards a particular emotion will have a tendency to display that emotion across a wider range of situations than someone who does not exhibit such a tendency. These predispositions towards the experience of emotion are termed traits. Traits can be used to reliably classify individuals as high or low in such dimensions as positive and negative affect, and allow for the prediction of future behaviors (Watson, Clark, and Tellegen, 1988).

Emotional traits may arise due to a combination of genetic influences and chronic state experiences. Research suggests that continuing styles of emotional expression lead to the development of personality traits (Izard, Libero, Putnam, et al., 1993; Malatesta and Wilson, 1988), indicating that the chronic experience of particular emotions allows for such emotions to become embedded into an individual's neurobiology in the form of a predisposition.

Differentiating Positive and Negative Emotions

Several models exist to define emotions. One model places emotions such as happiness, anger, sadness, and fear as basic, categorically distinct units (Ekman, 1992). The majority of models are dimensional models that involve a series of dimensions such as valence (Watson and Tellegen, 1985), or arousal (Russell, 1980). Another model places emotions on a concentric circle representation akin to a color wheel allowing for blending between emotions (Plutchik, 2001). One of the more useful distinctions of emotions is that of valence. Emotions which are negative in valence are referred to as negative emotions and those which are positive in valence are referred to as positive emotions. Negative and positive emotions have crucial differences that make each advantageous during very different circumstances. Negative emotions act to narrow a person's thought-action repertoire leading to discrete actions (Fredrickson, 1998). For example, fear is believed to narrow an individual's thought-action repertoire to the idea of removing oneself from a situation perceived as dangerous. This reduced thought-action repertoire may well explain why some individuals freeze and cannot move during fearful events. It can be argued that negative emotions aid in the immediate survival of an organism during dangerous high stress, fight or flight situations.

Whereas negative emotions typically arise during threatening situations, positive emotions occur when people are safe and satiated, affording long-term adaptive benefits rather than short-term action preparedness. Recent conceptualizations suggest that positive emotions act to expand one's thought-action repertoire rather than restrict it (Fredrickson, 1998). In fact, empirical evidence suggests that positive emotions act to rid individuals of the psychological and physiological sequelae of action readiness brought on by negative affect (Fredrickson and Levenson, 1998). Fredrickson and Levenson (1998) subjected participants to a fear-eliciting video excerpt followed by a second video that elicited happy, neutral, or sad mood. Compared to participants who viewed the neutral or sad mood excerpts, cardiovascular activation recovered to pre-film baseline levels more quickly among participants who viewed the happiness excerpt.

People with positive affect are free to pursue a wider range of actions and experiences because they are free from the restricted thought-action tendencies that accompany negative emotions. Positive emotions foster creativity; an effect that has recently been linked to increases in brain dopamine (Ashby, Isen, and Turken, 1999). According to the dopamine hypothesis, positive affect involves the release of dopamine in the brain that activate regions of the brain, including frontal areas responsible for high level cognition, executive function, attention switching, and conflict resolution (Isen, 2008).

Isen and colleagues highlight some of the various ways in which positive emotions broaden the scope of cognition. Initial research found that individuals experiencing positive affect access more unusual associations to neutral words than do individuals in neutral affect control conditions (Isen, Johnson, Mertz, et al., 1985). Further, being in a positive mood enhanced the ability to make connections between loosely associated objects. Individuals induced to experience positive affect were better able to categorize and associate loosely connected objects (for example, elevator and camel are weak exemplars of the category vehicle) (Isen and Daubman, 1984). Finally, Isen et al. (Isen, Daubman, and Nowicki, 1987) demonstrated that being in a positive mood enhances creative thinking during sentence completion and association tasks. Other investigators have reported that high positive affect improves compound remote association problem-solving using insight (Subramaniam, Kounios, Parrish, et al., 2009). This body of research indicated that positive emotions lead to efficient cognitive performance and creativity.

Some Characteristics of Positive Individuals

Individuals with a positive attitude tend to keep an optimistic outlook towards life. They look for the best in themselves and in those around them. Positive individuals have an uncanny ability to reframe negative outcomes into positive experiences. This is perhaps because these individuals focus on the positive rather than the negative aspects of life. Positive individuals are also more social, cooperative, and willing to help others.

Positive individuals see things from a different perspective. They tend to view problems as challenges rather than chores. Instead of focusing on what they are missing in life, positive individuals reflect on things that they have. They tend to appreciate the moments, items, and people in their lives, and be grateful for the blessings that come their way.

Is there a Threshold for the Benefits of Positivity?

Several investigators have tried to determine whether there is a minimum threshold for positive experience after which advantages are conferred. This threshold may represent a cut-score on a validated measure or it may represent a ratio of positive to negative emotions/experiences. There exists sound theoretical reasoning and ample empirical evidence to conclude that a positivity ratio exists that leads to beneficial outcomes.

Most humans experience a basal state of mild positive affect (Diener and Diener, 1996; Diener, Oishi, and Ryan, 2013). Yet, the experience of negative events are more potent than positive events (Baumeister, Bratslavsky, Finkenauer, et al., 2001; Rozin and Royzman, 2001), suggesting that the positivity ratio should exceed 1 if the goal is to overcome the toxicity of negative affect and remain positive. Much research confirms this hypothesis. Following two decades of observational research on marriages, Gottman concluded that flourishing marriages were characterized by a positive to negative affect ratio of approximately 5:1 while marriages on a cascade to dissolution were characterized by a ratio of approximately 1:1 (Gottman, 1994). As another example, mathematical models applied to data collected on business team dynamics indicated that the optimal positive to negative affect ratio characterizing high performing teams was 2.9:1 (Losada, 1999; Losada and Heaphy, 2004). This positivity ratio was later found to classify flourishing university students among two samples (Fredrickson and Losada, 2005). In a more novel approach to determine the dose of positive affect needed to counteract negative affect in daily life, Larsen and Prizmic reported that individuals have three days where the positivity ratio exceeds 1 for every bad day where the positivity ratio is below 1 (Larsen and Prizmic, 2008). Regression models used to predict subjective well-being indicated a ratio of approximately 3:1, indicating that daily negative affectivity contributes three-fold more than positive affectivity to overall well-being.

There is some evidence to suggest that low positive affect to negative affect ratios of less than 1:1 may contribute to mental illness. Results from an assessment of the affective balance of 66 depressed male outpatients receiving treatment indicate that depression is characterized by a positivity ratio of less than 1:1 (R.M. Schwartz, Reynolds, Thase, et al., 2002). Interestingly, following treatment with pharmacology and cognitive behavioral therapy the positivity ratio of remitted patients increased to about 2:1 and 4:1, respectively. This type of analysis has been extended to anxiety, anger, and stress, arriving at similar conclusions (Wong, 2010).

We do not mean to convey the message that negative affect is unimportant and a greater ratio of positive to negative experiences is always desirable no matter how high the ratio. In their initial conceptualization, Fredrickson and Losada (2005) reported that the benefits of a positivity ratio begin to break down at a ratio of approximately 11.1:1. More recent empirical findings suggest that this number may be lower. A cross-sectional study of 595 retail employees in Portugal reported that the positivity ratio is curvilinear in nature when applied to employee creativity (Rego, Sousa, Marques, et al., 2012). Creativity was enhanced among employees who exhibited a positivity ratio between approximately 2:1 and 5:1 with values falling outside this range becoming increasingly detrimental. A study of two samples of high stressed individuals (that is, gastric cancer patients and hospital personnel exposed to missile attacks) reported increasing benefits, and decreasing psychological distress as positivity ratios approached 3:1 (Shrira, Palgi, Wolf, et al., 2011).

The diverse range of empirical evidence assessing the threshold of positive affect needed to confer benefits has arrived at remarkably similar conclusions. A positive affect to negative affect ratio of approximately 3:1 appears optimal for most individuals, under most circumstances. Stated alternatively, negative experiences contribute approximately three times more influence to well-being and outcomes than do positive experiences, meaning that approximately three positive experiences are required to counteract each negative experience. These results should be interpreted with some degree of caution as these numbers may be somewhat different for different samples or across different outcomes.

How Harnessing the Power of Positive Affect Benefits the Self

Emotions can motivate people towards performing given actions, alter signals being transmitted through facial expressions, expand cognitive capacities, and change physiology to operate more efficiently. Thus, positive emotions afford the medium through which individuals can transform themselves to become more creative, resilient, knowledgeable, socially adept, and physically healthy.

Successful individuals who flourish in life appear to be capable of accessing the rich tapestry of information that emotions provide. Such individuals are able to harness the power of emotions and alter their thinking and behaviors in such a way that allows them to negotiate life's challenges in a more adaptive and productive manner (Matthews, Zeidner, and Roberts, 2004). A systematic review of the literature indicates that positive emotions benefit people by: increasing cognitive capacity and mental processing speed, enhancing social aptitude and amicability, and through fostering internal reward, greater task enjoyment, and persistence. As previously discussed, research has shown that positive emotions act to increase cognitive capacity by attenuating the restricted thought-action repertoires that accompany negative emotions. This increase in cognitive capacity and flexibility may be in part due to mental processing efficiency that occurs during positive moods.

Positive moods enhance mental processing speed and fluidity. Compared to those undergoing negative mood inductions and neutral controls, participants induced to feel positive moods are more likely to use rapid and efficient problem-solving strategies (Isen and Means, 1983). Happy people have been found to reduce their cognitive load and increase their decision-making time by relying on simple heuristics when asked to make decisions (Schwarz, 1990). These simple heuristics are often drawn from previous successful experiences that will likely lead to good future outcomes. Use of these heuristics affords greater cognitive resources which can then be applied to other tasks. However, simple heuristics do not always lead to good decisions and, in personally important and ecologically demanding situations, people in positive moods will allocate mental effort into careful deliberation in order to make creative and correct decisions (Isen, 2008). Thus, positive mood appears to afford individuals the flexibility to save cognitive resources when simple heuristics can be employed, and expend such resources to come up with creative solutions to high-risk decisions.

Positive emotions also benefit people socially by making them more personable and enhancing their social skill-set. Positive moods facilitate collaborative decision-making and compromise during social tasks. During negotiation, people in good moods are more likely to reach integrative solutions in which every party benefits rather than reaching compromise solutions where only one party benefits (Carnevale and Isen, 1986). It is easier for happy individuals to reach integrative solutions to problems because happy people are more willing to sacrifice in their decision-making strategies to achieve the best possible outcome for all parties, regardless of costs in effort and time (Schwartz, Ward, Monterosso, et al., 2002). It seems that positive moods facilitate a willingness to expend energy to help others during social situations. Indeed, individuals high in happiness, gratitude, and satisfaction with life are more likely to spend a portion of their free time volunteering (Bartlett and DeSteno, 2006; Thoits and Hewitt, 2001). In summary, positive emotions enhance an individual's social skill-set by facilitating cooperation, compromise, delay in gratification, and helping behaviors.

Finally, positive emotions appear to enhance success in life by promoting internal rewards and increasing task enjoyment. Individuals who are in good moods are more likely to derive greater enjoyment from instructed tasks (Hirt, Melton, McDonald, et al., 1996). Further, students induced to experience positive emotions have been found to set more lofty goals for themselves (Baron, 1990), describe themselves more positively, assess their performance as superior (Barsade, 2002), and recall more positive past experiences. Furthermore, when people believe that their actions will lead to positive outcomes they are more likely to engage in difficult and uncertain tasks, while also being more likely to persist through such tasks (Staw, Sutton, and Pelled, 1994). In summary, positive affect promotes greater enjoyment, self-appreciation, and persistence throughout life's circumstances, making even the most mundane or difficult work seem effortless and manageable.

Researchers have long been concerned that the benefits of positive emotions are merely reporting biases, with positive individuals inaccurately reporting better outcomes than their less positive counterparts. There is little research to address this concern. Much of the research assessing bias in memory and emotion has focused on negative affect and depression. From an examination of this literature it is possible to glean that the effects of emotion represent more than simple response biases. An experimental investigation of the association between depressed affect and the occurrence of positive and negative outcomes among undergraduate students over the course of a semester reported that students with depressed affect were less accurate at predicting the occurrence of positive outcomes, were more accurate when predicting negative outcomes, and experienced more negative outcomes (Dunning and Story, 1991). While not definitive, findings such as this suggest that positive and negative beliefs are not simply cognitive biases, but relate to behavioral outcomes in some tangible fashion. Additional rigorous research would be of benefit in order to adequately quantify the level of response bias evidenced by positive individuals.

How Positive Emotions Improve Physical Health

There is growing evidence that positive affect is associated with reduced risk of physical illness and prolonged survival. In some sense, this is not surprising given that serious illness often leads to deterioration in mood. The more interesting question is whether positive affect protects against future illnesses, inhibits the progression of chronic diseases, increases longevity, or promotes healthy lifestyle habits.

Prospective studies are required to examine the link between positive affect and subsequent disease onset. Healthy individuals or statistical controls must be selected and followed for a specified period of time during which they are monitored for the onset of the disease under consideration. Research of this nature has concluded that positive affect is associated with less risk of injury or illness, and better health. Most of this research has been conducted in relation to heart disease or stroke. In one case, the absence of positive affect among seniors over the age of 65 was associated with a greater risk of stroke incidence over a six-year follow-up (RR = 0.74; (Ostir, Markides, Peek, et al., 2001). This association was strongest among men and held after adjusting for age, income, education, marital status, body mass index, systolic blood pressure, smoking status, and history of heart attack or diabetes. In another trial, adults over the age of 55 who scored higher on a measure of positive affect following hospitalization for a heart problem were less likely to experience an unplanned readmission to the hospital at a 90-day follow-up (Middleton and Byrd, 1996). This effect persisted after controlling for additional chronic illnesses, length of initial stay, perceived health, and activities of daily living. Finally, a study of emotional vitality (that is, vitality, positive well-being, and emotional self-control) and coronary heart disease among a cohort of 6,025 men and women between the ages of 25 and 75 years who were free of heart disease at baseline concluded that higher emotional vitality reduced risk of coronary heart disease 15 years later (Kubzansky and Thurston, 2007). This effect persisted after adjusting for age, gender, ethnicity, marital status, education, blood pressure, cholesterol, smoking status, BMI, alcohol use, physical activity, diabetes, and psychological illness. All three components of emotional vitality contributed to health risk and together reduced the relative risk of heart disease by 26 percent. Emotional vitality was nearly as influential as exercise which reduced the risk of heart disease by 33 percent.

A small number of quasi-experimental studies have determined that positive affect reduces the risk of developing illness following experimental exposure to infectious agents (Cohen, Alper, Doyle, et al., 2006; Cohen, Doyle, Turner, et al., 2003). Volunteers were administered standard doses of the rhinovirus (common cold) or influenza virus and monitored in quarantine for the development of objective illness. Participants who remained very positive (that is, self-reported adjectives such as happiness, cheerful, lively, energetic) over several days had reduced risk of developing upper respiratory illness. In fact, positive individuals were nearly three-fold less likely to develop the illness and this relationship persisted after controlling for age, sex, immunity, education, and negative affect.

Prospective studies are also required to assess the relationship between positive affect and mortality. Populations are identified and followed for a specified number of years. At the end of this follow-up, the investigation identifies who is still alive. Several studies have assessed positive affect and mortality, supporting the theory that positive individuals live longer than their less positive counterparts. In one case, a nationally representative sample of 22,461 Finnish adults between 18 and 64 years of age were assessed at baseline and followed for 20 years (Koivumaa-Honkanen, Honkanen, Viinamaki, et al., 2000). Low scores on a measure of life satisfaction were linearly associated with increased all-cause, disease, or injury-related mortality. More dissatisfied individuals were nearly two-fold more likely to die within the 20-year follow-up. Results persisted after adjusting for age, marital status, smoking status, social class, alcohol use, and physical activity. In another case, Danner, Snowdon, and Friesen (2001) coded autobiographies written by nuns for emotion words and assessed mortality approximately 60 years later. Nuns who used more positive emotion words in their early 20s were less likely to succumb to age- and education-adjusted mortality in 60 years' time. In contrast, the number of negative emotions reported was not a predictor of mortality.

Studies specifically assessing positive affect and survival with terminal illnesses such as some cancers are less encouraging than those assessing long-term survival with chronic conditions such as AIDS. It appears that positive affect may negatively impact individuals in the end-stage of a disease characterized by high short-term mortality while benefiting those suffering from chronic diseases with low mortality rates (Pressman and Cohen, 2005). A study predicting survival among patients with AIDS (ages 25–53) over a seven-and-a-half-year follow-up period reported that positive affect at baseline was associated with an increased likelihood of survival (RR = 0.86) (Moskowitz, 2003). Similarly, positive affect was associated with survival in 356 individuals 10 years following a coronary angioplasty (van Domburg, Scmidt Pedersen, van den Brand, et al., 2001). Interestingly, this effect did not persist after adjustments were made for baseline measures of medical history and health. Only one of several studies assessing positive affect and survival in cancer patients reported positive findings. In this study, positive affect at baseline was a predictor of survival at a three-and-a-half-year follow-up in patients suffering from recurrent breast cancer (Levy, Lee, Bagley, et al., 1988). This pattern of findings suggests that positive affect may enhance survival in long-term disease situations where adherence to medical regimens and other behavioral factors could play a role.

While results are at times inconsistent, positive individuals appear to make healthier behavior choices. Higher positive affect is associated with improved sleep quality in healthy samples and narcoleptics (Bardwell, Berry, Ancoli-Israel, et al., 1999; Fosse, Stickgold, and Hobson, 2002), and with exercise engagement (Ryff, Singer, and Dienberg Love, 2004). In one large investigation, Grant et al. (Grant, Wardle, and Steptoe, 2009) sampled 17,246 students from 21 different countries in order to assess the relationship between life satisfaction and seven health behaviors, including smoking, physical activity, exercise, alcohol consumption, sun protection, fruit intake, fat consumption, and fiber intake. The authors classified the 21 countries into three geopolitical regions: Western Europe and the United States (Belgium, England, France, Germany, Greece, Iceland, Ireland, Italy, Netherlands, Portugal, Spain, and the United States), Central and

Eastern Europe (Bulgaria, Hungary, Poland, Romania, and Slovakia), and Pacific Asia (Japan, Korea, Taiwan, and Thailand). After controlling for age, gender, and clustering within countries, students who were very satisfied with their lives were less likely to smoke (mean OR = 1.75), and more likely to exercise (mean OR = 2.22), use sun protection (mean OR = 1.77), eat fruit (mean OR = 1.57), and limit fat intake (mean OR = 1.28). There was no association between life satisfaction and alcohol consumption or fiber intake. Results were consistent across regions for not smoking, exercising, and using sun protection.

Of course, it is also possible that happiness leads to beneficial health outcomes and longevity through beneficial biological correlates such as bolstered immune system functioning, lower cortisol levels, and better autonomic/cardiovascular functioning. The immune system is the body's first line of defense against infectious agents and diseases. Positive affect appears to bolster immune system functioning. Marsland et al. (Marsland, Pressman, and Cohen, 2007) reviewed the relationship between positive affect and immune system function, finding that state and trait positive affect is associated with increased cellular immune system competence. The induction of positive mood was found to up-regulate components of the innate immune system, including secretory immunoglobulin A, the abundance of immune cells in peripheral circulation, and natural killer cell activity. Trait positive affect was associated with greater natural killer cell number and activity, increased pro-inflammatory cytokines, and higher antibody responses to hepatitis B vaccination.

Positive individuals appear to be less sensitive to the negative physical consequences of stress. Cortisol is a well-established stress hormone that is involved in a range of chronic diseases, including diabetes, hypertension, heart disease, depression, and autoimmune conditions (McEwen, 2007; Raison and Miller, 2003). A number of studies have found an inverse relationship between positive affect and salivary cortisol. Steptoe and colleagues have collected salivary cortisol and ecological momentary assessment of positive affect among middle-aged workers. Results indicated that cortisol output during the day was lower among individuals who score higher in positive affect (Steptoe, Wardle, and Marmot, 2005), and that this effect occurs on working and nonworking days, and persists when the same individual is assessed during a three-and-a-half-year period (Steptoe and Wardle, 2005). This effect could not be explained by gender, age, grade of employment, smoking status, or body mass index. Lower cortisol levels suggest one of two explanations. Either positive individuals experience less stress, or they are less affected by stress.

Finally, positive affect has been found to improve cardiovascular and nervous system functioning. A cardiac measure providing important information about the functioning of the autonomic nervous system is heart rate variability. Heart rate variability reflects the variations in heart beat (that is, consecutive R-waves known as an inter-beat-interval) that result from the coordinated interplay between the sympathetic (which increases arousal and heart rate) and the parasympathetic (which reduces heart rate to promote rest and relaxation) branches of the autonomic nervous system. Heart rate variability, and parasympathetic cardiac control in particular, is a marker of cardiovascular health with higher levels reflecting reduced risk of mortality (see Thayer, Yamamoto, and Brosschot, 2010). The idea being that an individual with higher heart rate variability has a greater functional capacity from which they can draw upon to regulate the cardiovascular system during negative moods, stress, or danger. Positive affect is associated with a healthier profile of heart rate variability (Bhattacharyya, Whitehead, Rakhit, et al., 2008).

How Positive Emotions Improve Mental Health

Mental health is arguably as important as physical health, if not more so. The cardinal feature of optimal mental health appears to be the ability to modulate and regulate affect. Indeed, most mental health problems involve the dysregulation of negative affect (Gross, 1998). Emotion dysregulation is implicated in over half of the DSM-IV axis I disorders and in every axis II disorder (Gross and Levenson, 1997). Learning how to harness the power of positive emotion to attenuate and regulate negative affect has great potential for promoting proper mental health and staving off mental illnesses.

The recurrent experience of positive emotions may help develop psychological resilience (Fredrickson, 2000). Psychological resilience is characterized by the ability to recover from negative experiences using positive emotions, and adapt to the changing demands of life (Fredrickson, Tugade, Waugh, et al., ; Tugade, Fredrickson, and Barrett, 2004). In a study assessing psychological growth in the wake of the September 11th crisis in the United States, college students scoring high on psychological resilience prior to September 11th were found to experience more positive emotions (for example, gratitude, love, compassion), fewer depressive symptoms, and to develop greater positive meaning in the following months (Fredrickson, Tugade, Waugh, et al., 2003). Importantly, mediation analysis illustrated that positive emotions were the critical active ingredient underlying these benefits. Thus, it seems likely that positive emotions can be used to effectively cope with stress and overcome adversity; a belief supported by Tugade et al. (2004) who found that the ability to accurately label positive emotion experiences was associated with "proactive" and future-oriented coping.

Researchers at the Institute of HeartMath have performed studies examining the impact of a positive emotion-focused stress management program known as Inner Quality Management (IQM) on several indices of mental and physical health. IQM teaches individuals practical skills designed to reduce stress and negative affect, enhance health, and improve business performance, office climate, and job communication (McCraty, Atkinson, and Tomasino, 2003). The IQM is administered in a single eight-hour session or over the course of two four-hour sessions. Participants are taught how to refocus and restructure positive emotions, increase mental and emotional acuity, as well as how to reinforce healthy patterns of mental, emotional, and physiological activity (for a more thorough review see (McCraty Atkinson, and Tomasino, 2003) or (Barrios-Choplin, McCraty, and Cryer, 1997). The IQM has proved successful in relieving several indicators of poor mental health through teaching participants how to be in tune with their emotions, to detect and self-regulate negative affect, and to self-induce positive affect during stressful circumstances.

McCraty et al. (McCraty, Barrios-Choplin, Rozman, et al., 1998) administered the IQM to 45 working adult participants from the community (30 in a treatment group and 15 in a waitlist control) during a four-week period. Participants were encouraged to use techniques gleamed from the IQM during stressful situations and before important work events. Participants who underwent the IQM program experienced decreases in blood pressure, reductions in subjective and objective markers of stress (objectively measured using cortisol), as well as reductions in depressive symptoms, and enhanced markers of well-being. Reductions in stress were related to positive affective state while reductions in depression were associated with work satisfaction and lower levels of fatigue. Together, these findings suggest that learning to implement positive emotions during times of stress can offset mental illness and improve mental health.

Similarly, an examination of a six-week IQM training program among 54 volunteers (compared to 64 waitlist controls) found the positive emotion promoting technique to relieve symptoms of mental illness. Participants receiving the IQM program experienced less negative affect in terms of distress, fatigue, anger, sadness, and depression, and reported less sleeplessness, anxiety, and stress. Finally, two further examinations of the IQM have reported fewer physical symptoms of stress, tension, anxiety, and nervousness (Barrios-Choplin McCraty, and Cryer, 1997) as well as lower anger, fatigue, hostility, interpersonal sensitivity, and enhanced feelings of gratitude (McCraty, Atkinson, and Tomasino, 2003). In summary, being able to self-generate, sustain, and use positive emotions to attenuate negative affect has the potential to reduce the underlying symptoms of mental illnesses such as depression, stress, and anxiety.

Only recently have positive psychological interventions (aka. positive psychotherapies) been developed as a means of improving psychological well-being and treating mental illness. The theory underlying these interventions as well as their components have been described in detail elsewhere (see Seligman, 2002; Seligman, Rashid, and Parks, 2006; Seligman, Steen, Park, et al., 2005). In brief, intentional acts that cultivate positive feelings, behavior, and cognition can be used to address a lack of positive affect, engagement, and life meaning that characterizes such disorders as depression (Forbes and Dahl, 2005; Seligman, Rashid, Parks, et al., 2006). These interventions often include a piecemeal of positive psychological exercises (see Table 13.1).

Two meta-analytic reviews have evaluated the benefits of positive psychotherapy and provide encouraging evidence into its effectiveness relative to control conditions. A practice-friendly meta-analysis evaluating the effect of positive psychology interventions at enhancing well-being and ameliorating depressive symptoms identified 51 such interventions with 4,266 participants (Sin and Lyubomirsky, 2009). Forty-nine trials on psychological well-being resulted in moderate effects ($r = .29$) with 96 percent of effect sizes in the predicted positive direction. Positive psychology interventions also had a medium effect in ameliorating depression across the 25 trials identified ($r = .30$), with 80 percent of effects in favor of positive psychotherapy. Depression status, self-selection, age, and intervention format were found to be moderators of outcomes. Depressed, self-selecting, older individuals had greater benefits. Similarly, individual positive psychotherapy was more beneficial than was group practice.

In what is perhaps a more stringent comparison, Boiler and colleagues (2013) conducted a meta-analysis of 39 (n = 6,139) random controlled trials evaluating the effectiveness of positive psychological interventions on subjective well-being, psychological well-being, and depression (Bolier, Haverman, Westerhof, et al., 2013). Small to moderate average effect sizes were found for subjective well-being ($d = .34$; 95%CI = 0.22–0.45), psychological well-being ($d = .20$; 95%CI = 0.09–0.30), and depression ($d = .23$; 95%CI = 0.09–0.38). The effects for well-being were maintained over a 3- to 6-month follow-up period. The effect for depression was attenuated at follow-up ($d = .17$; 95%CI = -0.06–0.39).

Table 13.1   Description of positive psychology activities commonly used in positive psychotherapy

Positive Psychological Activity	Description
Gratitude visit	Write a letter thanking someone who made a meaningful contribution to your life who you have not properly thanked. Deliver this letter of gratitude in person. It may be helpful to read the letter aloud to this person.
Grateful contemplation	On three to four days each week, spend five minutes silently contemplating the people, moments, and events in your life that you are grateful for. Jot down these people, moments, and events following the exercise.
Three good things/blessings	Write a list of three to five good things that happen each day over the course of a week. In addition, provide a causal explanation for each good thing
Obituary/Biography	Imagine that you had passed away after living a fulfilling life. Think about how your obituary would read. Write a brief summary outlining what you would like to be remembered for.
You at your best	Write about a time that you were at your best and then reflect on the personal strengths displayed in the story. Revisit this story each day for one week and reflect on the identified strengths.
Using signature strengths in a new way	Take the inventory of character strengths available online at www.authentichappiness.org. Take one of your top five strengths provided through this website and use it in a novel way.
Active/Constructive responding	At least once a day, respond in a visibly positive and enthusiastic way to good news that you receive from someone else.
Savoring	Once a day, take time to enjoy something that you usually hurry through (e.g., a meal, a shower). When it is over, write down what you did, how you did it differently, and how it felt compared to how you do it when you rush through it.

It is important to note that the effect for depression at follow-up was limited by relatively few comparisons (n = 5). The two meta-analyses concluded that positive psychological interventions have small but reliable effects in improving psychological well-being and depression. These interventions may be particularly relevant due to their inherent appeal, ease of administration, and low participant burden.

How Positive Emotions Influences Work-Life

Positive affect appears to lead to desirable work outcomes, affording happy workers multiple advantages over their less happy peers. Individuals high in positive affect are more likely to perform well in school, secure job interviews, exhibit superior work performance and productivity, and excel in supervisor and managerial roles. Individuals high in positive affect are also less likely to engage in counterproductive workplace behavior, and experience stress-related burn-out.

Even before entering the workforce, people with high subjective well-being are more likely to graduate from high-school and partake in higher education (Frisch, Clark, Rouse, et al., 2005). People with high positive affect are also more likely to have success in acquiring interviews for employment. Longitudinal data indicated that positive affect measured four months before graduation predicted success at obtaining interviews in three months' time (Burger and Caldwell, 2000). In addition, positive individuals appear to be better at locating more desirable employment. Employees high in positive affect have been found to locate jobs that trained observers rate as having more autonomy, meaning, and variety (Staw, Sutton, and Pelled, 1994).

Employees with positive traits also experience greater success at work. In a study of 272 employees recruited from three organizations located in the Midwestern United States, high dispositional positive affect at pretest predicted more favorable supervisor evaluations for work quality, productivity, dependability, and creativity 18 months in the future (Staw, Sutton, and Pelled, 1994). Similarly, Wright and Staw (1999) conducted two studies assessing the happy-productive worker hypothesis. The first study followed 53 social welfare professionals over four years and concluded that high dispositional positive affect at time one predicted objectively rated work performance over four years ($r = .51$). Results of the second study were similar. Positive affect at time one predicted work performance after one year. Interestingly, state positive affect did not predict work performance in either study. In another study, higher psychological well-being among 60 social welfare professionals predicted performance on work facilitation, team building, and goal emphasis measures more than two years in the future (Cropanzano and Wright, 1999). The association was stronger when the time interval between evaluations was shorter, indicating that fluctuations in this relationship can occur over long-term time intervals. Evidence indicates that the effect of positive affect on optimal job performance is even more potent than that of job satisfaction. In two studies using one sample of human service workers and one sample of juvenile probation officers, psychological well-being was a positive predictor for supervisor rated work performance (Wright and Cropanzano, 2000). Importantly, this effect persisted beyond the effect of composite job satisfaction.

Staw and Barsade (1993) conducted a brilliant study designed to assess how positive affect might improve occupational performance: 111 first year Master in Business students were interviewed by a 12-member personality council followed by a six-member managerial council. Participants then underwent a decision-making simulation designed to parody real-world managerial decision-making, a leaderless group discussion exercise to assess interpersonal performance, and were rated on their managerial potential. Results were in support of a happier-but-smarter hypothesis. A positive association was observed between positive affect and accuracy, correctness of decisions, and analytical skills. There was also a positive association between positive affect and interpersonal skills, quality of participation, and leadership ratings. Finally, managerial potential was rated more favorably among participants higher in positive affect. It appears as though positive individuals are smarter and wiser in the work environment, a possible benefit of having a broader and more creative thought-action repertoire.

Perhaps unsurprisingly, positive affect also appears to have a direct bearing on job satisfaction. Connolly and Viswesvaran (2000) conducted a meta-analysis that synthesized the results of 27 studies that assessed the relationship between affect and job satisfaction. There was a strong positive association between positive affect and job satisfaction ($r = .49$), with positive affect accounting for 24 percent of the variance in job satisfaction. Further, this relationship was unaltered by moderators of age, organization sector, organization size, or tenure. Not only do they experience greater job satisfaction, individuals with a propensity to express positive affect also exhibit reduced work absenteeism and turnover. In a meta-analytic review of more than 200 studies, Thoresen et al. (Thoresen, Kaplan, Barsky, et al., 2003) reported that happy individuals are less likely to experience emotional exhaustion ($r = -.32$), and the intention to quit ($r = -.17$). Similarly, an inverse association has been found between positive affect and voluntary work absenteeism ($r = -.36$) among workers at an electronics company (Pelled and Xin, 1999). Positive affect accounted for 13 percent of the variance in absenteeism in this particular study.

Happy employees seem to acquire far more benefits than their negative counterparts. Perhaps happy people simply have more to be happy about. A diverse set of longitudinal findings indicate that individuals who are typified by a positive outlook towards life have a higher yearly income. A meta-analysis of 286 empirical investigations of older adults reported that happiness (r = .21), and life satisfaction (r = .18) were associated with higher income (Pinquart and Sorensen, 2000). Interestingly, this association was greater than the association between happiness, life satisfaction, and education. While happiness is associated with income one wonders if happiness leads to greater earning potential or vice versa. A large Australian panel study of over 20,000 participants found that higher ratings of happiness at the age of 17 or 18 predicted higher income 3 to 15 years in the future (Marks and Fleming, 1999). The effects were however small with a one standard deviation increase in happiness resulting in a 3 percent increase in income. A panel study of nearly 13,000 Russians came to a similar conclusion, finding that happiness in 1995 predicted higher income and lower unemployment in 2000 after adjusting for education, and other socio-demographic variables (Graham, Eggers, and Sukhtankar, 2004). Similarly, first year college students who were rated as more cheerful earned more money 16 years in the future, and this effect persisted after adjusting for parental income (Diener, Nickerson, Lucas, et al., 2002). The effect was however strongest for those whose parents were well-off and when parent income was high (that is, greater than $50,000 per annum). The most cheerful students later earned $25,000 more per annum than did the least cheerful students. While the relationship is likely bi-directional, being happy may lead to financial prosperity.

Individuals with a positive disposition are generally more sociable than their less positive counterparts and may cultivate a culture of sharing and reciprocity in the workplace. A review of the literature suggests that positive affect predicts organizational citizenship (for example, helping others with their jobs, supporting others, volunteering for additional responsibility) while negative affect is inversely correlated with it (Borman, Penner, Allen, et al., 2001). George (1991) examined the relationship between positive mood and prosocial behavior at work defined as behavior performed to benefit or help another individual. A total of 221 salespeople and 26 managers from a large retailer specializing in clothing and household appliances completed a self-report questionnaire package that contained measures of mood and prosocial behaviors. Employees who experienced positive moods at work were more likely to engage in prosocial organizational behavior regardless of whether this behavior was related to their occupational role. Further, employees who evidence high dispositional positive affect are more likely to elicit emotional and tangible support from their co-workers (Staw, Sutton, and Pelled, 1994). Thus, positive affect appears to cultivate a collegial working environment characterized by support and reciprocity.

Positive Psychology Interventions in Organizations

The aforementioned research on positive affect and work-life is nicely complimented by intervention studies, suggesting that positive psychology interventions can be used in a working context to improve work-related outcomes. A recent literature review identified 15 trials (n = 1,540) that assessed the effectiveness of positive psychology interventions delivered in organizations (Meyers, van Woerkom, and Bakker, 2012). Several interventions were delivered, including gratitude, loving-kindness meditation, resilience enhancement, psychological capital, and self-focused coping. These interventions were delivered in education, healthcare, information technology, resources, manufacturing, and government sectors. Positive psychology interventions were efficacious at improving well-being in 13 out of the 15 (87 percent) of studies included. The effects on work performance were encouraging with two out of four trials demonstrating performance enhancement. The use of positive psychology interventions to improve well-being seems particularly relevant given the wealth of empirical evidence indicating that positivity is related to beneficial outcomes.

Psychological Capital

A novel and interesting program of research has suggested that the benefits of positive affect may be more than a single trait such as happiness or optimism but rather may be a higher order constellation of positive state-like capacities. Luthans et al. have assessed the association between a constellation of positive psychological capacities and organization outcomes. It is believed that four positive psychological capacities—self-efficacy, optimism, hope, and resiliency—make up an employee's psychological capital defined as an individual's motivational drive, perseverance, and positive psychological state of development (Luthans and Youssef, 2004, 2007; Luthans, Youssef, and Avolio, 2007). These psychological capacities are viewed as state-like meaning that they are relatively malleable, and open to development, but are more fixed than momentary feelings. Importantly, these four psychological capacities are assessed using questions from both state and trait psychological questionnaires that are valid and reliable (Luthans, Avolio, Avey, et al., 2007).

Preliminary findings support a one factor solution for positive psychological capacities that is consistent with the theory of psychological capital (Luthans, Avolio, Avey, et al., 2007). Initial results also support an association between psychological capital, organizational commitment, and job performance

(Luthans, Avolio, Avey, et al., 2007; Luthans, Norman, Avolio, et al., 2008). A meta-analysis of 51 independent samples (n = 12,567) reported that psychological capital was associated with desirable employee attitudes, employee behaviors, and measures of performance (Avey, Reichard, Luthans, et al., 2011). Within the domain of employee attitudes, higher psychological capital was associated with greater job satisfaction (r = .45), higher work commitment (r = .40), better psychological well being (r = .40), less cynicism, (r = -.46), lower turnover intent (r = -.28), and less stress/anxiety (r = -.20). When examining behavior, psychological capital was associated with greater organizational citizenship behavior (r = .43), and less work deviance (r = -.43). Across measures of performance, higher psychological capital was associated with higher self-rated (r = .31), supervisor rated (r = .29), and objective indicators (r = .26) of work performance. In an examination of moderators, these associations were found to be stronger in the United States and in the service sector. In sum, psychological capital appears to be associated with a host of beneficial work outcomes but firm conclusions cannot yet be made. Without prospective studies it is impossible to determine whether psychological capital leads to better work outcomes or whether individuals with higher work outcomes have biased reporting of psychological capital. It is also important to understand why psychological capital is associated with beneficial work outcomes and these mechanisms of effect have yet to be tested. Finally, the effects reported on psychological capital may be overestimated due to the reliance on self-report methods which share common method error variance.

Perhaps more importantly, a psychological capacity intervention has been developed in an attempt to increase employee positive psychological capacity that may help to address some of the aforementioned limitations (see Luthans, Avey, Avolio, et al., 2006). This program consists of a two-hour workshop where a training facilitator utilizes eight modules to develop the four positive psychological capacities (see Luthans, Avey, Avolio, et al., 2010). Results following the delivery of this intervention are limited but encouraging. In a pilot study, management students randomly assigned to the intervention condition (n = 153) showed a small (d = .36) but significant improvement in their psychological capacity relative to a control condition (n = 89) focusing on group decision-making (Luthans, Avey, Avolio, et al., 2010). Similar results were found for a heterogeneous group of 80 managers who completed the intervention workshop. Managers who completed the workshop also evidenced improvement in self-report (d = .96) and manager-rated (d = .35) performance following the intervention (Luthans, Avey, Avolio, et al., 2010). These results are encouraging but limited for several reasons. The intervention improved psychological capital among students but the effects were small and no long-term follow-up was performed making it impossible to determine the durability of effects over time. The intervention was only found to improve performance in one sample of managers in which no control condition was delivered. Control conditions are essential in order to control for attention and expectancy effects. Thus, firm conclusions about this intervention will await future trials conducted with greater methodological rigor.

Positive Mood and Leadership

Leaders, managers, and supervisors dictate the office climate and influence group performance. They are responsible for setting examples of how to behave and motivating others to perform at their best. A good leader is one who motivates and inspires others, fosters positive attitudes at work, and creates a sense of contribution and importance among employees. It may be particularly beneficial for companies to hire and promote leaders, managers, and supervisors who have a tendency to experience positive affect, and cope well with stress. Leaders have higher expectations about their staff and are more optimistic about company performance when they are in a positive mood. These expectations have been found to enhance employee performance (Eden, 1990).

There is a special type of self-fulfillment prophecy known as the Pygmalion effect where raising managers' expectation in employee performance boosts performance. Eden (1990) examined the Pygmalion effect among soldiers at a military school who were undergoing 11 weeks of training. Ten platoon leaders were given high expectations about their squad with 19 platoon leaders given no instructions and serving as controls. Four areas of performance—theoretical specialty, practical specialty, physical fitness, and target shooting—were assessed through measures routinely administered at the school. Platoons with high expectancy leaders scored higher in areas taught by the platoon leader (theoretical specialty, practical specialty), and in natural areas (physical fitness, target shooting). While the mechanism of action is currently unknown, positive leader expectations have the potential to enhance the effectiveness of training and natural abilities.

George (1995) examined the association between leader positive mood and group performance among 53 sales managers who led teams of salespeople. Branch managers evaluated the performance of each group while positive mood at work was evaluated by each individual salesperson. Sales managers who experienced greater positive mood also experienced higher job performance, $r = .41$, better job satisfaction, $r = .60$, and greater job involvement, *r* = .41. Leader positive mood continued to predict higher job performance after adjusting for job satisfaction and involvement, indicating that leader positive mood is uniquely associated with job performance. This particular study did not evaluate what mechanisms might explain this relationship. Interestingly, leader positive mood was not associated with group affective tone but group affective tone also predicted job performance.

Refer to Figure 13.1 for a model detailing the benefits of positive employees and supervisors.

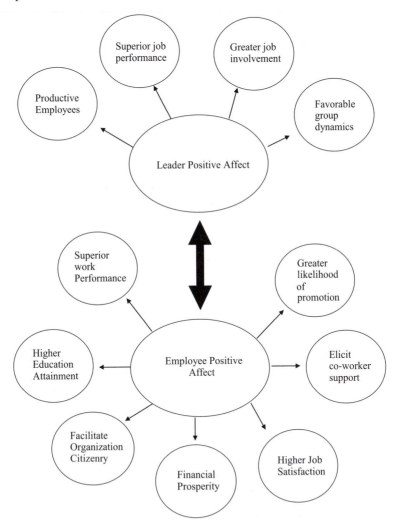

Figure 13.1   A model detailing the benefits of positive employees and supervisors

Beyond Positivity: Emotional Intelligence

Throughout this chapter we have illustrated the many benefits of positivity. Being inclined to experience positive emotions and to see the positive side of life can improve physical health, mental health, and work-life. At a physiological level, positive people recover more quickly from negative events and appear to be less susceptible to the adverse effects of stress and illness. At a fundamental level, positive individuals have a greater capacity for regulating their physiology following insults. At a psychological level, positive individuals seem to be better able to refocus their thoughts and manage their emotions. Our intention in this chapter was not to present an overly optimistic position about the benefits of positive affect. We do not wish to convey the message that an overly positive or optimistic attitude is always beneficial. Rather, we believe that a proclivity towards the experience of positive affect confers biopsychosocial benefits. This message should not be confused with the belief that the benefits of positive affect exist on a continuum with extreme positive affect being the ultimate goal. Rather, positive affect may be most beneficial in mild to moderate doses (see Isen, 2008). Research has found that unrealistic optimism may prevent proactive health behaviors and result in poor outcomes such as failure to quit smoking (Dillard, McCaul, and Klein, 2006), and engaging in risky behavior (Weinstein, 1982). The benefits associated with positivity may be most pronounced among individuals who are able to perceive, understand, self-generate, and manage their emotions. The literature reviewed may be capturing a construct referred to as emotional intelligence.

Although definitions vary, emotional intelligence is best conceptualized as a form of intelligence used to process and benefit from emotions (Matthews, Zeidner, and Roberts, 2004; Mayer, Caruso, and Salovey, 1999). From this perspective, emotional intelligence is composed of mental skills, abilities, and capacities. Specifically, emotional intelligence involves the ability to be aware of and perceive emotions, self-generate emotions to assist with thought, understand emotions and the ways in which they are used, and to regulate emotions to promote personal growth (Mayer, Roberts, and Barsade, 2008).

Emotional intelligence can be assessed using one of three techniques: ability-based measure, self-report measure, or some combination thereof. The first technique involves the use of ability-based tests such as the Mayer-Salovey-Caruso Emotional Intelligence Test II (MSCEIT-II; (Mayer, Salovey, and Caruso, 2002). Ability-based measures place emotional intelligence at the same level as cognitive intelligence (that is, emotional intelligence is subsumed by general intelligence or Spearman's g). These measures use a maximum performance approach where the goal is to measure the person at their maximum level of effort to find where their ability lies. Ability-based tests are lengthy to administer because enough questions must be given in order to determine where the true ability of the individual is in relationship to their peers. They involve external appraisal of performance having answers that are deemed as correct or incorrect. Finally, ability-based measures may be preferred in an employment setting because they have little to no response bias. The second technique involves the use of self-report measures such as the Schutte Emotional Intelligence Test (SEIT; Schutte, Malouff, Hall, et al., 1998) or the Trait Emotional Intelligence Questionnaire (TEIQue; Petrides, 2009). These tests presume that the construct is akin to a predisposition that can be measured using self-report. They are typically shorter than ability-based measures and presume typical effort or performance rather than maximal. Finally, self-report techniques are subject to response bias because employees can present themselves in a more or less favorable manner. The third techniques involve the measurement of both skills and abilities. Examples of these cross-over tests include the Emotional Quotient Inventory (EQi; Bar-On, 1997) and the Emotional Competency Inventory (ECI; Wolffe, 2005). Although there is debate among when and how to use the three different measures, there is good reason to believe that all three types of measures predict positive outcomes, including job performance and health outcomes. Several recent meta-analytic reviews suggest that emotionally intelligent individuals are less susceptible to physical, psychosomatic, and mental illnesses (for a review see Zeidner, Matthews, and Roberts, 2012).

Emotional intelligence is postulated to be a valid predictor of work performance. In his 1995 book championing emotional intelligence, Goleman cited research of over 500 organizations conducted by the Hayes Group to claim that emotional intelligence, rather than cognitive intelligence, accounts for over 85 percent of the performance in organizational leaders (Goleman, 1995). While there is no hard evidence to support such a statement, researchers such as Goleman do have reason to be excited because emotional intelligence does appear to predict optimal work and health outcomes. Yet this excitement needs to be tempered by the objective evidence, which suggests that effects are far more modest.

In a seven-year follow-up study of 58 managers in the United Kingdom and Ireland, emotional intelligence, cognitive intelligence, and managerial intelligence were assessed using self-report measures and used to predict career advancement (Dulewicz and Higgs, 2000). Emotional intelligence was a unique predictor of career advancement over and above cognitive and managerial intelligence, accounting for 36 percent unique variance. This proportion of variance was higher than that of cognitive (27 percent) and managerial (16 percent) intelligence. Unfortunately, this study did not utilize well-validated measures of emotional, cognitive, or managerial intelligence. More recent investigations corroborate these findings. Senior managers who scored higher on an ability-based measure of emotional intelligence cultivated better work relationships and scored higher on objective measures of performance as rated by higher-level managers and subordinates (Rosete and Ciarrochi, 2005). Importantly, this relationship persisted after adjusting for cognitive intelligence and personality. Similarly, higher emotional intelligence among 38 manufacturing supervisors was associated with higher managerial performance ratings made by 1,258 employees ($r = .38$) (Kerr, Garvin, and Heaton, 2006).

In a more empirically rigorous investigation, O'Boyle et al. assessed the relationship between emotional intelligence and job performance using a meta-analytic review (O'Boyle, Humphrey, Pollack, et al., 2011). A total of 43 (n = 5,795) studies were identified—nine using ability-based measures, seven using self-report measures, and 27 using some combination thereof. Studies were included if they used a measure of emotional intelligence, a quantifiable measure of job performance (for example, supervisor ratings, job performance), and a correlate of general intelligence or personality. Results indicated that higher emotional intelligence was associated with better job performance ($r = .27$). The magnitude of association did not differ as a function of assessment technique administered—ability-based ($r = .24$), self-report ($r = .30$), and combinatory ($r = .28$). The authors were interested in whether emotional intelligence predicted job performance over and above measures of general intelligence and personality. In order to test this question, a regression model was performed with cognitive and personality measures input as STEP 1 and emotional intelligence measures input as STEP 2. Cognitive abilities and personality measures predicted 42.3 percent of the variance in job performance. A substantial portion of the variance in job performance explained by ability-based measures of emotional intelligence was attributable to cognitive and personality measures. Ability-based measures of emotional intelligence did not explain additional variance in job performance beyond cognitive abilities and personality while self-report and combinatory measures accounted for an additional 5.2 percent and 6.8 percent of the variance in job performance, respectively.

While it must be remembered that not all studies have found positive results, the literature assessing the relationship between emotional

intelligence and optimal organizational outcomes indicates that a modest positive relationship exists that cannot be better accounted for by age, sex, education, cognitive intelligence, or personality. Additional research of a methodologically rigorous manner is required to explain the underlying mechanisms driving this association, but for the meantime organizations appear to benefit from the selection and advancement of emotionally intelligent employees.

Concluding Remarks

Until recently the field of Psychology has focused almost exclusively on mental illness and human suffering while largely ignoring positive virtues and strengths of character that allow resilience and flourishing. Positive emotions such as happiness, gratitude, or awe serve to broaden and build mental capacities allowing for creative and efficient cognition. Beyond this, the tendency to experience positive emotions across good and bad situations in life is associated with resiliency as well as biopsychosocial benefits. Relative to their less positive counterparts, positive individuals tend to live longer, are less likely to experience illnesses and major medical issues such as a heart attack, and show better immune, hormonal, and cardiac function. Positive individuals are also less likely to experience a mental illness and are more likely to show resiliency in the wake of particularly adverse events. The benefits of positive emotions permeate into the workplace as well where positivity is associated with higher earnings, better productivity, and fewer absences. The benefits of positivity may be the result of a larger constellation of positive capacities, or they may be reflective of the ability to use emotions in an intelligent manner. Either way, a proclivity towards positive affect appears to be a skill that can be developed through interventions, workshops, and diligent practice. Converging research evidence indicates that negative emotions are more salient than positive emotions with a ratio of approximately 3:1, suggesting that three positive experiences will offset each negative one.

Additional information can be found at the following sources:

Character strengths and virtues at http://www.viacharacter.org/www/

Positive psychology initiatives and practices at http://www.ippanetwork. org/

Center for positive organizational scholarship at http://www.centerforpos. org/

Emotional intelligence research in organizations at http://www. eiconsortium.org/

References

Ashby, F.G., Isen, A.M., and Turken, A.U. (1999). A neuropsychological theory of positive affect and its influence on cognition. *Psychol Rev*, 106(3), 529–50.

Avey, J.B, Reichard, R.J., Luthans, F., and Mhatre, K.H. (2011). Meta-analysis of the impact of positive psychological capital on employee attitudes, behaviors, and performance. *Human Resource Development Quarterly*, 22(2), 127–52.

Bar-On, R. (1997). *Emotional Quotient Inventory*. Toronto, ON: Multi Health Systems Inc.

Bardwell, W.A., Berry, C.C., Ancoli-Israel, S., and Dimsdale, J.E. (1999). Psychological correlates of sleep apnea. *J Psychosom Res*, 47(6), 583–96.

Baron, R.A. (1990). Environmentally induced positive affect: its impact on self-efficacy, task performance, negotiation, and conflict. *Journal of Applied Social Psychology*, 20, 368–84.

Barrios-Choplin, B., McCraty, R., and Cryer, B. (1997). An inner quality approach to reducing stress and improving physical and emotional wellbeing at work. *Stress Medicine*, 13(3), 193–201. DOI: 10.1002/(SICI)1099-1700(199707)13:3<193::AID-SMI744>3.0.CO;2-I.

Barsade, S.G. (2002). The ripple effect: Emotional contagion and its influence on group behavior. *Administrative Science Quarterly*, 47, 644–75.

Bartlett, M.Y. and DeSteno, D. (2006). Gratitude and prosocial behavior: helping when it costs you. *Psychol Sci*, 17(4), 319–25. DOI: 10.1111/j.1467-9280.2006.01705.x.

Baumeister, R.F., Bratslavsky, E., Finkenauer, C., and Vohs, K.D.. (2001). Bad is stronger than good. *Review of General Psychology*, 5(4), 323.

Bhattacharyya, M.R., Whitehead, D.L., Rakhit, R., and Steptoe, A. (2008). Depressed mood, positive affect, and heart rate variability in patients with suspected coronary artery disease. *Psychosom Med*, 70(9), 1020–7. DOI: 10.1097/PSY.0b013e318189afcc.

Bolier, L., Haverman, M., Westerhof, Ge J., Riper, H., Smit, F., and Bohlmeijer, E. (2013). Positive psychology interventions: a meta-analysis of randomized controlled studies. *BMC Public Health*, 13(1), 119.

Borman, W.C., Penner, L.A., Allen, T.D., and Motowildo, S.J. (2001). Personality predictors of citizenship performance. *International Journal of Selection and Assessment*, 9, 52–69.

Burger, J.M. and Caldwell, D.F. (2000). Personality, social activities, job-search behavior and interview success: distinguishing between PANAS trait positive affect and NEO extraversion. *Motivation and Emotion*, 24(1), 51–62. DOI: 10.1023/A:1005539609679.

Carnevale, P. and Isen, A.M. (1986). The influence of positive affect and visual access on the discovery of integrative solutions in bilateral negotiation. *Organizational Behavior and Human Decision Processes*, 37, 1–13.

Cohen, S., Alper, C.M., Doyle, W.J., Treanor, J.J., and Turner, R.B. (2006). Positive emotional style predicts resistance to illness after experimental exposure to rhinovirus or influenza a virus. *Psychosom Med*, 68(6), 809–15. DOI: 10.1097/01.psy.0000245867.92364.3c.

Cohen, S., Doyle, W.J., Turner, R.B., Alper, C.M., and Skoner, D.P. (2003). Emotional style and susceptibility to the common cold. *Psychosom Med*, 65(4), 652–7.

Connolly, J.J. and Viswesvaran, C. (2000). The role of affectivity in job satisfaction: a meta-analysis. *Personality and Individual Differences*, 29(2), 265–81. DOI: 10.1016/S0191-8869(99)00192-0.

Cropanzano, R. and Wright, T.A. (1999). A 5-year study of change in the relationship between well-being and job performance. *Counseling Psychology Journal: Practice and Research*, 51, 252–65.

Danner, D.D., Snowdon, D.A., and Friesen, W.V. (2001). Positive emotions in early life and longevity: findings from the nun study. *J Pers Soc Psychol*, 80(5), 804–13.

Diener, E. and Diener, C. (1996). Most people are happy. *Psychological Science*, 7(3), 181–5.

Diener, E., Nickerson, C., Lucas, R.E., and Sandvik, E. (2002). Dispositional affect and job outcomes. *Social Indicators Research*, 59, 229–59.

Diener, E., Oishi, S., and Ryan, K.L. (2013). Universals and cultural differences in the causes and structure of happiness: a multilevel review. *Mental Well-Being* (pp. 153–76): Springer.

Dillard, A.J., McCaul, K.D., and Klein, W.M. (2006). Unrealistic optimism in smokers: implications for smoking myth endorsement and self-protective motivation. *J Health Commun*, 11(1), 93–102. DOI: 10.1080/10810730600637343.

Dulewicz, V. and Higgs, M. (2000). Emotional intelligence: a review and evaluation study. *Journal of Managerial Psychology*, 15(4), 341–72. DOI: 10.1108/02683940010330993.

Dunning, D. and Story, A.L. (1991). Depression, realism, and the overconfidence effect: are the sadder wiser when predicting future actions and events? *J Pers Soc Psychol*, 61(4), 521–32.

Eden, D. (1990). Pygmalion without interpersonal contreast effects: whole groups gain from raising manager expectations. *Journal of Applied Psychology*, 75, 394–8.

Ekman, P. (1992). An argument for basic emotions. *Cognition & Emotion*, 6(3–4), 169–200.

Forbes, E.E. and Ronald, E. (2005). Neural systems of positive affect: relevance to understanding child and adolescent depression? *Development and Psychopathology*, 17(03), 827–50.

Fosse, R., Stickgold, R., and Hobson, J.A. (2002). Emotional experience during rapid-eye-movement sleep in narcolepsy. *Sleep*, 25(7), 724–32.

Fredrickson, B.L. (1998). What good are positive emotions? *Rev Gen Psychol*, 2(3), 300–319. DOI: 10.1037/1089-2680.2.3.300.

Fredrickson, B.L. (2000). Cultivating positive emotions to optimize health and well-being. *Prevention and Treatment*, 3(1), 1–25. DOI: 10.1037/1522-3736.3.1.31a.

Fredrickson, B.L. (2004). Gratitude, like other positive emotions, broadens and builds. In R.A. Emmons and M.E. McCullough (eds), *The Psychology of Gratitude* (pp. 145–66). New York, NY: Oxford University Press.

Fredrickson, B.L. and Levenson, R.W. (1998). Positive emotions speed recovery from the cardiovascular sequelae of negative emotions. *Cogn Emot*, 12(2), 191–220. DOI: 10.1080/026999398379718.

Fredrickson, B.L. and Losada, M.F. (2005). Positive affect and the complex dynamics of human flourishing. *American Psychologist*, 60(7), 678.

Fredrickson, B.L., Tugade, M.M., Waugh, C.E., and Larkin, G.R. (2003). What good are positive emotions in crises? a prospective study of resilience and emotions following the terrorist attacks on the United States on September 11th, 2001. *J Pers Soc Psychol*, 84(2), 365–76.

Frisch, M.B., Clark, M.P., Rouse, S.V., Rudd, M.D., Paweleck, J.K., Greenstone, A., and Kopplin, D.A. (2005). Predictive and treatment validity of life satisfaction and the quality of life inventory. *Assessment*, 12(1), 66–78. DOI: 10.1177/1073191104268006.

George, J.M. (1991). State or trait: Effects of positive mood on prosocial behaviors at work. *Journal of Applied Psychology*, 76, 299–307.

George, J.M. (1995). Leader positive mood and group performance: the case of customer service. *Journal of Applied Social Psychology*, 25, 778–95.

Goleman, D. (1995). *Emotional Intelligence*. New York, NY: Bantam Books.

Gottman, J.M. (1994). *What Predicts Divorce?: The Relationship Between Marital Processes and Marital Outcomes: John Mordechai Gottman*. Routledge.

Graham, C., Eggers, A., and Sukhtankar, S. (2004). Does happiness pay? an exploration based on panel data from Russia. *Journal of Economic Behavior and Organization*, 55, 319–42. DOI: 10.1016/j.jebo.2003.09.002.

Grant, N., Wardle, J., and Steptoe, A. (2009). The relationship between life satisfaction and health behavior: a cross-cultural analysis of young adults. *Int J Behav Med*, 16(3), 259–68. DOI: 10.1007/s12529-009-9032-x.

Gross, J.J. (1998). The emerging field of emotion regulation: an integrative review. *Review of General Psychology*, 2(3), 271–99. DOI: 10.1037/1089-2680.2.3.271.

Gross, J.J. and Levenson, R.W. (1997). Hiding feelings: the acute effects of inhibiting negative and positive emotion. *J Abnorm Psychol*, 106(1), 95–103.

Hirt, E.R., Melton, R.J., McDonald, H.E., and Harackiewicz, J.M. (1996). Processing goals, task interest, and the mood-performance relationship: a mediational analysis. *J Pers Soc Psychol*, 71(2), 245–61.

Isen, A.M. (2008). Some ways in which positive affect influences decision making and problem solving. In M. Lewis, J.M. Haviland-Jones, and L.F. Barrett (eds), *Handbook of Emotions* (3rd ed., pp. 548–73). New York, NY: Guilford Press.

Isen, A.M. and Daubman, K.A. (1984). The influence of affect on categorization. *Journal of Personality and Social Psychology*, 47, 1206–17.

Isen, A.M., Daubman, K.A., and Nowicki, G.P. (1987). Positive affect facilitates creative problem solving. *J Pers Soc Psychol*, 52(6), 1122–31.

Isen, A.M., Johnson, M.M., Mertz, E., and Robinson, G.F. (1985). The influence of positive affect on the unusualness of word associations. *J Pers Soc Psychol*, 48(6), 1413–26.

Isen, A.M. and Means, B. (1983). The influence of positive affect on decision-making strategy. *Social Cognition*, 2, 18–31.

Izard, C.E., Libero, D.Z., Putnam, P., and Haynes, O.M. (1993). Stability of emotion experiences and their relations to traits of personality. *J Pers Soc Psychol*, 64(5), 847–60.

Kashdan, T.B., Biswas-Diener, R., and King, L.A. (2008). Reconsidering happiness: the costs of distinguishing between hedonics and eudaimonia. *The Journal of Positive Psychology*, 3(4), 219–33.

Kerr, R., Garvin, J., and Heaton, N. (2006). Emotional intelligence and leadership effectiveness. *Leadership and Organizational Development Journal*, 27, 265–79. DOI: 10.1108/01437730610666028.

Koivumaa-Honkanen, H., Honkanen, R., Viinamaki, H., Heikkila, K., Kaprio, J., and Koskenvuo, M. (2000). Self-reported life satisfaction and 20-year mortality in healthy Finnish adults. *Am J Epidemiol*, 152(10), 983–91.

Kubzansky, L.D. and Thurston, R.C. (2007). Emotional vitality and incident coronary heart disease: benefits of healthy psychological functioning. *Arch Gen Psychiatry*, 64(12), 1393–1401. DOI: 10.1001/archpsyc.64.12.1393.

Larsen, R.J. and Prizmic, Z. (2008). Regulation of emotional well-being. *The Science of Subjective Well-being*, 258–9.

Levenson, R.W. (2011). Basic emotion questions. *Emotion Review*, 3(4), 379–86.

Levy, S.M., Lee, J., Bagley, C., and Lippman, M. (1988). Survival hazards analysis in first recurrent breast cancer patients: seven-year follow-up. *Psychosom Med*, 50(5), 520–528.

Losada, M. (1999). The complex dynamics of high performance teams. *Mathematical and Computer Modelling*, 30(9), 179–92.

Losada, M. and Heaphy, E. (2004). The role of positivity and connectivity in the performance of business teams a nonlinear dynamics model. *American Behavioral Scientist*, 47(6), 740–765.

Luthans, F. (2002). The need for and meaning of positive organizational behavior. *Journal of Organizational Behavior*, 23(6), 695–706.

Luthans, F., Avey, J.B., Avolio, B.J., Norman, S.M., and Combs, G.M. (2006). Psychological capital development: toward a micro-intervention. *Journal of Organizational Behavior*, 27(3), 387–93.

Luthans, F., Avey, J.B., Avolio, B.J., and Peterson, S.J. (2010). The development and resulting performance impact of positive psychological capital. *Human Resource Development Quarterly*, 21(1), 41–67.

Luthans, F., Avolio, B.J., Avey, J.B., and Norman, S.M. (2007). Positive psychological capital: Measurement and relationship with performance and satisfaction. *Personnel Psychology*, 60(3), 541–72.

Luthans, F., Norman, S.M., Avolio, B.J., and Avey, J.B. (2008). The mediating role of psychological capital in the supportive organizational climate—employee performance relationship. *Journal of Organizational Behavior*, 29(2), 219–38.

Luthans, F. and Youssef, C.M. (2004). Human, Social, and Now Positive Psychological Capital Management: Investing in People for Competitive Advantage. *Organizational Dynamics*, 33(2), 143–60.

Luthans, F. and Youssef, C.M. (2007). Emerging positive organizational behavior. *Journal of Management*, 33(3), 321–49.

Luthans, F., Youssef, C.M., and Avolio, B.J. (2007). Psychological capital: Investing and developing positive organizational behavior. *Positive Organizational Behaviour*, 9–24.

Lyubomirsky, S., King, L., and Diener, E. (2005). The benefits of frequent positive affect: does happiness lead to success? *Psychol Bull*, 131(6), 803–55. DOI: 10.1037/0033-2909.131.6.803.

Malatesta, C.Z. and Wilson, A. (1988). Emotion cognition interaction in personality development: a discrete emotions, functionalist analysis. *Br J Soc Psychol*, 27 (Pt 1), 91–112.

Marks, G.N. and Fleming, N. (1999). Influences and consequences of well-being among Australian young people: 1980–1995. *Social Indicators Research*, 46, 301–23.

Marsland, A.L., Pressman, S.D., and Cohen, S. (2007). Positive affect and immune function. In R. Adler (ed.), *Psychoneuroimmunology 4* (4th ed., pp. 761–79). Sandiego, CA: Academic Press.

Matthews, G., Zeidner, M., and Roberts, R.D. (2004). *Emotional Intelligence: Science & Myth*. Cambridge, MA: The MIT Press.

Mayer, J., Roberts, R.D., and Barsade, S.G. (2008). Human abilities: emotional intelligence. *Annu Rev Psychol*, 59, 507–36. DOI: 10.1146/annurev. psych.59.103006.093646.

Mayer, J., Salovey, P., and Caruso, D.R. (2002). *Mayer-Salovey-Caruso Emotional Intelligence Test: MSCEIT User's Manual*. Toronto, ON: Multi Health Systems.

Mayer, J.D., Caruso, D.R., and Salovey, P. (1999). Emotional intelligence meets traditional standards for an intelligence. *Intelligence*, 27(4), 267–98. DOI: 10.1016/S0160-2896(99)00016-1.

McCraty, R., Atkinson, M., and Tomasino, D. (2003). Impact of a workplace stress reduction program on blood pressure and emotional health in hypertensive employees. *Journal of Alternative and Complementary Medicine*, 9(3), 355–69.

McCraty, R., Barrios-Choplin, B., Rozman, D., Atkinson, M., and Watkins, A.D. (1998). The impact of a new emotional self-management program on stress, emotions, heart rate variability, DHEA and cortisol. *Integr Physiol Behav Sci*, 33(2), 151–70.

McCullough, M.E., Emmons, R.A., and Tsang, J.A. (2002). The grateful disposition: a conceptual and empirical topography. *J Pers Soc Psychol*, 82(1), 112–27.

McEwen, B.S. (2007). Physiology and neurobiology of stress and adaptation: central role of the brain. *Physiol Rev*, 87(3), 873–904. DOI: 10.1152/ physrev.00041.2006.

Meyers, M.C., van Woerkom, M., and Bakker, A.B. (2012). The added value of the positive: a literature review of positive psychology interventions in organizations. *European Journal of Work and Organizational Psychology* (ahead-of-print), 1–15.

Middleton, R.A. and Byrd, E.K. (1996). Psychosocial factors and hospital readmission status of older persons with cardiovascular disease. *Journal of Applied Rehabilitation Counseling*.

Moskowitz, J.T. (2003). Positive affect predicts lower risk of AIDS mortality. *Psychosom Med*, 65(4), 620–626.

Nelson, D. and Cooper, C.L. (2007). *Positive Organizational Behavior*. Sage.

O'Boyle, E.H., Humphrey, R.H., Pollack, J.M., Hawver, T.H., and Story, P.A. (2011). The relation between emotional intelligence and job-performance: A meta-analysis. *Journal of Organizational Behavior*, 32, 788–818. DOI: 10.1002/job.714.

Ostir, G.V., Markides, K.S., Peek, M.K., and Goodwin, J.S. (2001). The association between emotional well-being and the incidence of stroke in older adults. *Psychosom Med*, 63(2), 210–215.

Pelled, L.H. and Xin, K.R. (1999). Down and out: An investigation of the relationship between mood and employee withdrawal behavior. *Journal of Management*, 25, 875–95.

Petrides, K.V. (2009). *Technical Manual for the Trait Emotional Intelligence Questionnaire (TEIQue)* (1st, 4th printing ed.). London: London Psychometric Laboratory.

Pinquart, M. and Sorensen, S. (2000). Influences of socioeconomic status, social network, and competence on subjective well-being in later life: a meta-analysis. *Psychol Aging*, 15(2), 187–224.

Plutchik, R. (2001). The nature of emotions human emotions have deep evolutionary roots, a fact that may explain their complexity and provide tools for clinical practice. *American Scientist*, 89(4), 344–50.

Pressman, S.D. and Cohen, S. (2005). Does positive affect influence health? *Psychol Bull*, 131(6), 925–71. DOI: 10.1037/0033-2909.131.6.925.

Raison, C.L. and Miller, A.H. (2003). When not enough is too much: the role of insufficient glucocorticoid signaling in the pathophysiology of stress-related disorders. *Am J Psychiatry*, 160(9), 1554–65.

Rego, A., Sousa, F., Marques, C., and Cunha, M.P. (2012). Optimism predicting employees' creativity: the mediating role of positive affect and the positivity ratio. *European Journal of Work and Organizational Psychology*, 21(2), 244–70.

Rosete, D. and Ciarrochi, J. (2005). Emotional intelligence and its relationship to workplace performance. *Leadership and Organizational Development Journal*, 26, 388–99. DOI: 10.1108/01437730510607871.

Rozin, P. and Royzman, E.B. (2001). Negativity bias, negativity dominance, and contagion. *Personality and Social Psychology Review*, 5(4), 296–320.

Russell, J.A. (1980). A circumplex model of affect. *Journal of Personality and Social Psychology*, 39(6), 1161–78. DOI: 10.1037/h0077714.

Ryff, C.D., Singer, B.H., and Dienberg Love, G. (2004). Positive health: connecting well-being with biology. *Philos Trans R Soc Lond B Biol Sci*, 359(1449), 1383–04. DOI: 10.1098/rstb.2004.1521.

Schaufeli, W.B. and Salanova, M. (2007). Work engagement: An emerging psychological concept and its implications for organizations. In S.W. Gilliland, D.D. Steiner, and D.P. Skarlicki (eds), *Research in Social Issues in Management:*

Vol. 5. Managing Social and Ethical Issues in Organizations (pp. 135–77). Greenwich, CT: Information Age.

Schutte, N.S., Malouff, J.M., Hall, L.E., Haggerty, D.J., Cooper, J.T., Golden, C.J., and Dornheim, L. (1998). Development and validation of a measure of emotional intelligence. *Personality and Individual Differences*, 25(2), 167–77. DOI: 10.1016/S0191-8869(98)00001-4.

Schwartz, B., Ward, A., Monterosso, J., Lyubomirsky, S., White, K., and Lehman, D.R. (2002). Maximizing versus satisficing: happiness is a matter of choice. *J Pers Soc Psychol*, 83(5), 1178–97.

Schwartz, R.M., Reynolds, C.F., Thase, M.E., Frank, E., Fasiczka, A.L., and Haaga, D.A.F. (2002). Optimal and normal affect balance in psychotherapy of major depression: evaluation of the balanced states of mind model. *Behavioural and Cognitive Psychotherapy*, 30(4), 439–50.

Schwarz, N. (1990). Feelings as information: informational and motivational functions of affective states. In R.M. Sorrentino and E.T. Higgins (eds), *Handbook of Motivation and Cognition: Cognitive Foundations of Social Psychology* (2nd ed., pp. 527–261). New York, NY: Guilford Press.

Seligman, M.E.P. (1999). The president's address. *American Psychologist*, 54(8), 559–62.

Seligman, M.E.P. (2002). Positive psychology, positive prevention, and positive therapy. *Handbook of Positive Psychology*, 2, 3–12.

Seligman, M.E.P. and Csikszentmihalyi, M. (2000). Positive psychology: an introduction. *American Psychologist*, 55(1), 5.

Seligman, M.E.P., Rashid, T. and Parks, A.C. (2006). Positive psychotherapy. *American Psychologist*, 61(8), 774.

Seligman, M.E.P., Steen, T.A., Park, N. and Peterson, C. (2005). Positive psychology progress: empirical validation of interventions. *American Psychologist*, 60(5), 410.

Shrira, A., Palgi, Y., Wolf, J.J., Haber, Y., Goldray, O., Shacham-Shmueli, E., and Ben-Ezra, M. (2011). The positivity ratio and functioning under stress. *Stress and Health*, 27(4), 265–71.

Sin, N.L. and Lyubomirsky, S. (2009). Enhancing well-being and alleviating depressive symptoms with positive psychology interventions: a practice-friendly meta-analysis. *Journal of Clinical Psychology*, 65(5), 467–87.

Staw, B.M. and Barsade, S.G. (1993). Affect and managerial performance: a test of the sadder-but-wiser vs. happier-and-smarter hypothesis. *Administrative Science Quarterly*, 38, 304–31.

Staw, B.M., Sutton, R.I., and Pelled, L.H. (1994). Employee positive emotion and favorable outcomes at the workplace. *Organizational Science*, 5, 51–71.

Steptoe, A. and Wardle, J. (2005). Positive affect and biological function in everyday life. *Neurobiol Aging*, 26(1), 108–12. DOI: 10.1016/j. neurobiolaging.2005.08.016.

Steptoe, A., Wardle, J., and Marmot, M. (2005). Positive affect and health-related neuroendocrine, cardiovascular, and inflammatory processes. *Proc Natl Acad Sci U S A*, 102(18), 6508–12. DOI: 10.1073/pnas.0409174102.

Subramaniam, K., Kounios, J., Parrish, T.B., and Jung-Beeman, M. (2009). A brain mechanism for facilitation of insight by positive affect. *Journal of Cognitive Neuroscience*, 21(3), 415–32.

Thayer, J.F., Yamamoto, S.S., and Brosschot, J.F. (2010). The relationship of autonomic imbalance, heart rate variability and cardiovascular disease risk factors. *Int J Cardiol*, 141(2), 122–31. DOI: 10.1016/j.ijcard.2009.09.543.

Thoits, P.A. and Hewitt, L.N. (2001). Volunteer work and well-being. *J Health Soc Behav*, 42(2), 115–31.

Thoresen, C.J., Kaplan, S.A., Barsky, A.P., Warren, C.R., and de Chermont, K. (2003). The affective underpinnings of job perceptions and attitudes: a meta-analytic review and integration. *Psychol Bull*, 129(6), 914–45. DOI: 10.1037/0033-2909.129.6.914.

Tugade, M.M., Fredrickson, B.L., and Barrett, L.F. (2004). Psychological resilience and positive emotional granularity: examining the benefits of positive emotions on coping and health. *J Pers*, 72(6), 1161–90. DOI: 10.1111/j.1467-6494.2004.00294.x.

van Domburg, R.T., Scmidt Pedersen, S., van den Brand, M.J., and Erdman, R.A. (2001). Feelings of being disabled as a predictor of mortality in men 10 years after percutaneous coronary transluminal angioplasty. *J Psychosom Res*, 51(3), 469–77.

Watson, D., Clark, L.A., and Tellegen, A. (1988). Development and validation of brief measures of positive and negative affect: the PANAS scales. *J Pers Soc Psychol*, 54(6), 1063–70.

Watson, D. and Tellegen, A. (1985). Toward a consensual structure of mood. *Psychological Bulletin*, 98(2), 219.

Weinstein, N.D. (1982). Unrealistic optimism about susceptibility to health problems. *J Behav Med*, 5(4), 441–60.

Wolffe, S.B. (2005). *The Emotional Competence Inventory (ECI) Technical Manual.* Hay Group.

Wong, S.S. (2010). Balanced states of mind in psychopathology and psychological well-being. *International Journal of Psychology*, 45(4), 269–77.

Wright, T.A. (2003). Positive organizational behavior: an idea whose time has truly come. *Journal of Organizational Behavior*, 24(4), 437–42.

Wright, T.A. and Cropanzano, R. (2000). Psychological well-being and job satisfaction as predictors of job performance. *Journal of Occupational Health Psychology*, 5, 84–94.

Wright, T.A. and Staw, B.M. (1999). Affect and favorable work outcomes: two longitudinal tests of the happy-productive worker thesis. *Journal of Organizational Behavior*, 20, 1–23.

Zeidner, M., Matthews, G., and Roberts, R.D. (2012). The emotional intelligence, health, and well-being nexus: what have we learned and what have we missed? *Applied Psychology: Health and Well-Being*, 4(1), 1–30. DOI: 10.1111/j.1758-0854.2011.01062.x.

Conclusions

This book arose out of a frustration with the lack of resources that are available to address mental health issues in the workplace and out of the experience of being unable to even get workplaces to discuss mental health and what it would take to create mentally healthy workplaces. Despite the best efforts of many, mental illness and mental health remain taboo topics and persons with these issues continue to feel the stigma. So what is to be done? We decided that more information needs to be provided in order for there to be meaningful discussions about mental health in society and more specifically in workplaces. The issue needs to be named, clearly understood, and assertively confronted. As the World Health Organization has repeatedly pointed out, not doing so has been and will continue to be a very expensive proposition both on a monetary basis and to individuals on a personal basis. It is our hope that through this book such dialogue will occur and solutions posited and tested.

As a young psychologist many years ago one of the authors encountered a client who we shall call Shorty. Shorty was in his late 30s and had been in the woods all of his working life, most recently working as a tree faller. Shorty was married, had several children, and his family lived in town while he spent most of his time in various logging camps. This had been the case since Shorty was 15 years of age and he could legally leave school. Shorty was referred for psychological assistance because he was having difficulty sleeping which was interfering with his ability to participate in physical therapy after a worksite injury. Turns out that the 'incident' was that one of Shorty's work mates had been falling a tree and had dropped the tree right on Shorty. The tree had hit Shorty squarely on the head and had driven him into the ground like a nail. Luckily he had been standing on very soft ground and had been wearing his hard hat. His co-workers who witnessed the event assumed that no one could survive such a blow and didn't immediately seek to rescue him. They reported the incident and it wasn't until they were removing the tree to recover the body did they hear Shorty moaning and realized that he was still alive. On the one hand Shorty was lucky to be alive and actually to sustain only minor injuries. On the other hand he now had symptoms of post-traumatic stress that were affecting every part of his life. Those around him did not understand those symptoms, including the professionals involved in his recovery. His employer and work mates thought he should be heading back to work. After all, his physiological injuries had healed. He should just shake it off and get on with it. His family did not understand and his symptoms were causing difficulty with his wife and children. Shorty expressed that he wished he had died rather than face being alive and facing all of these issues and admitted that he had considered suicide as a way of dealing with it all.

This vignette, modified to protect privacy, contains many of the issues discussed in the book. It did not end well. The insurer essentially coerced Shorty back to work; his employer insisted that they could not accommodate his 'issues' so he had no job to go back to. Shorty stayed in town, an environment he was not suited for, and issues with his family escalated. Everyone involved washed their hands, saying that they had done what they could but clearly, from our perspective, not having done nearly enough. We believe that this result arose not out of malicious intent but rather out of ignorance. PTSD is much better understood and treated today and we hope that if the information presented in this book had been applied to this case a very different outcome would have ensued.

Extreme cases such as Shorty are actually the easy ones to discuss as everyone agrees that the incident was extreme enough to warrant PTSD. But what about cases where there is no such incident or where the etiology of the condition lies elsewhere?

People go to work unhappy, depressed, angry, and so on. You name it, they bring it to work. What does the workplace do about that: nothing? Well, actually it suffers from this transfer of ills through lost productivity, deceased morale, and a general decrease in employee health. We have a term for this: presenteeism. Originally, presenteeism referred to people who came to work sick. People with colds or the flu who were so committed to their jobs, or so insecure of their employment, that they struggled through rather than say at home. This type of thinking was often encouraged by employers with rewards such as money or a gift for perfect attendance. This kind of presenteeism was particularly challenged with the increasing prevalence of communicable diseases such as the flu and worksites now generally discourage such false bravado. The current use of the term presenteeism refers to workers who come to work with no intention of actually producing anything. Those who want to get paid simply for showing up. They are present but not productive. Most often, such behavior reflects mental illness issues.

Take the case of Mary, for example. By all accounts Mary was very bright and outgoing in high school. After graduating she tried college but found it difficult to work independently and did not do well. She soon met someone and got married. She dropped out of college when she got a job at a large processing plant. In this plant, Mary did the same job over and over again. She was bored but stayed in the job because it paid reasonably well and had health benefits. Slowly, over time Mary became depressed. The depression was not diagnosed and treated and manifested itself primarily in insomnia, irritability, and overeating. Mary became quite lethargic and her employer was concerned over the decrease in productivity and in particular her lack of attention to detail. Through her inattention Mary injured herself at work. She is now considered a cost to the system even though she has actually been a cost for many years. Helping Mary at this juncture may prove to be very difficult, since treating entrenched depression can be time-consuming. Also, returning her to the same work environment would likely exacerbate the problem and perhaps create a permanent disability. The workplace would need to change her duties or the way she does her duties in order to avoid repeating the situation. All too often we have looked to the worker to change rather than expecting workplaces to change. When it comes to mental health issues it requires change from both sides, but the onus lies on the workplace.

Creating mentally healthy workplaces is possible and we hope that we have provided the information and blueprints for doing so. More and more places of work and society require all of us to look to our own mental health. Society and workplaces have for years focused on providing physically safe environments but have ignored the mental environment. Some governments have grown impatient with worksites and their lack of efforts in this regard and are placing mental health safety and compensation into Workers' Compensation legislation. Hopefully, worksites will recognize the importance of addressing this issue from both a financial and human cost and will take action to create mentally healthy worksites.

We hope we have provided language, information and a forum for the discussion of mental health in the workplace to flourish. Mental health and mental health in the workplace is a critical issue facing all of us and should not be ignored simply because our systems are focused on physiological issues. We need to refocus and aggressively pursue effective solutions that will assist persons with mental illness to enter the workforce, stay in the workforce and re-enter the workforce post-injury and illness. However, the overarching goal should be to create mentally healthy workplaces for everyone.

Appendix A
Return on Investment (ROI) Equation Parameters for Depression

This section outlines parameter estimates utilized for the development of the Return on Investment (ROI) equation for depression in the workplace. This ROI equation can be found at the end of Appendix A and the electronic ROI files can be obtained by contacting the authors. The costs outlined in this ROI equation have been developed on a "per-employee" basis, assuming that accurate pre-screening and diagnosis have not yet been performed. Setting up an ROI equation in this manner means that employers do not need to know exactly which employees are going to develop depression in order to be useful. Instead, costs are broken down by the best available yearly prevalence estimates and given on a per-employee basis. For example, the ROI for an organization with ten employees paying an average salary of $20.00 per hour is $913.00 per month or $10,953 per year. This particular employer could spend up to $10,000 per year on depression screening, prevention, and treatment for his ten employees and still see an ROI. In order to use the ROI equation, simply review the evidence presented in this section, contact the authors for an electronic version of the ROI equation, and enter your organization characteristics of hourly wage and number of employees.

Prevalence Estimate: Depression is the most common mental illness worldwide. An estimated 12.9 percent of women and 7.7 percent of men (Fogel, Eaton and Ford, 2006) suffer from depression each year. These yearly prevalence estimates are close to the World Health Organization's 9.5 percent and 5.8 percent prevalence estimates among women and men, respectively. The prevalence estimates presented by Fogel et al. are likely higher because of an increase in reporting due to the anonymity in the study. We have elected to use prevalence estimates that combine the two sources at 11.2 percent in women and 6.75 percent in men. We assume that male and females represent equal workforce numbers giving us an overall prevalence of depression at 9 percent.

Savings due to a reduction in absenteeism: Various research has examined the effects that different degrees of depression has on workplace absenteeism. Key findings from North American researchers has found that depressed employees miss between 0.3–3.8 (Lerner and Henke, 2008) and 1.8–3.4 (Lerner, Adler, Chang et al., 2004a) additional work days per month. One well-conducted international study even found that depressed workers miss 7.7 additional workdays per month (Ormel, van den Brink, van der Meer et al., 1994). We have elected to use a conservative estimate of 2.5 missed work days per month. This figure equates to (2.5days*8hours/day) = 20 hours per month. To put this cost into an individual employee basis we multiply our absenteeism figure by the prevalence of depression to get (20hours*0.09prevalence) = **1.8**. Employers can expect a ROI of 1.8 hours per-employee per-month due to a reduction in absenteeism.

Savings due to a reduction in presenteeism: Studies have found that depression limits an employee's physical performance 20 percent of the time, with their mental performance suffering 35 per cent of the time (Lerner et al., 2004b; Lerner, Adler, Chang et al., 2004a; Adler, McLaughlin, Rogers et al., 2006). These studies have found that depression results in a loss of task focus of 18 percent and a loss of productivity of 7 percent for a combined effect of presenteeism ranging between 6–10 percent. Presenteeism of 8 percent during a 160-hour work month would result in a loss of (160 hours*0.08 presenteeism) = 12.8 productive work hours, a number just slightly higher than estimates from independent researchers (Kessler, White, Brinbaum et al., 2008). To put this cost into an individual employee basis we multiply our absenteeism figure by the prevalence of depression to get (12.8 hours*0.09 prevalence) = **1.15**. Employers can expect a ROI of 1.15 hours per-employee per-month due to a reduction in presenteeism.

Savings due to increased retention: One study directly measuring the link between job loss and depression found that 15 percent of depressed employees lost their job compared to 3.5 percent of controls (Lerner, Adler, Change et al., 2004b). This means that 11.5 percent of depressed employees are more likely to lose their jobs after six months than the expected 3.5 percent baseline job loss statistic. This means that (11.5 percent per 6 months * 2) 23 percent of depressed employees can be expected to lose their job in one year. Furthermore, the average estimate of replacing an $8/hr employee is $9,444.40 (Sasha-Corporation, January 2007). If we figure that 9 percent of employees suffer from depression each year and 23 percent of these employees will lose their job due to depression we get an estimated savings in retention of ($9,444.40 *.09*.23) = $195.50 per annum. This equates to a savings of ($195.50/12months) = **$16.30** per-employee per-month.

Savings due to a reduction in medical care costs: The direct medical care costs of depression due to inpatient and outpatient care were taken directly from Goetzel et al. (2004). Goetzel et al. obtained their estimates from the Medstat Marketscan Health and Productivity Management database between the 3-year period from 1997–99. The estimated medical care cost of depression, excluding prescription medication, on each individual of the population was $7.61 for inpatient costs and $25.47 for outpatient costs. This means that depression can be expected to increase employer's health care cost coverage an estimated **$33.08** per-year per-employee.

Savings due to a reduction in prescription claims: Cubic Health Inc. is a large drug plan management company in Canada that serves as an advisor to the Global Roundtable for Addictions and Mental-Health. Using data from Cubic Health Inc. and the Roundtable we are able to calculate an ROI benefit in terms of reducing the cost of antidepressant prescriptions. An estimated 70 percent of employees utilize their health prescription plan under medical coverage in Canada each year. Of this 70 percent, one in every seven employees makes an antidepressant claim each year. This means that 10 percent of the working population (70%*(1/7)) file prescription claims for antidepressants each year. Furthermore, claimants with depression have an annual drug expenditure of $1311 that far exceeds the drug expenditure of all other claimants at $514 (Cubic Health Inc., 2007). The 10 percent of all employees making prescription claims for depression then spend $797 more a year than do the average claimants. Placing this additional cost at a per employee basis we can see that depression costs employers an additional ($797*0.10) = **$79.70** a year in terms of prescription claims on a per-employee basis.

Savings due to a reduction in long-term disability premiums: A recent Globe and Mail Mental Health Roundtable Report states that 40 percent of short- and long-term disability claims in Canada involve a mental illness (Picard, 2008). The report found that mental illnesses cost Canadian employers and insurers $8.5 billion in terms of long-term disability each year. An expense of $8.5 billion among Canada's working population of 14.452 million equates to (8,500/14.452) = $588.15 spent per-employee in terms of mental illness. We can obtain the cost of long-term disability due to depression by multiplying this $588.15 by 60 percent, the percentage of mental illness disability cases found to be due to depression among one very large financial service company (Burton and Conti, 2008). This 60 percent estimate is once again a conservative estimate as the Mental Health Roundtable for Addictions and Mental-Health found depression to comprise 70 percent of mental health spending in 2004 (Cubic Health Inc., 2007). These equations give employers and insurers an estimated ROI of **$352.89** each year in terms of long-term disability costs alone.

References

Adler, D.A., McLaughlin, T.J., Rogers, W.H., Hong, C., Lapitsky, L., and Lerner, D. (2006). Job performance deficits due to depression. *American Journal of Psychiatry*, 163(9), 1569–76.

Burton, W.N. and Conti, D.J. (2008). Depression in the workplace: The role of the Corporate Medical Director. *Journal of Occupational and Environmental Medicine*, 50(4), 476–81.

Fogel, J., Eaton, W.W., and Ford, D.E. (2006). Minor depression as a predictor of the first onset of major depressive disorder over a 15-year follow-up. *Acta Psychiatrica Scandinavica*, 113(1), 36–43.

Kessler, R., White, L.A., Birnbaum, H., Qiu, Y., Kidolezi, Y., Mallett, D., et al. (2008). Comparative and interactive effects of depression relative to other health problems on work performance in the workforce of a large employer. *Journal of Occupational and Environmental Medicine*, 50(7), 809–16.

Lerner, D., Adler, D.A., Chang, H., Berndt, E.R., Irish, J.T., Lapitsky, L., et al. (2004a). The clinical and occupational correlates of work productivity loss among employed patients with depression. *Journal of Occupational and Environmental Medicine*, 46(6), S46–S55.

Lerner, D., Adler, D.A., Chang, H., Lapitsky, L., Hood, M.Y., Perissinotto, C., et al. (2004b). Unemployment, job retention, and productivity loss among employees with depression. *Psychiatric Services*, 55(12), 1371–8.

Lerner, D. and Henke, R.M. (2008). What does research tell us about depression, job performance, and work productivity? *Journal of Occupational and Environmental Medicine*, 50(4), 401–10.

Ormel, J., van den Brink, W., van der Meer, K., Jenner, J., and Giel, R. (1994). Prevalence, indication and course of depression in family practice. *Ned Tijdschr Geneeskd*, 138(3), 123–6.

Picard, A. (2008, June 23, 2008). The working wounded. *The Globe and Mail*, pp. 1–5. Retrieved July 22, 2009, from http://www.mentalhealthroundtable. ca/jun_2008/globeandmail.com_%20The%20working%20wounded.pdf.

Return On Investment (ROI) for Managing Workplace Depression on a Per Month Basis

	Hourly Savings	Hourly Wage	Total Savings $$$	Initial Figures	Correction Factors	Final Figures
Savings Due to a Reduction in Absenteeism	1.8		0			
Savings Due to a Reduction in Presenteeism	1.15		0			
Savings Due to Increased Retention			16.3			
Savings Due to a Reudction in Medical Care Costs			2.75			
Savings Due to a Reduction in long-term Disability			29.41			
Savings Due to a Reduction in Prescription Claims			6.64			
Only 80% of Depressed Individuals Respond to Treatment					0.8	
Average Monthly Savings per employee			55.1			
Total Monthly Savings Company Wide	Enter the number of people you employee here -->			0		0
Total Yearly Savings Company Wide				0		0

Appendix B

Return on Investment (ROI) Equation Parameters for Generalized Anxiety Disorder (GAD)

This section outlines parameter estimates utilized for the development of the Return on Investment (ROI) equation for GAD in the workplace. This ROI equation can be found at the end of Appendix B and the electronic ROI files can be obtained by contacting the authors. The costs outlined in this ROI equation have been developed on a "per-employee" basis, assuming that accurate pre-screening and diagnosis have not yet been performed. Setting up an ROI equation in this manner means that employers do not need to know exactly which employees are going to develop generalized anxiety in order to be useful. Instead, costs are broken down by the best available yearly prevalence estimates and given on a per-employee basis. In order to use the ROI equation, simply review the evidence presented in this section, contact the authors for an electronic version of the ROI equation, and enter your organization characteristics of hourly wage and number of employees.

Prevalence Estimate: Anxiety is the second most common mental illness worldwide. An estimated 3.1 percent of men and women suffer from GAD each year (Kessler, McGonagle, Zhao et al., 1994; Jacobi, Wittchen, Holting et al., 2002). This estimate was derived from two population-based surveys sampling more than 64,000 individuals in North America and Europe, arriving at the same figure.

Savings due to a reduction in absenteeism: Estimates from the US have reported that individuals with GAD experience 5.5 (Kessler, Greenberg, Mickelson et al., 2001), and 4.1 (Kroenke, Spitzer, Williams et al., 2007) additional days each month where they could not work due to disability. International estimates place absenteeism at 2.6 (Wittchen, Carter, Pfister et al., 2000), 4.6 (Weiller, Bisserbe, Maier et al., 1998), 0.89 (Bijl and Ravelli, 2000), and 3.7 (Hunt, Slade and Andrews, 2004) additional days per month. We have elected to use the average of these estimates and placed GAD-attributable workplace absenteeism at 3.6 additional days absent from work each month. This figure equates to (3.6days*8hours/day) = 28.8 hours per month. To put this cost into an individual employee basis we multiply our absenteeism figure by the prevalence of GAD to get (28.8hours*0.051prevalence) = **1.47**. Employers can expect a ROI of 1.47 hours per-employee per-month due to a reduction in GAD associated absenteeism.

Savings due to a reduction in presenteeism: While there is consensus that anxiety disorders negatively impact employee productivity, few trials have assessed the subject in a rigorous manner. Only two studies reviewed were deemed to quantify GAD-associated presenteeism in a manner that would inform the present ROI equations. One trial found that treatment-seeking anxiety patients with mild to severe anxiety experience between 24 percent and 45 percent impairment while at work (Erickson, Guthrie, Vanetten-Lee et al., 2009). A second population-based survey indicated that 34 percent of patients with pure-GAD reported a reduction of work productivity of greater than 10 percent (Wittchen, Carter, Pfister et al., 2000). We elected to use an estimate of presenteeism for anxiety disorders provided by Loepkke et al. (2009). Anxiety disorders were found to result in an additional 10.5 presenteeism days per year when compared to employees without a physical or mental illness. While this estimate was ascertained for any anxiety disorder it is reasonable to presume that GAD would result in similar presenteeism. This figure equates to (10.5days*8hours/day) = 84 hours per year or (84hours/12months) = 7 hours per month. To put this cost into an individual employee basis we multiply our presenteeism figure by the prevalence of GAD to get (4.87hours*0.051 prevalence) = **0.36**. Employers can expect an ROI of 0.36 hours per-employee per-month due to a reduction in GAD-associated presenteeism.

Savings due to increased retention: Two studies ascertained nationally and community representative unemployment rates of patients with GAD attending primary care networks. In the United States, pure-GAD was associated with a 10.7 percent unemployment rate (Wittchen, Kessler, Beesdo et al., 2002) which is 4.6 percent greater than the 1994 US national average unemployment rate of 6.1 percent (the time at which the survey was completed). The pure-GAD associated unemployment rate of 9.2 percent (Ansseau, Fischler, Dierick et al., 2008) was 1.7 percent higher than 7.5 percent average rate of unemployment observed in Belgium in 2002. We have elected to use the average of these two estimates, placing pure-GAD associated unemployment at 3.7 percent above the national average. The average estimate of replacing an $8/hr employee is $9,444.40 (Sasha-Corporation, January 2007). This means that employers can expect an employee with GAD to be slightly more likely to lose their job each year. Employers could expect to save an estimated ($9,444.40 *.051 *.037) = $17.82 per annum as a result of retaining employees with GAD. This equates to a savings of ($17.82/12months) = **$1.48** per-employee per-month.

References

Ansseau, M., Fischler, B., Dierick, M., Albert, A., Leyman, S., and Mignon, Annick. (2008). Socioeconomic correlates of generalized anxiety disorder and major depression in primary care: The GADIS II study (Generalized Anxiety and Depression Impact Survey II). *Depression and Anxiety*, 25(6), 506–13. DOI: 10.1002/da.20306.

Bijl, R.V. and Ravelli, A. (2000). Current and residual functional disability associated with psychopathology: findings from the Netherlands Mental Health Survey and Incidence Study (NEMESIS). *Psychological Medicine*, 30(03), 657–68. DOI: null.

Erickson, S.R., Guthrie, S., Vanetten-Lee, M., Himle, J., Hoffman, J., Santos, S.F., et al. (2009). Severity of anxiety and work-related outcomes of patients with anxiety disorders. *Depress Anxiety*, 26(12), 1165–71. DOI: 10.1002/da.20624.

Hunt, C., Slade, T., and Andrews, G. (2004). Generalized Anxiety Disorder and major depressive disorder comorbidity in the National Survey of Mental Health and Well-Being. *Depress Anxiety*, 20(1), 23–31. DOI: 10.1002/da.20019.

Jacobi, F., Wittchen, H.U., Holting, C., Sommer, S., Lieb, R., Hofler, M., and Pfister, H. (2002). Estimating the prevalence of mental and somatic disorders in the community: aims and methods of the German National Health Interview and Examination Survey. *Int J Methods Psychiatr Res*, 11(1), 1–18.

Kessler, R.C., Greenberg, P.E., Mickelson, K.D., Meneades, L.M., and Wang, P.S. (2001). The effects of chronic medical conditions on work loss and work cutback. *J Occup Environ Med*, 43(3), 218–25.

Kessler, R.C., McGonagle, K.A., Zhao, S., Nelson, C.B., Hughes, M., Eshleman, S., et al. (1994). Lifetime and 12-month prevalence of DSM-III-R psychiatric disorders in the United States. Results from the National Comorbidity Survey. *Arch Gen Psychiatry*, 51(1), 8–19.

Kroenke, K., Spitzer, R.L., Williams, J.B., Monahan, P.O., and Lowe, B. (2007). Anxiety disorders in primary care: prevalence, impairment, comorbidity, and detection. *Ann Intern Med*, 146(5), 317–325. DOI: 146/5/317 [pii].

Weiller, E., Bisserbe, J.C., Maier, W., and Lecrubier, Y. (1998). Prevalence and recognition of anxiety syndromes in five European primary care settings. A report from the WHO study on Psychological Problems in General Health Care. *Br J Psychiatry Suppl*, (34), 18–23.

Wittchen, H.U., Carter, R.M., Pfister, H., Montgomery, S.A., and Kessler, R.C. (2000). Disabilities and quality of life in pure and comorbid generalized anxiety disorder and major depression in a national survey. *Int Clin Psychopharmacol*, 15(6), 319–28.

Wittchen, H.U., Kessler, R.C., Beesdo, K., Krause, P., Hofler, M., and Hoyer, J. (2002). Generalized anxiety and depression in primary care: prevalence, recognition, and management. *J Clin Psychiatry*, 63 Suppl 8, 24–34.

Return On Investment (ROI) for Managing Workplace Anxiety on a Per Month Basis

	Hourly Savings	Hourly Wage	Total Savings $$$	Initial Figures	Correction Factors	Final Figures
Savings Due to a Reduction in Absenteeism	1.47		0			
Savings Due to a Reduction in Presenteeism	0.36		0			
Savings Due to Increased Retention			1.48			
Savings Due to a Reudction in Medical Care Costs						
Savings Due to a Reduction in long-term Disability						
Savings Due to a Reduction in Prescription Claims						
Only 80% of Depressed Individuals Respond to Treatment					0.8	
Average Monthly Savings per employee			1.48			
Total Monthly Savings Company Wide	Enter the number of people you employee here -->			0		0
Total Yearly Savings Company Wide				0		0

Appendix C

Return on Investment (ROI) Parameters for Companies Addressing Workplace Bullying

Around 10 percent of employees are currently bullied at work and 25 percent of employees have been bullied in the last five years. The negative impact of bullying has been found to persist for around five years, making a 15 percent estimate of the prevalence of workplace bullying a conservative estimate (Hoel, Sparks and Cooper, 2001).

Savings due to a reduction in absenteeism: Victims of bullying take on average seven more absence days than do their non-bullied counterparts (Hoel and Cooper, 2000). That equates to 56 hours of lost work a year; 4.67 lost working hours each month. To place this cost at a per employee basis we simply multiply the increase in absenteeism per month (4.67 hours) by the prevalence of those affected by bullying (15%) = **0.70**.

Savings due to increased productivity of victims: Victims of bullying self-rate their productivity 7 percent lower than do non-victims (Hoel and Cooper, 2000). A 7 percent reduction in productivity during an 160 hour work month equates to (0.07*160) = 11.2 lost work hours each month. To place this cost at a per employee basis we simply multiply the reduction in presenteeism per month (11.2 hours) by the prevalence of those affected by bullying (15%) = **1.68** hours/month.

Savings due to increased productivity of witnesses: Witnesses of workplace bullying rate their level of productivity 2 percent lower than do employees who do not witness workplace bullying (Hoel and Cooper, 2000). An estimated 11 percent of employees witness workplace bullying to a degree that can be considered harmful (Lutgen-Sandvik, Tracy and Alberts, 2007). A 2 percent reduction in productivity during a 160 hour work month equates to (0.02*160) = 3.2 lost work hours per month. To place this cost at a per employee basis we simply multiply the reduction in presenteeism per month (3.2 hours) by the prevalence (11%) = **0.36** hours/month.

Savings due to retention: Independent estimates have placed the number of victims who leave their job as a result of bullying at 25 percent (Rayner, 1997, 2000). Victims of workplace bullying do not leave their jobs immediately; however they are likely to leave their current job within the first three years. We can therefore place a yearly estimate of employee resignation due to workplace violence at 8 percent (25% / 3-years) of victims. Multiplying this statistic by the prevalence of bullying we obtain the estimated per-employee rate of resignation due to workplace bullying (0.08*0.15) = 0.012 or 1.2 percent of employees. Employee turnover is a costly affair in terms of direct costs (recruitment, loss of experienced staff, overtime pay to cover shifts, testing and training new hires) and indirect costs (decreased morale, insufficient staffing, loss of social networks). The average low-end estimate of replacing an $8/hr employee is $5,505.80 (Sasha-Corporation, January 2007). The per-employee low-end yearly cost of turnover then is (5505.8*.012) = $66.07 making the monthly ROI estimate at **$5.50** per employee per month.

Savings due to reductions in medical care: Bullying accounts for approximately 27 percent of the variance in reported mental health symptoms and also 10–20% of the adverse effects of stress. Furthermore, 23 percent of psychosomatic symptoms among victims can be explained by exposure to bullying. However, eradicating bullying will not alleviate its total effect on ill-health because the effects of bullying are cumulative and long-lasting. Therefore, employing conservative estimates, it is reasonable for employers to anticipate lower ROI's in the way of 15 percent of mental healthcare premiums and some 10 percent of medical care costs among victims of bullying. This translates to a per employee savings of 2.25 percent for mental healthcare and 1.5 percent for medical care.

Savings due to production and quality of work: It is very difficult to estimate the potential savings that employers may accrue by increasing the quality of employee products and services. Furthermore, these numbers will show a wide fluctuation depending on the field of employment. At present, any number placed herein would be simply a speculation.

Risk of workplace bullying by service sector: The most comprehensive data pertaining to the prevalence of bullying in various occupational sectors was available from an unpublished study in Britain and was used as the basis of the risk factor calculation (Hoel and Cooper, 2000). A global prevalence of bullying by occupational sector was created by averaging the prevalence of bullying in the last six months and in the last five years into one global score of workplace bullying. This prevalence of workplace bullying score was put into SPSS and standardized z-scores were created to control for sample size. The standardized z-scores represent standard deviations above and below the mean that were multiplied by the standard deviation in the prevalence of workplace bullying (4.28 percent). This number was then turned into a risk factor representing the increase or decrease in prevalence of workplace bullying depending on the service sector of the employees.

References

Hoel, A. and Cooper, C.L. (2000). *Destructive Conflict and Bullying at Work*. Manchester, UK, University of Manchester Institute of Science and Technology.

Hoel, H., Sparks, K., and Cooper, C.L. (2001). The cost of violence/stress at work and the benefits of a violence/stress-free working environment. *Geneva: International Labour Organization*.

Lutgen-Sandvik, P., Tracy, S.J., and Alberts, J.K. (2007). Burned by bullying in the american workplace: Prevalence, perception, degree and impact. *Journal of Management Studies*, 44(6), 837–62.

Rayner, C. (1997). The incidence of workplace bullying. *Journal of Community & Applied Social Psychology*, 7(3), 199–208.

Rayner, C. (2000). *Building a Business Case for Tackling Bullying in the Workplace: Beyond a Basic Cost-benefit Approach*. Transcending Boundaries, Griffith University, Brisbane, Australia.

Return On Investment (ROI) for Managing Workplace Bullying on a Per Month Basis

	Hourly Savings	Hourly Wage	Total Savings $$$
Savings Due to a Reduction in Absenteeism	0.7		0
Savings Due to a Reduction in Presenteeism	1.68		0
Savings Due to a Reduction in Presenteeism Among Witnesses	0.36		0
Savings Due to Increased Retention			5.5
Savings Due to a Reudction in Medical Care Costs			12.04
Savings Due to a Reduction in Disability			
Average Monthly Savings per employee	Enter the number of people you employee here -->		17.54
Total Monthly Savings Company Wide			0
Total Yearly Savings Company Wide			0

Enter your company wide savings next to the company's designated service sector in column D

Service Sector	Risk Factor Index	Adjusted Savings
Postal Service / Telecommunications	1.043	0
Prison	1.063	0
Teaching	1.08	0
Other	1.000	0
Dance and Performing Arts	1.039	0
Police Services	1.028	0
Voluntary Organization	1.008	0
Banking	1.002	0
Health Occupations	1.001	0
Local Authority	0.981	0
Civil Services	0.99	0
Fire and Rescue	0.966	0
Hotel Industry	0.943	0
Higher Education	0.965	0
Retailing	0.944	0
Manufacturing	0.939	0

Index

Bold page numbers indicate figures,
italic numbers indicate tables.

New Directions in Organizational Psychology and Behavioral Medicine
Edited by
Alexander-Stamatios Antoniou and Cary Cooper
Hardback: 978-1-4094-1082-9
e-book: 978-1-4094-1083-6 (PDF)
e-book: 978-1-4094-6023-7 (ePUB)

Occupational Health and Safety
Edited by
Ronald J. Burke, Sharon Clarke and Cary L. Cooper
Hardback:978-0-566-08983-1
e-book: 978-1-4094-3207-4 (PDF)
e-book: 978-1-4094-8663-3 (ePUB)

Safety Culture: Assessing and Changing the Behaviour of Organisations
John Bernard Taylor
Hardback: 978-1-4094-0127-8
e-book: 978-1-4094-0128-5 (PDF)
e-book: 978-1-4094-5996-5 (ePUB)

Visit **www.gowerpublishing.com** and

- search the entire catalogue of Gower books in print
- order titles online at 10% discount
- take advantage of special offers
- sign up for our monthly e-mail update service
- download free sample chapters from all recent titles
- download or order our catalogue